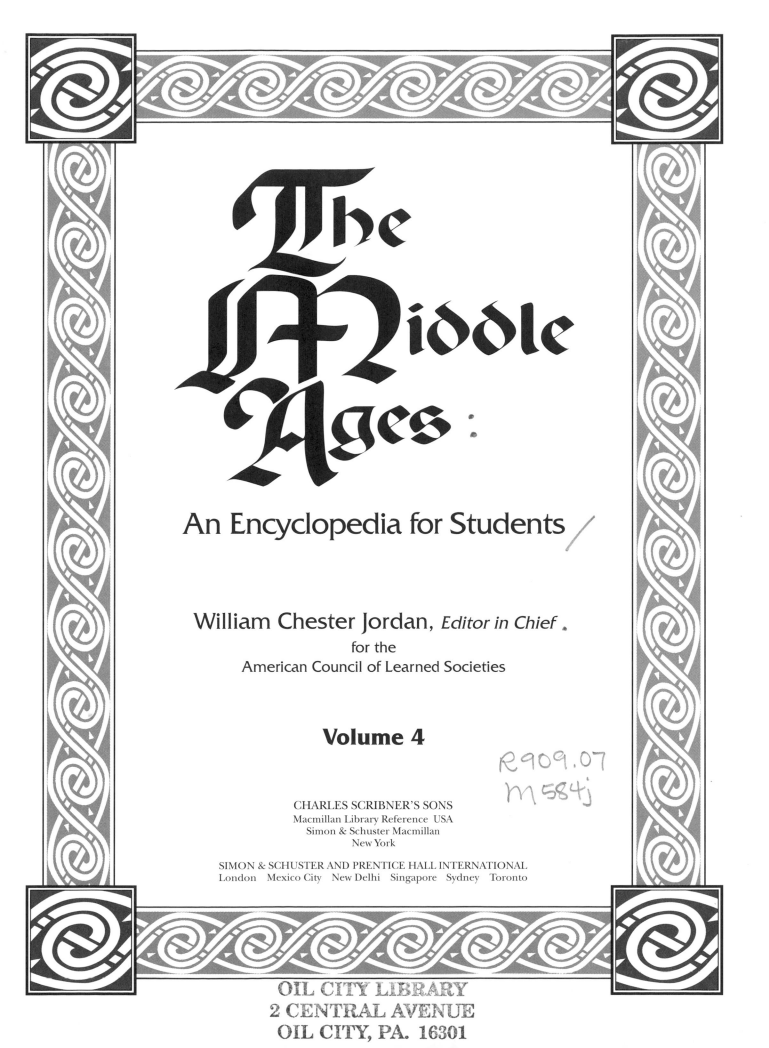

The Middle Ages:

An Encyclopedia for Students

William Chester Jordan, *Editor in Chief*.
for the
American Council of Learned Societies

Volume 4

CHARLES SCRIBNER'S SONS
Macmillan Library Reference USA
Simon & Schuster Macmillan
New York

SIMON & SCHUSTER AND PRENTICE HALL INTERNATIONAL
London   Mexico City   New Delhi   Singapore   Sydney   Toronto

Developed for the American Council of Learned Societies by
Charles Scribner's Sons and Visual Education Corporation.

PRINTING
  3 4 5 6 7 8 9 10

Library of Congress Cataloging-in-Publication Data

The Middle Ages / William Chester Jordan, editor in chief for the
American Council of Learned Societies.
        p.   cm.
    Includes bibliographical references and index.
    ISBN 0-684-19773-1   (hard/libr. bind. : alk. paper)
    1. Middle Ages—Encyclopedias, Juvenile.   I. Jordan, William C.,
1948– .   II. American Council of Learned Societies.
D114.M54 1996
909.07´03—dc20   95-49597
                                                            CIP

ISBN 0-684-80483-2 (vol. 1)
ISBN 0-684-80484-0 (vol. 2)
ISBN 0-684-80485-9 (vol. 3)
ISBN 0-684-80486-7 (vol. 4)

Psellos, Michael

1018–ca. 1078
Scholar, statesman, and historian

* **patron**   person of wealth and influence who supports an artist, writer, or scholar

Michael Psellos was one of the most important scholars in the history of the BYZANTINE EMPIRE. His works covered a wide range of subjects, including SCIENCE, MATHEMATICS, MUSIC, astronomy, MEDICINE, LAW, and philosophy. His work helped to preserve ancient Greek learning and to popularize it for his 11th-century readers. His most important work was *Chronographia,* a history of the Byzantine imperial court from 976 to 1077.

Born in CONSTANTINOPLE to parents of modest means, Michael Psellos attracted the attention of imperial patrons* while he was still a young man. After Emperor Michael IV (who reigned from 1034 to 1041) appointed him to his first high office, he continued to serve at court until about 1054. Then he left the capital and retired to a monastery on Mount Olympus. However, soon the empress THEODORA I recalled him to court, and he reached the height of his political power during the reign of his former pupil, Emperor Michael VII Doukas (who reigned from 1071 to 1078). However, he fell out of favor for reasons that are unclear and was forced to leave. (*See also* **Astrology and Astronomy; Byzantine Literature; Classical Tradition in the Middle Ages; Historical Writing.**)

Ptolemy

See *Classical Tradition in the Middle Ages.*

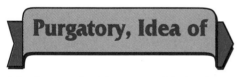

Purgatory, Idea of

* **theology**   study of the nature of God and of religious truth

* **penance**   an act of repentance for sin

* **doctrine**   principle, theory, or belief presented for acceptance

The idea of purgatory—a place where human souls reside temporarily after death—developed during the medieval period in both the Christian and Islamic religious traditions. Each religion has a somewhat different view of purgatory, which is based on the sacred writings and theology* of each faith.

In Christianity, the idea of purgatory developed from two early customs: praying for the dead and performing penance* to atone for one's sins. According to early church doctrine*, after a sin was committed, the sinner was readmitted into the church only after years of severe penance. From this came the idea that atonement for every sin was required, either during one's lifetime or afterward. At the same time, St. AUGUSTINE taught that prayers and the celebration of a Mass for the dead were effective substitutes for the punishment of sin in this world. However, the prayers of the living could not help the damned. Together, these ideas suggested the existence of a place between heaven and hell. This place eventually became known as purgatory, a "place of cleansing," where sins were cleansed by fire.

According to Christian doctrine, the righteous entered heaven at death, while the wicked entered hell. The imperfectly righteous—sinners who had neglected penance during their lives, or who were unable to perform penance before they died—had to atone for their sins after death, in purgatory. Purgatory was only a temporary state. While there, sinners would suffer various terrible pains, part of which was the pain of

* **resurrection** coming to life again; rising from the dead

Purgatory was a place of cleansing, where the souls of the unforgiven went before entering heaven. The length of a soul's stay in Purgatory and the intensity of suffering depended on the number of unforgiven sins and how serious they were. This illumination from the 1300s shows the pope praying for the deliverance of souls from Purgatory into heaven.

a separation from God. The duration of suffering depended on the number of sins a person had committed. The intensity of the suffering depended on the seriousness of the sins. The pain and suffering of purgatory were made more bearable by the knowledge that the dead would enter heaven as soon as their souls were cleansed.

During the Middle Ages, a few Christian sects rejected the idea of purgatory, and the issue was hotly debated at several church councils. Following the medieval period, the doctrine became a significant feature of the Roman Catholic tradition, although it was largely abandoned by Protestants.

In the Islamic religion, the closest parallel to the Christian doctrine of purgatory is the idea of *barzakh*. This word refers to both the place where the dead live prior to Judgment Day and the indefinite period of time between death and resurrection*. *Barzakh* is thus an intermediary realm where the soul awaits judgment. Unlike Christian doctrine, the dead in *barzakh* do not atone for their sins in order to ascend to heaven. The Muslim soul's ultimate destiny is already fixed at the time of death, and no prayers or atonement can change its fate. *Barzakh* is simply a period and place in which both the righteous and the wicked wait to enter either heaven or hell. For the virtuous, *barzakh* is a preview of paradise. For the wicked, it is a preview of hell. This idea is comparable in some ways to the beliefs of the Eastern Orthodox Church. (*See also* **Death and Burial in Europe; Islam, Religion of; Mass, Liturgy of the; Paradise, Idea of.**)

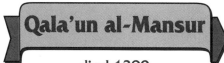

died 1290
Sultan of Egypt and Syria

* **sultan** political and military ruler of a Muslim dynasty or state

See map in Fatimid Empire (vol. 2).

* **crusader** person who participated in the holy wars against the Muslims during the Middle Ages

Qala'un al-Mansur, sultan* of Egypt and Syria from 1279 to 1290, is considered one of the most important rulers of the MAMLUK DYNASTY. During his reign, he helped make the Mamluk state the great power of the Middle East, a position it maintained until its conquest by the Ottomans in the early 1500s.

Born near the Black Sea, Qala'un was purchased as a slave while only a young boy. He was sent to CAIRO, where he received military training under the AYYUBIDS. Qala'un completed his military training in the 1240s, a turbulent time in which power was being transferred from the Ayyubids to the Mamluks. During that time, he also developed a close relationship with BAYBARS AL-BUNDUQDARI, who later became the fourth Mamluk sultan.

In 1260, Qala'un helped Baybars prevent the Mongol invasion of Syria and North Africa. Later that year, Baybars succeeded to the sultan's throne, and he promoted Qala'un to the highest ranks of the military. Baybars died in 1277, and, after two years of struggles over who would become the next sultan, Qala'un took the throne.

Qala'un is best known for his aggressive campaigns against the Mongols and the crusaders* and for his policies to promote international trade. In addition, Qala'un built some of Cairo's most impressive monuments. It was largely his efforts that brought an end to the crusader era in the Middle East. During the 11 years of Qala'un's reign, Mamluk power became firmly entrenched in Egypt and Syria, and both regions prospered. (*See also* **Crusades; Mamluk Dynasty; Ottomans and Ottoman Empire.**)

Qur'an

The Qur'an (sometimes spelled Koran) is the book of sacred writings of Islam. It contains divine revelations to the prophet MUHAMMAD, recited to the people of MECCA and Medina from 610 until his death in 632. The term *qur'an* itself means recitation and reflects the fact that its contents first appeared in oral form. In recited form, it is memorized by Muslims and essential to daily prayer.

The origins and early development of the Qur'an were closely related to Muhammad's prophetic experiences and his various roles as founder of the Muslim community. In Mecca, Muhammad received his divine messages from God at night and then recited them during public rituals each morning and evening. In Medina, he led the worshipers at weekly religious services. These services became the setting for the public recitation of new revelations as well as revised and expanded versions of old ones. While in Medina, Muhammad adapted the collected revelations in the form of a written scripture, or holy book, for Muslims. His responsibilities as a political leader, however, forced him to leave this work unfinished.

During Muhammad's lifetime, some of his followers made their own collections of his revelations. By the time of his death, several collections existed. The first official version of the Qur'an was prepared under caliph Uthman ibn Affan, in the mid-600s. However, other versions gradually emerged. In the late 700s, a version known as the Kufan version became the standard text. This version is still used throughout most of the Islamic world.

The Qur'an is written in Arabic. It consists of 114 chapters called suras, which vary in length from 2 lines to more than 700. The suras are divided into loosely rhymed verses that also vary considerably in length and style. Some suras are longer literary pieces with main themes, a consistent form, and other unifying features. Most suras, however, consist of sections with different themes and from different dates, often loosely joined with little unity of thought. This disjointedness probably reflects the fact that the Qur'an had no set form during its early oral stage.

The Qur'an became the ultimate authority in all Islamic legal and religious matters, and its interpretation (called *tafsir*) became an important branch of Islamic learning. Since the 900s, the Qur'an has been translated into many languages. However, translations are not considered to be the Qur'an itself, but only interpretations of it. The Arabic Qur'an is the only authoritative version. (*See also* **Islam, Political Organization of; Islam, Religion of; Islamic Art and Architecture; Tabari, al-.**)

This page is from a medieval manuscript of the Qur'an. Islamic custom did not allow images of people or animals to be used in religious texts. Muslim scribes used calligraphy, or beautifully designed lettering, to write the sacred words of Islam and to make the pages beautiful. Calligraphy was an important art form in Islamic texts.

Ramadan

See *Feasts and Festivals.*

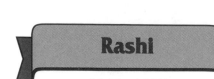

Rashi

1040–1105
Rabbi and scholar

* **Talmud** large body of collected writings on Jewish law and tradition

* **Pentateuch** first five books of the Old Testament; also referred to as the Torah in Jewish tradition

See color plate 4, vol. 1.

Rabbi Solomon ben Isaac, known as Rashi, was a rabbi and scholar whose commentaries on the Talmud* and the BIBLE have had a tremendous influence on Jewish thinking from the Middle Ages to the present. His Talmudic commentary is among the most inclusive and authoritative in Jewish thought, and his commentary on the Pentateuch* is considered a masterpiece.

Born in Troyes in northeast France, Rashi studied at Jewish academies in Worms and Mainz, which were the major centers of Talmudic studies in medieval Germany. After completing his studies, he spent the remainder of his life working on his commentaries on the Talmud and the Bible.

Rashi's commentary on the Talmud is unequaled in its brevity and clarity. Within a century after Rashi's death, it became the basis for almost all Talmudic studies. Rashi not only addressed the central issues of each Talmudic text. He also commented on the grammar, the writing style, and the strength of the argument. The end result was that text and commentary became inseparably interwoven.

Rashi's commentary on the Pentateuch combined the literal meaning of the text (as understood by Rashi) with earlier interpretations and oral Jewish law. The commentary had a huge impact on European Jewish life. It was taught to Jews in early childhood, and the images of biblical figures and the messages established by Rashi influenced the Jewish imagination for almost a thousand years. Rashi's work also influenced medieval Christian thinking on the Bible. (*See also* **Hebrew Literature; Jewish Communities; Judaism; Maimonides, Moses.**)

Ravenna

* **baptistery** room or hall for holding baptisms. Early Christian baptisteries were often large, freestanding buildings.

* **basilica** oblong building with rows of columns dividing the interior into a nave, or central aisle, and side aisles

Ravenna is a city on the northeastern coast of Italy. It is renowned for its large collection of monuments from the 400s and the 500s, which show a Byzantine architectural style beginning to differentiate itself from the styles of the West.

An important port city under the Romans, Ravenna became the capital of the Western Empire in 402. In 493, the OSTROGOTHS seized the city and made it the capital of their kingdom. In 540, Ravenna was recaptured by the Byzantines and served as the seat of Byzantine governors until 751, when it was taken by the LOMBARDS. Five years later, Ravenna and its surrounding lands were seized by the FRANKS and given to the PAPACY, which maintained control of the region until the 1200s. After that, the city was ruled by a dynasty of local lords and dominated by VENICE for about the next 200 years. In 1509, Ravenna once again came under papal control.

Ravenna's historic architecture reflects its turbulent early history. The city is famous for the colorful MOSAICS in its late Roman and Byzantine buildings. Its most celebrated Byzantine-style church is San Vitale, which was begun after 525. Octagonal in shape, San Vitale is similar to churches in CONSTANTINOPLE. It is considered a showpiece of Byzantine influence in Italy.

Ravenna is also noted for its Orthodox baptistery*, built around 400, and several basilicas* that date from the late 400s. Also notable are the

Ravenna, Italy, is famous for its collection of monuments dating from the Roman era and from the early Middle Ages. The basilica of Sant'Apollinare in Classe was consecrated by Archbishop Maximian in 549. While the brick exterior is unadorned, the interior is richly decorated with mosaics. The cylindrical, freestanding campanile, or bell tower, was added later, in the 800s or 900s.

See color plate 7, vol. 2.

* **mausoleum**   memorial building to house a tomb

mausoleum* of THEODORIC THE OSTROGOTH, with its massive dome carved from a single huge piece of rock, and the tomb of Dante Alighieri. (*See also* **Byzantine Architecture; Byzantine Art; Byzantine Empire.**)

Razi, al-

ca. 854–925 or 935
Islamic physician and philosopher

* **treatise**   long, detailed essay

* **pharmacology**   science of drugs, their properties, uses, and effects

Al-Razi was born in Iran. He studied mathematics, astronomy, philosophy, Arabic literature, and medicine and became a great medieval philosopher and physician. His medical writings include a diary published after his death and a celebrated treatise* on smallpox, which defined for the first time the difference between that disease and measles. As a physician, al-Razi based his learning on previously recorded case studies and on evidence that he himself observed. He contributed to the development of ALCHEMY through his classification of various substances, and he is credited with helping develop pharmacology* as a discipline separate from medicine.

Most of al-Razi's philosophical writings are lost, but many of his ideas are known through the writings of other medieval Islamic thinkers, most of whom were highly critical of his views. Al-Razi believed that the creation of the world occurred when God caused the one eternal soul to unite with disorganized matter to form individual living beings. God then endowed some of these living beings (humans) with reason. Al-Razi argued that salvation is achieved only through reason and philosophy. He said, therefore, that there was no need for revelation. This idea put him at odds with most Islamic thinkers, who stressed the importance of divine revelation in achieving salvation. These philosophical ideas were fiercely debated during the Middle Ages. However, al-Razi's greatest influence in both the Islamic world and in Europe was on the development of medicine and science. (*See also* **Islam, Religion of; Medicine; Science.**)

Relics

* **veneration** profound respect or reverence

The relics of Christian saints were kept in special containers called reliquaries. Many reliquaries were small enough to be carried, and they came in a variety of shapes. They were often beautiful works of art, made of gold, silver, or ivory, and encrusted with precious stones. The value of the reliquary was a reflection of the value of the relic it contained.

Many people believe that saints and their remains possess special powers. People pray to saints to ask for help in urging God to answer their requests. Relics—such as bones, crosses, or pieces of clothing—help the faithful to feel connected to departed saints.

The veneration* of relics was very popular in the Middle Ages. Memorial rites were performed at the tombs of venerated Christians, such as St. Peter in Rome. Many people believed that being buried near a saint's remains increased their chances of salvation on Judgment Day. For that reason, large cemeteries grew up around the graves of saints. People also thought that saints protected the communities in which they were buried. When the Byzantine emperor Leo I sought to move the remains of St. Simeon from Antioch to CONSTANTINOPLE, the people of Antioch objected. They insisted that the saint's relics kept their city safe from harm.

In the early Middle Ages, these cemeteries fell into disuse, and the saints' tombs were endangered by ruin or attacks by non-Christians. In Rome and elsewhere, the remains were dug up and relocated for safekeeping. Soon a brisk trade in the buying and selling of relics developed. Some people even tried to steal relics or to buy them for their personal use. Others tried to "find" new ones, and disputes arose concerning ways to identify true relics from fake ones.

The relics of especially famous saints attracted pilgrims and gifts of money and land from the faithful. Churches and monasteries that had such relics kept them in special containers, called reliquaries, which were often exquisitely crafted from precious materials. (*See also* **Canonization; Christianity; Indulgences; Pilgrimage; Purgatory, Idea of; Saints, Lives of.**)

Religious Instruction

In the early Middle Ages, most people did not know how to read. They learned about religion by memorizing prayers and by listening to SERMONS in church. Parents taught their children the most important prayers. The church expected that, by age seven, children would know the Lord's Prayer and the Apostles' Creed, which contained the basic principles of CHRISTIANITY. MISSIONARIES spread these same principles to adult converts. In the late 12th century, the church also required people to learn the Hail Mary, a prayer to the mother of Jesus. The church taught Christians the correct way to make the sign of the cross (a devotional gesture made with the hand). Some children, usually boys, received further religious instruction at school, where they learned how to read simple prayers.

CLERGY members were responsible for teaching people how to better understand and practice Christianity. In church, priests often read stories about the lives of saints, and, several times a year, they delivered sermons about the life and teachings of Jesus. By the 1200s, Dominican and Franciscan friars frequently visited churches to preach and give sermons.

Works of art were also effective forms of religious instruction. People who could not read learned BIBLE stories from statues, carvings, stained glass windows, and paintings. Beginning in the 1200s, religious plays became popular. They presented moral lessons and biblical tales in a dramatic and entertaining way. In the later Middle Ages, when more people among the middle and upper classes could read, books of religious instruction in Latin and in vernacular* languages became available.

* **vernacular** language or dialect native to a region; everyday, informal speech

For Jews, religious instruction of the young (particularly sons) was regarded as a father's duty. This applied to wealthy and poor households alike. Teaching was often begun by the father and later taken over by a private instructor. Students, sometimes as young as three, would begin by learning the Hebrew alphabet. After basic reading skills were mastered, students studied the first five books of Hebrew Scripture (the Pentateuch), which were read publicly in the synagogue*. This initial training was followed by some study of the Talmud*. Jewish culture put special value on higher religious study, which usually meant a more detailed study of the Talmud. Some attention was paid to girls' education as well, although girls usually did not go on to advanced studies.

* **synagogue** building of worship for Jews
* **Talmud** large body of collected writings on Jewish law and tradition

Islamic religious teaching relied heavily on memorization of the Qur'an and hadith*. From childhood on, Muslims of different races and languages committed the Qur'an to memory in Arabic and recited it to set patterns. Primary schooling was held in the elementary school, known as the *kuttab* or *maktab*, where children learned grammar, reading, and writing by studying the Qur'an. At the age of 15, male Muslims could begin study of Islamic law at a college, or madrasa. (*See also* **Dominicans; Drama; Franciscans; Glass, Stained; Sacraments; Saints, Lives of; Schools; Sermons.**)

* **hadith** collected traditions of the words and deeds of Muhammad

Rhetoric

Rhetoric is the art of speaking and writing persuasively. It is based on principles and rules of composition that were developed by the ancient Greeks and Romans. Rhetoric was an important branch of learning throughout the medieval world for Europeans, Byzantines, Muslims, and Jews.

Western European Rhetoric. Medieval Europeans based their ideas about rhetoric mostly on the works of Roman scholars, especially Marcus Tullius Cicero, who lived in the first century B.C. Cicero believed that the chief use of rhetoric was to persuade an audience through speech. He identified the main settings for speeches as law courts and political assemblies. Cicero provided detailed instructions on the correct way to prepare for the delivery of various types of speeches and listed the elements of an effective speech. Other Roman writers and later medieval scholars expanded Cicero's work into a large body of scholarship dealing with such subjects as oratory*, poetry, and figures of speech.

* **oratory** public speaking

* **secular** nonreligious; connected with everyday life

Rhetoric was one of seven subjects that formed the basis of secular* education in the Middle Ages. The other six subjects were grammar, dialectic (logic), geometry, arithmetic, astronomy, and MUSIC. Medieval Europeans advanced the study of rhetoric well beyond speech making. The three main types of rhetoric they recognized were poetry, preaching, and letter writing. The formal study of letter writing was a medieval innovation inspired by the growth of government and the church, which made written communication increasingly vital. Medieval scholars wrote many books in Latin on the art of letter writing, about 300 of which have survived. The center of letter-writing studies was the Italian city of Bologna.

Rhetoric is a good example of the way people in the Middle Ages used the past to meet their needs. They relied on the works of Cicero and other ancient scholars, but they also added to this body of knowledge to develop new skills.

Byzantine Rhetoric. The Byzantines found rhetoric most useful for teaching men in public life how to make speeches, which nearly always followed a carefully structured format. Speeches were to the Byzantines what journalism is today—a source of news and information and a way to influence popular opinion. As Christianity spread, the Byzantine CLERGY adopted this formal approach to religious speaking, and they applied it in their delivery of elaborate sermons. Many sermons were collected into books for other clergy members to study.

Arabic Rhetoric. In the Islamic world, rhetoric was partly a literary subject, partly a religious one, and partly a practical tool. Unlike Byzantine or western European rhetoric, Arabic rhetoric was not influenced by the ancient Greek or Latin tradition. The first known book about Arabic literary rhetoric was written about 887 and compared old and new styles of poetry. Muslim religious scholars used rhetoric to study how language is used in the QUR'AN, the sacred book of Islam. On a practical level, the study of rhetoric taught government clerks how to write proper letters and documents. Many Arabic manuals on rhetoric contained sample letters for various occasions that clerks used as models. Arabic rhetoric was the foundation for other rhetorical traditions in the Islamic world. Although Persian was important as a language for poetry, only a few books on the art of poetry writing were composed in the Persian language, and they are based on Arabic texts.

Hebrew Rhetoric. Although there was a flourishing tradition of Hebrew poetry in Spain, southern France, and Italy, the only work on rhetoric and poetics from the Jewish community that survives was written in Arabic. This is the *Book of Discussion and Conversation* by Moses ibn Ezra (who died about 1140). Ibn Ezra's book followed the tradition of Arabic rhetoric. It contained a long section on rhetorical techniques, as well as suggestions about the topics a poet should study and about the elements of a good poem. In addition, Ibn Ezra tried to answer questions about Hebrew literary history, such as why the Hebrew language had fewer words than the Arabic language. He believed that the reason was that most JEWISH COMMUNITIES lived in exile.

Later Jewish scholars used rhetoric to examine the BIBLE. The most comprehensive work on this subject was written in the 1400s by Judah

> **Remember:** Consult the index at the end of Volume 4 to find more information on many topics.

ben Jehiel, who based his work on the ancient Latin rhetorical tradition rather than on the Arabic tradition. (*See also* **Astrology and Astronomy; Classical Tradition in the Middle Ages; Encyclopedias and Dictionaries; Sermons.**)

Richard I the Lionhearted

1157–1199
King of England

See map in Crusades (vol. 2).

Although Richard I was king of England from 1189 until his death in 1199, the course of his life was largely determined by events in France. Richard was raised and educated in France and ruled large territories there. He belonged to the Plantagenets, the ruling family in England that was descended from the Norman invader, William I the Conqueror. During his reign as king of England, disputes with the French king PHILIP II AUGUSTUS led to a series of fierce battles. Richard's skill on the battlefield and his courage during the CRUSADES earned him the nickname "Lionhearted."

Richard's mother, ELEANOR OF AQUITAINE, was the heiress to a vast region in France, and Richard became duke of AQUITAINE at age 11. His father, King HENRY II OF ENGLAND, also ruled large parts of France. Henry had been duke of Normandy and count of Anjou before claiming the English throne. In his late teens, Richard began having bitter disputes with his father.

When Henry died in 1189, Richard inherited the English throne and his father's French territories. Richard traveled to England just long enough to receive his crown and establish his royal government. Less than a year later, he left on a crusade. On his way to the Holy Land, Richard joined the French king, Philip II Augustus, in SICILY. At the time, Richard was betrothed to Philip's half sister Alice, but he asked Philip to release him from the betrothal. Richard wanted to marry Berengaria, the

Treachery at home forced Richard the Lionhearted to make a truce with Saladin to end the Third Crusade. Philip II of France had seized some of Richard's French territories. Returning to defend his lands, Richard was imprisoned by German emperor Henry VI, an ally of Philip. He was ransomed after more than a year in captivity. This illumination shows Richard being brought as a prisoner before the emperor.

daughter of the king of NAVARRE. Philip agreed to the request in return for a large payment and some of Richard's lands in France. Richard then went to CYPRUS, where he married Berengaria.

Richard finally reached the Holy Land, joined forces with Philip, and together they captured the port of Acre. Richard then captured Jaffa, scoring another important victory for Christianity. In the meantime, Philip was plotting to seize more of Richard's French possessions to increase his own power in France. Pretending to be ill, Philip abandoned the crusade and returned to France.

* **crusader** person who participated in the holy wars against the Muslims during the Middle Ages

Learning of Philip's treachery, Richard made plans to return to England. But first he agreed to a truce with the Muslim leader SALADIN that allowed Christian pilgrims to visit JERUSALEM safely and protected the lands the crusaders* had captured in SYRIA. On his return journey, Richard avoided France, fearing that Philip might try to block him. However, when he traveled through Austria and Germany instead, the duke of Austria captured him and turned him over to the German emperor, Henry VI, an ally of Philip. The emperor kept Richard captive for more than a year and demanded a large ransom for his release. Upon the payment of 150,000 marks of silver, the emperor released Richard on February 4, 1194, in the city of Mainz.

Within six weeks, Richard was back in England, where he made immediate plans for a war of revenge against Philip. On May 12, 1194, leaving the government of England in the hands of Hubert WALTER, the archbishop of CANTERBURY, Richard crossed the English Channel to France, never to return to England. For the next five years, he campaigned against Philip, and, in the course of winning every battle, he reclaimed all the French lands he had lost. To celebrate his victories, Richard built himself an impressive castle in Normandy. True to his character as a warrior, he died in France from a wound he received in battle. (*See also* **Angevins; England; Normans; Warfare.**)

Richard II

1367–1400
King of England

* **depose** to remove from high office
* **chancellor** official who handles the records and archives of a monarch

In 1377, at age 10, Richard II became king of England after the death of his grandfather, Edward III. His own father, EDWARD THE BLACK PRINCE, had died in 1376. A council of barons advised the young king, but in the 1380s, while still a teenager, Richard began taking a more active role in the affairs of state. During the Peasants' Rebellion of 1381, Richard acted courageously by meeting with the rebels. The concessions he made were later revoked, and the rebels were ruthlessly suppressed.

In 1386, a baronial group opposed to his policies, led by his uncle, Thomas, duke of Gloucester, deposed* Richard's chancellor* and established a commission to supervise the king. Richard tried unsuccessfully to counteract this threat to his power.

Two years after Richard's wife, Anne of BOHEMIA, died, he strengthened his truce with France by marrying Isabelle, the eight-year-old daughter of the French king, CHARLES VII. During two expeditions to IRELAND, Richard assembled an army of followers to confront his opponents in England. They captured the duke of Gloucester, who died in

custody, and brought some of the duke's allies to trial before parliament. Two other allies, the duke of Norfolk and Henry Bolingbroke, were exiled, and the king confiscated the property of the duke of Lancaster, Bolingbroke's uncle.

In 1399, Henry Bolingbroke returned from exile. Richard, who was unable to raise a sufficient force to oppose him, surrendered the crown, and Bolingbroke became King Henry IV. Richard died several months later in February 1400. (*See also* **England; Hundred Years War; Peasants' Rebellions and Uprisings.**)

Richard III

1452–1485
King of England

Richard III served briefly as king of England after the death of his older brother, King Edward IV, who reigned from 1461 to 1483. Richard, the youngest son of the duke of York, lived during the WARS OF THE ROSES, the extended struggle for control of the English monarchy by members of the House of York and the House of Lancaster. In 1461, Edward seized the throne from the Lancastrian king, HENRY VI. When Richard became duke of Gloucester upon his brother's coronation, he was only nine years old. Richard served his brother faithfully to the end of Edward's reign.

In October 1470, a rebel group led by the earl of Warwick and Richard's other brother, George, drove Edward and Richard into exile and restored Henry VI to the throne. Edward and Richard returned the following March and defeated the rebels in battles at Barnet and Tewkesbury. Edward imprisoned Henry VI in the Tower of London, where Henry was murdered, probably on orders from Edward and Richard.

For the rest of Edward's reign, Richard served as lieutenant general for northern England. When Edward died in 1483, the crown was supposed to pass to Edward's 12-year-old son as Edward V, but Richard seized the crown for himself. He then proceeded to put his nephews, Edward V and his younger brother Richard, in the Tower of London, where they too were subsequently murdered. The Lancasters took their revenge in 1485 when Henry Tudor landed in Wales and killed Richard in battle on Bosworth Field to become the new king of England as Henry VII. With the death of Richard, the last Yorkist king, the Wars of the Roses ended.

Roads and Bridges

The Byzantines and the Muslims did not have extensive systems of roads and bridges in the Middle Ages, preferring rather to travel by sea or by camel, respectively. In the early Middle Ages in Europe, few roads and bridges existed. In the centuries following the fall of the Roman Empire, no strong central governments existed to build or maintain them. However, by the 1100s, when trade increased and CITIES AND TOWNS developed, roads and bridges became important features of life in medieval Europe.

Byzantine and Islamic Roads. Located at the crossroads between Europe and Asia, the BYZANTINE EMPIRE's capital, CONSTANTINOPLE, was the

This French illumination from the 1400s shows the importance of roads and bridges during wartime. They made it easier for armies to travel from one place to another, and they played an important role in military defense. The side that controlled a road or bridge could keep the enemy from moving soldiers or supplies.

hub of dozens of land and sea routes, including many roads inherited from the Romans. The crusaders of medieval Europe, bound for the Middle East, used the Byzantine roads that ran through BULGARIA and southern ANATOLIA (present-day Turkey). Since the mountainous terrain of Byzantine lands made it difficult to build and maintain roads, and transport by land was notoriously slow, the Byzantines much preferred to travel and transport their goods by sea.

In the Islamic world of ARABIA, the Middle East, and North Africa, virtually all wheeled transportation had disappeared prior to the rise of Islam. The main reason for this was the economic advantage of using pack camels. Camels could travel long distances and cross desert terrain, and wheeled carts were expensive and the wood needed to build them was scarce. By the 500s, camels had replaced oxcarts. Muslim roads were caravan routes, and since camels could walk on almost any type of surface, the routes received little or no maintenance. Camels with their loads could get through narrow passageways, so Muslim towns and cities could have narrow, winding streets—a feature that can still be seen today in much of the Islamic world.

European Roads.   Medieval people inherited the remains of the extensive road system that the ancient Romans had built, especially in ITALY, FRANCE, ENGLAND, and western GERMANY. While the Romans had built some bridges, they were chiefly interested in making straight, wide roads to carry their military forces swiftly from one end of the empire to the other. While some Roman roads remained in use through the Middle Ages, most had become unusable, either because of lack of maintenance or because local people had carried away the paving stones for use as building materials. A few new roads were constructed when a new town developed or when traffic increased to popular destinations—such as PILGRIMAGE shrines and FAIRS. Although stretches of road leading into and out of major towns were sometimes paved, most roads were dirt paths that became muddy when it rained or snowed. To make the roads passable, people put gravel, logs, or bundles of sticks in the muddy places. In some

Bridge Life

In the Middle Ages, bridges were more than just a way to get across a river. Many were lined with stores, public buildings, and other structures. At different times and places in medieval Europe, a person could go to school, live in a house, shop in a market, go to church, or even be born in a hospital—all on a bridge. A person could raise fish in a pond under a bridge and grind corn in a mill attached to a bridge. He or she could be tried in court—and even executed—on a bridge. Bridges were often the center of a town's life.

* **patron saint** saint held as guardian of a group's spiritual life

* **indulgence** release from all or part of a punishment for a sin

* **guild** association of craft and trade workers that set standards and represented the interests of its members

spots, especially in Germany, roads across marshes and swamps were built with wooden planks.

A French chronicler, writing in the 1200s, listed five kinds of roads: 4-foot-wide paths too narrow for carts; 8-foot-wide roads on which carts could travel but two carts could not pass; 16-foot-wide roads on which two carts could pass; 32-foot-wide roads that were wide enough for herds of cattle; and 64-foot-wide roads like those built by the Roman emperor Julius Caesar.

Smaller roads often belonged to the estates of local lords, churches, or monasteries, which collected tolls from people who used them. The large roads usually belonged to the king. By the 1200s, it had become customary for the tolls paid by travelers to be used to maintain and improve the roads. If the tolls on large roads were insufficient, the king might order towns along the way to contribute money or labor for the upkeep of the roads.

European Bridges.   The Romans had been much more interested in building roads than bridges. When they came to rivers, they were more likely to look for a shallow, safe place to cross on foot or by barge than to build a bridge. The medieval period, however, was a great age of bridge building. Medieval people built hundreds of impressive timber and stone bridges, some of which are still in use today. They believed that bridges were pleasing in God's sight because they helped travelers, many of them pilgrims, to cross dangerous and difficult places.

Medieval people wanted their bridges to be protected by SAINTS, and a chapel to a bridge's patron saint* was often built on or near the bridge. Building and caring for bridges was considered an act of religious merit. In fact, the church granted indulgences* to those who donated their labor or money for the construction of bridges.

Church-related institutions such as chapels, hospitals, monasteries, and convents were often built on or near bridges, and sometimes these institutions received a share of the bridge tolls. In some communities, people formed guilds* or brotherhoods to raise money for their local bridge. Bridges also were funded by taxes and charitable gifts.

Although most medieval bridges were neither fortified nor designed for defense, some were built for military use. These bridges had forts on them from which troops could defend against enemy soldiers who wanted to cross the bridge or pass under it. Bridges sometimes played an important role in military defense. For example, armed men on London Bridge prevented Danish invaders from advancing up the Thames River in 1016.

In the early Middle Ages, most bridges belonged to the church or to local lords and were made of wood, but in the 1100s two significant changes took place. First, as towns sprang up and grew in size, townspeople assumed responsibility for the construction and upkeep of local bridges. Bridge maintenance became more of a civic duty than an act of religious devotion. Second, bridge builders used stone for their larger and more ambitious ventures. Although stone bridges were more costly and difficult to construct than wooden ones, they lasted longer, and there was less chance of their being destroyed by fire or flood. The Ponte Vecchio in Florence, Italy, and the Old London Bridge are two examples of great medieval stone bridges. (*See also* **Crusades; Trade; Travel and Transportation; Warfare.**)

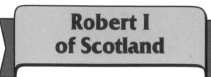

Robert I of Scotland

1274–1329
King of Scotland

See map in England (vol. 2).

Robert I was a member of the Bruce family, one of several families that claimed the Scottish throne in the 1200s. Robert spent much of his life fighting opponents, including the English king, EDWARD I, who claimed authority over Scotland. Robert finally won the right to rule an independent Scotland free of English control.

Robert was still in his 20s when he first participated in these conflicts. He fought alongside his father, who sought to depose the Scottish king, John Balliol. After the king was ousted, several prominent Scotsmen competed to replace him. In 1306, Robert quarreled with and subsequently murdered John Comyn, lord of Badenoch and a leading Scottish patriot. Robert then claimed the monarchy for himself and traveled to Scone, where he had himself crowned. Scone was the place where Scottish kings were traditionally crowned.

A few months later, English forces confronted Robert at Methven, where the Scots were defeated. Robert fled to the remote Western Isles, but his three brothers were captured and executed. After the death of King Edward I in 1307, Robert launched a campaign to regain control of Scotland. Beginning in the north, he advanced south, defeating his enemies and taking one region after another. In 1313, he captured Perth. A year later he met the large army of the English king, Edward II, on the battlefield. Robert and his much smaller force inflicted a crushing defeat on the English at Bannockburn.

Since the English refused to make peace and recognize Robert as Scotland's legitimate ruler, Robert raided northern England. In 1328, a weakened English government finally agreed to a peace treaty that recognized Robert as the independent king of Scotland. The treaty also arranged for the marriage of Robert's son David to the sister of EDWARD III OF ENGLAND.

While seeking to win Scotland's freedom, Robert also tried to strengthen and unify the country. To help govern, he appointed two capable assistants—his nephew, Thomas Randolph, whom he made the earl of Moray, and Sir James Douglas. By establishing an order of succession to the throne—his son David (King David II) followed by his grandson (Robert II)—he solidified Scotland's position as an independent kingdom. (*See also* **Scotland.**)

Robert d'Arbrissel

ca. 1047–1117
Founder of French religious order

Robert d'Arbrissel was a French religious reformer and preacher who founded a religious order that was respected for its piety and its creation of leadership roles for women. Born in the village of Arbrissel in BRITTANY, Robert studied literature and philosophy in PARIS. In 1089, the bishop of Rennes summoned him to assist with efforts at church reform in Brittany. Robert campaigned vigorously against various corrupt church practices, such as clerical marriage (it was becoming customary in this period for priests not to marry) and simony (buying and selling church positions). Robert spent four years preaching against these practices, as he became more strict about his own religious life.

In 1095, he went to live in the forest as a hermit. Whenever a large enough group of his followers expressed the desire to join him, Robert founded a monastery for them. He did this with the approval of Pope URBAN II.

In 1098, Robert left the monastery to devote himself exclusively to public preaching. His powerful sermons attracted many followers from all social classes—from lepers* and peasants to nobles, including many women. In 1101, Robert established a new religious order at Fontevrault, near Poitiers, with separate facilities for men and women. (ELEANOR OF AQUITAINE, queen of France, retired to Fontevrault after the death of her husband.) Robert refused the title of abbot and instead named two women to head the order.

During his extended travels as a preacher in western France, he founded other religious communities associated with Fontevrault. In 1115, Robert formally placed the order under the leadership of an abbess, and he himself continued preaching until his death in 1117.

* **leper** person who has leprosy

Robin Hood

One of the most popular and enduring legends of medieval England is the story of Robin Hood. According to the legend, Robin Hood was an outlaw who lived in Sherwood Forest with his gang and stole from the rich to help the poor. But this image of Robin Hood, created by writers and playwrights in the 16th and 17th centuries, differs from the earlier accounts of the man. The original Robin Hood who appeared in a handful of medieval BALLADS was a shadier figure.

Scholars have tried to identify the real-life Robin Hood, the historical figure who might have served as the basis for the legends, but no such identification has been possible. It seems that the Robin Hood story is a composite loosely based on the exploits of a group of outlaws who operated in the vicinity of Barnsdale, a town in the Yorkshire region of northern England. Apparently, the MINSTRELS who sang ballads about the exploits of these criminals combined tales about them with stories about the sheriff of Nottingham, which is actually 50 miles south of Barnsdale. Gradually, the sheriff and characters from the other ballads merged and became part of the Robin Hood legend. The legend's characters included a jolly monk named Friar Tuck and a beautiful woman named Maid Marian, both of whom had appeared in English and French poems, stories, and ballads long before Robin Hood.

The Robin Hood stories were probably composed in the early 1300s and spread by traveling minstrels. A reference to Robin Hood occurs in *Piers Plowman,* an English poem written in 1377. That poem describes a lazy priest who cannot say his prayers properly but can remember rhymes about "Robyn Hood." Another early reference dates from 1439 when the people of the Derbyshire district asked the English parliament to arrest a troublemaker who was living in the woods in the manner of "Robyn Hode." These and other early references suggest that the figure of Robin Hood was not admired by the general public. He was regarded more as an outlaw than as a hero. One medieval Scottish historian wrote that only foolish people celebrated him, and another chronicler described him as an assassin.

By the 1500s, the image of Robin Hood underwent an important change. The darker aspects of the legend faded, and the "new" Robin

Hood was portrayed as kind, brave, and generous. He remained an outlaw, but he was seen as the honorable victim of an unjust and corrupt society, as represented by the evil sheriff of Nottingham. This Robin Hood was a new type of hero. Unlike the aristocratic heroes of older romances, he was neither a prince nor a knight. Instead, he was a freeman of ordinary status who reflected the growing self-confidence of the English peasantry, a group that felt increasingly free to criticize the social ills caused by weak monarchs and corrupt local officials.

The Robin Hood stories appealed to a wide audience that included all levels of society. He was, and continues to be, regarded as a noble-hearted bandit committed to setting right the wrongs of society and securing justice for the downtrodden. (*See also* **England; English Language and Literature; Outlaws and Outlawry.**)

Roger of Salisbury

ca. 1065–1139
Bishop and statesman

* **chancellor** official who handles the records and archives of a monarch

* **fiscal** pertaining to financial matters and revenues

The man whom some called "Roger the Great" rose from obscure beginnings to become the bishop of Salisbury and one of England's most effective statesmen. As a priest in Normandy, Roger met and impressed the young future king of England, HENRY I. When Henry crossed the English Channel to England, he brought Roger with him and quickly put his administrative skills to work. In 1101, Henry appointed Roger royal chancellor*. Roger soon became bishop of Salisbury as well.

Henry I, who reigned from 1100 to 1135, spent most of his time dealing with troublesome matters in Normandy, relying on Roger to govern England in his absence. As the king's JUSTICIAR, or representative, Roger streamlined the government, making it more efficient, especially its finances and its court system. His most lasting contribution to English government was his creation of the EXCHEQUER, the department that manages the royal finances and public revenues. By doing so, Roger established the first effective fiscal* system in Europe. Roger also brought the government closer to the people by sending royal justices out into the countryside to hear pleas and complaints.

As bishop of Salisbury, Roger rebuilt the cathedral at Old Sarum (an ancient fortress town located one mile from the later town of Salisbury) on a grand scale and erected many new churches, monasteries, and castles. Roger's power and influence did not long outlive King Henry, however. King Stephen, who reigned from 1135 to 1154, turned against Roger and had him imprisoned. Roger and his family were forced to give up their money and property. Roger died in poverty on December 11, 1139. (*See also* **Angevins; Chancery; England; Normans.**)

Roland, Song of

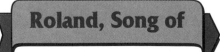

The *Song of Roland* is a French epic poem about the deeds of the Frankish emperor CHARLEMAGNE and his nephew Roland, who was one of his lieutenants. The 4,002-verse poem was written around 1100, although earlier versions of the story may have existed.

The *Song of Roland* is the oldest known example of the CHANSON DE GESTE, a type of medieval poem that celebrated CHIVALRY and noble deeds. The poem is based on an event that occurred in 778 when Muslims

The *Song of Roland,* a masterpiece of world literature, was written around 1100. It tells the story of the emperor Charlemagne and his nephew, Roland, and celebrates their noble deeds against the Saracens. This illumination showing Charlemagne and Roland comes from a later medieval manuscript.

See color plate 8, vol. 3.

ambushed Charlemagne's army as it was returning from a military campaign against Muslim Spain.

The *Song of Roland* sets Roland against his evil stepfather, Ganelon, who conspires with the treacherous Muslim leader Marsile. Marsile pretends to make peace with Charlemagne but then attacks the Frankish army from the rear. Roland and his friend Oliver hold off the attack as long as possible before blowing the horn to summon help. Charlemagne arrives to discover that his nephew has died a hero's death fighting the enemy.

Written in French about the time of the First Crusade* and soon translated into other languages, the *Song of Roland* portrays CHRISTIANITY as superior to other faiths, especially Islam—a view shared by the European nobles fighting in the CRUSADES. For modern scholars, the poem serves as a window into the past, offering a close look at the ideas and values of the medieval aristocracy. The poem, with its exciting story and memorable characters, is considered a masterpiece of world literature. (*See also* **Franks; French Language and Literature; Islam, Religion of; Nobility and Nobles.**)

* **crusade** holy war declared by the pope against non-Christians. Most were against Muslims, but crusades were also declared against heretics and pagans.

Roman de la Rose

* **allegory** literary device in which characters represent an idea or a religious or moral principle

The *Roman de la Rose* (called the *Romance of the Rose* in English) is a long French poem that many medieval writers imitated. It became the most influential allegory* of the Middle Ages.

The poem consists of two parts, written by different authors. The first and shorter part of the poem was written by Guillaume de Lorris around 1237 and is about COURTLY LOVE. The narrator describes a dream in which he enters a beautiful garden of pleasure and meets joyous figures who represent Youth, Wealth, Beauty, and Courtesy. In the garden, the narrator falls in love with a beautiful Rose. His attempts to win the Rose are aided by the God of Love, who gives him advice about proper behavior for a lover. In this first section of the *Roman de la Rose,* the narrator also meets such enemies as Jealousy and Fear. This first part of the poem ends with the narrator pining away for his unattainable love.

Between 1275 and 1280, Jean de Meun wrote a long conclusion to the *Roman de la Rose,* in which he continued the story of the lover's quest to win the Rose. Using such allegorical figures as Jealousy and Reason, he changed the poem from a hymn of praise for courtly love to a philosophical discussion about the nature of love. This part of the poem includes many passages that offer the writer's views on various subjects, such as the unfaithfulness of women and the greed of the clergy*. The poem ends with Venus, the goddess of love, setting fire to the castle in which the Rose is hidden, thus allowing the narrator to possess the Rose at last. (*See also* **Allegory; French Language and Literature.**)

* **clergy** priests, deacons, and other church officials qualified to perform church ceremonies

Roman Numerals

* **decimal system** system of numeration that is based on units of ten

* **abacus** device for making arithmetic calculations consisting of a frame with rows of counters or beads that slide back and forth

Roman numerals are the letter symbols used by the ancient Romans to represent numbers. These symbols continued to be used throughout the Middle Ages until they were finally replaced by the ARABIC NUMERALS used today.

Roman numerals were based on a decimal system* that used different symbols for tens, hundreds, and thousands and for the halfway point of each order (5, 50, and 500). The seven symbols of the Roman numeral system were I (1), V (5), X (10), L (50), C (100), D (500), and M (1000). The Romans calculated with an abacus* and did not use zero because the abacus did not require it as a place holder.

Arabic numerals and arithmetic were introduced into Europe in the late 1100s. However, people continued to use Roman numerals along with the new Arabic numerals, and many medieval manuscripts have both Roman and Arabic numerals in the same text. In the 1100s, the works of the great Arab mathematician al-KHWARIZMI were widely translated into Latin and adapted for Europeans. Although these works showed the advantages of Arabic numerals for more advanced mathematical calculations, the Arabic system of written arithmetic using the new notation only gradually took the place of Roman numerals. Roman numerals remained in use in Europe until the early 1400s. Since that time, Roman numerals have been used only for ornamental purposes. (*See also* **Mathematics.**)

Romanesque Architecture

Romanesque was the dominant architectural style of Europe from the early 1000s to the mid-1100s. The term *Romanesque* was chosen to describe this style by later art historians because of certain similarities with ancient Roman architecture, most notably the use of vaults and round arches. Visually, the round arches contrast dramatically with the pointed arches that were a prominent characteristic of the GOTHIC ARCHITECTURE that followed. Romanesque architecture is known primarily

The most notable characteristics of Romanesque architecture were the use of vaults and round arches and the regular division of interior spaces into bays. Solid, massive walls featured small windows that allowed little light to enter. This photograph shows Notre-Dame du Port in France, which was built before 1150.

from churches. Few domestic and public buildings from the period remain. Those that have survived, however, suggest that the secular architecture and the religious architecture of the period were quite similar.

Characteristics of Romanesque Architecture.   A fundamental feature of Romanesque architecture is the division of the interior spaces of a building into modular units called bays*. These spatial divisions are marked on the interior by projecting vertical elements, such as pilasters*, attached to the walls. These projections break up the interior spaces—the nave* and aisles in Romanesque churches—at equally spaced points along the length of the church. Overhead, the projecting elements are often connected by masonry* arches. On exterior walls, the bays are marked by buttresses* that correspond to the pilasters or columns inside. This articulation of interior and exterior wall surfaces was a clear break

* **bay**   section of a church or cathedral, defined by stone supports or columns

* **pilaster**   shallow, rectangular pillar projecting from a wall and serving as a support or decoration

* **nave**   main part of a church or cathedral between the side aisles

* **masonry**   referring to stone or brick

* **buttress**   stone or wood structure that supports a wall or building

* **vault** section of a three-dimensional arched ceiling of stone

* **pier** stone pillar used to sustain vertical pressure

* **apse** vaulted, semicircular section of a church, usually at the east end

* **basilica** oblong building with rows of columns dividing the interior into a nave, or central aisle, and side aisles

* **transept** the shorter part of a cross-shaped church, at right angles to the nave

* **choir** part of a church near the altar that is reserved for the singers

* **ambulatory** passageway around the choir and altar sections of a church

* **capital** uppermost portion of a column

* **barrel vault** round arched ceiling made of stone or brick

* **crypt** underground room of a church or cathedral, often used as a burial place

* **facade** front of a building; also, any side of a building that is given special architectural treatment

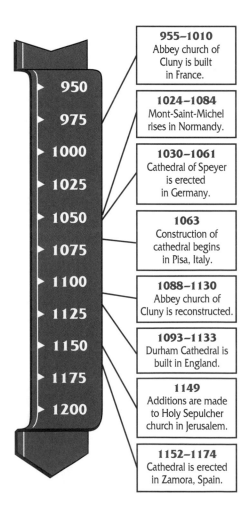

950	**955–1010** Abbey church of Cluny is built in France.
975	**1024–1084** Mont-Saint-Michel rises in Normandy.
1000	**1030–1061** Cathedral of Speyer is erected in Germany.
1025	**1063** Construction of cathedral begins in Pisa, Italy.
1050	
1075	
1100	**1088–1130** Abbey church of Cluny is reconstructed.
1125	**1093–1133** Durham Cathedral is built in England.
1150	**1149** Additions are made to Holy Sepulcher church in Jerusalem.
1175	
1200	**1152–1174** Cathedral is erected in Zamora, Spain.

from earlier architectural styles, in which flat, continuous wall surfaces were standard.

Another characteristic of Romanesque architecture is the regular use of large masonry vaults* over interior spaces. Such large-scale vaults were a common feature of ancient Roman architecture, but they were not used widely in the pre-Romanesque period. Pre-Romanesque buildings typically had wooden roofs, which were a fire hazard. Builders during the Romanesque period tried to eliminate this danger by rediscovering the vaulting techniques of the ancient Romans. Large masonry vaults must bc supported by solid, massive walls and piers*, and these features became characteristic of Romanesque architecture as well. There is relatively little light in Romanesque interiors. Romanesque builders seem to have thought that wall openings would weaken their structures, so they did not pierce windows through their heavy vaults and thick walls. This problem led to architectural experimentation and ultimately contributed to the development of the Gothic style in architecture.

Romanesque churches follow two basic ground plans. One is the echelon apse* plan. Churches of this type consist of a cross-shaped basilica* with small apses that open off the east walls of the transept*, the choir*, and the choir aisles. The other ground plan features an ambulatory* and radiating chapels. In this plan, the aisles next to the choir come together in a semicircular passage, called an ambulatory, that surrounds the central apse. Small chapels radiate off these passages, and worshipers can walk through the passage to visit the chapels without disturbing services in the main part of the church. The ambulatory and radiating chapel plan often was used for large churches, such as cathedrals and pilgrimage churches.

Variations in Romanesque Style. The Romanesque style had three basic sources. The first was Roman architecture. In addition to the round arch, the architects of Romanesque churches borrowed Roman decorative elements, such as moldings, grooved pilasters, and elaborately sculpted capitals* on columns. A second source of Romanesque architecture was the pre-Romanesque architecture of northern Spain, southern France, and northern Italy dating from 950 to 1020. Many buildings in these areas had features that were developed more fully in the Romanesque period, including heavy supporting walls, large barrel vaults*, and rudimentary bays. The third major source for Romanesque architecture was Ottonian architecture, the name given to architecture of the Holy Roman Empire from 950 to 1050. Ottonian buildings are close in size to the major structures of the Romanesque period. Many had semicircular crypts* similar to the ambulatories of Romanesque churches. Others had wall articulation that suggested the beginnings of the bays that were a basic characteristic of Romanesque. The Ottonian emphasis on elaborate facades*, often incorporating towers, was also carried over to the Romanesque period.

Building from these sources, Romanesque architects evolved a variety of regional styles. While all reflected the basic characteristics of the Romanesque, these styles also exhibited unique characteristics that became identified with certain geographic areas. The Romanesque style reached its fullest expression in France, where the regions of NORMANDY

and BURGUNDY were especially influential. Among the most important Romanesque buildings in France were the successive churches of the great BENEDICTINE abbey of Cluny, the first built between 955 and 1010 and the second between 1088 and 1130. The later church was at one time the largest in Christendom. Other parts of Europe—including England, Spain, Italy, and Germany—developed local variations on the Romanesque style. In Spain, for example, Islamic architecture was an important influence. In Italy, the architectural heritage of the early Christian era remained a powerful influence on the Romanesque style.

Spread of Romanesque Architecture.   As Romanesque architecture developed, it spread throughout Europe and even into the Holy Land*. In time, it became a truly international style, the first in Europe since the fall of the Roman Empire. Monastic orders, particularly the CISTERCIANS, helped to spread the Romanesque style as they did missionary work and established new monasteries.

* **Holy Land** Palestine, the site of religious shrines for Christians, Jews, and Muslims

The Romanesque architecture that developed around the edges of the European heartland tended to reflect the nearest major regional style. In Scandinavia, for example, German influence was very strong. The architecture of the region of Dalmatia, along the coast of the Adriatic Sea, relied heavily on Italian Romanesque designs. Finally, the Romanesque architecture of the Holy Land reflected the French Romanesque style, a result of the considerable French presence there. (*See also* **Construction, Building; Romanesque Art.**)

Romanesque Art

A style of art known as Romanesque flourished in western Europe from around 1000 to 1150. Romanesque art developed in close association with Romanesque architecture, and much of it was produced as decoration for buildings constructed during this period. Its origins were linked with the reform of religious life that began in the 900s, and, as a result, most Romanesque art is religious in subject matter. The greatest innovations in art during the Romanesque period occurred in sculpture adorning monuments and in mural painting. Other art forms—such as manuscript illumination, stained glass, and metalwork—also exhibited features of the Romanesque style.

Characteristics of Romanesque Art

There are distinct regional differences in the Romanesque style within western Europe. Yet there also are some elements common to almost all Romanesque art. Romanesque art, especially painting and sculpture, is both expressive and dramatic. Figures may be distorted and lines are irregular and twisted, creating a sense of agitation. In addition, movement is often exaggerated, creating a sense of extreme liveliness and visual excitement. Romanesque art emphasizes emotion, particularly religious excitement, and it presents rich images drawn from daily life. It also exhibits a taste for fantasy and the grotesque*. The stone walls of cathedrals and the pages of illuminated manuscripts are sometimes filled with grotesque and fanciful creatures. Most of these characteristics are especially evident in Romanesque sculpture.

* **grotesque** fanciful style of decorative art using distorted, ugly, or unnatural forms of people, animals, or plants

Among the earliest Romanesque sculptures in France were reliefs carved into the walls of the church of St. Sernin in Toulouse. This sculpture of Christ with the four symbols of the evangelists dates from around 1096. Most Romanesque art was religious in subject and was used to decorate cathedrals, churches, and monasteries.

* **reliquary**   container or shrine in which sacred relics are kept

* **tympanum**   ornamental space or panel on a building, usually the triangular section between the two slopes of a roof

* **evangelists**   writers of the Gospels—Matthew, Mark, Luke, and John

* **capital**   uppermost portion of a column

* **ambulatory**   passageway around the choir and altar sections of a church

* **facade**   front of a building; also, any side of a building that is given special architectural treatment

Romanesque Sculpture

Relief sculpture, in which the figures and ornaments project from the surface from which they are cut, had been used to decorate certain parts of ancient Roman buildings, but in the early Middle Ages it was used only for small, portable objects such as crosses and reliquaries*. It was not until the Romanesque period that large-scale, monumental sculpture based on ancient Roman models began to appear. The sculpture of the early Romanesque period was less three-dimensional than ancient Roman sculpture. It often was used as an element of architectural decoration on cathedrals, churches, and monasteries. Although Romanesque sculpture was found throughout much of western Europe, it probably made its greatest impact in Spain, France, and Italy.

France.   In general, Romanesque sculpture in France can be classified according to various regions. The sculpture of LANGUEDOC in southwestern France reflects one Romanesque tradition. Among the earliest Romanesque sculptures in this region are figures carved in relief on walls in the church of St. Sernin in TOULOUSE. The monastery of St. Pierre at Moissac, also near Toulouse, contains one of the masterpieces of Romanesque art. This is a tympanum* relief showing Christ surrounded by symbols of the evangelists* and other religious figures. All the figures are filled with life, exaggerated movement, and intense expression.

In BURGUNDY, Romanesque sculpture flourished at the BENEDICTINE abbey of Cluny, which was among the greatest architectural achievements of the Romanesque period. Sculptures on the huge capitals* that once decorated columns in the ambulatory* of the church depict subjects related to music and scenes of Adam and Eve. The carvings reflect the Burgundian taste for flattened surfaces and strong lines. A second phase of Burgundian sculpture is found at the church of La Madeleine at Vézelay. Its sculptures—which show scenes from the life of Christ, the apostles, and John the Baptist—contain figures of exaggerated length with garments consisting of elegant swirls and patterns of thin lines.

Another French Romanesque tradition is found in PROVENCE. The sculpture of Provence is more classical in style and suggests ancient Roman relief sculpture. It was no doubt influenced by the many remainders of Roman civilization in this region. The art of Provence resembles Roman art, for example, in the more realistic human anatomy of its figures.

Sculptures at the abbey of St. Denis were among the earliest in the Romanesque style in the region around PARIS. CHARTRES CATHEDRAL demonstrates the transition between the Romanesque and Gothic styles of architecture. The figures on its west facade* are some of the last that can be called Romanesque, with their planar, linear treatment and relative rigidity. Yet, the expressive faces and the exquisite delicacy of the detail of the figures herald the Gothic style.

Italy.   In the northern Italian region of Lombardy, most Romanesque sculpture had a classical appearance. As in Provence, this was probably due to the influence of Roman remains in the area. Unlike most Romanesque artists elsewhere, the sculptors of this region sometimes signed their works. A sculptor named Master Wiligelmo created reliefs for the Cathedral of Modena around the year 1100. His figures are heavy, stumpy, and somewhat three-dimensional. The contrast between bulky figures and

a lack of background space is typical of the Romanesque style in Lombardy. An unusual feature at the Cathedral of Modena is the representation of secular* subjects as well as religious scenes. The south portal* of the cathedral contains scenes from Aesop's fables, and arches have scenes of King Arthur and his knights.

Another Lombard sculptor, Niccolò da Verona, created figures that were smaller and better proportioned than those of Wiligelmo. His works have more persons in historical scenes, more suggestions of background of city and landscape, and more decorative details. His masterpiece, signed and dated 1135, appears in the Cathedral of Ferrara. It depicts the legendary St. George as a knight in armor killing a dragon, as well as figures of the biblical prophets that have such intensity of feeling that they seem to be shouting their prophecies.

In TUSCANY, relief sculpture did not appear until the mid-1100s. This was because the Romanesque architecture of the region favored a purely architectural mode of decoration and did not have a place for sculpture. When relief sculpture appeared, it was on pulpits, fonts*, and other types of church furniture rather than on the surfaces of buildings. This sculpture was more classical in style than that of any other region.

In southern Italy and Sicily, Romanesque sculptors drew from several cultural traditions. For example, the sculptures in the cloister* of the magnificent abbey cathedral of Monreale, which date from the late 1100s, display the influence of ancient Roman art, BYZANTINE ART, and IS-LAMIC ART.

Romanesque Painting

The walls of Romanesque churches often were decorated with mural paintings in fresco* or with MOSAICS. The large, often unbroken expanses of wall in these churches provided excellent surfaces on which painters could work. Romanesque mural paintings were often monumental in scale and bold in color and form. There were many regional styles of wall painting in Europe during the Romanesque period.

Rome and Italy.   The churches of Rome abound in splendid fresco and mosaic paintings from the 1100s. The unique style of these works reflects the early Christian traditions of the city. Among the best preserved of these decorations are the mosaics and frescoes in the church of San Clemente. Elsewhere in Italy, Byzantine influence was very strong, especially in small churches in southern Italy, in Sicily, and in VENICE.

Spain.   Many small churches in CATALONIA in northeastern Spain contain fresco decorations. Their lively and expressive style, with vigorous and contorted shapes and figures, is typically Romanesque. At the same time, many murals also reflect a strong Byzantine influence. Paintings on panels of wood from the region portray scenes of Christ, the Virgin Mary, and various saints. Their vivid colors make them brilliant examples of Romanesque art.

France.   The most complete set of Romanesque frescoes in France, dating from the early 1100s to the mid-1100s, is in the abbey church of St. Savin-sur-Gartempe, near the city of Poitiers. The colors of the frescoes include vivid shades of yellow, red, and green against light backgrounds.

* **secular** nonreligious; connected with everyday life

* **portal** large doorway or entrance

* **font** basin for holy or baptismal water

* **cloister** covered passageway around a courtyard in a monastery or convent

* **fresco** method of painting in which color is applied to moist plaster and becomes chemically bonded to the plaster as it dries; also refers to a painting done in this manner

The Worldly Versus the Unworldly

Romanesque sculpture can be appreciated from both a religious and a secular point of view. In the 1100s, Bernard of Clairvaux denounced Romanesque sculpture as too worldly. He worried that it was so excessively ornate that it would distract monks from their contemplation of God. Abbot Suger of St. Denis, on the other hand, believed that people could best understand God through the contemplation of worldly things, such as ornate sculptural decoration and other elaborate works of art.

* **nave** main part of a church or cathedral between the side aisles

Frescoes in the nave* of the church are especially impressive. They depict scenes from the Old Testament, beginning with the Creation and continuing to the story of Moses.

Frescoes of Christ and the saints in the small chapel at Berzé-la-Ville in Burgundy reveal Byzantine influence in the use of dark backgrounds and highlights. They also reflect the restless, agitated quality that is such an important characteristic of the Romanesque style.

Manuscript Illumination

During the Romanesque period, many illuminated manuscripts were produced by church schools and monasteries. Among the most popular books produced were large Bibles and the lives of SAINTS. In general, manuscript illumination shows the characteristics of Romanesque painting: strong colors; exaggerated postures and movement; some Byzantine influence in figure types, drapery, and lighting effects; and a mix of highly traditional and fantastic subjects. England especially was a prolific center of Romanesque manuscript painting. (*See also* **British Isles, Art and Architecture; Gothic Architecture; Gothic Painting; Gothic Sculpture; Romanesque Architecture.**)

Rome

The Germanic invasions of the 400s and the 500s that hastened the collapse of the Roman Empire left the once mighty capital, Rome, a shadow of its former self. During the Middle Ages, Rome became the center of a long power struggle between popes, German emperors, foreign invaders, and the city's nobility. By the end of the Middle Ages, Rome was the headquarters of the powerful PAPACY and the international capital of the Roman Catholic Church.

Early Middle Ages. The Byzantines who captured Rome from the OsTROGOTHS in 553 found the city depopulated and disorderly. The problems worsened 20 years later, when another Germanic group, the LOMBARDS, invaded Italy. The Lombard invasion had the effect of almost cutting off Rome from the rest of the Italian peninsula, which remained in Byzantine hands. By the late 500s, much of Rome's administration and social organization had collapsed. The civic offices responsible for managing the city and maintaining its aqueducts*, walls, and imperial palaces had declined or disappeared. Even the Roman Senate ceased to function.

* **aqueduct** channel, often including bridges and tunnels, that brings water from a distant source to where it is needed

Pope GREGORY I THE GREAT, concerned about the disrepair of the aqueduct system and the frequent collapses of ancient buildings, assumed leadership. Although he never had political control of Rome, he used church land to supply the city with food and essential services, including the care of refugees. Severe flooding of the Tiber River and the PLAGUE that followed added to his difficulties.

The Lombard threat against Rome intensified in the 700s, when the Lombards seized towns in the Tiber River valley north of Rome and threatened to attack Rome. Pope Zacharias I appealed to the FRANKS for help. In 756, the Lombards attacked Rome and plundered the sanctuaries until the Franks arrived and drove them back. When the Lombards attacked

Monuments of the old Roman Empire, including the circular Colosseum, can be seen in this panoramic view of the medieval city. In the later Middle Ages, the Roman government enacted laws to protect its ancient monuments from being dismantled or built over.

 See map in Italy (vol. 3).

* **militia** army of citizens who may be called into action in a time of emergency

Relics of Ancient Greatness

Many of the temples and monuments built by the ancient Romans were still standing in Rome in the early 500s. Around that time, however, the people of Rome began removing blocks of stone from the ancient structures for use in new construction. They also began building churches and homes over the sites of theaters, arenas, and other structures from pre-Christian Rome. In the late Middle Ages, Rome's governing body enacted laws to protect the city's ancient heritage, as people began to see the monuments of antiquity as a priceless legacy from the past.

Rome again in 771 and 773, the Frankish king CHARLEMAGNE intervened. His arrival in Rome in 774 marked the beginning of a long period of Frankish protection for the city. On Christmas Day 800, Pope LEO III crowned Charlemagne the new Roman emperor. Frankish support allowed the popes to construct churches and other public works, giving rise to a PAPAL STATE in Rome.

As the papal state emerged under Frankish protection, the interests of the great Roman nobles often clashed with those of the papacy. These clashes became especially violent during the papacies of Paul I (757–767) and Stephen III (768–772). When the reorganization and expansion of the papal estates threatened noble power, the nobles burned the estates. In the early 800s, Pope Paschal I tried to fight back against the nobles with the help of a rural church militia* called the *familia sancti Petri* (Holy Family of St. Peter).

After the death of Charlemagne, the imperial government tended to side with the Roman nobles, as reflected in Rome's constitution of 824. Rome prospered during this time, until a Muslim army sacked the city in 846. A period of decline set in, and the papacy came under the control of the local nobility. When the German king OTTO I THE GREAT entered Rome in 962 to restore imperial control of the papacy and to protect the pope from unruly citizens, the grateful pope crowned Otto emperor. Otto's coronation was the formal beginning of the HOLY ROMAN EMPIRE (although that name came later).

The German emperors tried to keep order in Rome, but the constantly feuding Roman nobles were the real rulers of the city. In 996, Emperor OTTO III tried to establish a permanent imperial government in Rome with the popes under his control, but his policies were not effective. The noble factions once again ruled the city, choosing the popes who suited them best.

Growth of the Papacy. By the 11th century, the papacy and the COLLEGE OF CARDINALS (the group of CLERGY that helped the pope manage the church) had become stronger and were taking control. Even after the Roman nobles ceased to run the city, the popes gave them some governmental authority by inviting them to attend papal councils. Toward the end of the century, the German ruler Henry IV became locked in a bitter struggle with Pope GREGORY VII over which of them had the right to

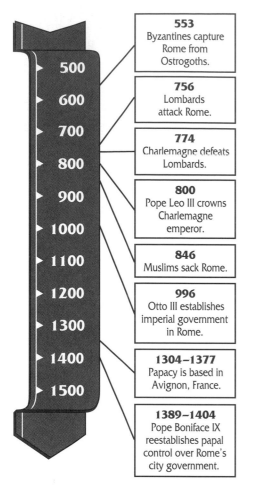

553
Byzantines capture Rome from Ostrogoths.

756
Lombards attack Rome.

774
Charlemagne defeats Lombards.

800
Pope Leo III crowns Charlemagne emperor.

846
Muslims sack Rome.

996
Otto III establishes imperial government in Rome.

1304–1377
Papacy is based in Avignon, France.

1389–1404
Pope Boniface IX reestablishes papal control over Rome's city government.

choose German bishops. In 1084, Henry entered Rome and appointed a new pope, Clement III, to replace Gregory. Clement in turn crowned Henry emperor. Several weeks later, the NORMANS arrived in the city to support Gregory. They defeated the Germans, but they also looted and set fire to parts of the city.

Control of Rome soon returned to the German emperors, who gave the Roman people the right to elect their own magistrates and senators and to control their economic resources. Friction emerged between the papacy and the Roman COMMUNE, or city government. This friction erupted into civil war under Pope INNOCENT III. In the mid-1200s, Rome's city government was fiercely against the papacy. During this period, Roman churches were financially exploited and sometimes even destroyed.

Between 1304 and 1377, the papacy was based in AVIGNON in southern France. Rome's economy suffered because, with the pope absent, there was less reason for pilgrims to visit that city and to spend money there. The popes tried to control their Italian lands from Avignon, but the power and independence of the Roman commune remained strong.

In the late 1300s, Pope Boniface IX limited the authority of the commune by forcing it to recognize his right to appoint city officials. The city senator became a papal official, and Roman judges came under papal influence. The papacy even gained the power to set aside city laws. By the early 1400s, the commune had lost its financial independence, and the papacy had established itself as the unofficial financial administrator of the city. Boniface had succeeded in establishing a papal authority over the Roman city government that would last for the rest of the Middle Ages.

The papacy of Pope Martin V marked the beginning of a new chapter in Rome's history. As the Middle Ages drew to a close, Rome was set to enter the Renaissance as the financial and administrative center of the Roman Catholic Church. Rome was also beginning to wield considerable political power, as European rulers sought papal endorsement of their right to govern. (*See also* **Christianity; Cities and Towns; Holy Year; Italy; Migrations, Germanic; Nobility and Nobles; Papal States; Pilgrimage; Schism, Great.**)

Royal Households

The growth of medieval kingship increased the size and scope of royal households. Royal households had existed since ancient times, when kings were surrounded by followers who saw to the king's comfort and helped him perform his duties. In the early Middle Ages, the kings of Europe were surrounded primarily by their military officers and advisers. However, as they became involved in activities other than fighting—such as managing their land and finances and administering justice—the kings delegated some of their duties to the members of their household. Food, drink, and clothing had to be provided. Horses needed to be looked after. The many details connected with moving the king, his family, and his household from residence to residence had to be taken care of.

Royal and noble households employed many people to tend to the needs and comforts of the aristocratic families. This banquet scene from the 1400s shows trumpet players performing at a noble household. As feudal courts became larger and wealthier, nobles spent more money on personal luxuries such as permanent minstrels to entertain the household.

* **falconer**   person who breeds and trains falcons for hunting

* **squire**   aide to a knight

Royal households in early medieval Europe had four major officials. The SENESCHAL, or steward, was in charge of obtaining food for the royal household. The butler was responsible for obtaining wine. The CHAMBER-LAIN administered the royal chamber (bedroom) and wardrobe (dressing room). The marshal cared for the king's horses and made his travel plans. Most royal households also included members of the CLERGY, whose job it was to take care of the religious needs of the king and his family. These clergy members said MASS and heard confessions, and they gave religious instruction to the king's children.

At first, these royal officials were responsible only for domestic matters, but gradually they were given public responsibilities as well. Trusted officials of the royal household administered the royal treasury and supplied and transported the army. As the king's advisers and assistants, these royal officials became the core of government. Chamberlains had such enormous influence on royal policy that in the 1300s the English BARONS had PARLIAMENT enact laws that curbed the power of these officials.

A document called the *Establishment of the Royal Household,* written about 1135, provides much information about the intricate workings of the English royal household and its officers. Although the size of English royal households varied, it was never less than several hundred persons. These included senior officials and their assistants, royal priests and doctors, clerks, minstrels, falconers*, messengers, kitchen and stable workers, palace servants, and the king's bodyguard of about 20 KNIGHTS and their squires*.

Members of the royal household staff, who often had an annual allowance as well as their food and lodging, were appointed by the king or his officers. Staff members who served the king outside the royal estate were reimbursed for their expenses. Emperors in Germany and Byzantium had huge households. During peacetime, however, the staff was much smaller than when the ruler was preparing to go to war.

Membership in the royal household was considered a great honor and sometimes a great danger. The French kings often preferred not to appoint high seneschals or chancellors (keepers of records) for fear that they might become rivals for the throne. However, for any ambitious individual, no matter how lowly his duties, service close to the king and his family meant economic and social advancement. (*See also* **Chaplain; Kingship, Theories of.**)

Royal Touch

* **leper** person who has leprosy

In the late Middle Ages, the kings of France and England were thought to have the ability to cure people with scrofula simply by touching them. Scrofula was called the "king's evil." It is an infection that enlarges the lymph glands. The term was also applied to jaundice, leprosy, and other disorders of the neck and face.

In *Vita Aedwardi regis,* a biography of King EDWARD THE CONFESSOR of England, the young king was said to have performed a healing miracle on a woman whose throat glands were infected. The biographer of King Robert II the Pious of France reported that the king healed sick people, including lepers*, by touching the diseased part of their bodies and making the sign of the cross.

Around 1124, Abbot Guibert of Nogent reported seeing King LOUIS VI of France perform his "customary miracle," healing crowds of people who came to him with scrofula. Guibert remarked that Louis's father, Philip I, had also performed miracles until his sins deprived him of his healing power.

By the late 13th century, royal touching to cure the "king's evil" was a regular practice in both France and England. English public records show that in 1276/1277 Edward I's confessor gave a penny to each of the 627 people cured of scrofula. In 1307/1308, many sufferers came to King PHILIP IV THE FAIR of France from as far away as Spain and Italy. The custom of royal touching continued in England until 1714 and in France until 1789. (*See also* **Kingship, Theories of; Medicine.**)

Rublev, Andrei

ca. 1360–1430
Monk and artist

* **fresco** method of painting in which color is applied to moist plaster and becomes chemically bonded to the plaster as it dries; also refers to a painting done in this manner

* **icon** Christian religious image of a saint, often painted and placed on a screen in the church; most common in the Eastern Church

Andrei Rublev was the most famous Russian artist of the Middle Ages. A monk at the Trinity–St. Sergius Monastery at Zagorsk near Moscow, he was frequently mentioned in both medieval chronicles and later sources.

Rublev's first known works, which date from 1405, were the frescoes* and icons* of the Annunciation Cathedral in the Kremlin (in Moscow). He worked on the cathedral with two other artists. In 1408, he and his friend Daniel Chorny painted decorative works in the Dormition Cathedral in Vladimir. Several years later, Rublev and Chorny worked together on the Trinity Cathedral at Zagorsk.

The most famous of Rublev's surviving icons were found in 1918 under some firewood in a barn near the Dormition Cathedral of Zvenigorod. Although the icons had been damaged, they show Rublev's great skill. The best known of the icons is the Old Testament Trinity, now

in the State Tretyakov Gallery in Moscow. Rublev's creative artistry influenced many later Russian icon painters. (*See also* **Byzantine Art; Icons; Muscovy, Rise of.**)

Ruiz, Juan

1283–1350
Spanish poet

* **parody** to ridicule by imitating; a work produced in this way

Spanish poet Juan Ruiz wrote the *Libro de buen amor (The Book of Good Love),* a long poem that was one of the most important literary works of medieval Spain. Little is known about Ruiz except that he was a priest in a small town near Guadalajara in central Spain. The *Libro,* written in the early 1300s, expresses the author's thoughts on pure (good) love and impure (evil) love. The poem has always delighted readers because of Ruiz's artistry in combining different themes and poetic styles and its sense of exuberance and joy. At the same time, the *Libro* has annoyed some critics because of the difficulties in categorizing the work with a particular literary tradition and in assessing its true meaning. Accurate interpretation is hindered by the poet's constantly changing stance and by his tendency to parody* established literary and cultural traditions. The text can be understood in a number of ways. It deals with the distinction between truth and falsity, and between the apparent and the real. This concern characterized Spanish literature up to the late 1600s.

The *Libro* combines philosophical argument with parodies of religious works, fables, praises of the Virgin Mary, stories of amorous adventures, and new compositions based on medieval, classical, and Islamic tales. Together, they form a vivid, humorous, but critical view of medieval Spanish society that is similar in tone to the *Canterbury Tales* of Geoffrey CHAUCER. Because of this similarity, Ruiz has often been called the "Spanish Chaucer." (*See also* **Spanish Language and Literature.**)

Rumi

1207–1273
Persian mystical poet

* **mystical** referring to the belief that divine truths or direct knowledge of God can be experienced through meditation and contemplation as much as through logical thought

* **theologian** person who studies religious faith and practice

Jalal al-Din, known as Rumi in the West, was the greatest mystical* poet in the Persian language. His works have had a profound and enduring influence on the spiritual life of Muslims in Iran, Turkey, central Asia, and India. Rumi also founded a mystical brotherhood known as the Mawlawiya, which still exists. Members are sometimes known as Whirling Dervishes because dancing and music are part of its spiritual practices.

Born in Balkh, a town in present-day Afghanistan, Rumi later moved to ANATOLIA. Although he seemed destined to become a theologian* and teacher like his father, several important spiritual relationships dramatically changed his life and transformed him into a great mystical poet. The first and most important of these was his relationship with Shams-i Tabrizi, a wandering mystic whom Rumi met in 1244. Rumi's affection for Shams inspired a hidden poetic talent. Under Shams's influence and encouragement, Rumi began writing poems in great abundance. His poems were eventually collected in a single volume called the *Divan.* His most significant work, the *Mathnawi,* was a long narrative poem, containing more than 25,000 couplets, which became the most important Persian mystical work. (*See also* **Iran; Islam, Religion of; Mysticism.**)

Runes

* **pagan** word used by Christians to mean non-Christian and believing in several gods

* **incantation** magical chant

Runes were the letters used by Vikings to write on wood and stone. Thousands of runic inscriptions have been found in northern Europe. Most predate the introduction of Christianity and the Latin alphabet into Scandinavia. Runic inscriptions have been of great value in the study of Germanic and Scandinavian culture.

Runes are letters of the runic alphabet, a system of writing native to medieval Scandinavia, England, and regions in northern Europe where Germanic languages were spoken. Runes were used extensively during the era of the VIKINGS. Their use declined after the establishment of Christianity and the introduction of the LATIN LANGUAGE and alphabet from which time runes were considered a pagan* form of writing. By the end of the 1300s, they were no longer a living tradition except in isolated parts of rural Scandinavia.

Scholars believe that runes developed sometime during the first century after the birth of Christ. They were probably invented by the Goths, a Germanic people of northern Europe, who are thought to have derived them from the alphabets of the Greek and Etruscan languages. The word *runes* itself derives from *runa,* a Gothic translation of the Greek word *mysterion,* and the term came to mean secret or private communications. This suggests that the earliest runes were known by only a small elite within the Germanic tribes.

Runes were adapted to carving on wood and stone. They consisted of perpendicular and slanted lines with few curves. The runic alphabet was known as the *futhark,* a term derived from the initial letters of the alphabet. A rune could appear upside down or reversed, and runic inscriptions could be read from left to right, from right to left, or even in alternating directions. Words or groups of words generally were not separated by spaces or punctuation marks. The oldest form of the alphabet consisted of 24 symbols. By the late 800s, the number of symbols had decreased to 16 as a result of significant changes in form and structure.

Scholars have discovered thousands of runic inscriptions in northern Europe. These provide an interesting glimpse into the life and culture of the early Germanic and Viking peoples. Many inscriptions are found on raised memorial stones in Sweden and date from the 900s and 1000s. Runic inscriptions also are found in Norway, in Denmark, on islands off the coasts of Scotland and Ireland, and as far away as Greenland and Iceland. They appear on such diverse objects as stone crosses, weapons, tools, jewelry, and gold medallions. They also appear on wooden sticks used to send messages, to record business transactions, and to mark down magical words or incantations*. (*See also* **Magic and Folklore; Scandinavia; Scandinavia, Culture of.**)

Rurik

ca. 800s
Founder of the
Russian state

* **mercenary** soldier who fights for payment rather than out of loyalty to a lord or nation

Rurik was a Viking chieftain who was credited with founding the early Russian state. Rurik grew up in Friesland (in the present-day Netherlands), a region controlled by his father. After raiding coastal areas of France, England, and Germany in the 840s, Rurik gained control of Jutland (in present-day Denmark). However, he soon lost this land to rivals.

Between 854 and 856, Rurik led an expedition into northwest Russia and established a settlement at Ladoga (near present-day St. Petersburg). Soon after, he became the leader of a mercenary* group that protected the nearby city of NOVGOROD. According to tradition, Rurik had come to Russia at the invitation of the people of Novgorod to govern them. He

eventually moved his seat of power to that city, where he built a fortress and became a genuine ruler of Russian lands. His rule extended as far south as the city of Kiev.

Rurik left Russia in 873 to take over his father's land in Friesland. He left his Russian realm to his kinsman Oleg because his son Igor was very young. Russian princes from this time on claimed descent from Rurik. One line of descendants supplied the grand princes and tsars* of Moscow until the late 1500s. (*See also* **Kievan Rus; Muscovy, Rise of; Scandinavia; Vikings.**)

See map in Kievan Rus (vol. 3).

* **tsar** Slavic term for emperor

Russia

See *Kievan Rus; Muscovy, Rise of; Novgorod.*

Sacraments

* **consecrate** to declare someone or something sacred in a church ceremony

Sacraments are the sacred practices or ceremonies of the Christian church. They are considered a form of grace given to the faithful by God, through Christ, in order to keep the faith alive and growing.

The word *sacrament* is derived from the Latin word *sacrare,* which means to consecrate* or to make a mystery. In the early history of the church, the word came to mean a sacred mystery, and it was used to describe any ritual of the church. This meaning was later narrowed to include only certain rituals. Over the course of the Middle Ages, the Christian church came to recognize seven sacraments: baptism, penance or confession, the Eucharist or Holy Communion, confirmation, holy orders, matrimony, and extreme unction.

Baptism is the first rite of joining the church, during which an individual is cleansed of sin and prepared for his or her eventual entrance into the Kingdom of Heaven. Penance or confession is a means by which sinners receive forgiveness for their sins through prayer, fasting, or some other action. Confession, penance, and forgiveness of sins traditionally have been necessary in order to partake of the Eucharist. The Eucharist, or Holy Communion, is the core of the Mass at which the faithful celebrate Christ and join him in spiritual union. Confirmation is the ritual in which one's joining the church at baptism is confirmed and strengthened. At first, confirmation was a part of the baptismal rite, but it became a separate ritual in the late 700s. Matrimony, or marriage, is the sacred union of two people with the blessing of the church. Holy orders refers to the ordination of clergy*. When a person takes holy orders, he vows to serve and obey God and carry out the duties of the church. Extreme unction is the last rite of the church, in which a priest grants a dying person forgiveness for sin. The rite was (and still is) of great importance because it removed an individual's remaining sin and prepared him or her for entrance into the Kingdom of Heaven.

By the end of the Middle Ages, these seven sacraments had become standardized rituals within the Roman Catholic Church. After the Reformation in the 1500s, the newly formed Protestant churches rejected most of the sacraments. They accepted only baptism and Communion as sacred. (*See also* **Anointing; Christianity; Death and Burial in Europe; Religious Instruction.**)

* **clergy** priests, deacons, and other church officials qualified to perform church ceremonies

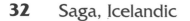

See *Scandinavia, Culture of.*

* **veneration** profound respect or reverence

* **liturgy** form of a religious service, particularly the words spoken or sung

* **martyr** person who suffers and dies rather than renounce a religious faith

* **asceticism** way of life in which a person rejects worldly pleasure and follows a life of prayer and poverty

Veronica, a pious Jewish woman, accompanied Christ to his Crucifixion. She comforted him by wiping his face. His image remained on the material, which became known as the Veil of Veronica. The lives of many saints, such as St. Veronica, became legendary. Facts gradually became inseparable from legend.

A basic belief of Christianity is the idea that all Christians, both living and dead, are bound together through the life and suffering of Christ. During the Middle Ages, the most prominent expression of this belief was the widespread veneration* of saints—men and women who lived their lives in the spirit of Christ. The cult of the saints, as it was called, led to the remembrance of saints at shrines, in the liturgy*, and in a body of literature about their lives that was meant to preserve their memory among the faithful and to inspire people to emulate their behavior.

Devotion to the saints originated in the veneration of early martyrs* whose deaths or spiritual asceticism* made them living examples of Christian heroism. The names and places of veneration of these martyrs were entered into a church calendar according to the date of their death, and these "feast days" were celebrated annually. The faithful also prayed to the saints and visited shrines dedicated to them.

Many of the earliest writings on the lives of saints were about the early martyrs. One of the most famous of the early saints' biographies was the *Life of St. Martin,* about a beloved monk and early bishop. Written in the late 300s by Sulpicius Severus, this work was widely imitated by writers throughout the Middle Ages. These early works were characterized by an absence of normal time references, since saints were thought to inhabit a world of eternal truth. As a result, these early lives presented little accurate historical information. In time, individual saints' lives were gathered together in collections. These collections formed the basis for narratives that were read aloud in church on each saint's feast day.

During the 500s, the ideal of Christian heroism began to shift, and saints were drawn largely from the ranks of the nobility. They were the people who maintained and spread the Christian faith and protected the church against the ungodly. As the number of saints increased, the church realized that it had to exert some sort of control over their public veneration, so it established certain regulations concerning sainthood. This led to the practice of CANONIZATION, which became formalized by the church in the 1100s.

In the 1100s and the 1200s, there was a tremendous increase in faith and spirituality in western Europe. New religious orders, the FRANCISCANS, DOMINICANS, and CISTERCIANS, were founded. The founders of these orders were quickly viewed as saints, and works were written about their lives. At this same time, saints' lives were collected in single volumes for popular use. Unlike earlier periods when saints' lives were used primarily for moral improvement, they now became a form of entertainment. This led to an emphasis on literary style rather than accuracy of content. The number of lives of women saints also increased significantly during this period.

Writing about the lives of saints was also a rich literary tradition in the BYZANTINE EMPIRE. It developed along much the same lines as in western

See color plate 5, vol. 3.

See color plate 6, vol. 3.

Europe, except that here it remained more focused on individual saints than on collections of saints' lives. The 800s and the 900s were considered a golden age for this type of writing. Many saints' lives were written at this time to remember missionaries, women saints, and the founders of monasteries.

Muslims and Jews also wrote about the lives of their saints. The most complete source book about the lives of the early Islamic mystics is *Hilyat al-awliya (The Ornament of the Saints)*. Written about 1000, it preserved the sayings and teachings of early Sufi masters as well as details about their lives. Jewish literature also contains many stories about leading zaddikim (saints), who symbolized both strict adherence to Jewish law and a love of God and of other people. (*See also* **Bede; Books, Manuscript; Byzantine Literature.**)

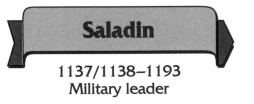

Saladin

1137/1138–1193
Military leader

* **crusader** person who participated in the holy wars against the Muslims during the Middle Ages

The Muslim leader Saladin is best known for his victory over Christian crusaders* at the Battle of HITTIN, his recapture of JERUSALEM in October 1187, and his defensive struggle against the enemies of Islam during the Third Crusade. To many in the Islamic world, Saladin was a model of piety, humility, generosity, and chivalry. His exploits gained him the admiration of Muslims and the respect of many Christians.

Saladin belonged to an ambitious Kurdish family with roots in ARMENIA, but he rose to prominence in IRAQ and SYRIA. His father, Ayyub, and his uncle, Shirkuh, were in the service of powerful Syrian leaders, including the famous Nur al-Din. The prestige and influence of Saladin's father and uncle were helpful in promoting Saladin's own career.

In 1156, Saladin was put in charge of the security forces of DAMASCUS. He soon became an officer in charge of communication between Nur al-Din and his military commanders, a position that helped Saladin gain first-hand experience in running a military organization. Saladin's political power grew as a result of the significant role he played in three military expeditions against the FATIMID EMPIRE of Egypt between 1164 and 1169. During these campaigns, he displayed superior organizational talent, distinguished himself in battle, and helped seize control of the Fatimid CALIPHATE by killing its treacherous VIZIER. With his reputation firmly established, he became commander of the Syrian army in Egypt, and he was appointed vizier of the Fatimid caliphate.

In this position, Saladin quickly launched a series of military, economic, and administrative reforms in Egypt. He also organized successful military operations in Yemen, NUBIA, and North Africa and put down local rebellions. By 1171, he had emerged as a powerful force in the AYYUBID family, and he suppressed the Fatimid caliphate. When Nur al-Din died in 1174, Saladin rushed to Damascus to take control. This attempt to expand his power led to rivalries between Saladin and Nur al-Din's descendants and to years of internal struggles. By 1186, he had defeated his opponents and gained control of northern Syria, Iraq, and eastern ANATOLIA.

Saladin next turned his attention to the Christian crusaders. In July 1187, his Muslim army won a great victory over the crusaders at the Battle

Saladin was one of the most famous warriors of the Middle Ages. He was a hero to the Muslim people and won the respect of many Christians as well. Although much of his fame rests on his battles with Richard the Lionhearted during the Third Crusade, Saladin led many military campaigns, including victories in Syria, Iraq, and Egypt. Saladin's army is shown here in this French illumination from the 1300s.

* **Holy Land**   Palestine, the site of religious shrines for Christians, Jews, and Muslims

* **Sunnites**   Muslim majority who believed that the caliphs should rule the Islamic community

of Hittin. With the loss of military protection, crusader territories in the Holy Land* quickly fell to Saladin's army. The high point in the struggle came in October 1187, when Jerusalem surrendered to Saladin.

Despite Saladin's victories, he never succeeded in expelling the crusaders from the Middle East. Crucial fortresses along the Mediterranean coast remained in Christian hands, and the defense of these strongholds eventually led to the Third Crusade. Although Jerusalem was never reconquered, crusader attacks inflicted crippling blows to Saladin's status. The Egyptian navy was destroyed and Egypt's resources were severely strained. After losing several battles to RICHARD I THE LIONHEARTED, Saladin signed a three-year truce with the crusaders in 1192. He died in Damascus soon afterward, following a brief illness. Although Saladin had failed to destroy the crusaders, his recovery of Jerusalem won him the lasting admiration of Muslims. Among his other great achievements were the reestablishment of the Sunnite* branch of Islam in Egypt and the founding of Ayyubid rule in Egypt, Syria, and Iraq. (*See also* **Crusades; Egypt; Jerusalem.**)

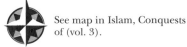

See map in Islam, Conquests of (vol. 3).

Samarkand is an ancient city located in central Asia (in present-day Uzbekistan). It is thought that the city was originally founded in the mid-500s B.C. by the Persian king Cyrus the Great. Cyrus reportedly established Samarkand as a frontier outpost to protect Persia from attacks by central Asian nomads.

Throughout much of its early history, Samarkand drifted in and out of the political influence of Persia. It was usually dominated locally by Turkish and Mongol groups. The importance of the city was its location. It was a major stopping place on the main trade route between Asia and the West, and it was one of the last outposts for merchants traveling east.

After its conquest by the Arabs in the early 700s, Samarkand became one of the easternmost outposts of Islam. At first a part of the Islamic

* **dynasty** succession of rulers from the same family or group

* **artisans** skilled craftspeople

Empire of the UMAYYADS and ABBASIDS, the city was eventually ruled by a succession of local dynasties*. During a revival of Iranian culture in the 900s, Samarkand became a flourishing center of Islamic learning and Persian artistic and literary activity. After the late 900s, the city was ruled by a succession of Turkish dynasties. Then, in the early 1200s, it was conquered by the Mongols and incorporated into the MONGOL EMPIRE. Under Mongol rule, Samarkand went into a period of decline, and much of the city fell into ruin.

By the mid-1300s, Mongol rule of the region around Samarkand gave way to a period of anarchy. Out of this chaos emerged a local chieftain named TAMERLANE. Tamerlane reestablished order and made Samarkand his capital. Although responsible for unprecedented and unparalleled horrors in the Middle East, Russia, and India, Tamerlane brought a period of renewal to Samarkand. He spared no expense in transforming the half-ruined city into a showcase of his rule. Tamerlane brought captive craftsmen and artisans* from the lands he conquered to Samarkand and put them to work on building projects. This period saw the construction of impressive Islamic architectural works throughout the city. Some of these buildings and monuments still distinguish some of the older parts of Samarkand today. (*See also* **Genghis Khan; Iran; Iraq; Islam, Conquests of.**)

Samarra

* **caliph** religious and political head of an Islamic state

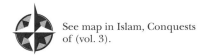
See map in Islam, Conquests of (vol. 3).

* **mosque** Muslim place of worship

Samarra was the second great capital city of the ABBASIDS. Situated along the Tigris River north of BAGHDAD, the city was founded by caliph* al-MU'TASIM in 835. It served as the administrative center of the Abbasid Empire until caliph al-Mu'tadid returned the government to Baghdad in 892.

Samarra was probably founded because of the hostility of the population of Baghdad to al-Mu'tasim's Turkish guard. To help reduce public anger toward these foreign troops, the caliph decided to leave Baghdad and to establish a new city. The site he chose was situated on a large plain and did not offer any commercial, geographic, or strategic advantages. It is possible that the site had been settled at various periods going back to ancient times. One legend says that al-Mu'tasim built the city in fulfillment of an ancient prophecy.

Samarra consisted of a series of isolated settlements extending like a ribbon for about 20 miles along both banks of the Tigris River and outside the perimeter of the city. The city was planned very carefully. Al-Mu'tasim built three palaces, numerous dwellings for his staff and Turkish army, and an extensive economic system, including a market area surrounding the main mosque*. Careful attention was paid to keeping the military separate from the general population. Military settlements were situated a considerable distance from the main markets, and slave girls were imported to provide wives for the Turkish troops, who were forbidden to marry other women.

The main thoroughfare of Samarra was called the al-Sarijah. This road extended the entire length of the city, and government buildings, the main mosque, and city markets were all situated along it. All important roads ran parallel to it. The absence of major bisecting roads was probably a deliberate effort to discourage movement between military settlements and civilian areas. Samarra was thus essentially a series of military camps kept separate from one another.

Samarra grew and expanded under later caliphs, and the distinction between military settlements and other neighborhoods gradually blurred. Increasingly, Samarra took on the features of an integrated city and lost those of a military camp. Despite the expansion and changes that occurred in the mid-800s, caliph al-Mu'tadid abandoned Samarra in 892 and moved the government back to Baghdad. Thereafter, Samarra declined rapidly. (*See also* **Caliphate; Iraq.**)

Sanctuary, Right of

* **abbey** monastery under the rule of an abbot or abbess

In the Middle Ages, fugitives from the law had the right to protection and shelter in churches. This was called the right of sanctuary. Every church or chapel, including its churchyard, was considered a sanctuary—a place where the accused could claim asylum and not be pursued. Some abbeys* had large areas of sanctuary, with limits clearly marked by signs, such as stone crosses.

The fugitive in sanctuary had to surrender any weapons, make confession to church officials, and place himself under their supervision. Then he had a set time, often 40 days, to make a choice: surrender to the law and stand trial, or publicly confess guilt and go into exile. The sanctuary was guarded by a group of villagers who would be fined if the fugitive escaped. If he failed to decide after the allotted time, the church was forbidden to give him any more food or drink.

Fugitives who chose exile lost all their possessions. They had to walk to the borders of the kingdom, bareheaded and barefoot, keeping to the highway and carrying a cross as a sign of protection. Even so, their enemies might lie in ambush. If they left the highway or returned from exile without the king's permission, they could be executed.

In many countries, the right of sanctuary existed until modern times. Though France suppressed it in the 1400s, churches could still offer sanctuary in England until 1623 and in Prussia until 1794. (*See also* **Law.**)

Santiago de Compostela

* **apostle** early follower of Jesus who traveled and spread his teachings

* **pilgrimage** journey to a shrine or sacred place

Santiago de Compostela is a city in the province of Galicia in northwestern Spain. The city dates from the early 800s, when an ancient tomb was discovered there. The tomb was thought to be that of the apostle* James. According to tradition, James's body was brought to the area because he had Christianized the region through his preaching. Shortly after the discovery of the tomb, a small church was built above it, and James was eventually declared the patron saint of Spain.

The tomb of James immediately became an important pilgrimage* site, and a city developed around it. In the late 800s, the original church was replaced by a larger one, but that one was destroyed by the Arab caliph al-MANSUR when he captured and destroyed the city in 997. Construction

* **Romanesque** referring to a style of architecture developed in Italy and western Europe between the Roman and Gothic periods and characterized by round arches, thick walls, and small windows

* **consecrate** to declare someone or something sacred in a church ceremony

* **ambulatory** passageway around the choir and altar sections of a church

* **relic** object cherished for its association with a martyr or saint

of a large, Romanesque* cathedral began around 1075, and this church was consecrated* in 1211. The design of this church, often called the "pilgrimage plan," was shared by certain other pilgrimage churches of the period. It had galleries over the aisles as well as an ambulatory* with chapels situated away from the center to accommodate large crowds of worshipers moving through the church to visit the relics*.

In the 1100s and the 1200s, Santiago de Compostela was one of the most important spiritual centers of Western Christianity, attracting thousands of pilgrims each year. Only Jerusalem and Rome were more important pilgrimage centers. The city and its cathedral also served Christians as a counter to the Muslims in the rest of Spain. Santiago became a vivid symbol of the ancient roots and current vitality of the Christian church in Spain. (*See also* **Mass, Liturgy of; Pilgrimage; Relics; Romanesque Architecture.**)

Sasanians

* **dynasty** succession of rulers from the same family or group

 See map in Islam, Conquests of (vol. 3).

* **pagan** word used by Christians to mean non-Christian and believing in several gods

* **bureaucracy** large departmental organization such as a government

* **magistrate** ruling official of a town

For more than four centuries (from 224 to 651), the Sasanian dynasty* ruled Persia, the region of present-day IRAN and IRAQ. Sasanian rule ended in the mid-600s when the Arabs conquered the region.

The founder of the Sasanian dynasty was Ardesir I, who came to power in about 224. Ardesir had killed the former king and acquired the title "king of kings" by winning the support of other local rulers. He further strengthened his position by placing members of his family in government. Ardesir's son, Sabuhr I, led Persia's military struggle against the Roman Empire—a conflict that would continue throughout Sasanian history. In 259, Sabuhr I defeated the Romans and captured the Roman emperor Valerian.

The Sasanians established the Zoroastrian religion—founded by the prophet Zoroaster in the sixth century B.C. and practiced in western Persia at that time—as the state religion. This decision led to the persecution of non-Zoroastrians, including Manichaeans, Christians, and native Persian pagans*, whom the Zoroastrian church condemned as worshipers of demons.

Sabuhr II, who reigned from 309 to 379, succeeded in centralizing the Sasanian Empire by establishing a state bureaucracy* to administer the region. The government bureaucracy was run by a chief civil official, and most of its members were recruited from the lower ranks of the priesthood and the nobility. However, doctors, astrologers, poets, and musicians also served the government.

When ARMENIA converted to Christianity and developed close ties to the Roman Empire in the 300s, Sabuhr II invaded Armenia, which at that time divided its loyalty between Rome and Persia. Sabuhr II also encouraged the Zoroastrian campaign against other religions. During his reign, taxes on Christians doubled, and persecutions against Jews and Manichaeans increased. Despite periods of persecution, Christianity flourished. Some Sasanian rulers tolerated Christians, and some actually favored them, appointing Christians to positions of authority as magistrates*, tax collectors, bankers, doctors, and ambassadors. The top jobs, however, were reserved for the Zoroastrian clergy.

Xusro I (pronounced Khusrau), whose reign began in 531, was considered the model of a wise and just ruler. He was known for his support of scholars. His grandson, Xusro II, undertook successful military campaigns against the BYZANTINE EMPIRE. He invaded deep into Byzantine territory, taking JERUSALEM in 614 and EGYPT in 619. In 622, the Byzantines defeated the Sasanians, weakening the empire, which was beginning to feel growing pressure from ARABIA. Arab forces raided Sasanian territory several times and then attacked in full force in the 630s. The Arabs defeated the Sasanians in major battles in 636 and 642, opening the Iranian plateau to Arab conquest. This marked the beginning of the Islamic era in Iran.

The Sasanian cultural heritage survived the Arab onslaught and enriched the Islamic civilization that developed after the 600s. Many Islamic writers and rulers admired the Sasanians, and some later Islamic dynasties in Iran traced their ancestry to the Sasanians. Unlike many other lands conquered by the Arabs, Iran never adopted the Arabic language. (*See also* **Arabic Language and Literature; Islam, Conquests of; Islam, Religion of; Islamic Art and Architecture.**)

Scandinavia

See map in Vikings (vol. 4).

Aside from scattered references in ancient sources, Scandinavia was little known to the rest of the world before the VIKING raiders from the region began terrorizing Europe in the 800s. The Christianization of the Scandinavian nations—Denmark, Sweden, Norway, and Iceland—between about 950 and 1100 linked the area more closely to European civilization.

Early History

The earliest surviving reference to Scandinavian peoples appeared in a work by the Greek geographer Strabo, who described the writings of a sailor's journey to the far north around the fourth century B.C. The Roman writer Pliny, writing in the first century A.D., used the name *Scadinavia* (the *n* was added later) to refer to the Germanic tribes who lived around the Baltic and North Seas. The Roman historian Tacitus, writing in his *Germania* in A.D. 98, discusses the kingdom of Sweden, the Lapp people of northern Scandinavia, and the Finns. Other references to Scandinavia appear in the early medieval period. However, it was not until the 800s—when CAROLINGIAN Europeans traveled to Scandinavia and the Vikings raided Europe—that Scandinavia entered European history.

The Scandinavians did not write about their early history. What little is known about them (from before 800) comes from archaeological remains and artifacts found at settlement sites, graves, and other places. Among the articles discovered were spears, swords, horns, pictorial stones, and gold jewelry.

In the early Middle Ages, the common political unit in southern Scandinavia was the *herred,* or district. Decisions were made by yeomen (free farmers) who met at regular intervals at a local public assembly. A central assembly generally approved a new king's right to rule, and when the king attended such assemblies, he did so as a guest. The assemblies

Scandinavian Society

Yeomen, or free farmers, formed the basis of medieval Scandinavian society. Those yeomen who owned their own land had greater status than those who rented from or worked for others. Yeomen, at their public assemblies, made decisions affecting the community and gave judgments in lawsuits.

Local leaders rose to positions of power by means of noble birth, wealth, marriage to a woman of noble family, or royal favor. Men could also achieve leadership through personal qualities—especially bravery, which Scandinavians deemed the highest virtue.

* **bishopric** office of or area governed by a bishop

* **archbishopric** church district headed by an archbishop

could replace the monarch if he broke the law or failed to bring prosperity and success to the region. Over time, the king played a greater role in defense—building fortifications, guarding coasts, and constructing roads and bridges. As his power increased, so did the size of his entourage (those who went with him when he moved from place to place).

During the Middle Ages, the peoples of Scandinavia were united by shared language and customs. For a time, they were politically unified as well. However, Denmark, Sweden, Norway, and Iceland did not maintain their unity. Iceland was most distinctive in being ruled by chieftains in a "democracy" until it came under the authority of the Norwegian king.

Denmark

The first reference to Denmark appears in Carolingian chronicles of the ninth century, which report frontier skirmishes against a Danish king named Godfred. Soon after, Vikings from Denmark and other parts of Scandinavia came from the north to explore, raid, colonize, and trade in Europe. The first Vikings set out in small groups under the leadership of war chieftains. Gorm the Old and his son Harald II Bluetooth were the first to launch full-scale attacks beyond the Baltic and North Seas.

In the 980s, Harald's son, Sweyn I Forkbeard, set out to conquer England and became the English king in 1014. Sweyn was succeeded by his son Cnut I the Great, who spent most of his time in England and greatly admired English civilization. He not only allowed ANGLO-SAXON customs to continue in England, he also introduced them in Denmark. Danish interest in England died with Cnut and his sons. Succeeding Danish kings concentrated on raising the standard of living in Denmark. However, European interest in Scandinavia increased after the mid-1000s. Several historical sources reported the growing contact between Scandinavia and the rest of Europe. Adam of Bremen's *History of the Bishops of the Church of Hamburg*, written in the 1070s, described in detail the missionary work carried out in Denmark by the German church. The most outstanding of the Danish historians who emerged at this time was Saxo Grammaticus. His *Gesta Danorum*, a massive history of the Danes from the beginning of the monarchy to about 1185, compares in size and worthiness to BEDE's great *Ecclesiastical History of the English People.*

Sweyn II Estridsen, Cnut's nephew and an Anglo-Saxon earl, was the first and most important Danish king. In 1042, he received Denmark as his share of Cnut's vast North Sea empire and ruled it until his death in 1074. Sweyn promoted the growth of Christianity in Denmark. Working with the archbishop of Hamburg, he organized the Danish church into eight bishoprics*—an act that greatly impressed Pope GREGORY VII, who wrote Sweyn a series of friendly letters. The church was further strengthened in 1103 when a Danish archbishopric* was established in Lund.

For 60 years following Sweyn's death, Denmark was ruled by his five sons, who were elected king in succession. After the last son died in 1134, family members fought bitterly for the crown. Family rivalries led to the election of two kings. Both candidates appealed to the German emperor FREDERICK I BARBAROSSA, who tried to divide the kingdom between them. Family rivalries resurfaced many times until one member of the family, Waldemar I, finally emerged as the sole ruler.

A stela is a freestanding stone that is carved or inscribed. It is used to mark a grave or to commemorate an important event. Stelae are an ancient art form. The one shown here is from Gotland, a Swedish island in the Baltic Sea, and dates from before the year 1000. Scandinavian stelae sometimes depicted scenes from Viking mythology.

* **pagan** word used by Christians to mean non-Christian and believing in several gods

* **diocese** church district under a bishop's authority

The Waldemar Age—from 1157 to 1241 and including the reigns of Waldemar I and his sons Cnut VI and Waldemar II—was the high point of Danish medieval history. The kings and the archbishops of Lund worked together to strengthen both church and state. Denmark expanded its power in the Baltic, conquering Estonia and German coastal areas. Eventually, tensions developed between church and state, the nobility revolted, and the monarchy fell.

The monarchy enjoyed a brief revival under Waldemar IV in the mid-1300s. His remarkable daughter Margaret, married to the Norwegian king, established the Nordic Union that united Denmark, Norway, and Sweden into a single Scandinavian government in 1397. Her son, Olaf, ruled both Norway and Denmark, and her grandnephew, Eric of Pomerania, served as king of Sweden. The union prospered under Margaret, but after her death, the Swedes withdrew and chose their own king. Denmark and Norway remained united for four centuries.

Sweden

In the early Middle Ages, Sweden was virtually unknown to the rest of Europe. Historians Jordanes (a Goth) and Procopius (a Byzantine) recorded stories of sailors, traders, and Scandinavian officers who served in the armies of Gothic Italy and Byzantium. According to their accounts, three major tribes lived in Sweden—Goths, Swedes, and Ostrogoths. Other, smaller tribes in western Sweden were part of the Danish Empire.

The peoples of Sweden lived in small villages and engaged in farming, herding, hunting, and fishing. The climate was favorable for AGRICULTURE, and trade was also important to the economy. Archaeological evidence shows that the inhabitants of Sweden traded with the Romans and Greeks and later with the FRANKS, ANGLO-SAXONS, and Irish. Birka, a new town built on an island in Lake Mälar, became a center of international trade and a temporary residence of the king of Sweden.

During the Viking era (800–1000), the kingdom of Sweden was a loose federation of the three main tribes. The Swedes chose the king, and the other tribes then decided whether to accept or reject the Swedish choice. The Swedish king, in fact, had little power except in time of war, and sometimes the Goths preferred to have their own king. From earliest medieval times, the Swedish people were linked by water. They traveled readily along the ocean coast and on rivers and lakes. Scandinavian ships—light, swift, and seaworthy—both united the Swedes and other Scandinavian peoples and allowed them to sail across the seas and down the rivers of Europe.

In the 900s, Sweden was Christianized, probably by English missionaries. Swedish kings were Christian, although several early kings were expelled by their pagan* opponents. In the mid-1000s, Christianity gained a stronger foothold in Sweden when a diocese* was established in the new city of Skara.

During the later Middle Ages, the Swedish kingdom expanded eastward. Sweden established settlements on both sides of the Gulf of Finland, attempted to control trade in northern Russia, and colonized the sparsely populated northern parts of Sweden. The 14th century brought civil war between the Swedish kings and the nobility who opposed them. The conflict ended when Margaret of Denmark was recognized as ruler of all three

Scandinavian kingdoms. However, later, the Swedes left the Nordic Union, and Sweden remained an independent kingdom until the close of the Middle Ages.

Norway

Medieval Norway was an agricultural society with few villages and fewer towns. Most people lived on farms and supplemented their farming with fishing, hunting, and wood cutting. Fish made up a large part of the daily diet of the people who lived in the northern and western coastal districts.

As the population of Europe increased after 1000, so did the demand for Norwegian stockfish (fish dried in the open air without salt). In addition, the fasting rules of the church banned the eating of meat on certain days, which meant that many people ate fish instead. This further increased the demand for Norwegian stockfish, which accounted for as much as 80 to 90 percent of Norway's exports. With the money they made from selling stockfish, the Norwegians imported much-needed grain and malt. The western port of Bergen became a bustling center of foreign trade, especially with England and Germany.

As the population of medieval Norway increased, settlement expanded into the interior and into the sparsely populated north. Overpopulation in the southern and western coastal areas may have been the main force behind the Viking colonization of the Shetland, Orkney, Hebrides, and Faeroe Islands in the North Atlantic. Even after the Viking emigrations from Norway, the country's population continued to grow. In the early 1300s, the population was between 300,000 and 500,000. However, the BLACK DEATH of 1349–1350 and the epidemics that followed drastically reduced the Norwegian population.

The unification of Norway, which had begun with the reign of King Harald I Fairhair in the late 800s, proceeded with periods of military struggle that pitted the king against local chieftains who resisted his rule. In the late 1300s, Olaf IV (the son of Norway's King Haakon VI and the Danish princess Margaret) became king of Denmark even before he inherited his father's Norwegian throne. Olaf's reign strengthened the Danish-Norwegian union that eventually lasted for more than four centuries.

Iceland

Iceland is an island in the North Atlantic Ocean. In the mid-800s, it was inhabited by only a few Irish hermits. A Scandinavian explorer discovered Iceland by mistake when a fierce wind blew him off course as he sailed to the Faeroe Islands. His chance discovery of the remote island led to further exploratory visits and then to large-scale colonization.

Between 870 and 930, thousands of Scandinavians settled in Iceland. Most were Norwegian, but some came from Denmark, from Sweden, and from Scandinavian settlements in SCOTLAND, IRELAND, and the North Atlantic islands. The main reasons for the large-scale emigration from Scandinavia seem to have been overpopulation and the dissatisfaction of local chieftains in western Norway with policies of King Harald I Fairhair. By 930, more than 30,000 Scandinavians had settled in Iceland.

Fearful of allowing a king to gain too much power, the settlers established a government that gave local chieftains the authority to control the legislative and judicial processes. The chieftains gave land to their followers

See color plate 12, vol. 2.

Remember: *Words in small capital letters have separate entries, and the index at the end of Volume 4 will guide you to more information on many topics.*

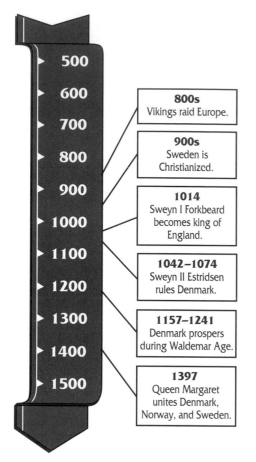

800s
Vikings raid Europe.

900s
Sweden is
Christianized.

1014
Sweyn I Forkbeard
becomes king of
England.

1042–1074
Sweyn II Estridsen
rules Denmark.

1157–1241
Denmark prospers
during Waldemar Age.

1397
Queen Margaret
unites Denmark,
Norway, and Sweden.

in exchange for allegiance and the payment of taxes. The chieftains also provided their followers with protection, settlement of disputes, and places of worship. As more settlers came to Iceland and the number of disputes between neighbors increased, judicial assemblies became necessary for areas larger than those controlled by a single chieftain.

The most important assembly was the Althing, an islandwide assembly that had been established by 930. It met for two weeks every June. The legislative body associated with it—the Lögrétta—had 144 members, two bishops (after Christianity was introduced to Iceland), and a "lawspeaker" whose main duty was to recite the laws to the assembly from memory. (Iceland's laws were first written down around 1117.)

When Iceland was divided into four regions in 965, the Althing had four Quarter Courts whose members were chosen from the island's 36 chieftaincies. The Fifth Court was introduced in the early 1000s to serve as an appeals court. After the Lögrétta adopted Christianity in about 1000, the chieftains found a way to control the new religion the way they had controlled the old pagan religion—by building their own churches and becoming priests themselves or appointing their own priests. After two dioceses were established at Skálholt (1056) and Hólar (1106), the Althing chose the bishops, who were usually relatives of the chieftains. When a TITHE (church tax) was imposed in 1097, the chieftains kept half the money they collected in their districts.

Iceland's main product was a rough wool cloth, but the island never seemed to have enough cloth to export in exchange for the grain it needed. Despite Iceland's attempt to trade with other places, its only consistent trading partner was Norway. Iceland's commercial tie to Norway was strengthened in 1022 by a trading agreement.

In the 1200s, strife among Icelandic chieftains became so intense, and their opposition to church reforms so extreme, that the people called on the king of Norway for help. In 1262, the island's leading chieftains agreed to a political union with Norway. In return for an annual tax, the king kept peace on the island and passed no laws that were burdensome to the Icelanders. However, after the union, Norwegian laws were introduced, and the authority of the Althing and the Lögrétta was reduced.

By the end of the Middle Ages, there was peace in Iceland, and the island was receiving basic necessities—but at a price. Although the island had been settled in part to escape royal power, it was now dependent on the united kingdom of Denmark and Norway. (*See also* **Fishing, Fish Trade; German Language and Literature; Historical Writing; Kievan Rus; Law; Migrations, Germanic; Scandinavia, Culture of; Ships and Shipbuilding.**)

Scandinavia, Culture of

The literary culture of medieval Scandinavia consisted of two types of material: the old mythology and sagas (long tales or poems about heroes from Scandinavia's pre-Christian past), and the newly created material such as rhymed chronicles, saints' lives, sermons, and other religious works written on Christian themes.

Mythology and Sagas.   Most of what we know about pre-Christian Scandinavian culture comes from medieval Icelandic poems called Eddas,

Golden Hoards

Early Scandinavian culture encompassed more than literature. Scandinavian artists and craftspeople produced magnificent weapons and jewelry. Long two-edged swords, spearheads, battle-axes, pins, bracelets, and necklaces have been found in graves and settlement sites throughout the region. The most spectacular finds are superbly decorated gold necklaces. Bracteates—thin gold disks meant to be sewn onto clothing—have also been found. Many bracteates were stamped with figures of heroes or gods; their wearers believed that the bracteates had supernatural powers.

See map in Vikings (vol. 4).

* **heathen** not believing in the God of the Bible

which recorded the Norse legends about heroes, gods, giants, and the origins of the world. One important source of information about Norse legend and myth is a manuscript called the Codex Regius of the *Poetic Edda*. Another is the *Prose Edda*, a handbook of poetry compiled by Icelander Snorri Sturluson around 1220.

The chief god of the pre-Christian Scandinavians was called All-father. He was supreme over 12 other gods, the best known of whom were Odin and Thor. Odin—later equated with All-father—was the highest and oldest of these gods. Wednesday (Woden's day in Old English) was named for him. Thor, the strongest of the gods, was often pictured in battle against evil forces represented by giants, trolls, wolves, and other creatures, such as the Midgard serpent, who lived in the ocean and was coiled around the earth. Thursday (Thor's day) was named for this god. Two other weekdays bear the names of Scandinavian dieties. The name of Tyr, the boldest of the gods, was given to Tuesday (Tyr's day), while the name of Odin's wife, Frigg, the preeminent goddess, was given to Friday.

The sagas are long narratives that describe the deeds of notable Vikings and other Scandinavians. Although the sagas are concerned mainly with events of the 10th and the 11th centuries or earlier, they were not written down until the 1200s and the 1300s. Because the sagas were passed along orally and preserved only in memory for many years, there are various versions of each popular tale. The *Greenlanders' Saga* and the *Saga of Erik the Red* are of special interest to modern historians. They tell how Norse adventurers founded a colony on Greenland, a large island off the coast of North America, and how Vikings became the first Europeans to see the Americas.

Rhymed Chronicles. The rhymed chronicle originated on the European Continent in the late 1100s and appeared in Scandinavia in the late 1200s and the early 1300s. A rhymed chronicle is an account in verse of a historical event or series of events, usually in honor of an aristocrat or aristocratic family. The style and structure of the medieval Scandinavian chronicles were based on models from elsewhere in Europe, especially from Germany.

The first and perhaps the finest of the Scandinavian rhymed chronicles is *Erikskrönikan (The Chronicle of Erik)*. Composed anonymously between 1322 and 1332, *Erikskrönikan* set the pattern for all later Scandinavian chronicles. The longest surviving version of the chronicle contains 4,545 lines. It opens with the following lines: "May God grant you honor and praise./He is the source of all comely virtue,/All earthly pleasure and heavenly grace,/For he reigns over them both."

Erikskrönikan chronicles Sweden's history from the rule of Erik Eriksson in 1249 to the selection of Magnus II Eriksson as king in 1319. Most of the first part of the poem, which chronicles events to the year 1301, is about a war against the heathen* Finns. The next section narrates the events of the next few decades, including a 1309 sea battle between the king of Norway and Duke Erik, the brother of King Birger Magnusson of Sweden. The last part of the chronicle describes a feast at Nyköping Castle to which King Birger invites his brothers Erik and Waldemar. The king imprisons and executes his brothers in a scene that forms the emotional core of the chronicle and raises it to the level of a true epic poem. None of the other Scandinavian chronicles comes close to achieving its high artistic standard.

Of the Scandinavian chronicles that followed *Erikskrönikan*, only *Karlskrönikan*, the longest of the rhymed chronicles (9,628 lines), is of special interest. This is because it contains valuable historical information. Completed in 1452, *Karlskrönikan* chronicles Sweden's history from 1390 to 1452. The poem seems to contain two distinct chronicles and is probably the work of two anonymous authors.

Religious Works.   The medieval religious literature of Scandinavia and Iceland consisted of commentaries on the BIBLE, translations, SERMONS, lives of saints, accounts of visions and revelations, theological* handbooks, prayer books, and other devotional writings. These works were not fundamentally Scandinavian. They closely resemble Latin sources and were part of the teaching and preaching of missionaries who Christianized Scandinavia.

CHRISTIANITY was introduced to Scandinavia in the 800s, first to Denmark and Sweden, and later to Norway, Iceland, and Greenland. St. Ansgar, the first archbishop of Hamburg in northern Germany, is credited with bringing Christianity to Denmark and Sweden about 830. However, missionaries from the British Isles also went to Scandinavia. They may have been the ones who inspired Scandinavian writers to use their native languages. The missionary period lasted until 1104, when the church established an archbishopric* in Lund, in southern Sweden, to serve the needs of Sweden and Denmark. In the mid-1100s, two additional archbishoprics were created in Scandinavia.

Medieval Scandinavians were deeply interested in stories about the lives of saints. More than 100 saints and groups of saints had their stories told in Icelandic and Norwegian sagas, and collections of saints' lives were constantly revised and expanded to make the legends fuller and better. Literature about Mary, the mother of Jesus, was also extremely popular in Scandinavia, especially legends about the miracles she was said to have performed. Stories about her life circulated in Iceland as early as the 1100s, and a long series of Swedish tales about her miracles was also found.

Two nearly complete manuscripts from about 1200—one Icelandic and the other Norwegian—are the best surviving source of medieval Scandinavian sermons. Theological handbooks, schoolbooks, prayer books, and other works used in worship from the medieval period were mainly in Latin or translated from Latin. As with most Scandinavian religious literature, inspiration for these works came from abroad, particularly from Germany. (*See also* **Anglo-Saxons; English Language and Literature; Handbooks (Fachschrifttum); Latin Language; Saints, Lives of; Scandinavia; Vikings.**)

* **theological**   pertaining to the nature of God, the study of religion, and religious beliefs

* **archbishopric**   church district headed by an archbishop

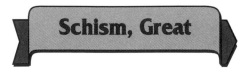

Schism, Great

* **papacy**   office of the pope and his administrators

From 1378 to 1417, the Roman Catholic Church was divided by allegiances to rival papacies*: one centered in AVIGNON in France, the other in ROME, Italy. Known as the Great Schism, this division was not about matters of faith; it involved a conflict between persons and politics.

The papacy had moved to Avignon in 1308 because of political conflicts. For the next 70 years, the Avignon popes, all of whom were French, had the support of all Catholics. In 1378, Pope Gregory XI moved the papacy

(*See also* **Papacy, Origins and Development.**)

* **cardinal** high church official, ranking just below the pope

back to Rome. He died shortly thereafter. The people of Rome, who feared that the papacy would be returned to Avignon, demanded the election of an Italian pope. Under pressure, the cardinals* chose an Italian archbishop, who became Pope Urban VI.

Urban VI soon lost the support of many church leaders because of his policies and his abusive behavior. The cardinals declared his election invalid and elected a French cardinal as Pope Clement VII. Urban VI, however, refused to step down, so Clement fled to Avignon, where he set up a rival papal court. These rival courts at Rome and Avignon had the support of different parts of Europe. Support for Avignon came from France, Scotland, parts of Spain, and Sicily. The Roman papacy was recognized by England, Ireland, and most other states of Europe. Some states remained neutral.

* **abdication** giving up the throne voluntarily or under pressure

* **depose** to remove from high office

The existence of two papacies, each with substantial support, caused tensions and problems throughout western Europe. Finally, in the 1390s, some European leaders began pressing for an end to the schism. In 1394, the French sought a diplomatic solution to the problem: the voluntary abdication* of both reigning popes and the election of a single new one. When both popes refused, a general church council was convened. The Council of Pisa of 1409 deposed* both the Avignon pope, Benedict XIII, and the Roman pope, Gregory XII, and elected a new pope, Alexander V, to head a united church. Although this solution was supported by most European rulers, the deposed popes still had many followers, and they refused to step down. The result was that instead of two popes, there were now three. Neither Alexander V nor his successor, John XXIII, could gather enough support to establish a unified papacy.

* **doctrine** principle, theory, or belief presented for acceptance

The Great Schism was resolved finally in 1417 at the Council of Constance. The Roman pope, Gregory XII, was persuaded to resign. The Avignon pope, Benedict XIII, and the other pope, John XXIII, were deposed. A new pope, Martin V, was chosen to head a unified papacy. Martin had substantial support throughout Europe, and the schism ended. While it lasted, the Great Schism delayed church reforms and raised important questions concerning papal authority. On this last issue, the Council of Constance proclaimed the doctrine* of "conciliarism"—the idea that a general council representing the whole church was the supreme religious authority to which even popes had to submit. (*See also* **Papacy, Origins and Development.**)

Scholasticism

* **theology** study of the nature of God and of religious truth

* **philosophy** study of ideas, including science

Scholasticism was a way of thinking that sought to combine classical, Christian, and worldly knowledge into a single belief system. The term *Scholasticism* comes from the Latin word *schola,* which originally meant a learned conversation or debate but later came to refer to a school. Scholasticism was a way of teaching and learning that was widely used in the UNIVERSITIES of Europe, especially in the disciplines of theology* and philosophy*.

The Scholastic method originated in the work of European scholars of church law and theologians of the 11th and the 12th centuries.

Albertus Magnus was a major figure in the Scholastic movement of the 13th century. Albert was interested in the ideas of Aristotle and tried to bring these ideas into harmony with the Christian faith. Scholasticism was a way of teaching and learning that was widely used in medieval European universities.

Scholasticism developed as these scholars tried to find agreement among the authorities. The Bible was, for many people, the highest authority. Yet some sections of the Bible seemed to contradict other sections. Furthermore, the ideas of other respected authorities, such as the ancient Greek philosopher Aristotle, did not always agree with the Bible. The theologian's task was to closely examine these conflicting texts and then to interpret them in such a way as to make them agree with one another.

Scholars of church law faced a similar task when confronted with centuries-old statements from church councils, popes, and other religious authorities. Sometimes, these statements were in conflict with one another. However, since all such statements were believed to be inspired by true Christian faith and human reason, agreement was very important. Scholasticism grew out of the need to find harmony among different authorities. Scholastics often used the principles of logical argument developed by Aristotle to accomplish their work.

By 1200, Scholasticism was flourishing in the universities of Europe. In these centers of learning, Scholasticism found expression in three types of writing that were popular in the medieval schools—commentary, question, and summa. The commentary consisted of a detailed examination of a textual passage. The question consisted of a written debate or discussion of an issue. The summa was a summary of an issue that was used to introduce a subject to new students. All three types of writing reflected two basic principles of Scholasticism—belief in the importance of authoritative religious and scholarly texts, and close attention to detail. After the 1500s, Scholasticism changed when summaries came to be used more frequently than commentaries and questions, and agreement among different sources ceased to be the main purpose of study. (*See also* **Aquinas, Thomas, St.**)

Schools

See color plate 13, vol. 1.

During the Middle Ages, schools played an important role in both western European and Islamic society. In general, schools made no attempt to provide a broad public education. Instead, they provided a private, specialized education aimed at promoting LITERACY among certain groups of the population and training young people for specific roles, especially religious roles, within their society.

European Schools

There were various types of schools in medieval Europe, including cathedral schools, monastic schools, grammar schools, and palace schools. Throughout the medieval period, education at these schools was a luxury generally available to only a small minority of the male population, and schools were established and supported primarily by the church.

Cathedral Schools. Medieval cathedral schools existed to train CLERGY for their religious duties. Thus, education was largely practical and emphasized knowledge of Latin and church law, singing of hymns, preparation of documents, performance of the liturgy*, and administration of the SACRAMENTS. Literature, the liberal arts, theology, and philosophy were

* **liturgy** form of a religious service, particularly the words spoken or sung

sometimes included as part of the curriculum as well, but only to make the study of the BIBLE easier.

The beginnings of cathedral schools date from the late Roman Empire. Before that time, clergy members were educated in secular* Roman schools, and they learned religious skills through practice and imitation while serving in the church. As Roman schools closed, bishops established schools of their own. The first bishops' schools were founded in the 300s and the 400s. By the 600s and the 700s, cathedral schools had become important centers of learning in northern Italy and elsewhere in Europe. In the early 800s, CHARLEMAGNE ordered all cathedrals to provide schools for training religious leaders. As a result, cathedral schools were opened in all the cathedral towns of his realm. As these towns grew, so did the schools. Many gained a reputation for the excellence of their teaching and curriculum. Cathedral schools began to dominate medieval education and intellectual life in the late 900s. By the 1000s and the 1100s, cathedral schools at PARIS, Rheims, Chartres, Liège, TOLEDO, COLOGNE, and CANTERBURY had become leading centers of European intellectual life.

The intellectual excellence of schools depended on the master, or head teacher. Until the 1100s, when a license to teach was required, no specific standards governed the choice and conduct of the master. He usually had to be at least 25 years old, although younger masters were known. His classroom might be located in the cathedral itself, in a room in the bishop's palace, or in a special building reserved for his use.

Curriculum varied from school to school, depending on the resources available and the special interests of the master. Elementary instruction always included learning to read and write basic Latin, to sing, and to calculate. Instruction in reading began with recognition of the letters of the alphabet. This went hand in hand with writing, as students learned to copy letters on parchment or wax tablets. Students used books of psalms* as their first reading texts, and they memorized the contents. While learning the psalms, students were introduced to singing and chanting.

Calculation was another basic skill students had to master. In addition to learning how to perform simple arithmetical functions, students also learned how to determine the time of day and the date of important holy days, which required understanding complicated formulas related to the movement of the sun, moon, and other heavenly bodies. Students also learned how to measure fields, tally harvests, and perform various financial transactions.

As students learned basic skills, they also were introduced to the study of Latin, the language of the church. The study of Latin began in earnest after reading, writing, calculation, and chant were mastered. Students were expected not only to be able to read Latin, but also to write and speak it with ease. These skills often took many years to acquire.

From the 6th to the 13th century, learning was commonly divided into the seven liberal arts, consisting of the trivium (grammar, rhetoric*, and logic) and the quadrivium (arithmetic, geometry, music, and astronomy). Some students also pursued studies in history, geography, law, science, and medicine. The main purpose of all training was to better understand the Christian faith. Uncovering the meanings of the Bible was a

* **secular** nonreligious; connected with everyday life

* **psalms** sacred songs from the Old Testament of the Bible

* **rhetoric** art of speaking or writing effectively

Medieval schools were supported primarily by the church. In the later Middle Ages, universities developed as important new places of education. They were independent of church authority and could determine their own courses of study. This detail from the 1100s shows a law seminar in Bologna, Italy, the location of medieval Europe's leading law school.

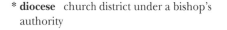

* **diocese**   church district under a bishop's authority

basic endeavor for both masters and students, and each group used their accumulated knowledge to achieve this goal.

In the 1000s and the 1100s, the fame of certain cathedral schools attracted students from beyond the limits of the diocese*. Some schools, such as those in Paris, attracted an international student body. Schools became crowded with students, masters competed for teaching positions and students, and bishops complained that they were losing authority over their own schools. In this turbulent atmosphere, several cathedral towns developed a new educational institution—the university. The first UNIVERSITIES were medieval "corporations" of masters or of students, who determined their own administrative structure, academic requirements, and curricula.

Monastic Schools.   Schooling was an integral part of monastic life. Since the study of Scripture required literacy, early monks found a need to gather together for group study as well as for prayer. As in cathedral schools, the purpose of monastic schools was to provide Christian instruction.

By the late 500s, monastic schools played an important role in training individuals for service in the church. Training often included the study of Christian writings, Latin, and grammar. In the late 700s and the early 800s, monasteries helped spread education to the public. Kings often were taught by monks, and large abbeys began to designate qualified monks as schoolmasters. Learning in monastic schools was based on the seven liberal arts, with astronomy and arithmetic being taught in addition to religious studies. Under Charlemagne, monastic schools, like cathedral schools, were charged with teaching boys psalms, writing, singing, calculation, and grammar.

Charlemagne's successor, Louis I the Pious, led reforms to remove all secular influences from the monasteries and to limit monastic schooling to future monks. Such reforms, continued through the Middle Ages, tended to push the responsibility for public education onto other types of schools. Monasteries that continued to teach secular students separated them from the novices* by creating classrooms in town or outside the monastery walls. Over the course of the Middle Ages, monastic schools declined in importance, but they were still essential for the education of monks into the 11th century.

*** novice** person in a religious order during a period of probation before taking vows

Grammar Schools.   Medieval grammar schools taught young people the crafts of writing and reading. The most basic type of grammar school was a simple, casual meeting between a student and any literate person. Beginning in the 500s, grammar schools were incorporated within monastic schools. Many of these schools offered education to outsiders as well as to young novices and others connected with the monastery.

In the 800s, ALCUIN OF YORK, the tutor of Charlemagne's son, initiated reforms that led to the development of grammar schools in cathedrals. These schools were modeled after those in the monasteries. In 1215, a church council made grammar schools mandatory for all cathedrals. Around the same time, religious orders of FRANCISCANS and DOMINICANS established grammar schools in cities. These schools offered the basics of learning to townspeople and recruited future members for the order. Some of the more important urban grammar schools provided the elementary preparation for future university students, and Franciscan and Dominican schools were crucial in the founding of the early universities.

*** monarchy** nation ruled by a king or queen

Palace Schools.   Schools were an important feature of court life in many early medieval monarchies*. By educating the children of nobles, these schools helped secure the loyalty of noble families to the king. Instruction at palace schools was quite elementary, and much of the training was vocational. The children were educated in the military and bureaucratic duties of a court noble for the roles they would assume when grown up. The atmosphere in palace schools was informal. There was no fixed curriculum, and instruction could take place anywhere in the palace and at any time. Relationships among students and between students and their teachers was close.

*** patronage** the support of an artist, writer, or scholar by a person of wealth and influence

The best-known palace school was that of the CAROLINGIANS, particularly during the reign of Charlemagne. Royal patronage* attracted scholars to this school from all over Europe. In the 1000s and the 1100s, the academic functions of palace schools were taken over by monastic and cathedral schools, and later by universities.

Islamic Schools

The most important type of school in the Islamic world was the Muslim college. Developed by Muslims in the 600s and the 700s, the college was unknown in western Europe until the late 1100s. Education at a Muslim college consisted mainly of studies of the QUR'AN, Islamic law, and Arabic grammar and rhetoric. In the early Islamic era, colleges were located in mosques*, and students came from home to attend classes. In the 900s, a new type of college developed in which an inn was added to house students

*** mosque** Muslim place of worship

Fernando, the Boy Wonder

In 1445, a young student came to study at the College of Navarre. Masters at the college were truly impressed by his prodigious skills. He sang beautifully and excelled in mathematics. He was an exceptional artist, and he could swing a sword so mightily that none would fight with him. He had mastered medicine, law, and theology. He spoke fluently in Latin, Greek, Hebrew, Arabic, and several other languages. One teacher described him this way: "So shrewdly did he reply to all the questions which were proposed that he surpassed belief. . . . Indeed, he filled us with deep awe, for he knew more than human nature can bear."

* **synagogue** building of worship for Jews

from out of town. This became necessary since students might require many years to finish their education.

By the 1000s, another form of Muslim college was developed—the madrasa. The madrasa was a private institution located in a building complex that combined the teaching function of a mosque with housing for students. Madrasas flourished, and a network of them was established throughout the Islamic world. The curriculum remained the same as that of the earlier colleges.

Besides the mosque and the madrasa, education also was available at monastery colleges and at institutions that combined the various functions of the mosque, madrasa, and monastery. All these Muslim colleges taught only subjects that related to Islamic religion and law. Greek sciences, including philosophy and mathematics, were taught privately in the homes of scholars or in other institutions, such as hospitals.

Jewish Schools

Education was very important among the Jews, and various forms of private and community-sponsored institutions developed in JEWISH COMMUNITIES throughout the medieval world. As with Christian and Muslim education, Jewish education also was focused on religion. Jewish schools, however, reflected major cultural differences between the Jewish communities of northern Europe and those of Spain and the Islamic world. In northern Europe, Jewish schools emphasized piety and the study of the Talmud, the body of religious writing relating to Jewish tradition. In Spain and the Islamic world, Jewish schools combined a study of the Bible, Hebrew grammar, Jewish law, and the Talmud with studies of sciences, philosophy, logic, mathematics, music, and medicine.

To provide their sons with an education, many Jewish fathers hired private tutors. Synagogues* also supplied schoolrooms with teachers paid for by parents or the community. Jewish communities throughout the medieval world were very involved both in providing educational opportunities and in supervising curriculum and instruction. (*See also* **Classical Tradition in the Middle Ages; Judaism; Law Schools; Religious Instruction.**)

Science

* **optics** branch of physics that deals with the properties and phenomena of light

* **theology** study of the nature of God and of religious truth

* **philosophy** study of ideas, including science

Islamic and Jewish scholars studied and preserved the scientific, philosophical, and medical works of ancient Greece, and then they went on to develop their own scientific traditions. Europeans, who benefited both from the learning of the ancient Greeks and from Islamic science, made many further scientific contributions, particularly in such fields as mechanics and optics*. For many European scholars, science was a means of understanding God's creation, and scientific principles were often examined in relation to theology* and philosophy*. For more about European science, see the articles listed at the end of this entry.

Islamic Science.   Scientific endeavors in the Islamic world began in the mid-700s, as scholars in BAGHDAD translated ancient Greek texts into Arabic. Work on translating ancient texts continued into the 900s, and Islamic

science reached its greatest levels of achievement at different times and places over a period that extended to the early 1400s.

Those who embraced the medieval scientific tradition came from various parts of the Islamic world and were of different backgrounds. Some were Christians, others were Jews, and still others were Muslims. A common factor was that Arabic was the predominant language of scientific expression and communication. The use of Arabic was the major reason for the spread of scientific knowledge throughout the Islamic world.

The early translations of Greek texts were supported by the rulers and elite classes of Islamic society. Although some translations were made under the UMAYYADS in DAMASCUS, it was not until the rise of the ABBASIDS in the mid-700s that the job of translation developed into a major undertaking. Among the first scientific texts translated into Arabic were astronomical works originally written in Sanskrit* and Persian. During the reign of HARUN AL-RASHID, great works of Greek science by Euclid and Ptolemy were made available in Arabic. Soon, Islamic scholars had access to an enormous amount of ancient science and philosophy, including works by Aristotle and Plato.

* **Sanskrit** ancient sacred and literary language of India

At the same time that Abbasid power declined, centers of learning multiplied across the Islamic world. A large public library, the Dar al-Ilm (House of Science), was founded in CAIRO in 1004. In the 12th century, scholars of astronomy, philosophy, and medicine flourished in Muslim Spain. In SAMARKAND (in southwest Asia), a scientific observatory was founded in the 1400s.

One factor in the spread of scientific knowledge was the greater availability of relatively inexpensive manuscripts as a result of a papermaking technique learned from the Chinese in the 700s. Another factor was the rapid growth of libraries throughout the Islamic world. Many private libraries were accessible to some scholars, and libraries attached to mosques* and schools were open to all. The observatory—a scientific institution with a permanent staff, library, and astronomical instruments—contributed to the spread of scientific knowledge.

* **mosque** Muslim place of worship

The achievements of Islamic science were significant. In mathematics, Islamic scholars devised and applied new techniques of numerical calculation and expanded various mathematical concepts that were already known. Islamic astronomers made many observations of the planets and constructed sophisticated and reliable observation instruments, such as sundials and ASTROLABES. Islamic engineers designed and built mechanical devices, such as CLOCKS and fountains, and explained the principles of mechanics in simple, nonmathematical ways. Islamic scholars were concerned not only with scientific concepts, but also with the practical application of scientific principles. Thus, science was used to build better SCIENTIFIC INSTRUMENTS and to determine direction and time more accurately.

Jewish Science. Jewish scholars, many working within the Islamic world or along its borders with Europe, made important contributions to medieval science. Jewish scholars researched and wrote on various branches of science and did scientific translations, mainly from Arabic into Hebrew. Some also translated Arabic works into Latin, often at the

* **patron**   person of wealth and influence who supports an artist, writer, or scholar

request of Christian patrons*. This helped spread Islamic science to western Europe.

Many Jewish scholars focused on astronomy, acquainting themselves with the works of the Greeks in Arabic translation and with the contributions of the Arabs. The most important and original Jewish astronomer was Levi ben Gershom of southern France, known for his accurate calculations of planetary distances. Some Jewish scholars, famous for their work in astronomy, also made important contributions in mathematics. The astronomer Abraham bar Hiyya, for example, wrote the earliest European work on algebra. Several Jews were well-respected authorities on medicine, translating medical works from Arabic and other languages into Hebrew.

Toward the end of the Middle Ages, Jewish science was affected by several factors. The expulsion of the Jews from scientific centers in Spain and southern France and their exclusion from European universities had an adverse affect. In the end, Jews shared with their Muslim neighbors the decline of Arab science that took place in the late medieval period. (*See also* **Alchemy; Aquinas, Thomas, St.; Artillery; Astrology and Astronomy; Bacon, Roger; Calendars; Grosseteste, Robert; Heating; Jews, Expulsion of; Khwarizmi, al-; Lenses and Eyeglasses; Lighting Devices; Maps and Mapmaking; Mathematics; Medicine; Metals and Metalworking; Navigation; Oresme, Nicole; Technology; Waterworks.**)

Scientific Instruments

* **Hellenistic**   referring to Greek history, culture, or art after Alexander the Great

After the fall of the Roman Empire in the 400s, knowledge of ancient scientific instruments was generally lost to the West. Such knowledge continued in the East for a time, but eventually religious and political upheaval caused many scholars to flee to the Islamic world. Science flourished in the medieval Islamic world, and, from there, knowledge of ancient Hellenistic* science and technology was dispersed again to medieval Europe.

Beginning in the 800s, many technological advances were made in the Islamic world as a result of developments in mathematics, astronomy, navigation, and other related fields. Among the scientific instruments that came to the Muslims from the ancient Greeks and Romans were the armillary sphere (for determining the time of equal day and night and the motions and positions of heavenly bodies), the globe, and the ASTROLABE. Other scientific instruments included the quadrant (for measuring altitude), the equatorium (for finding the positions of the planets), and the torquetum (a type of astronomical compass for measuring the stars or angles along the horizon). The Muslims used and improved these devices to suit their own scientific needs. Many of the astronomical instruments were used in observatories—institutions in which professional astronomers worked. Such observatories are thought to have developed in the Islamic world.

Most of these scientific instruments came to medieval Europe through SICILY in the 900s and the 1000s and through SPAIN in the 1100s and the 1200s. Europeans also made important contributions to the development of scientific instruments during the Middle Ages. One of the most important instruments was the compass, which may have originated

The astronomers in this illumination are studying the heavens from atop Mount Athos in Greece. They are using an astrolabe to observe and calculate the position of heavenly bodies, as others record their findings. Many scientific instruments used during the Middle Ages were Muslim improvements on Greek and Roman devices. These devices later came into use in medieval Europe.

in China and may have come to Europe over early trade routes. Europeans improved the compass, and it became the indispensable tool of navigators. Another important navigational instrument developed in Europe was the cross-staff. This device, which was first used by astronomers to measure the distance between two stars, was used by mariners to measure the elevation of the sun or a star above the horizon. The time glass, or hourglass, probably came into use in Europe in the late 1200s. The time glass consisted of two glass bulbs connected by a narrow neck through which sand slowly ran down. It took an hour for the sand to pass from the top bulb to the lower one.

During the late 1400s in Europe, the making of scientific instruments developed into an art. The demand for scientific instruments increased the need for craftsmen who could produce them. Several European cities became known for their instrument makers, and GUILDS formed to meet the needs of these highly skilled workers. Clockmakers, who constructed mechanical clocks, often made scientific instruments as well; the skills needed to make each were similar. Toward the end of the medieval period, however, instrument making became a separate and more specialized craft. (*See also* **Astrology and Astronomy; Clocks and Reckoning of Time; Navigation; Science.**)

Scotland

Scotland, in the northernmost part of the British Isles, is a land of steep mountains, rugged coastlines, and long sea inlets called firths. The region emerged as an independent kingdom during the Middle Ages. In the early medieval period, the area had been occupied by a number of small kingdoms. In the 11th century, these small states united to become the kingdom of Scotland. Although Scotland remained independent for the rest of the Middle Ages, its history was shaped by its relationship with England, its powerful neighbor to the south.

Friendship with England.   At first, relations between medieval England and Scotland were friendly. When England came under the rule of the NORMANS in 1066, the Scottish kings welcomed Norman noblemen and churchmen to Scotland. The Norman newcomers and the Anglo-French influence they brought to Scotland strengthened the ties between the Scottish and English crowns and broadened the horizons of Scottish culture and society.

Unlike some of the independent-minded Scottish lords, the Norman settlers were loyal to the crown. By giving them titles and estates, the Scottish kings created a band of strong followers who helped the crown control uprisings and rebellions of the old families. In the 1100s and the 1200s, the Scottish monarchy* grew steadily more powerful. Between 1220 and 1260, Scotland enlarged its borders by annexing* some western islands and mainland territory in the north previously held by Norway.

Scotland's economy also grew during these years as new towns and cities were formed, some by royal decree. People from FLANDERS who settled in Scotland brought with them not only their experience in trade and commerce but also their knowledge of the wool industry. Scottish wool became a valuable export and the basis of Scotland's economy. (The industry suffered greatly in the late 1200s and the early 1300s when disease struck the sheep herds of Scotland and England.)

Wars of Independence.   In 1290, King Edward I of England claimed supreme power over Scotland, marking a new phase in Scottish history. Several years earlier, the Scottish king Alexander III had died without leaving an heir. When 13 Scottish noblemen claimed the throne, Edward I was asked to settle the problem. He took the opportunity to claim overlordship of Scotland for himself.

The first great leader of Scottish resistance to English rule was a knight named William Wallace, who was supported by the "middling folk" of Scotland—the growing middle class of small landholders, merchants, and townspeople. For the first time in Scottish history, ordinary people participated in the political affairs of the country.

In 1298, the English defeated Wallace and his supporters in the Battle of Falkirk, and the leadership of the resistance passed to the aristocrat Robert Bruce. He was one of several nobles who had tried to claim the throne after the death of Alexander III. In 1306, Bruce seized the crown. As king, he continued to resist the English, keeping Scotland free of English control until his death in 1329.

War broke out again when King EDWARD III OF ENGLAND invaded Scotland in 1341. Scottish independence was seriously threatened until Edward turned his attention to war against France instead. In the late 1300s, Scotland's independence became more secure after the landowners in southern Scotland drove the last of the English from the border territories.

* **monarchy**   nation ruled by a king or queen

* **annex**   to add a territory to an existing state

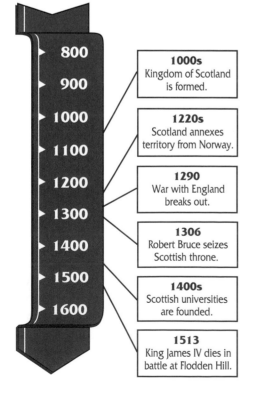

1000s	Kingdom of Scotland is formed.
1220s	Scotland annexes territory from Norway.
1290	War with England breaks out.
1306	Robert Bruce seizes Scottish throne.
1400s	Scottish universities are founded.
1513	King James IV dies in battle at Flodden Hill.

The Scottish wars for independence lasted from the late 1200s until the mid-1300s. This illumination shows King David II of Scotland at the Battle of Neville's Cross in 1346, where he was captured by the English forces when he attempted to invade England. He was released after 11 years in captivity. By this time, the English had turned their attention to problems in France, and fighting with Scotland ended.

Expanding Contact with Europe.   The final phase of medieval Scottish history lasted from the end of the wars of independence in the mid-1300s to the early 1500s. Scotland was not at war during this period, and the Scottish rulers had time to reflect on their country's place in the world. Scotland had been regarded as a small, poor, backward country on the fringe of Europe, but now its rulers were determined that the country should become an important European kingdom.

To enhance Scotland's reputation, Scottish kings built castles and maintained courts that were as grand as the courts of France. With the support of the Scottish crown, the arts flourished. Musicians traveled to Europe to study and returned to train new singers and musicians. Poets Robert Henryson and William Dunbar gained fame and popularity for their works. The UNIVERSITIES founded in the 1400s at St. Andrews, Glasgow, and Edinburgh became respected institutions of learning and scholarship.

In spite of the ambitions of its rulers, however, Scotland remained a poor country with little arable* farmland and few natural resources. Because the wool trade remained in decline from the late 1200s until the mid-1400s, cloth making failed to develop into as important an industry in Scotland as in Flanders. Nonetheless, Scotland did find other products to export, mainly fish and leather. Scottish merchants also expanded their trade by venturing to new ports in Spain and around the Baltic Sea.

Since Scotland's main political alliance was with France, many Scottish aristocrats spent time at the French court, and Scottish soldiers fought in the French army. Kings James III and James IV of Scotland helped arrange treaties between France and Denmark. The ties between

* **arable** suitable for plowing and producing crops

See color plate 14, vol. 3.

France and Scotland were a source of displeasure for England, which was France's great rival of that period.

In the early 1500s, Scotland's alliance with France brought disaster to the Scottish monarchy and army. King James IV, who ruled Scotland from 1488 until 1513, tried to strengthen his country's ties with England by marrying a daughter of the English royal family while remaining loyal to France. James's involvement in the politics of other European countries also helped bring about his downfall.

In 1513, while England was at war with France, James led a Scottish army of 30,000 into England, hoping to help the French by diverting English troops from attacking France. English and Scottish troops met at Flodden Hill, where the Scots were roundly defeated. The battle ended with James IV and 10,000 of his followers—including most of the ruling elite of Scotland—lying dead in the mud. This devastating defeat marked the end of medieval Scottish history. (*See also* **England; Nobility and Nobles; Wool.**)

 Sculpture

See *British Isles, Art and Architecture; Byzantine Architecture; Gothic Sculpture; Islamic Art and Architecture; Romanesque Art; Spanish Art and Architecture.*

 Seals and Charters

* **mandate** official command or decree

* **dynasty** succession of rulers from the same family or group

Seals are marks or symbols pressed into wax or metal and attached to various types of documents. During the Middle Ages, seals commonly were used to close a package or text, guaranteeing that its contents were not tampered with, and to show that documents were authentic. Seals were especially important on charters—official documents that recorded and provided proof of legal action, such as deeds, contracts, constitutions, privileges, or mandates*. Used throughout medieval Europe and the Islamic world, seals were a mark of authority as well as a claim and proof of ownership.

Seals were used widely in ancient Rome, and the practice was adopted by people in the early Middle Ages. During the period of the MEROVINGIAN dynasty*, for example, rings engraved with names or symbols were used to make impressions on seals that closed letters or served as marks of office. Beginning perhaps in the 500s, the placing of wax seals on documents as a mark of authentication became a practice solely of a king. In the 800s, bishops were the first nonroyal individuals to prove that documents were true by using personal seals. Then, in the 900s, dukes, princes, and other members of the nobility used seals of their own.

At first, seals had no legal standing, but they were useful in authenticating documents. However, as the use of seals on documents became more widespread, a fundamental change occurred. Increasingly, authority became associated with the seal itself rather than with an individual's personal power. As a result, the seal soon evolved as a symbol of legal proof, and it became a convenient way to validate written records and to

* **secular** nonreligious; connected with everyday life

* **parchment** writing material made from the skin of sheep or goats

Pictured here is the Golden Charter, or Golden Bull, of German emperor Charles IV, which was issued in 1356. This important constitutional document set rules for the election and coronation of German kings. The golden seal, or bulla, was used to authenticate very important documents issued by medieval rulers.

guarantee their authenticity. By the mid-1200s, religious communities, UNIVERSITIES, members of the CLERGY, local officials, merchants, craftswork- ers, GUILDS, and landowners all sealed documents routinely.

As their use spread, seals came to serve special functions. Some seals ensured that a signature was genuine, while others were used by various secular* or religious officials as a mark of their particular area of authority or jurisdiction. Private seals were used by the church, the nobility, and cities for sealing letters and other documents.

By the end of the Middle Ages, the use of seals declined as a means of authentication, and they were replaced by a simple handwritten signa- ture. Kings, royal courts, and nobles continued to use private seals as a sign of status, but they had little legal significance by the end of the me- dieval period.

Most medieval seal impressions were made of colored wax, although some were made of metal, including silver and gold. The size and shape of seal impressions varied, as did the method for attaching seals to docu- ments. From the 1100s to the 1400s, wax seals often were hung from parchment* documents with cord. These hanging seals allowed for two- sided impressions. As parchment was gradually replaced with more fragile paper beginning in the 1400s, hanging seals were replaced with lighter im- pressions made directly on the paper. This became the rule except on ma- jor state documents.

Sealing also was common practice in the Islamic world. Islamic seals were used to validate documents, to mark property, and to secure pack- ages. Every individual with business to transact had a seal, usually worn as a ring or on a neck cord or carried in a small bag. Personal Islamic seals contained the owner's name and, often, short religious sayings. Official Is- lamic seals had more detail. (*See also* **Archives; Heraldry.**)

Seljuks

* **Sunnites** Muslim majority who believed that the caliphs should rule the Islamic community

* **mercenary** soldier who fights for payment rather than out of loyalty to a lord or nation

* **sultan** political and military ruler of a Muslim dynasty or state

* **Shi'ites** Muslims who believed that Muhammad chose Ali and his descendants as the rulers and spiritual leaders of the Islamic community

The Seljuks were a Turko-Muslim dynasty that ruled over much of IRAN, IRAQ, SYRIA, Asia Minor, and parts of central Asia from the mid-1000s to the mid-1200s. They originated among the Turkish- speaking nomadic tribes that controlled a vast area from Mongolia to the Black Sea. The Seljuks traced their descent from a tribe living east of the Caspian Sea in the 700s. According to tradition, the founder of the dy- nasty was Seljuk ibn Doqaq, a tribal warlord. In the late 900s, the Seljuks migrated to northeast Iran, where they came into contact with the Is- lamic Empire. They soon embraced the Sunnite* branch of the Muslim faith and served as mercenaries* in power struggles among regional Is- lamic dynasties.

In the early 1000s, the Seljuks conquered much of Iran, and one of their leaders, Toghril, declared himself sultan*. In 1055, Toghril entered Baghdad at the invitation of the Abbasid caliph and deposed the Buyids, a Shi'ite* dynasty that had controlled Iraq since 945. Under Toghril's succes- sor, his nephew Alp Arslan, the Seljuks conquered GEORGIA, ARMENIA, and much of Asia Minor. They also overran Syria and defeated the Byzantines at the Battle of Manzikert in 1071. This victory opened much of the Byzan- tine Empire to Turkish occupation.

The Seljuk sultanate reached the height of its power in the late 1000s under Alp Arslan's son, Malikshah. The Seljuks ruled a vast empire from the Mediterranean to central Asia and from Arabia to the Caucasus region. After Malikshah's death, a domestic crisis rocked the Seljuk state. Malikshah's successor, his son Berkyaruq, was faced with rebellious relatives who sought either the sultanate or their own independent domains. Internal divisions eventually tore apart the sultanate, and local tribal chieftains established their own independent states.

Less-powerful branches of the Seljuks founded other Turkish dynasties during the period. A Seljuk dynasty in ANATOLIA, known as the Seljuks of Rum, was founded in the 1070s. This dynasty withstood challenges from Turkish lords, the Byzantines, and crusaders*, but it finally fell to the Mongols in the late 1200s and the early 1300s. Another Seljuk dynasty ruled in Syria from 1078 to 1117. This short-lived line, founded by a brother of Malikshah, gave way to local tribal leaders. A fourth Seljuk state was established in Kirman, a region in southeastern Iran. Founded in the 1040s by a brother of Alp Arslan, it remained a relatively untroubled, isolated area for most of its history. Dynastic strife in the late 1100s led to a period of anarchy, followed by occupation by other rebellious Turkish tribes.

The Seljuk states were marked by two contrasting features. On the one hand was the Iranian tradition of absolute monarchy and Muslim legal tradition. Opposed to this were the ideas of the Turkish tribesmen—social equality, a nonrestrictive form of government, and laws based on traditional custom. The Seljuks were never able to settle these differences. As they moved further from their tribal roots, their tribesmen became increasingly dissatisfied. Internal struggles and dynastic strife gradually reduced their power and authority and led to their downfall. Despite their eventual downfall, the Seljuks were successful in introducing large numbers of Turkish peoples into Anatolia and the Middle East. In doing so, they changed forever the ethnic composition of the region. Turkish culture and language have remained dominant up to the present day. (*See also* **Anatolia; Iran; Iraq; Sultan.**)

* **crusader** person who participated in the holy wars against the Muslims during the Middle Ages

Seneschal

In the Middle Ages, a seneschal was a senior official who advised a lord or a king and managed his estates. In some parts of Europe, the seneschal wielded great power and had wide-ranging responsibilities.

In the early Middle Ages, great lords traveled frequently and their household servants and officials traveled with them. In time, the administration of manors and estates became more complex, and it became necessary for some household officials to remain behind to supervise their lord's affairs. This was the origin of the seneschal.

In England and Germany, the seneschal was just an estate manager of a monarch or rural lord. In France, however, a household official known as the royal seneschal emerged as the most important administrator after the king. In addition to supervising the royal court and advising the king, the royal seneschal often was put in command of feudal armies and was given various judicial and ceremonial responsibilities. Lesser

seneschals also existed at some of the courts of other French lords and nobles. Seneschals also served as salaried governors of provinces in southern France.

In some places, the post of seneschal was hereditary, and ambitious seneschal families sometimes threatened the power of monarchs. As a result, the power of the seneschal was steadily reduced, and the position became largely ceremonial after the 1200s. (*See also* **Bailli; Castellan; Chamberlain; Constable of the Realm.**)

Serbia

* **dynasty** succession of rulers from the same family or group

* **annex** to add a territory to an existing state

In this Serbian fresco from the 1300s, a raven brings food to the prophet Elijah. This Old Testament prophet was an important figure in Christian, Jewish, and Islamic art and literature. The Eastern Church revered him as a saint. Medieval Serbian art and architecture were influenced by the Byzantines. Churches were often lavishly decorated with representations of religious figures.

Located in the Balkan Mountains of southeastern Europe, Serbia became an independent state during the Middle Ages. Its size and borders changed as a result of conflicts with neighboring states until the mid-1400s, when it lost its independence.

Early Middle Ages. In the early 600s, a people called the Serbs migrated into a part of the Balkans inhabited primarily by SLAVS. Little is known about the early history of the Serbs, but it is believed that they originated in IRAN.

By the late 700s, the Serbs occupied the area that is now known as Serbia. Although they continued to call themselves Serbs, they intermarried with the Slavs, and after a few generations they spoke the Slavic language and were considered to belong to the Slavic ethnic group. In the 800s, several Serbian tribes united in opposition to the Bulgarians, who were pressing westward and enslaving the Slavic people. The BYZANTINE EMPIRE, which also wanted to stop the Bulgarians, encouraged Serbian unity. The Bulgarians invaded Serbia in the 840s, but the Serbians drove them back. The Serb leader, Vlastimir, who had defeated the Bulgarians, expanded his state to the west. When he died, his realm was divided among his three sons. In 853, the Bulgarians attacked again, and once more the Serbs defeated them. Serbians captured the son of the Bulgarian king. His father ransomed him back, and peace between Serbia and Bulgaria was maintained for much of the rest of the century.

In the 900s, Serbia was involved in a three-party struggle with Bulgaria and Byzantium. Each side tried through diplomacy and war to gain the advantage over the other two. Serbia and Bulgaria sometimes joined forces against Byzantium, while at other times Serbia joined Byzantium to make war on Bulgaria. During this period, Serbia's borders expanded into the regions that are today known as BOSNIA and Montenegro. At this same time, the Serbs adopted the form of Christianity practiced in the Byzantine Empire. By the late 900s, the Serbian state had disintegrated.

A new Serbian state emerged in the mid-1000s when a powerful family of Serbian nobles founded a new dynasty*. One member of this dynasty, Vukan (who ruled from about 1084 until 1125), sought to annex* Byzantium's Balkan territories, including Macedonia. Although the Byzantines managed to quell Serbia's challenges, they were unable to bring peace to the region.

Late Middle Ages. A new dynasty—the Nemanja family—rose to power about 1166. In 1190, Byzantium recognized Serbia's independence. The

* **pilgrimage** journey to a shrine or sacred place

* **relic** object cherished for its association with a martyr or saint

Nemanjic rulers, who remained on the throne until 1371, turned Serbia into a significant power in the Balkan region. Under their rule, religion and culture flourished. In exchange for the church's support, Nemanjic rulers gave the church large tracts of land and built many MONASTERIES. The Byzantine Church appointed Sava to be Serbia's first archbishop in 1219. Sava died in Bulgaria in 1235 on his return from his PILGRIMAGE to the Holy Land. His body was brought back to Serbia and buried in the monastery of Milesevo, which had been built by the Nemanjic ruler Vladislav. Sava was declared a saint by the Byzantine Church. His shrine was a popular pilgrimage* site, and his relics* had a reputation for working miracles.

Serbia's economy flourished during the Nemanjic dynasty. The Nemanjic encouraged trade, coined money, and developed Serbia's natural resources—silver, lead, gold, copper, and iron. Under their rule, Serbia became the leading producer of silver in the Balkans.

The Nemanjic were often at war, both to defend Serbia against Bulgaria and Byzantium and to gain new territory. During their long reign, the Nemanjic suffered no major defeats and added Albania, Macedonia, and parts of Greece to the Serbian state. Serbia reached its greatest size under Dusan, who reigned from 1331 to 1355. He gave the country its first official code of laws. Dusan's dream of conquering Byzantium was never realized because he died before he could begin his campaign.

Despite the creation of a strong state with a well-organized central government, Serbia suffered from internal conflict during the two centuries of Nemanjic rule. Power struggles among members of the dynasty often led to revolts and civil war. After Dusan's death, Serbian unity was threatened when various members of the royal family seized territories for themselves.

In the mid-1300s, a new threat appeared when the Ottoman Turks from northwestern ANATOLIA began their campaign to conquer Byzantium and the Balkans. The Ottomans defeated Serbian troops in key battles—at Marica in 1371 and at Kosovo in 1389. In the early 1400s, Serbia and Hungary united briefly to check the Ottoman advance, but soon Serbia was fighting for its survival against a new Ottoman offensive.

When the last Serbian government fell to the Ottomans in 1459, the Serbian state disappeared as an independent state. Serbia remained part of the Ottoman Empire until the 1800s. (*See also* **Bulgaria; Christianity; Nobility and Nobles; Ottomans and Ottoman Empire; Relics.**)

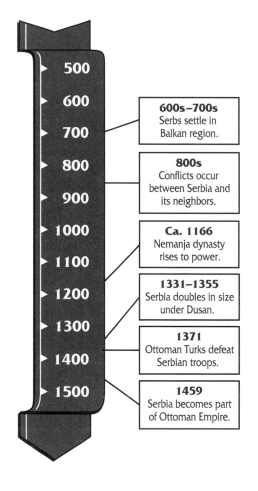

500	
600	**600s–700s** Serbs settle in Balkan region.
700	
800	**800s** Conflicts occur between Serbia and its neighbors.
900	
1000	**Ca. 1166** Nemanja dynasty rises to power.
1100	
1200	**1331–1355** Serbia doubles in size under Dusan.
1300	
1400	**1371** Ottoman Turks defeat Serbian troops.
1500	**1459** Serbia becomes part of Ottoman Empire.

Serfs and Serfdom

* **hereditary** passed on from parent to child

* **feudal** referring to the social, economic, and political system that flourished in western Europe during the Middle Ages

In medieval Europe, large numbers of peasant workers were bound to the land in a state of semi-bondage. These workers, known as serfs, were required to perform various types of farm and household labor for their masters. The status of serfs was usually hereditary*, and serfdom was distinguished from slavery in that serfs usually had limited rights. The conditions of serfdom varied from time to time and from place to place. In western Europe, it arose during the feudal* period and disappeared around 1300. In eastern Europe, particularly in Russia, serfdom was not fully established until the late 1500s and the early 1600s, and it was not abolished there until the 1860s.

This illumination from the 1100s shows two serfs plowing fields with a wheeled plow. The status of the serf was only slightly better than that of a slave. Serfs were required to work for their lords and had little personal liberty. A serf was not considered a full member of peasant society, although, as the Middle Ages progressed, the difference between a serf and a peasant became less distinct. By the 1200s, serfdom had begun to decline.

* **pagan** word used by Christians to mean non-Christian and believing in several gods

From Slavery to Serfdom. Around the time of CHARLEMAGNE, a basic distinction existed between two categories of people: free persons and slaves. Free persons were subject only to the authority of public officials and were, in principle, protected by them. Slaves, on the other hand, were the property of a master and had no rights of their own.

After the fall of the Roman Empire, the number of slaves within the old imperial domains declined. This was due in part to the spread of Christianity, which taught that all people are equal in the eyes of God. In the 500s, the church forbade the enslavement of Christians. The only people who could be used as slaves were pagans* captured along the northern and eastern frontiers of the Christian Germanic kingdoms. As the number of slaves decreased, they became more expensive, and the slave trade dwindled.

During the 700s, the demand for slaves increased in the rich Mediterranean lands conquered by the Muslims. This led to a new increase in the price of slaves. Most of the slaves of this period were Slavic peoples from eastern Europe. (The English word *slave* comes from the word for these enslaved peoples.) These slaves were taken to Muslim SPAIN or to VENICE, where they were transported to the Middle East. Christians were still exported as slaves, but only in very small numbers.

By the 800s, a fundamental change had occurred in the situation of slaves. Because of worsened economic conditions in Europe and changes in the management of rural estates, gangs of slaves began to disappear. Instead, landlords settled slave families on small plots of land. During plowing and harvest, the lord required the services of the slave families who had become his tenants. At other times, the tenants could work their own land. The slave and his family subsisted on the crops grown on the land granted to him by his lord. In return, the family owed the lord an annual payment, usually in agricultural products. The relationship between slave and master was thus profoundly changed. The rights of the slave over his family were recognized, and he had gained a degree of economic independence. Little by little, the slave had become a serf.

The Status of Serfs. The status of serfs, like that of slaves, was marked by a lack of personal liberty. Serfs could gain freedom only through a formal ceremony known as manumission. Serfdom was hereditary, and serfs increasingly were considered the property of their lord. The lord could sell serfs, pass them on to heirs, require services whenever desired, and take back land he had given them. The lord had the duty of protecting and defending his serfs against any and all dangers. The bond between master and serf could not be broken, even if a serf ran away or if a female serf married a serf on another estate and went there to live. In the latter case, the two lords usually reached a compromise, perhaps by agreeing to divide the couple's children between them or by one lord's buying out the other's claim. In order to control the migration of serfs, masters generally exercised their right to approve or disapprove the marriages of their serfs.

Even when serfs held land, they were not full members of peasant society. They could not join the CLERGY or enter a monastery, and they were excluded from all public institutions, such as the courts of law. The lord, rather than the courts, had full power to punish a serf for misdeeds or crimes.

The political developments that led to the feudal system had important effects on legal and social class distinctions. As public institutions lost power, it became impossible to prove one's freedom in the courts. As a result, the legal barrier that separated free persons from the unfree was weakened, and old concepts of liberty and servitude were destroyed. Thus, between 1000 and 1200, there was a slow but steady disappearance of social customs and laws that set the serf apart from other peasants. From the 1000s on, serfs were no longer only the descendants of slaves. More and more peasants sought protection from local lords and relinquished the rights to their property in return. In this way, many free peasants became serfs. Serfdom became based not only on ancestry but also on varying degrees of obligation to the lord and dependency on him.

The Decline of Serfdom. Beginning in the 1200s, the number of serfs in western Europe declined, as a great movement to free them developed. In many parts of rural France, serfs became a minority of the population. In Spain, where the granting of privileges was essential to the resettlement of lands conquered from the Muslims, monarchs encouraged the decline of serfdom. The same was true in the Italian regions of Lombardy and TUS-CANY, where the great towns led the movement to end serfdom. In order to weaken the power of nobles and to acquire more taxpayers, the governments of those towns abolished all forms of personal servitude and eliminated other obstacles to freedom. In England, meanwhile, the number of villeins—the English term for unfree persons—remained at a high level for a long time.

After 1300, it became increasingly difficult to distinguish between serf and free peasant because both were almost always at the same economic

Hiding from Ivan

Ivan IV's terrorism and violence against the Russian people led to a mass flight from central and northeastern Russia. Entire districts were emptied of their inhabitants. In some areas, as many as 97 percent of the farm homesteads were vacated. Most of the migrants fled east and south into regions that had only recently been opened to Russian settlement. Others went into the freezing woods of northern Russia. Some, however, went no farther than the forests and marshes surrounding their old neighborhoods.

 See map in Kievan Rus (vol. 3).

* **tsar** Slavic term for emperor

level. The burdens imposed by the lord were only slightly heavier for serfs, and most serfs were simply small landholders like most other villagers. In addition, because the lord had a strong connection to his serfs, he often appointed them to minor offices, such as policeman, BAILIFF, keeper of the oven, or operator of the winepress. Through such favored treatment, some serfs were able to improve their positions, becoming village leaders and even acquiring modest wealth. As the distinction between serf and free person became increasingly unclear, a new distinction arose—one based on the size of one's landholding.

By the middle of the 1300s, and for about a century thereafter, the situation of serfs changed everywhere in western Europe. Repeated outbreaks of the BLACK DEATH, rebellions, urban and rural uprisings, economic depression, and the difficulties of lords in trying to deal with these problems led to the decline of serfdom in many regions. In eastern Europe, however, serfdom became more deeply rooted and continued to exist for hundreds of years.

Serfdom in Russia. The roots of serfdom in Russia reach back to the period of KIEVAN RUS, when the status of many peasants declined as a result of the growth of large-scale private landownership. Land that had belonged to peasants was absorbed into large estates owned by princes, other lords, and the church, and the peasants were reduced to renters or landless laborers. As time went on, a distinction was drawn between these landless peasants and other peasants, with the former considered inferior even though they had not yet lost their personal freedom.

In the 1200s, many peasants in Kievan Rus fled north to escape the Mongol invasions. These peasants sought protection from local princes, other lords, and monastery officials, who allowed them to settle as free renters on land in exchange for various services, such as clearing forests. The practice of placing oneself under the protection of lords became more and more widespread, and it played a significant role in the eventual transformation of the Russian peasant into a serf.

By the mid-1500s, the judicial powers of the lords over their peasant renters had become an established institution. The conditions of peasants worsened during the reign of Tsar* Ivan IV in the mid-1500s. Ivan decreed that all landholders had to perform military service for him or pay additional money. In order to meet their obligations to the tsar, the landholders demanded increased rents and services from their peasants. In the late 1500s, Russia was torn by political and social upheaval caused by Ivan's insane drive for absolute power. He confiscated the estates of princes and executed thousands of people. The terror and turmoil caused many peasants to flee and caused others to sell themselves into slavery for protection.

The final act in the transformation of the Russian peasant to serf occurred in the 1600s against a backdrop of terrorism, foreign and civil wars, political chaos, and economic disaster. During this time, the movement of peasants was completely restricted, and legal codes gave the landlords nearly unlimited authority over their peasants. By the mid-1600s, the once free Russian peasant was bound to his lord, and the only rights he possessed were those allowed by his master. (*See also* **Agriculture; Feudalism; Nobility and Nobles; Slavery.**)

* **laity** those who are not members of the clergy

* **vernacular** language or dialect native to a region; everyday, informal speech

* **heresy** belief that is contrary to church doctrine

* **Gospels** accounts of the life and teachings of Jesus as told in the first four books of the New Testament

* **ordination** church ceremony in which a person becomes a member of the clergy

* **consecration** church ceremony declaring someone or something sacred, as when a bishop is ordained

* **theological** pertaining to the nature of God, the study of religion, and religious beliefs

* **synagogue** building of worship for Jews

* **parable** simple story that illustrates a religious or moral lesson

In the Middle Ages, sermons contributed greatly to the spread of religion. In all three major religions—CHRISTIANITY, JUDAISM, and ISLAM—preaching was used to instruct, reinforce, and spread the faith.

Western European Sermons. In medieval Europe, large numbers of people were illiterate. Therefore, sermons by the CLERGY were the primary means of educating the laity*.

Although church fathers such as AUGUSTINE and Pope GREGORY I recognized the importance of preaching, there were few distinguished preachers in the early Middle Ages. Almost all clerical preaching was done in Latin before audiences of other clergy. In the 900s and the 1000s, nearly all sermons were delivered in MONASTERIES twice daily, either by the abbot or by one of the monks. In the 1100s, church scholars also known for their preaching included ANSELM OF CANTERBURY, BERNARD OF CLAIRVAUX, and Peter ABELARD.

Preaching to lay audiences, not in Latin but in the vernacular*, became more widespread in the late 1100s, especially when such sermons were seen as a way of combating heresy*. The emergence of the FRANCISCAN and DOMINICAN preaching orders in the early 1200s contributed to the trend toward popular preaching. After sermons in the vernacular were delivered, they were often written down and preserved in Latin, sometimes in an abridged form. Collections of sermons and handbooks on preaching circulated widely in the 1200s and the 1300s.

Sermons were preached throughout the church year—at Mass on Sunday and on feast days as well. Mass sermons, which followed the reading of the Gospel* for the day, were usually explanations or interpretations of the meaning of the passage. However, sermons were not delivered just on those occasions. Bishops and other church leaders frequently preached when they visited monasteries and parishes and attended church assemblies. Sermons were also preached to highlight such special occasions as ordinations*, consecrations*, dedications, elections, coronations, and PILGRIMAGES.

Theological* education emphasized the importance of preaching. At the University of Paris, for example, theology students were required to deliver at least one sermon a year and had to show competence in preaching as a requirement for being granted a degree. Both teachers (called masters) and students were expected to attend university sermons.

Jewish Sermons. The purpose of Jewish sermons was to explain the meaning of texts from the BIBLE. Tied to the weekly readings from the Five Books of Moses (Torah), they were usually given in the vernacular rather than in Hebrew and were delivered in the synagogue* and at festivals and weddings as well.

The preacher (darshan) began the sermon with a preface that contained a quotation from the Bible or some other religious text, which he then related to the Scripture reading of the day. In the sermon itself, he explained various verses from the day's reading and usually ended with a message of encouragement or comfort. The preacher often introduced stories and parables* to illustrate the meaning of the text.

Great Preacher

Ibn al-Jawzi was a leading Muslim scholar and a remarkable preacher. At the height of his career, tens of thousands of people flocked to hear him. According to his own estimate, he converted 100,000 people to Islam during his lifetime.

A Spanish visitor to Baghdad in 1184 who heard Ibn al-Jawzi preach at three separate rallies described him as "the wonder of all time." Many of the younger preachers he trained took up preaching posts in Cairo, Damascus, and other large Muslim cities.

---

* **rabbi** teacher of Jewish law and religion and spiritual leader of a Jewish congregation

* **caliph** religious and political head of an Islamic state

---

From the 600s through the 1100s, great efforts were made to collect the sermonic teachings of the great rabbis* of the first four centuries, even though these anthologies often contained only prefaces or summaries rather than complete texts. A Jewish work from the Islamic world known as the *She'iltot (Questions)* from Ahai of Shabha (680–752) consisted of legal questions and answers that were then expanded into sermons.

Late medieval Jewish anthologies were encyclopedic works that were used as handbooks for preaching. The most original of these from northern Europe was the *Sefer Hasidim (Book of the Pious)* by Rabbi Judah he-Hasid, who died in 1217. Sermonic literature from southern France and Spain showed a special interest in philosophical issues. The influence of ARISTOTLE and MAIMONIDES can be seen in the sermons of Abraham bar Hiyya, who died about 1136, and Jacob ben Abba Mari Anatoli, who died in 1256. The last great Jewish medieval sermon collection that attempted to harmonize philosophy and Judaism was the *Aqedat Yitzhaq (Binding of Isaac)* of Isaac Arama, who died in 1494.

Islamic Sermons.   Preaching also played an important role in the spread of Islam. Although Islamic preachers were active during the lifetime of MUHAMMAD, their role in spreading the new religion increased after his death in 632.

Two distinct kinds of Islamic preaching emerged early—the Friday sermon and the popular sermon. During the first Islamic century, the Friday sermon became an established Muslim tradition. UMAYYAD caliphs* and their provincial governors gave sermons in the main mosques in connection with Friday noon prayers. However, by the end of the Umayyad period, responsibility for these Friday sermons was delegated to a special class of preachers appointed by the CALIPHATE. The length of the Friday sermon varied; generally it was brief, no more than 10 or 15 minutes.

In addition to the Friday sermon, another quite different kind of preaching emerged. Although some of the popular preachers who emerged were appointed by governmental officials, most of them operated without official authorization. Since they were not confined to the mosque by law or custom, they were able to preach beyond the reach of the authorities at times of their own choosing.

These lay preachers gave sermons that told stories with religious lessons such as those found in the QUR'AN. In fact, the Arabic word for such a preacher—*qass*—literally means a storyteller. These preachers believed that it was their responsibility to teach, support, and, when necessary, criticize the Muslim community. They also regarded the conversion of non-Muslims as one of their most important duties. Some *qassas* (plural of *qass*) accompanied Muslim armies on their military campaigns to inspire the troops and convert captured prisoners.

Although these lay preachers were often criticized by traditional Muslim leaders and authorities who tried to control them, they remained active and respected in the Muslim community until the late Middle Ages, when their popularity began to decline. (*See also* **Arabic Language and Literature; Clergy; Feasts and Festivals; Hebrew Literature; Jewish Communities; Jews, Expulsion of; Latin Language; Mass, Liturgy of the; Monasticism; Parish; Religious Instruction; Rhetoric.**)

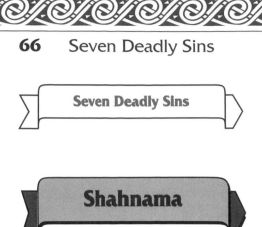

Seven Deadly Sins

See *Virtues and Vices.*

Shahnama

* **succession** the transmission of authority on the death of one ruler to the next

* **dynasty** succession of rulers from the same family or group

The *Shahnama* is an epic poem that narrates the story of the Iranian people from the Creation of the world until the mid-600s. It includes the stories of kings, legendary heroes, and romances. This scene, showing the cavalry charge of Faramouz, is from a manuscript of the *Shahnama* dating from the 1300s.

The *Shahnama (Book of Kings)* is the greatest epic poem of IRAN. Written in the Persian language in the early 1000s by Abu'l-Qasim Firdawsi, the *Shahnama* recounts the history of the Iranian people from the Creation of the world until the conquest of the SASANIANS by the Arabs in the 600s. Firdawsi uses the unifying theme of Iranian kingship and royal succession* to tie together tales of kings, mythical heroes, and legendary characters.

The *Shahnama* presents a history of events in the order in which they occurred in four Iranian dynasties*, one following another, including two early ones that are considered mythical or legendary. Each dynasty is broken down into the reigns of each of its kings, and the stories of these kings form the basic storytelling units of the poem. Woven into these stories are exciting tales and romances about mighty heroes of a foreign dynasty that invaded Iran in ancient times. Over the centuries, the tales of these heroes and their family histories became integrated with the stories of the Iranian royal dynasties.

The world depicted in the *Shahnama* is vast. War and hunting expeditions take Persian heroes beyond Iran to Arabia, the Byzantine Empire, central Asia, China, and India. In the stories of each dynasty, one theme remains constant—the conflict between settled Iranians and their nomadic enemies. Firdawsi adds to this the struggle between good and evil. Firdawsi also uses the work to preach the virtues of wisdom, justice, and honesty and to point out the values of honor, patriotism, and freedom. (*See also* **Chronicles; Historical Writing; Iran.**)

Sheriff

* **reeve** administrative assistant or steward

* **secular** nonreligious; connected with everyday life

In medieval England, each county (or shire) was headed by an agent of the king called the sheriff (from shire-reeve*). This position was established throughout most of England by about the year 1000. The traditional head of the county was the earl, who presided over the county court along with the bishop and the sheriff. Earls and bishops often were busy with other matters, however, and sheriffs gradually gained greater responsibility for county affairs. The increased power of the sheriff became apparent after the Norman conquest in 1066, when earls lost their links to the counties, and bishops' courts were separated from secular* institutions. Thereafter, the sheriff emerged as the general governor of the county. He became head of the county court and was in charge of defense, the police, and the collection of county revenues.

The office of sheriff was commonly given to earls and important barons, and in some counties the position was hereditary. Beginning in the 1200s, however, it became customary to appoint local knights. Gradually, the royal government sought to curtail the power of the sheriff, and one responsibility after another was taken away. By the 1300s, the sheriff had ceased to be the true head of the county. He became an agent of royal

justices of the peace, with responsibility to collect the king's debts, decide on bail for prisoners, and organize juries. (*See also* **England; Law; Normans; Parliament, English; Shire.**)

Shi'ites

See *Caliphate.*

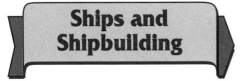

Ships and Shipbuilding

See map in Crusades (vol. 2).

The Viking ship was the greatest accomplishment of early medieval shipbuilding. It made Viking exploration, trade, and colonization possible. The ship in this photograph is from Norway and dates from about the year 800. It is believed to have been a pleasure craft used in protected waters and was not designed for use on long expeditions.

D uring the Middle Ages, Mediterranean shipping was based on Greek and Roman traditions. In northern Europe, shipbuilding began as a simple industry carried on by a few men and developed into a technically advanced enterprise. In the late Middle Ages, increased contact between northern and southern Europe led to an exchange of information that greatly improved the design of sailing ships.

Mediterranean Shipbuilding.   The ancient Romans used a ship propelled by oars, called a galley, for both warfare and transport. The galley was well suited for a sea such as the Mediterranean, which was relatively calm during the warm-weather sailing season. Although the galley had sails that could be raised for cruising, the ship's oar power was what made it effective for combat. During the Middle Ages, the galley kept its special status as a combat vessel, but improvements in sail design and the construction of sailing ships led to its eventual decline.

By the early Middle Ages, the square, cross-rigged sail began to be replaced by the triangular, fore-and-aft rigged (or lateen) sail. Fore-and-aft rigging provided sailing ships and galleys with greater ability to move and change direction, especially when heading into the wind, and its use spread throughout the Mediterranean.

Another important development was the skeleton-first technique of ship construction. Ships had been constructed from the outside in—with the outer shell built before the internal framework. Using the new technique, the basic framework was constructed first, and then the hull planking was nailed to it. This change saved time and money and paved the way for more ambitious ship designs.

In the 1100s, shipping on the Mediterranean greatly increased as a result of the CRUSADES. Although most European participants in the First Crusade went to the Holy Land by land routes, Italian ships were enlisted to supply the armies, to rescue trapped forces, and to keep the crusaders in contact with western Europe. In later crusades, Italian ships transported entire armies. Between crusades, there was a steady flow of maritime traffic to and from the newly won crusader territories. The result of all this traffic was a boost to the economies of VENICE, GENOA, PISA, and other Christian Mediterranean ports.

As the amount of Mediterranean shipping increased, so did improvements in ship materials and design. In the 13th century, cotton, which dried quickly, was introduced from Arabia and replaced linen as sailcloth. In the 14th century, Mediterranean sailors had increased contact with northern European ships, and Mediterranean shipbuilders began to make

These sailing vessels in Venice harbor show the mixed-rig designs of the later Middle Ages. The large sails near the front of the vessel are cross rigged (perpendicular to the keel) to catch the wind from behind and propel the ship forward. Lateen (fore-and-aft) rigging places a triangular sail along the mast. It can be manipulated to catch the winds from either side, thus increasing the maneuverability of the ship.

See color plate 7, vol. 1.

design modifications based on these northern ships. Some ships were built with the high sides of the northern cog ship, which provided protection during attack. Others were mounted with a stern-post rudder, instead of the traditional steering oars.

Northern European Shipbuilding.   Even after the Roman occupation of Gaul and Britain, Celtic and Viking shipbuilders continued to use their traditional designs for ships that sailed in certain waters or had specific functions. The main northern European ships were the curragh, the cog, the pram, the hulk, and the Viking ship. The cog was a simple, flat-bottomed sailing ship with one square sail in the middle. It was used primarily as a cargo ship. The Viking ship, descended from a long barge used in SCANDINAVIA and northern GERMANY, was a low, narrow barge with a single mast and square sail. The Viking ship was the greatest accomplishment of early medieval shipbuilding.

Around 1100, the cog was transformed into a larger and more efficient seagoing ship by the addition of a keel and improvements to the rig (the arrangement of sails, masts, and ropes). A major improvement in controlling large ships came in the late 12th century with the introduction of the rudder at the rear. This rudder made the vessel easier to control, and it became a standard fixture on all cogs. Since the cog could carry more men than any other ship, it became the main northern European warship.

Cogs were the principal carrier of men and goods in northern Europe. They were used to transport men and supplies from northern European ports to the eastern Mediterranean for crusades. Their extensive use contributed to the development of towns and commerce along the northern coast of Germany that led to the creation of the HANSEATIC LEAGUE.

Significant development in ship design occurred in the late medieval period, with increased contact between northern and southern Europe.

Northern shipbuilders adopted many of the best features of Mediterranean shipbuilders, and vice versa. For example, the Mediterranean method of skeleton-first construction began dominating shipbuilding in northern Europe in the 1400s.

Full-Rigged Ship.   In the 15th century, the ultimate refinement of the sailing ship took place. The carrack, the first true full-rigged ship, appeared on the western shores of Europe, perhaps on the Bay of Biscay. A half century later, full-rigged ships could be found sailing the North and Baltic Seas of northern Europe as well.

The best features of northern and southern building methods were combined in the construction of the full-rigged ship. This new type of large, wooden ship had three masts—the foremast and the mainmast, carrying square sails, and the mizzenmast, having a triangular sail. Its improved speed, flexibility, durability, and safety made the full-rigged ship better than any ship before it. Features of its design dominated European shipbuilding for the next three centuries. (*See also* **Exploration; Navigation; Technology; Trade; Vikings.**)

Journey Long and Dangerous

A round trip by sea across the Indian Ocean to Asia usually took two winters (with the summer spent ashore). If the trip went as far as China or the East Indies, or included East Africa, it might take three or more years.

Ships traveled in convoys for protection against pirates, who launched their attacks from islands along shipping routes. Pirates, reefs, and overloading resulted in frequent shipwrecks.

Shire

By the early 800s, much of England was divided into administrative districts called shires. The origins of these shires depended on local history. In western England, they formed around towns and countryside once ruled by various Anglo-Saxon chieftains. In other parts of England, they were formed from independent kingdoms, recently conquered territories, tax districts, or tribal divisions, or by the unification of provinces.

In the late 800s, King ALFRED THE GREAT organized the shires along standard patterns that made governing easier. Each shire was directed by ealdormen (later known as aldermen) who represented royal authority. These officials often were members of royal families who had ruled earlier territories; others were relatives of the king. The ealdormen were responsible for gathering warriors, presiding over shire courts and assemblies, and enforcing royal decrees.

By the mid-900s, shires were subdivided into smaller areas, called hundreds or wapentakes, to make governing more manageable. Some of these units were subdivided even further. After the Norman conquest of 1066, the term *shire* was replaced with *county,* from a French term for a similar type of district in France. (*See also* **Commune; Count, County; England; Law.**)

Shota Rustaveli

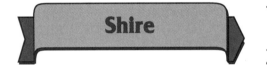

1172–ca. 1216
Georgian poet

* **courtier** person in attendance at a royal court

Shota Rustaveli is the most renowned poet of GEORGIA. Almost nothing is known about his life. Legend says that he was a courtier* of Queen TAMAR, that he was deeply in love with her, and that he ended his days in a monastery. Rustaveli's great epic poem, the *Vep'khistqaosani (The Man in the Panther's Skin),* is considered a Georgian national treasure. Dedicated to Queen Tamar, it dates from the early 1200s.

The poem tells the story of a hero named Tariel who falls in love with Nestan-Darejan, the daughter of a king of India. She returns his love but is promised to another, whom Tariel kills. The princess is taken away to an inaccessible fortress, and Tariel, dressed in a panther's skin, wanders the world in search of his beloved. In the end, he finally succeeds in rescuing her.

The poem's major themes are love, friendship, and devotion to the service of women. Unlike most medieval Georgian literature, the *Vep'khistqaosani* does not contain Christian themes and references. Its originality made it extremely popular throughout Georgia, and for centuries Georgian brides traditionally included a copy of the epic in their dowries. (*See also* **Kievan Rus; Muscovy, Rise of; Novgorod.**)

The island of Sicily, in the center of the Mediterranean Sea near the coast of North Africa, is an extension of the Italian peninsula. In the Middle Ages, Sicily had great strategic importance. Rulers who controlled the island and its ports had valuable military and commercial advantages.

Sicily in Early Middle Ages

At the beginning of the Middle Ages, Sicily was a province of the BYZANTINE EMPIRE (together with the southern and eastern parts of the Italian peninsula). However, the rise of ISLAM and its subsequent spread soon ushered in a new era in the island's history.

See map in Islam, Conquests of (vol. 3).

Muslim Conquest of Sicily.   The Muslim forces that conquered North Africa in the 600s raided Sicily and removed the island's valuable property. The raids continued for more than a century.

In 827, Ziyadat Allah I, the Aghlabid ruler of Ifriqiya (which included eastern Algeria, Tunisia, and Tripolitania), launched a military campaign against the island that captured the city of Mazara and established a permanent Muslim foothold on the island. From their base in Mazara, the Muslims extended their rule over the island during the next 75 years. They took Palermo in 831, Castrogiovanni (the island's Byzantine capital) in 859, and Syracuse in 878. When Taormina fell in 902, nearly all of Sicily was in Muslim hands.

Islamic Sicily.   A series of emirs, or governors, administered Sicily as a province of Ifriqiya. During the two and a half centuries Sicily remained under Muslim control, Ifriqiya was controlled by three important dynasties—the Aghlabids until 909, the FATIMIDS until about 1050, and the Zirids until the NORMAN conquest of the island in the late 1000s.

For almost a century, beginning in the mid-900s under the Fatimids, a semi-independent, hereditary dynasty* of governors called the Kalbites ruled Sicily. During this period, the island became a prosperous center of Mediterranean trade and a major producer of both raw and woven SILK. During the years of Muslim rule, a flourishing Islamic culture developed in Sicily, and it continued well after the Norman conquest of the island.

* **dynasty** succession of rulers from the same family or group

Kingdom of Sicily

Following conquests in northern France in the 900s and England in 1066, the Normans turned their attention to the Mediterranean. The Norman

Roger II assumed control of Sicily and southern Italy in 1101. He was finally accepted and crowned king on Christmas Day in 1130. Under Roger's leadership, the Kingdom of Sicily became an important Mediterranean power. In this mosaic from Palermo, Italy, Roger is being crowned by Christ.

* **sultan** political and military ruler of a Muslim dynasty or state

See map in Italy (vol. 3).

* **coronation** ceremony during which a leader, king, or queen is crowned

conquest of southern Italy and Sicily happened gradually. In 1030, the duke of Naples rewarded the Norman leader, Rainulf, with the nearby county of Aversa in return for Rainulf's help against the LOMBARDS. (Rainulf's nephew, Richard, who succeeded him, became the prince of Capua in 1058.) Farther south, the sons of TANCRED of Hauteville carved out domains for themselves in Apulia at the expense of the Byzantines.

The Hauteville domination in southern Italy over the other Norman lords began with the arrival of Robert and Roger Guiscard. Concerned with the growing Norman influence in Italy, the PAPACY at first tried to stop the growing power and influence of the Guiscard brothers. Then, in 1059, Pope Nicholas II decided to make the Guiscards papal vassals—Robert as duke of Apulia and Calabria (as well as future duke of Sicily) and Roger as prince of Capua. In return, the brothers promised to defend the PAPAL STATES and drive the Muslims from Sicily.

Although the conquest of Sicily was the joint effort of both brothers, Roger did most of the fighting because Robert increasingly turned his attention to the Adriatic Sea on the other side of Italy. Roger took advantage of feuding among Sicilian Muslims by joining with the sultan* of Syracuse to capture Messina in 1061. After Robert Guiscard captured Bari in 1071 and ended Byzantine rule in southern Italy, he and Roger, supported by a fleet of 58 ships, captured Palermo and Catania. However, not until 1095 was Norman control of Sicily secure.

The main result of Norman conquest on the island was the spread of Roman influence—Latin culture, church beliefs and practices, papal power, and western MONASTICISM. On the Italian mainland, the monastery of Monte Cassino, under the leadership of Abbot Desiderius, became an important center of learning and culture.

Roger II and His Successors.   Following the death of Roger Guiscard in 1101, his son, Roger II, assumed control of both Sicily and southern Italy. After summoning an assembly to Salerno that declared his right to be king, he was crowned (by a representative of a claimant to the papal throne) in the cathedral of Palermo on Christmas Day in 1130, although the true pope withheld confirmation until 1139.

Faced with the difficult task of uniting the different peoples and regions in southern Italy and Sicily into a single kingdom, Roger II drew together the leaders of the various Muslim, Lombard, Byzantine, and other communities and found a way to use existing institutions in the interests of his kingdom. Under his successful leadership, the Kingdom of Sicily (called the *Regno*) became the chief European power in the Mediterranean region west of Greece and remained so until Roger died in 1154.

During the rule of his grandson, William II, who reigned from 1172 to 1189, the kingdom's chief rival was FREDERICK I BARBAROSSA, emperor of the HOLY ROMAN EMPIRE, who wanted to dominate Italy. In 1184, William II made a treaty with Frederick that gave his aunt and heir, Constance (daughter of Roger II), in marriage to Frederick's son, Henry. This fateful marriage paved the way for passage of the Kingdom of Sicily into the hands of the German Hohenstaufen dynasty.

Following Frederick's death, his son Henry went to Rome in 1191 for his coronation* as emperor. He then invaded the *Regno* and, in Palermo,

Protected Minorities

During the 250 years of Muslim rule in Sicily, the majority of the island's inhabitants were Christians who did not want to convert to Islam. Islamic law granted them the status of a protected minority. In return for payment of a poll tax, Christians were guaranteed safety for themselves and their property and freedom to practice their religion. The same status was accorded to the island's small Jewish community.

* **excommunicate** to exclude from the rites of the church

* **monarchy** nation ruled by a king or queen

* **depose** to remove from high office

had himself crowned king of the Kingdom of Sicily. His brief reign—from 1194 to 1197—was important because it connected the Kingdom of Sicily to the Holy Roman Empire for the next two generations. After Henry died, his wife, Constance, forced the Germans out of the kingdom. Shortly before her death in 1198, she sought the protection of Pope INNOCENT III for her four-year-old son, Frederick Roger.

Emperor Frederick II.   Young Frederick married Constance of ARAGON in 1208 and allied himself to Pope Innocent III, who at the time was engaged in a struggle with the Holy Roman Emperor Otto IV over the issue of papal rights in Italy and Germany. When Otto moved against the Kingdom of Sicily in 1210, Innocent excommunicated* him and with French support undermined his position in Germany.

In November 1211, when a group of German representatives came to Palermo and informed the 17-year-old Frederick of his election to the German monarchy*, he hurried to Germany, where the princes and bishops eagerly made him the new German ruler. He spent the next eight years in Germany dealing with state matters before returning to Italy to be crowned emperor by the pope in 1220. When he returned to the *Regno* after his long absence, Frederick took steps to reestablish strong monarchical rule in the kingdom in the face of opposition from the nobility, the church, and the Muslims of Sicily. Frederick only then kept the promise he had made to the pope to go on a CRUSADE to the Holy Land. While there, he joined the force that made it possible to negotiate the return of Jerusalem to Christian control.

On his return from the East, Frederick issued the Constitution of Melfi of 1231, which reestablished royal power in the *Regno* by using Roman law and tradition to support the idea that within the kingdom there was no higher power than the king. From his base in the Kingdom of Sicily, Frederick sought to strengthen his authority as emperor. Conflict between himself and the papacy eventually led to Frederick's excommunication, and then to Pope Innocent IV's being exiled from Italy. Innocent summoned a council that met in Lyons in 1245. There he condemned and deposed* Frederick. Two years later, Frederick suffered a major military defeat near Parma, and he died in Apulia in 1250.

Angevins and Aragonese.   The papacy, determined to end Hohenstaufen rule in Italy and Sicily after Frederick's death, persuaded Charles of Anjou, the brother of the French king LOUIS IX, to come to Italy and rule the kingdom. Charles's defeat of Frederick's grandson in battle put an end to Hohenstaufen rule in Italy. As a result of the papal policy that successfully checked the power of the German emperor in Italy, French influence increased.

After Charles moved the capital of the Kingdom of Sicily from Palermo to NAPLES, he sought to expand his influence. Growing resentment against the French eventually caused the Sicilians to force the ANGEVINS from the island and to invite Pedro of ARAGON to be their king instead. Aragonese rule lasted about a century, and then Sicily and the Italian part of the kingdom were ruled separately—the island by the Aragonese and the mainland by the Angevins.

Aragonese rule over Sicily brought increased Spanish involvement in the affairs of the island. By the time Alfonso of Aragon became the ruler

See map in Italy (vol. 3).

* **annex** to add a territory to an existing state

* **patronage** the support of an artist, writer, or scholar by a person of wealth and influence

* **treatise** long, detailed essay

of Sicily, Spanish domination of the island was complete. When he annexed* the kingdom of Naples in 1443, the two parts of the Kingdom of Sicily reunited. This time, however, the kingdom was under Aragonese rule, a sign of the growing power of Spain.

Cultural Achievements.   During the Middle Ages, the Kingdom of Sicily played an important cultural role by bringing Greek and Arab learning to Europe. During the 1100s and the 1200s, Sicilians paid for translations from Arabic of works on philosophy, astronomy, and medicine, which then passed into the mainstream of European scholarship.

The royal court at Palermo was a center of intellectual life that attracted Arab, Greek, and Latin scholars. The English scholar, Adelard of Bath, who translated the works of Euclid (the mathematician) and the astronomical tables of al-KHWARIZMI, was one of the great scholars who visited Sicily. The most famous and important Arabic work produced on the island was the universal geography of al-Idrisi, completed in the 1150s and written at the request, and under the patronage*, of Roger II, to whom it was dedicated. Scholars in the kingdom were responsible for translations of works by PLATO, ARISTOTLE, Ptolemy, Euclid, and others, either directly from the Greek or from Arabic translations of the Greek.

The court of Frederick II was especially lively because of the emperor's strong intellectual pursuits. He was interested in mathematics and had personal contacts with the mathematician Leonardo Fibonacci of PISA. He discussed philosophical issues with Muslim scholars. He wrote a treatise* called *De arte venandi cum avibus (On the Art of Hunting with Birds).* In 1224, Frederick founded the University of Naples, which quickly became a respected European center for the study of law and medicine. (*See also* **France; Germany; Italian Language and Literature; Italy; Medicine.**)

Siena

Siena is a hill town in the Italian region of TUSCANY. Located about 30 miles south of the great city of FLORENCE, it might have seemed inevitable that Siena would become dependent on its powerful neighbor. Yet, for centuries, Siena remained independent and was famous throughout Europe for its banking and commerce.

Little is known of Siena's early history. There is some evidence to suggest that a community existed in pre-Roman times. According to legend, the town became Christian in the late third century as a result of the preaching of a Roman noble, St. Ansano. The people of medieval Siena believed in the legends that linked them to the greatness of ancient Rome. They believed that Siena was founded by sons of Remus, one of Rome's legendary founders. The emblem of medieval Siena, which is similar to that of Rome, strengthened the connection to that city.

From the 700s to the 1100s, Siena was involved in bitter disputes with its arch rival, the town of Arezzo, presumably over territorial claims. During the 800s and the 900s, the bishop of Siena played a prominent role in the town's political development and was more influential than the CAROLINGIAN counts who controlled the region.

In the 1100s and the 1200s, Siena became embroiled in quarrels between the popes and the Holy Roman Emperors. In 1167, during struggles

In the late 1100s, Siena became a commune, a self-governing city that was not under the control of a duke or other noble. It was given important privileges by the emperor. By the mid-1200s, Siena had become a major banking center. This manuscript illumination from the 1400s shows the commune's employees being paid.

* **depose** to remove from high office

* **secular** nonreligious; connected with everyday life

* **magistrate** ruling official of a town

* **imperial** pertaining to an empire or emperor

* **excommunication** formal exclusion from the church and its rituals

between Emperor FREDERICK I BARBAROSSA and Pope Alexander III, the town seized the opportunity to depose* its bishop and to create a COMMUNE headed by secular* officials. In 1185, the Sienese were granted important privileges by the emperor, including the right to elect magistrates* and to coin money. Siena's leaders in the 1100s and the 1200s, many of whom were involved in commerce, banking, and industry, helped lay the foundations for the town's success. By the mid-1200s, Sienese bankers were prominent throughout Europe. One Sienese family, the Bonsignori, became the bankers for the PAPACY.

During the conflict between the GUELPHS AND GHIBELLINES, Siena became involved in a fierce rivalry with Florence. The Guelphs of Florence favored the pope, and the Ghibellines of Siena supported the empire. For more than a century, the two cities struggled for power and position. In 1260, Siena, with the aid of imperial* troops, won a great military victory over Florence in the Battle of Montaperti. The victory was short-lived, however. Papal forces soon overpowered the imperial side, and, in 1269, Siena was defeated by Florence. As the Guelph-Ghibelline struggle drew to a close, papal displeasure at Siena's pro-imperial position led to the excommunication* of Sienese public officials and the loss of the papal banking business. Sienese families involved in banking

and commerce switched their support to the papacy, and the city became allied with Florence.

In 1287, a new political regime took control of Siena's government and ruled for nearly 70 years. This new government—the Nine Governors and Defenders of the Commune and the People of Siena—was known simply as the Nine. The Nine was an oligarchy* of powerful merchants and bankers from the noble and middle classes who supported the Guelph position. The Nine focused on hard work, dedication to detail, and a practical approach to government. They developed and standardized many of Siena's most important governmental institutions and policies. The Nine also supervised town planning projects, which included widening and straightening the streets and unifying the architectural style of the city. The rule of the Nine coincided with the greatest era of Sienese art.

In 1355, a pro-imperial revolution broke out in Siena and overthrew the government of the Nine. Nearly two centuries of political instability followed, which led to the town's increasing dependence on Florence and its eventual loss of independence. By 1530, Siena had become a satellite of Holy Roman Emperor Charles V, and in 1557 it was sold to Cosimo de' Medici, the duke of Florence. Two years later, the once-independent Siena became part of the grand duchy* of Tuscany. (*See also* **Banking; Commune; Florence; Italy; Medici Family; Tuscany.**)

* **oligarchy** form of government in which a few people hold all the ruling power

* **duchy** territory ruled by a duke or a duchess

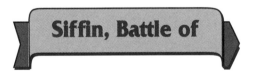

Siffin, Battle of

* **succession** the transmission of authority on the death of one ruler to the next

* **caliph** religious and political head of an Islamic state

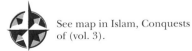 See map in Islam, Conquests of (vol. 3).

* **arbitration** settlement of a dispute by referring it to a person(s) whose decision the conflicting parties agree to accept

Beginning on July 19, 657, Muslim fought Muslim in a fierce conflict known as the Battle of Siffin. The issue behind the battle was the succession* to the Islamic CALIPHATE. The battle was the climax to a series of events that began a year earlier with the assassination of caliph* Uthman. The assassins proclaimed ALI IBN ABI TALIB as the successor. Uthman's cousin MU'AWIYA, the powerful governor of SYRIA, first withheld his allegiance from Ali and then broke openly with him. He became the leader of a movement to avenge Uthman's death, and he called for a council to choose a new caliph.

Faced with this challenge to his leadership, Ali assembled an army and marched against Mu'awiya. Both sides met at Siffin in May 657. For two months, the rival armies faced each other while the leaders negotiated. Neither side really wanted to fight. Members of the same families or tribes were on both sides, and all feared that bloodshed might lead to continuing revenge. Negotiations failed, however, and fighting began.

The battle was long, bloody, and indecisive. After ten days, fighting was stopped when some of Mu'awiya's troops held up copies of the QUR'AN and asked that it be used to judge the issue. Reluctantly, Ali agreed to arbitration*. Many of his supporters were furious and asked him to withdraw his agreement. When Ali refused, they left. This break with Ali marked the beginnings of a group known as the Kharijites and led to Ali's death at the hands of a Kharijite assassin a few years later. Mu'awiya, meanwhile, returned to Syria unopposed and began amassing power that enabled him to gain the empire for himself after Ali's death. (*See also* **Iran; Iraq; Islam, Conquests of; Islam, Religion of.**)

Sigismund, Emperor

1368–1437
Emperor and king

* **crusades** holy wars declared by the pope against non-Christians. Most were against Muslims, but crusades were also declared against heretics and pagans.

* **sultan** political and military ruler of a Muslim dynasty or state

Sigismund was a man of great ambition and energy who considered himself a second CHARLEMAGNE. He lacked the skills his ambition required, however, and his life was a long series of conflicts and half-realized aspirations that took him throughout Europe and beyond.

In 1387, Sigismund became king of Hungary after marrying Mary, the daughter of Hungary's King Louis the Great. At this time, the Ottoman Turks were advancing on Europe, and in 1395 they invaded Hungary. Sigismund organized a crusade* against them, which ended in a crushing defeat by the sultan* BAYAZID I at Nicopolis (in present-day Bulgaria) in 1396.

In 1410, Sigismund was elected Holy Roman Emperor. Among his most important goals was to resolve the Great Schism in the Christian church and to end the HUNDRED YEARS WAR. Sigismund was a major figure at the Council of Constance, which restored unity to the Western Church. However, his attempts to end the Hundred Years War were unsuccessful.

Sigismund's most bitter struggle was with Bohemia, where he was crowned king in 1420. Bohemia was embroiled in a political and religious upheaval inspired by the reformer JAN HUS. Sigismund promised Hus safe conduct to the Council of Constance so that Hus could plead his case before church leaders. But Sigismund failed to defend Hus while there, and Hus was arrested and burned at the stake. The incident led to 20 years of internal struggle in Bohemia, which Sigismund tried to end with anti-Hussite crusades against his own subjects. Finally, in 1436, Sigismund granted Hussites the right to preach their doctrines, and they, in turn, reluctantly accepted him as their king. (*See also* **Bohemia-Moravia; Germany; Hungary; Hus, Jan; Ottomans and Ottoman Empire.**)

Silk

See map in Trade (vol. 4).

Medieval Europeans valued silk greatly for its luxurious, soft texture and its beautiful design patterns. During the early Middle Ages, Europeans imported their silk from China. Then, Italy developed the silk-weaving techniques that made it a leader in silk production. Northern Italy maintained almost exclusive control of Europe's silk industry through the end of the Middle Ages.

Sericulture (the production of raw silk by the raising of silkworms) began in ancient China. The Chinese method involved collecting the eggs of silk moths. After hatching, the caterpillars, or silkworms, fed on chopped mulberry leaves for 42 to 45 days. Toward the end of the feeding period, the silkworms secreted a liquid that solidified when it came into contact with the air. The filament that was formed was spun into a cocoon.

The cocoon filament was then converted into silk yarn for weaving by two processes: reeling and throwing. To provide greater strength and uniformity, three or more filaments were slowly unwound or "reeled" together from their cocoons by a hand crank onto a circular reel. To make the silk suitable for weaving, a twist was added to the yarn (throwing).

Sericulture and silk production remained a closely guarded secret of the Chinese government for more than 2,000 years. Around 140 B.C., some

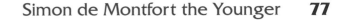
silk moth eggs and the secrets of sericulture were smuggled out of China to central Asia, India, Japan, Korea, and SASANIAN Persia. The West, however, did not learn the secrets of sericulture until the 500s, when two BYZANTINE monks succeeded in smuggling silk moth eggs and mulberry seeds—the two essential ingredients for silk making—into CONSTANTINOPLE. There it became a state monopoly and one of the Byzantine Empire's most important industries. After the Islamic conquests, the Arabs introduced sericulture to SPAIN and SICILY.

By the 1200s, silk weaving was well established in Italy. Two Italian cities, Lucca and Bologna, became famous for the development of a silk-throwing machine, one of the most important new technologies in the history of textiles. Invented in Bologna by an exile from Lucca by the name of Borghesano, the machine allowed two to four people to replace several hundred hand-thrower workers and to produce fine, strong silk yarn. Advanced models of the machine appeared in silk-throwing mills in FLORENCE and VENICE in the 14th century.

Another important development was the introduction of the drawloom from Persia. The key feature of this machine enabled weavers to produce complex, detailed designs and led to the manufacture of a wide variety of silks, silk-based fabrics woven with other fibers, and silks interwoven with gold or silver. During the late Middle Ages, northern Italian towns exercised a virtual monopoly over the European silk industry. (*See also* **Clothing; Iran; Islam, Conquests of; Italy; Technology; Textiles; Trade.**)

Simon de Montfort the Younger

ca. 1200–1265
Political leader and reformer

* **duchy**　territory ruled by a duke or a duchess

Simon de Montfort the Younger, a longtime associate of King HENRY III OF ENGLAND, broke off his close relationship with the king when he tried to restrict royal power. Simon's attempt to control the king led to the constitutional crisis of 1258–1265 and to his fatal confrontation with Henry's son, Prince Edward (EDWARD I).

Montfort was the son of a French nobleman, Simon de Montfort III, leader of the ALBIGENSIAN crusade. In 1230, the younger Montfort went to England, where he won the favor of Henry III. He became earl of Leicester in 1231, and seven years later he married Henry's sister Eleanor. In 1239, after he quarreled with Henry over a financial matter, he returned to France with his wife and then went on a CRUSADE. When he came back to England, he settled his differences with Henry and served as peacemaker between Henry and dissatisfied barons. At Henry's request, Montfort agreed to act as administrator in the troubled duchy* of Gascony in southwestern France. He left, however, when Gascon nobles, and later Henry himself, accused him of financial wrongdoing.

Montfort made peace with Henry again in 1253, but at the PARLIAMENT at Oxford in 1258 he supported the demand of the barons for reform of the government. In 1263, convinced that there was no peaceful road to reform, the barons asked Montfort to lead them in their attempt to carry out the reforms proposed by the Oxford parliament. Montfort's forces, composed mostly of younger barons and men from the towns, defeated the royal army and captured King Henry and his oldest son, Edward.

Montfort then broadened his base by calling for two parliaments to reform the royal government. He ordered each shire (county) to elect four knights as representatives to the parliament that met in London in 1264. For the second parliament in 1265 he called for two burgesses* from each borough*.

Montfort's plan for the formation of a small group to direct operations, consisting of only a few barons and himself, convinced other barons to support Henry's son, Edward, who had escaped from captivity and was able to lead the royal forces. In the military battles that followed, Edward first defeated Montfort's son Simon, and then Montfort himself and his other sons at Worcestershire. Montfort was killed and his head was cut off. Thus his attempt to restrict royal power was ended. (*See also* **England; Nobility and Nobles.**)

* **burgess** a representative of a borough

* **borough** medieval town with special duties and privileges, such as sending representatives to parliament

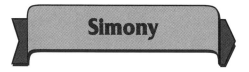
Simony

* **apostle** early follower of Jesus who traveled and spread his teachings

* **ordination** church ceremony in which a person becomes a member of the clergy

Simony refers to the buying and selling of church offices and holy orders. The term *simony* comes from Simon the Magician, a New Testament figure who tried to buy sacred powers from the apostle* Peter.

Simony became a serious problem in the fourth century when the Christian church was transformed into a wealthy institution whose offices were valuable enough to be bought and sold. Until the 500s, simony was understood as the giving or taking of money in return for ordination* or appointment to church office. In the 500s, however, Pope GREGORY I THE GREAT broadened the idea to include the transfer of a valuable object, the use of flattery or influence to gain favor, and the giving of service in expectation of reward.

Although prohibitions against simony were incorporated into church law, they were seldom enforced until the 11th century. At that time, a vigorous reform movement, known as the Investiture Controversy, made simony one of its central issues. Old laws against simony were refined and expanded, and many established payments were abolished. Some actions, such as the purchase of a priesthood, were condemned outright. Others, such as trading one benefice* for another, were considered wrong but tolerable. Despite the reforms, simony persisted through the Middle Ages and well beyond, and it became one of the central issues of the Protestant Reformation of the 1500s. (*See also* **Benefice; Church-State Relations.**)

* **benefice** church office to which property or income is attached

Slavery

Slavery, which had been widespread in the ancient world, continued into the Middle Ages. However, by the last years of the Roman Republic the legal position of slaves had improved, and in the Islamic world slavery was largely limited to urban households. Although medieval slavery continued in the Mediterranean world in both Christian and Muslim countries, it ceased to be significant in FRANCE, GERMANY, ENGLAND, and SCANDINAVIA.

The Military Elite

The Janissaries were the regular infantry troops of the Ottoman Empire. Technically the sultan's slaves, they were first recruited from his legal share (one-fifth) of war booty. In 1395, forcible induction into the army of non-Muslim males, ages 8 to 20, began. Recruits received years of rigorous training, including instruction in the Turkish language and customs and conversion to Islam. Isolated from the Muslim population because of their non-Muslim birth, and from the Christian population because of their conversion to Islam, they were dependent on the sultan. Charged with guarding him at home and in battle, the Janissaries came to be regarded as the elite military force within the empire.

 See map in Trade (vol. 4).

* **dynasty** succession of rulers from the same family or group

European Slavery

The medieval Christian attitude toward slavery was based on the idea from the BIBLE that slavery should not exist when master and slave belong to the same race and religion. However, it took several centuries for that idea to gain wide acceptance in Europe.

Early Middle Ages. When the VISIGOTHS and OSTROGOTHS ruled parts of Italy in the 400s and the 500s, they kept their slaves in a constant state of terror. For example, a slave could be killed if he was involved in a lawsuit that concerned his master, and he could be burned alive if he started a fire or had intercourse with a widow (even if she consented).

The clash of Christians and non-Christian populations of central and northern Europe before the Christianization of those lands resulted in the enslavement of the Saxon tribes in Germany and England and the peoples of Scandinavia. After the Carolingians established the policy that banned Christian slaves in a Christian society, European slavery declined, and the number of SERFS (rural workers subject to the will of their landowners) increased.

The European slave trade flourished through the sale of large numbers of non-Christian slaves to Muslim Spain and North Africa. In the 800s and the 900s, large numbers of SLAVS were transported by slave traders through Christian Europe to the Muslim world. As the Slavic people of KIEVAN RUS, POLAND, BOHEMIA-MORAVIA, CROATIA, SERBIA, and BULGARIA converted to Christianity, the slave trade in these regions declined.

Later Middle Ages. The clash of peoples of different religions was the main reason for the persistence of slavery and the slave trade in the late medieval period. The confrontation between Christianity and Islam provided slaves to both sides since those captured in battle were usually enslaved.

In the BYZANTINE EMPIRE, slavery eventually disappeared, even though it was never officially abolished. Captured prisoners of war had been the chief source of slaves, and, after the 1300s, Byzantine war efforts were largely unsuccessful. In this way, Byzantine slavery gradually decreased.

From the 1100s through the 1400s, the international slave trade turned to the shores of the Black Sea and, eventually, to Africa. In the 12th century, Italian merchants from VENICE and GENOA bought slaves in the Black Sea region and supplied them to the AYYUBID and MAMLUK dynasties* of EGYPT. By the 1300s, Genoese and other Italian merchants had a virtual monopoly on the international slave trade. They exported Turks, Mongols, and other peoples from the Caucasus and Crimea regions and blacks from Africa, at first through Muslim ports in North Africa and later from Portuguese trading posts in Africa.

This trade supplied slaves to the Mediterranean world to both Christian and Muslim countries. The number of slaves in Italian towns grew in the late Middle Ages. In the 1100s, slaves accounted for perhaps 10 percent of the population of Genoa and, by the late 1300s, perhaps 15 percent. On Mediterranean islands, such as Crete and Majorca (where escape was difficult), the percentage of slaves was even higher and the conditions much harsher. Some Majorcan landowners owned more than 60 slaves. Many slaves were chained and locked in cellars for the night. In addition, a special police force was established to capture runaways and to put down

The clash between people of different religions was the main reason for the persistence of slavery in Europe during the Middle Ages. In this bronze relief from the 1100s, St. Adalbert of Prague intercedes with King Boleslaw I of Poland for the release of his subjects from slave traders.

revolts. In 1328, the 21,000 slaves on Majorca made up 36 percent of the island's population. Slavery persisted in the Mediterranean world past the end of the Middle Ages.

Islamic Slavery

The assumption that one human being has the right to own and rule another human being was taken for granted in Islam. The QUR'AN and Muslim law assume that the inequality between master and slave, like the inequality between man and woman, is ordained by God. However, the Qur'an also advocates that slaves—male and female—be treated with kindness and encourages masters to free their slaves as an act of charity.

Urban Slaves.   Because slaves in the Islamic world generally worked in urban households, their lives were often less harsh than those in other societies where slaves were used for agricultural production or major CON-STRUCTION projects. In medieval Islamic society, workers employed on labor-intensive projects received payment for their work. A rare attempt to use slave labor in Iraq in the 800s ended in disaster when a revolt by East African slaves, forced to work in the marshland of lower Iraq under harsh conditions, was violently put down.

Although slaves accounted for only a small percentage of the total Islamic population, they played a vital role in Muslim towns and cities. In almost every aspect of urban society, enslaved men, women, and children of diverse origin, background, and training provided their masters with a wide range of services—from cleaning, cooking, and child care to managing the financial affairs of great merchant houses. Some even commanded Islamic military forces.

The fate of slaves depended mostly on the conditions in the household in which they served and on the status of their masters, who might be rulers, scholars, merchants, or craftsmen. Since Muslim law prohibited the enslavement of Muslims, Jews, and Christians living under Islamic rule, slaves were by definition outsiders from beyond the Islamic world.

The newly acquired slave (children were preferred) was given a distinctive slave name. Then he or she was trained, educated, and socialized into Islam and into the master's household. The nature of the training varied greatly from household to household. The future slave soldier was trained in the use of weapons. The future business agent was trained in accounting. Some young slaves were even trained to be professional musicians. Those trained from their earliest years in religious studies sometimes became recognized scholars as adults.

Adult males, often acquired as prisoners of war, were not considered good investments since they were more difficult to subdue into slavery. Adult female slaves were viewed more favorably because they could bear children, who could then be trained as needed. Slaves who earned their own capital through their service were in a position to buy their freedom.

Manumission. The ultimate goal of Islamic slavery was freedom for the slave (called manumission) and his or her integration into Muslim society. Slavery was not meant to be permanent, and second-generation slavery was rare. Islamic slavery was regarded as a way to convert outsiders into insiders, and the training of young slaves usually ended with their manumission in early adulthood. The freed slave was reborn as a member of the Muslim community, integrated into its social network, and linked even more strongly with the former master. Manumission was not a severance of the master-slave relationship as much as it was a remaking of the relationship into an even deeper relationship of clientage, which was a type of artificially created kinship. The freed slave became a loyal client, and this new relationship might extend for generations. (*See also* **Agriculture; Islam, Conquests of; Islam, Religion of; Warfare.**)

Slavic Literature

See map in Kievan Rus (vol. 3).

During the Middle Ages, the people known as SLAVS spread out into many parts of eastern Europe and western Russia. As the Slavs established new communities in many different areas, the Slavic language evolved from a single language into the dozen or so different languages that Slavic peoples speak today.

A written Slavic language began among the West Slavs when CYRIL AND METHODIOS, two missionary monks from the BYZANTINE EMPIRE, traveled to Moravia (which later became part of the former Czechoslovakia). They created a Slavic alphabet, using mostly Greek letters. Then they translated biblical and religious texts into Slavic, using this new alphabet. Thus, the Moravians were the first Slavs to have their own written language. A modified form of this Cyrillic alphabet (named in honor of St. Cyril) is used today by Russians, Ukrainians, Belorussians, Bulgarians, and most of the peoples of the former Yugoslavia.

By 1000, this earliest Slavic written language—now called Old Slavic or Old Church Slavonic—was used throughout those parts of the Slavic world that were under Byzantine influence. However, some western

Russian Literary Renaissance

A great burst of Russian literary activity occurred as the medieval period ended. In the late 1400s, churchmen in Novgorod produced the first complete Slavic translation of the Bible. A merchant named Afanasii Nitikin wrote a remarkable travel account called *Journey Beyond Three Seas*. A military narrative called *Tale of the Taking of Constantinople* was widely read because it predicted that Russia would free Constantinople from the Turks. Also, the first Russian version of the Dracula story—a tale that is still popular today—appeared around 1475.

* **Gospels**   accounts of the life and teachings of Jesus as told in the first four books of the New Testament

* **secular**   nonreligious; connected with everyday life

* **annals**   written account of events year by year

* **chronicles**   record of events in the order in which they occurred

See color plate 1, vol. 1.

* **theologian**   person who studies religious faith and practice

* **ecclesiastical**   pertaining to a church

Slavs, such as the Czechs and the Poles, used LATIN rather than Old Slavic because they had adopted the Roman rather than the Byzantine form of Christianity. For this reason, the modern Polish and Czech languages use the Latin alphabet instead of the Cyrillic. In addition to the church texts that Cyril and Methodios translated into Old Slavic for the Moravians, the western Slavs produced original works, including biographies of Cyril and Methodios, poems placed at the beginning of Gospel* translations, and prayers.

After the Byzantines were expelled from Moravia, Czech literature came under the Western influence of Latin, German, French, and Italian. The little surviving Czech literature from the medieval period consists of religious writings based on Latin models from Germany and Italy. The most accomplished poetry of the period was an anonymous hymn to St. Wenceslas, the martyred patron saint of the Czechs.

Eastern Europe's first university was founded in PRAGUE in 1348, ushering in a golden age of cultural activity. Many secular* works were published during this time. These were mostly love poems, satirical verses, and student drinking songs. Czech prose consisted mostly of translations of the BIBLE, the travels of Marco POLO, the autobiography of the emperor CHARLEMAGNE, and other works. The leading Czech prose writer of the Middle Ages was Tomás ze Stítného (ca. 1325–1400), who wrote on various religious subjects. In the 1400s, JAN HUS and his followers wrote sermons, letters, and pamphlets in Czech (instead of Latin) in order to communicate their ideas about church reform to the greatest number of people.

Medieval Polish literature was religious. It consisted of annals*, chronicles*, saints' lives, religious songs, and sermons. Most were written in Latin. The first works in Polish, written during the late Middle Ages, were also about religion.

Bulgaria created a flourishing Old Slavic literature, which it passed on to the eastern Slavs and Serbs. Medieval Bulgarian religious and philosophical works, written in Old Slavic, reflected a strong Byzantine influence. In Croatia, the Latin alphabet was preferred over the Cyrillic. Medieval Croatian literature consisted mostly of translations of Latin religious texts. Serbia remained closely linked to Bulgaria and Byzantium, and Serbian monks translated many Byzantine works, including sermons, hymns, and religious poems as well as histories of Alexander the Great and the Trojan War. After Turkey occupied Serbia and made it a Turkish province in 1459, Serbian literary activity decreased dramatically.

Works translated into Old Slavic in KIEVAN RUS were mostly religious works, such as saints' lives and the sermons of early Greek theologians*. However, Russian writers also made their own original contributions, such as the masterful *Slovo o zakone i blagodati (Sermon on Law and Grace)*, written about 1050 by Ilarion, the first native Russian to head the Russian Christian church.

The last major Old Russian work before the Mongol conquest was *Patericon,* a large collection of tales about the monks of Kiev's Monastery of the Caves. Filled with tales of miracles, demons, and divine interventions, the work was eagerly read by later generations of Russian readers. Literature continued to be produced in many centers, especially Moscow, after the Mongol conquest. Works of this period include translations of ecclesiastical* works, travel accounts, philosophical and medical texts, and historical epics. The most famous epic is the *Zadonshchina* of the late 1400s, which is about the famous Battle of Kulikovo. (*See also* **Historical Writing; Mongol Empire: Saints, Lives of; Sermons.**)

Slavs

* **nomadic** wandering from place to place to find food and pasture

See map in Kievan Rus (vol. 3).

Since the Middle Ages, the people called Slavs have been the largest cultural and language group in eastern Europe. No one knows for sure where the original Slav homeland was located. Most scholars think that it was somewhere between the Baltic Sea in the north, the Black Sea in the south, the Volga River in the east, and the Oder River in the west.

In the mid-500s, nomadic* tribes called the Turkic Avars moved from central Asia into the area north of the Black Sea. Later, they pushed westward to the basin of the Danube River in eastern Europe. The Slavs who lived in these areas were either conquered by the Avars or forced to move elsewhere. The eastern Slavs—ancestors of the Ukrainians, Russians, and Belorussians—migrated north into southern Ukraine. The southern Slavs—ancestors of the Bulgarians, Serbians, Croatians, Macedonians, and Slovenes—migrated south into the Balkan Mountains. Other Slavs went west and north along the Danube as far as the Baltic coast, some of them as allies of the Avars. These became the western Slavs—ancestors of the Czechs, Slovaks, and Poles. (In the Middle Ages, all Slavic tribes on the borders of Germany were called Wends).

Slavs considered land to be communal, and movable possessions (such as livestock, slaves, weapons, and tools) to be personal property. The oldest Slavic law codes make little reference to land ownership. One such code of laws, the *Russkaya pravda*—which greatly influenced the law codes of Poland, Lithuania, and other eastern European countries—does not mention land boundaries or landed property in its oldest form. The only mention of land in this oldest version is about protecting forests.

The Slavs, who worked the land communally as members of large extended families or clans, had no individual land ownership until the end of the Middle Ages. Late in the Middle Ages, with the rise of kings and princes who wanted to reward their supporters with estates, Slavic law began to recognize land rights. (*See also* **Bohemia-Moravia; Bosnia; Bulgaria; Croatia; Kievan Rus; Muscovy, Rise of; Poland; Serbia; Serfs and Serfdom; Slavic Literature.**)

Snorra Edda

See *Scandinavia, Culture of.*

Social Classes

Before the 11th century, sharp distinctions between social classes did not exist in western European society. There were many groups, each group blending into those above and below it. The groups that existed in early medieval France, for example, consisted of great lords, CLERGY (ranging from archbishops to doorkeepers), CASTELLANS (governors of forts and castles), KNIGHTS (some were mercenaries), tenants, free peasants, and those in varying degrees of servitude and

Rapid commercial expansion after 1000 led to the growth of towns and cities. A new urban social class evolved, which did not have the traditional feudal relationship with the nobility. This illumination from the 1300s shows merchants and nobles riding past peasants tilling the soil. Free peasants and other noncitizens of a town could become citizens with the approval of the town's government.

See color plate 14, vol. 1.

dependency—shepherds, peddlers, servants, and beggars. In the later Middle Ages, clearer social classes evolved. In the Byzantine Empire, social classes also grew more distinct and rigid as the Middle Ages progressed.

Western Europe.   In the early Middle Ages, lords controlled most of the land and earned their income from it without having to actually work it. On the other hand, peasants did the work and were subject to the will of the lord. Together, these two groups accounted for about 90 percent of the population.

By the 12th century, NOBILITY was based more on family ties and prestige than on the amount of land owned. Knighthood was one way to achieve prestige and power, and many nobles were knights. However, not all knights were nobles; some were from humble peasant backgrounds with little or no land and few resources.

In the 1100s, the high costs of the knight's equipment—a horse, coat of mail, armor, shield, sword, and helmet—drew a line between those who could afford to equip and train themselves and those who could not. Those who became knights were considered aristocrats*, especially if they married into a noble family or had a castle. Those who could not afford to become knights faded into the peasantry. During the Middle Ages, the number of nobles increased, as free peasants, officeholders, and even prosperous serfs found means to buy their way into the nobility. The growth of the noble class, combined with a sense of privilege and

* **aristocrats** people of the highest social class

See
color plate 10,
vol. 1.

* **charter** written grant from a ruler
conferring certain rights and privileges

* **apprentice** person bound by legal
agreement to work for another for a specific
period of time in return for instruction in a
trade or art

* **vassal** person given land by a lord or
monarch in return for loyalty and services

Swedish Peasants

Sweden was home to Europe's
most successful peasant class.
Land, forests, and lakes were
abundant. Feudal lords were few
and weak. Serfdom in Sweden did
not begin until the 13th century.

Swedish peasants owned about
half of the country's farmland. They
had a share of the political power
as well. In 1319, when it was time
to choose a new king, peasant representatives were called to vote.
Later in the century, the Swedish
crown established the Riksdag, the
country's first parliament. The
peasants were given their own
chamber or house in the Riksdag.

responsibility among the nobles, made this the dominant group in medieval European society.

The peasants did not achieve the same sense of class identity. Most
peasants felt isolated. Some left the land and moved to towns and cities. In
many parts of Europe, the peasantry itself was divided into several groups:
independent plowmen who lived and worked on their own land; laborers
who worked the land of others for wages; and serfs who generally were
bound to the land as tillers of the soil. Depending on the size and quality
of their landholdings, some serfs were better off than freemen.

The rapid commercial expansion in western Europe after 1000 stimulated the growth of towns and cities. It also increased the number of
townspeople who supported themselves by trade and manufacturing and
were able to save and invest money. As towns achieved some degree of independence, especially in Italy and Germany, the new urban class began
to express itself politically. The citizens of towns stood apart from the feudal relationship between lord and peasant. Residents of towns and cities
demanded the right to govern themselves. Residents of many communities pressured kings into granting them town charters*.

Not everybody who lived in a town was a citizen. Citizenship was reserved for artisans, merchants, and others who owned property, paid taxes,
and contributed to the defense of the town. Wage earners, apprentices*,
and servants were not considered citizens. Most townsfolk inherited their
citizenship, although free peasants and other noncitizens could acquire
citizenship with the approval of the town government. Those who were not
citizens were prohibited from attending assemblies, standing guard duty,
or participating fully in the life of their towns.

Although citizens formed a distinct social group within each town,
townspeople as a whole did not form a social class across a region or country. Differences that existed regarding towns and their charters, difficulties
of communication, and the lack of government or social standards prevented townspeople from joining forces for a common cause with people
of other towns. Although there were exceptions, such as in the HANSEATIC
LEAGUE, most urban dwellers pursued their interests locally.

As with townspeople, the status of the clergy was also separate from
the fundamental feudal relationship between lord and vassal*, although
the church drew its support from both groups. In a society in which the
church was an extremely powerful and influential institution, clergymen
enjoyed prestige and special privileges. The clergy included several sub-
classes. At the top of the hierarchy were bishops and abbots, usually from
noble families or those with large landholdings. At the other end were village priests, usually from peasant origins. Clergy members who lacked
BENEFICES (church positions supported by endowments) were wage earners
who made their living by assisting at parishes or conducting church services for fees.

Byzantine Empire.   Politically, the Byzantine Empire was a continuation
of the ancient Roman Empire. Byzantine society was shaped by the actions
of the early emperors Diocletian (who reigned from 284 to 305) and CON-
STANTINE (who reigned from 307 to 337). In an attempt to reorganize the
Roman Empire and to return the region to its former glory, these emperors placed strict controls on farmers and city workers. In Byzantine cities,

workers engaged in labor that the empire considered essential—such as shipbuilders, bakers, pork dealers, and state factory workers—were tied for life to their trades, and these trades were hereditary. Byzantine workers, as well as farmers, were legally obliged to follow the trade of their fathers. These restrictions were loosened later in the Middle Ages, although many people continued by custom to follow the family trade.

People who worked the fields were tied to the soil for life. Many peasants were oppressed by heavy taxes and by local officials who exploited them. Many peasants ran away or became serfs on the large estates of landowners, hoping for better treatment. They were often disappointed since many landowners also exploited them with little regard for their well-being. Serfs had few rights.

In the early Middle Ages, some Byzantine villages were inhabited by free peasants who owned and farmed their own land. By the 900s, however, the landed aristocracy and the MONASTERIES had taken over most of these areas. Several emperors enacted laws designed to protect the villages, but these laws did little to halt the growth of large estates. As in European society, the Byzantine clergy also became a powerful class in society. Clergy members were considered a strong spiritual force on which the safety of the empire depended. The emperors were unable to keep the monasteries from expanding their holdings, as once-free villages became church property.

By the 1300s, the disintegration of the Byzantine countryside was complete. Peasants were oppressed, villages were deserted, and there was open rebellion against greedy landowners. When Turkish armies marched from the east to conquer the empire, the countryside lay weak and defenseless. One Turkish invader wrote, "God has decreed that we should take the land from the Christians because they do not conduct their affairs . . . with justice, because they look to wealth and favor, and the rich treat the poor with haughtiness, and do not help them either with gifts or with justice." (*See also* **Chivalry; Commune; Inheritance Laws and Practices; Land Use; Peasants' Rebellions and Uprisings; Serfs and Serfdom; Slavery; Trade.**)

Spain, Muslim Kingdoms of

See map in Aragon (vol. 1).

* **caliph** religious and political head of an Islamic state

After the Muslims conquered Spain (called al-Andalus in Arabic) in the early 700s, they occupied and dominated all but the northern-most regions of Spain and Portugal for much of the medieval period. Beginning in the 1200s, the Christian Spanish states in the north asserted themselves against the Muslims and drove them from Spain.

Conquest and Reconquest.   According to Islamic accounts, Tariq ibn Ziyad (who had just conquered North Africa) invaded Spain in 711 with an army of Arab officers and about 12,000 BERBERS. Following the conquest, an 18,000-man force led by Musa ibn Nusayr, the Arab governor of North Africa, occupied Seville, Saragossa, and most of the rest of Spain.

The UMAYYAD caliph* of DAMASCUS ordered both Tariq and Musa home from Spain. Between 714 and 756, the Muslim territory in Spain had 20 governors. Many of these governors fell from power as a result of an older Arab feud that was transported to Spain.

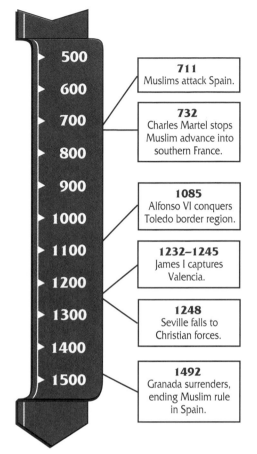

500
600
700
800
900
1000
1100
1200
1300
1400
1500

711
Muslims attack Spain.

732
Charles Martel stops Muslim advance into southern France.

1085
Alfonso VI conquers Toledo border region.

1232–1245
James I captures Valencia.

1248
Seville falls to Christian forces.

1492
Granada surrenders, ending Muslim rule in Spain.

* **mosque**   Muslim place of worship

* **sultan**   political and military ruler of a Muslim dynasty or state

* **principality**   region that is ruled by a prince

At first, the Muslims viewed Spain as a launching place for the conquest of Europe. They seized the city of BARCELONA in northern Spain and advanced into southern France as far as Poitiers until CHARLES MARTEL and Eudes of AQUITAINE stopped their advance in 732. By this time, the borders of al-Andalus were firmly set. Only a narrow strip of unconquered Christian states remained in northern Spain. These included CASTILE, ARAGON, NAVARRE, and CATALONIA.

The first emir (military ruler) of al-Andalus was Abd al-Rahman I. During his long reign from 756 to 788, he repelled Christian raiders, crushed revolts, and brought more Syrian supporters to Spain. More revolts and VIKING attacks from the north plagued the emirs of al-Andalus in the 800s. However, the 900s brought a kind of golden age to the emirate under Abd al-Rahman III (who ruled from 912 to 961) and under his son al-Hakam II (who ruled from 961 to 976).

Abd al-Rahman III, who boldly gave himself the title of caliph in 929, made al-Andalus a mighty sea power. His ships raided the islands and coasts of the western Mediterranean and plundered the Rhône valley in southern France. His attacks along the North African coast convinced the FATIMID rulers to move their capital to EGYPT at the opposite end of the Mediterranean. Abd al-Rahman III also undertook ambitious building projects and began the first regular minting of gold coins.

Abd al-Rahman III's reign was notable for the splendor of the palaces, baths, country estates, castles, and mosques* that were built. One impressive example is the Great Mosque of CÓRDOBA, which was decorated with gold imported from Africa. With the help of Berber sultans*, the rulers of al-Andalus had access to trade routes through the Sahara desert and south of the Sahara. Along these routes, gold was transported. From the mid-800s to the mid-1200s, African gold bolstered the economic prosperity of al-Andalus and helped make its capital of Córdoba as splendid as CONSTANTINOPLE and BAGHDAD.

Around 1000, the Spanish Muslim CALIPHATE split into a patchwork of 20 to 30 principalities* ruled by local dynasties. The five major principalities were Badajoz, TOLEDO, and Saragossa in the north and Seville and GRANADA in the south. These principalities often fought among themselves. Occasionally the Christian states of Europe became involved in these struggles.

In 1085, the Christian ruler Alfonso VI of Castile conquered the border region of Toledo. Around the same time, the Christian warrior known as the CID captured the coast of VALENCIA. Worried representatives of several Muslim principalities asked for aid from the Almoravids, an Arab dynasty from North Africa. Not only did the Almoravids drive the Castilians back, but they also seized control of Seville, Granada, Valencia, Saragossa, and other principalities, thus making al-Andalus part of their empire. The Almoravids were in turn replaced by the Almohads, who took control of Morocco and Spain. They made Seville the capital of a vast territory that stretched from the Atlantic Ocean to Tripoli.

The conquest of Muslim Spain by the Christian states in the north began in earnest in the early 1200s. JAMES I THE CONQUEROR of Aragon and Catalonia raided Valencia in 1225, captured the island of Majorca in 1229, and then conquered the Valencian lands in 1232–1245. Meanwhile, Ferdinand III and his son ALFONSO X EL SABIO of Castile and León captured Córdoba (1236), Jaén (1246), Seville (1248), and Cadiz (1262).

In 1085, King Alfonso VI of Castile conquered the border region of Toledo, Spain, and took it back from Muslim control. This mosque in Toledo was converted into a Christian church in the early 1100s. By the end of the 1200s, most of the Muslim kingdoms of Spain had been reconquered by Spanish Christians.

See color plate 11, vol. 2.

* **enclave** country or part of a country contained within the boundaries of another country

As the Christians advanced south through Muslim Spain, they followed the Muslim example of maintaining conquered communities as independent enclaves*. The conquered Muslims, called Mudejars, had their own religious institutions, laws, and internal government. The Spanish Muslim principality that lasted the longest was Granada. Its position behind sheltering mountains allowed it to survive until it was finally forced to surrender in 1492.

Diverse Population.   The population of Muslim Spain was both an ethnic and a religious mix. It included the Arab elite, mostly from Syria and Yemen; Berber farmers and herders from North Africa; slaves brought in to serve the army and bureaucracy (these were generally freed when they converted to Islam); and Jews and Mozarabs. (Mozarabs were Spanish Christians who were traditionally Arab in their language and customs but retained their Christian faith.) The majority of the population consisted of native Spanish people who were born into or converted to Islam. The social classes included nobles, CASTELLANS (those who administered castles and forts), city officials, farmers, artisans, laborers, and household slaves.

Under Islamic law, Jews and Mozarabs were generally tolerated and allowed to associate with Muslims. Jewish and Christian communities were

self-governing, with their own leaders and laws. Because of this fairly tolerant attitude, Jewish immigration to Muslim Spain increased substantially. Spanish Jews held important positions in Spanish Muslim society as statesmen, scholars, physicians, and merchants.

This diversity of peoples and traditions helped make al-Andalus a leader in astronomy, geography, metaphysics, music, mysticism*, poetry, law, theology*, history, medicine, travel, agricultural and botanical research, and architecture. Muslim Spain's high level of scholarship and culture brought new ideas to western Europe and contributed to the development of scholasticism and health care. Many great thinkers and writers lived and worked in Muslim Spain, including the Arab philosopher IBN RUSHD and the Jewish philosopher MAIMONIDES. (*See also* **Arabic Language and Literature; Historical Writing; Islam, Conquests of; Islam, Religion of; Islamic Art and Architecture; Jewish Communities; Jews, Expulsion of; Medicine; Science; Scientific Instruments.**)

* **mysticism** belief that divine truths or direct knowledge of God can be experienced through faith, spiritual insight, and intuition

* **theology** study of the nature of God and of religious truth

See color plate 15, vol. 3.

Spanish Art and Architecture

D uring the Middle Ages, Spain's art and architecture reflected the country's unique blend of Islamic, Christian, Jewish, and other traditions. The brilliant heritage created by this ethnic variety made a deep and lasting impression on the medieval culture of western Europe.

Islamic Influence.   Spain was ruled by Muslims for nearly eight centuries during the Middle Ages. The style of Islamic Spanish art (called Hispano-Mauresque art) was established during the peak of North African Arab rule in Spain, from 756 to 1031. The two major architectural achievements of this early period are the Great Mosque* of CÓRDOBA and the palace city of Madinat al-Zahra. Both were created in terms of rectangular units, and, in both, this regular geometry is disguised by lavish, colorful decoration, such as patterns of alternating wedge-shaped pieces of white stone and red brick.

Construction of the Great Mosque began in 785 under the rule of Abd al-Rahman I. The mosque has a simple stone exterior, an open courtyard, and a covered area containing 11 parallel aisles. Separating the aisles, and supporting the flat ceiling, are unique two-tiered arcades*. The lower, horseshoe-shaped arches rise from short columns, and the upper arches rise close above the lower ones. The builders of the mosque combined fine masonry of specially cut stones and columns that were taken from the ruins of earlier buildings of the Romans and VISIGOTHS. Additions were made to the mosque in 848, 969, and 987.

A palace was built next to the Great Mosque, so that the caliphs* could enter the mosque through a private door from the palace. Soon, there were also secondary palaces erected outside the city. The earliest and most important of these "suburban" palaces was Madinat al-Zahra. This was a vast and sumptuous structure, built for the caliph Abd al-Rahman III (who reigned from 912 to 961), on a hillside six miles northwest of Córdoba. Begun in 936 and used until 981, Madinat al-Zahra was an administrative center as well as a royal residence for the ruler and his court. It had a mint* and workshops for various luxury items, such as elegantly carved ivory boxes. Madinat al-Zahra contained a series of separate courtyards

* **mosque** Muslim place of worship

* **arcade** long, arched passageway

* **caliph** religious and political head of an Islamic state

* **mint** to make coins by shaping and stamping metal; the place where coins are made

Islamic Tiles

The Islamic taste for ornamentation gave rise to the medieval Spanish ceramics industry. Muslims used tiles to cover the lower part of the walls of their buildings.

Tiles from the Alhambra are shaped like polygons. Made of a single color, each small piece was either sawed into shape after firing or set into a mold before firing. The pieces were then set into bands of blue, green, white, brown, and black patterns.

The Visigoths were Germanic people who settled in Spain in the early Middle Ages. They were conquered by the Moors in 711. Like many Germanic tribes of the period, they were known for portable objects of gold inlaid with colored glass and precious gems. The fibulas and buckle shown here are from Visigothic Spain in the 500s. They are made of gold-plated bronze and inlaid with green glass.

* **crusades** holy wars declared by the pope against non-Christians. Most were against Muslims, but crusades were also declared against heretics and pagans.

* **Romanesque** referring to a style of architecture developed in Italy and western Europe between the Roman and Gothic periods and characterized by round arches, thick walls, and small windows

* **synagogue** building of worship for Jews

linked by corridors. Around the largest courtyard were several lavishly decorated reception rooms.

Beginning in the 11th century, two North African dynasties, the Almoravids (1054–1147) and the Almohads (1130–1269), ruled parts of Spain and brought with them architectural ideas from their native regions. One of Spain's greatest monuments, the ALHAMBRA, reflects these influences. The Alhambra—the royal palace of MUHAMMAD V—was built inside a fortified enclosure on a hill overlooking GRANADA. Begun sometime after 1354, the Alhambra survived as a monument to Islamic power in Spain. The Islamic and North African influences in Spanish art lived on long after Muslim power in that region ended.

Christian Art. The most original works of art in medieval Christian Spain were the manuscript illuminations of a text called the *Commentary on the Apocalypse,* compiled about 776 by Beatus of Liébana, a monk in ASTURIAS-LEÓN. The *Apocalypse* concerns a final victory over the powers of evil, which Christians interpreted as a prediction of the Christian crusade* against Muslim Spain. This made Beatus's text so popular that it was recopied and illustrated many times. More than 20 illustrated manuscripts of the Beatus text, dating from the 900s to the 1200s, have survived.

Ferdinand I the Great, who ruled León and CASTILE from 1037 to 1065, helped end Christian Spain's artistic isolation from the rest of Europe. Through his connections with the abbey of Cluny in France, new styles appeared in Spanish art. The Romanesque* artistic style that was popular elsewhere in Europe began to appear in Spanish architecture, and Spain contributed to its development. The cathedral in SANTIAGO DE COMPOSTELA is Romanesque in its architectural design and decorative sculpture. The carvings in the cloister of Santo Domingo de Silos are also fully Romanesque in style.

Jewish Art. Among the surviving examples of Jewish medieval art are two beautiful synagogues* in TOLEDO. The older synagogue was built in the 1200s and is now the church of Santa María la Blanca. The other, built in the 1350s as a private synagogue, is now the church of El Tránsito. Spanish Hebrew religious manuscripts from the 1300s have also survived. Some of these have full-page illustrations from the book of Exodus in the BIBLE. (*See also* **Books, Manuscript; Crusades; Hebrew Literature; Jewish Art; Jewish Communities; Metals and Metalworking; Spain, Muslim Kingdoms of.**)

Spanish Language and Literature

* **vernacular** language or dialect native to a region; everyday, informal speech

* **dialect** form of speech characteristic of a region that differs from the standard language in pronunciation, vocabulary, and grammar

Old Spanish was the vernacular* of the various inhabitants of medieval Spain—Spanish Muslims, Christians, and Jews. Although they all spoke Old Spanish, Muslims and Jews wrote in Arabic and Hebrew. Little is known about Spanish language and literature of the early Middle Ages, but both are well documented for the later Middle Ages.

Language. Old Spanish refers to the closely related group of dialects* that were spoken, and later written, in the central part of medieval Spain. Scholars divide Old Spanish into three periods: early, classical, and late.

The early Old Spanish period is represented by a few poems and prose texts that were written between 1100 and 1250. The language of these works was greatly influenced by local dialects. These early works are highly individual, and scholars do not consider them to follow any particular literary tradition.

Classical Old Spanish (sometimes referred to as standardized Old Spanish) was spoken and written from 1250 to 1400. During this period, the differences among dialects disappeared, and the language became more standard and universal. The texts that survive from this period include a few poems and several types of didactic* prose, such as SERMONS and HANDBOOKS of morals. Standardized Old Spanish was encouraged by Alfonso XI, king of CASTILE, and his nephew Don Juan MANUEL.

* **didactic** designed or intended to teach

Late Old Spanish (1400–1500) came under Portuguese, French, and Italian influences. These languages added many words and phrases to Spanish. Once again, dialects appeared, but this time more because of foreign influences than because of differences among the regions of Spain.

Old Spanish has been traced to 1100, but scholars believe that an even older form of Spanish existed. Called Archaic Spanish, it is thought to have been in use from about 900 to 1100. There are very few documents in Archaic Spanish—only a few charters, contracts, and assorted fragments of other written works. A few scholars believe that a still older form of Spanish, from the period between 400 and 900, was the link between the LATIN LANGUAGE of the Roman Empire and Archaic Spanish. However, no actual evidence of this intermediate language has been found.

See map in Aragon (vol. 1).

Spoken Old Spanish had many dialects. The three major ones were those of the kingdoms of ASTURIAS-LEÓN, CASTILE, and NAVARRE and ARAGON. As these northern Spanish-Christian kingdoms expanded southward through Muslim Spain, the characteristics of their speech mixed. There was also a distinct dialect spoken by the Mozarabs, who were Spanish Christians who adopted some aspects of Arab culture.

Remember: Words in small capital letters have separate entries, and the index at the end of Volume 4 will guide you to more information on many topics.

In addition to its vernacular language, Spain had several literary languages. For much of the Middle Ages, Latin, Arabic, and Hebrew were the languages of learning and literature in Spain. Poetry and prose in the Spanish vernacular appeared around the middle of the medieval period. However, Spanish did not replace Latin as the chief literary language of Spain until the 1300s.

Latin Literature.   The major figure of Spanish literature in Latin during the early medieval period was Isidore of Seville (ca. 560–636). Isidore's religious writings and histories greatly influenced medieval European scholars, and his 20-volume encyclopedia of ancient learning established him as the "schoolmaster to the Middle Ages." Another important writer of the early Middle Ages was Eugenius II, bishop of Toledo, who wrote poetry in Latin.

After the Muslim conquest of Spain in the early 700s, education in Latin declined—not just in Islamic southern regions of Spain but also in the Christian north. In the Muslim city of CÓRDOBA, a Christian writer named Paulus Alvarus (ca. 800–ca. 861) praised contemporary Christian martyrs*, and he expressed regret that many young Christians were turning away from Latin and studying Arabic instead. One important Christian work from this period was the *Chronica* of King Alfonso III of Asturias,

* **martyr** person who suffers and dies rather than renounce a religious faith

Alfonso X was king of Castile from 1252 to 1284. Many significant cultural developments occurred at his court. He established the Castilian version of Spanish as the language of prose, and he was the author of several books, including a history of Spain. This miniature is from Alfonso's *Cantigas de Santa María,* a collection of songs in praise of the Virgin Mary.

written about 883. It was the first of a series of official court histories that continued for the rest of the Middle Ages.

Medieval Spain, especially the city of Toledo, became the major center of translation of ancient Greek and medieval Arabic works on science and philosophy. Translated into Latin, these works had an enormous impact on European learning, beginning in the 1100s. Muslim Spain was the cultural bridge between the Arabic and Latin worlds and produced two of the leading philosophers of the Middle Ages—IBN RUSHD (also called Averroës) and Moses MAIMONIDES.

As elsewhere in Europe, Latin as a literary language was replaced by the vernacular from the 13th century on. Nevertheless, Latin remained the preferred language of scholars and the church. Leading Spanish literary figures of this later period who wrote in Latin included Raymond Sabunde of BARCELONA, a priest at the University of TOULOUSE. He was the author of *Theologia naturalis,* a work that inspired the 16th-century French writer Montaigne.

Spanish Literature from 900 to 1300.   Spanish vernacular literature appeared around 900 in Islamic Spain. The mixed population of Christians, Muslims, and Jews was largely bilingual, speaking Old Spanish and probably one other language, such as Arabic or Hebrew.

According to Arabic historians writing in the 1100s, a type of poem called a *muwashshah* was invented about 900 by Muhammad of Cabra, who built his poems around popular verses and songs in the language of the people. The first surviving *muwashshah* that contains some Spanish vernacular is a Hebrew poem by Yosef al-Katib, written not later than 1042. Some surviving *muwashshahs* have only a few Spanish phrases. Others, in Arabic and Hebrew, have more than 60 songs or verses in Spanish. Scholars now think that the *muwashshahs* and other early Spanish poems are related to a

type of poem called "the women's love song" that is at least as old as the Roman Empire and perhaps older. Similar poems occur in French, Portuguese, and Slavic literature.

Spanish writers produced several epic poems about the deeds of heroes, national pride, and ancient or historic events. The earliest Spanish epic poem was probably *Siete infantes de Lara,* which may have been written before 1000. It was the story of a family feud that resulted in murder and revenge. Although all but a few verses have been lost, it is clear from these fragments and from later chronicles* that *Siete infantes de Lara* was one of the masterpieces of medieval Spanish literature. This lost work influenced later Spanish writers of epic poems, ballads, and plays.

The "counts cycle" was a series of epic poems that dealt with real and imagined events during the time of the first counts of Castile. Although some of these poems have been lost, their stories were summarized in other texts. One interesting aspect of these poems is that women were featured in prominent roles and dominated much of the action. Although the poems originated in Christian northern Spain, Muslims are not cast as villains. Muslims are portrayed as enemies in battle, but the real villains of these epics are other Christians, often members of the hero's own family. Muslims often appear as generous and honorable characters.

The longest and best of the surviving Spanish epic poems is the *Poema de mío Cid,* written by an unknown author about 1207. It tells the story of the real-life warrior Rodrigo Díaz de Vivar (ca. 1043–1099), who was called the Cid (Arabic for lord). The style and tone of the poem are unusually dignified and restrained. For example, the number of warriors in the battle scenes is realistically small, not improbably large as in many other epic poems, and the heroic deeds described are not so exaggerated as to be incredible.

A new form of Spanish poetry called *clerecía* emerged in the early 1200s. The *clerecía* poems were associated with monasteries and universities in the Christian north. (The first Spanish university was founded at Palencia in the 1220s.) The earliest and longest of these poems was the *Libro de Alexandre.* The poem, which is about Alexander the Great, was intended to be a lesson for rulers. Its concerns a hero of dazzling talent and achievement who conquers the world but, through a flaw in his character, brings about his own downfall. Part romance and part epic, the poem is one of the best of the many medieval works about Alexander the Great.

Although the most important prose continued to be written in Latin, vernacular prose works appeared in the late 1100s. King Ferdinand III of Castile (who reigned from 1217 to 1252) helped to establish vernacular Spanish as a language of scholarship by having the law codes translated into Spanish. His successor, ALFONSO X EL SABIO, established the Castilian version of Spanish as a language for learned prose by forming an international body of scholars, translators, and artists to write essays in Spanish on law, history, science, and religion. One of Alfonso's most ambitious works was an encyclopedia of law, which had a significant effect on later Spanish history.

Spanish Literature from 1300 to 1500. The two major figures of Spanish literature in the early 1300s were Don Juan Manuel in prose and Juan

* **chronicles** record of events in the order in which they occurred

Happy Ending

The *Poema de mío* Cid, unlike most other medieval epics, has a happy ending. The hero of the poem is the Cid, who has been exiled by his enemies in the royal court. The king restores him to favor and suggests that the Cid give his daughters in marriage to nobles called the Infantes de Carrión. The marriages end disastrously when the nobles beat and abandon their young wives in a forest. With the king's help, the daughters are saved, their honor is restored, and they are happily remarried to royal husbands.

RUIZ in poetry. Manuel, a nephew of Alfonso X el Sabio, wrote two major works: *Libro del conde Lucanor et de Patronio* (completed in 1335) and *Libro de los estados* (written about 1327–1332). They deal with the need to save one's soul by living a good life. The poet Juan Ruiz collected the lyric poems he wrote over many years in a single book, *Libro de buen amor,* which appeared in 1330. Ruiz's poems display a remarkable variety of styles, moods, and subjects. They also reflect influences of western European, Arabic, and Hebrew cultures. Ruiz's poems helped establish Spain's tradition of lyric poetry*.

* **lyric poetry** poetry that has the form and general effect of a song

One of the great philosophical poems of the late 1300s was the *Proverbios morales* of Rabbi Shem Tov ben Yitzhak Ardutiel. Shem Tov was the only medieval writer who produced major literary works in both Castilian and Hebrew. The *Proverbios morales* is a long, melancholy, carefully organized poem about wisdom, with occasional touches of personal feeling.

During the reign of John II of Castile in the early 15th century, poems were collected in *cancioneros* (songbooks). One of the best poets of this period was Íñigo López de Mendoza (1398–1458), who wrote many different kinds of poems as well as a history of European poetry. Another exceptional poet was Juan de Mena (1411–1456), whose political allegory*, *Laberinto de Fortuna* (written in 1444), is considered a literary masterpiece.

* **allegory** literary device in which characters represent an idea or a religious or moral principle

The 1400s also brought a great outpouring of prose literature, including SERMONS, satire, chronicles, biographies, and travel accounts. *Memorias,* an autobiography that Leonor López de Córdoba (1362/1363–ca. 1412) dictated at the end of her life, is the first surviving book in Spanish literature by a woman author. At the end of the century, many works were written to celebrate the deeds of Ferdinand of Aragon and Isabella of Castile, whose marriage paved the way for a single Spanish monarchy.

Thousands of poems were written in the late 1400s. One of them, considered the greatest elegy* in the Spanish language, was *Coplas que fizo por la muerte de su padre,* written in 1479 by Jorge Manrique. Florencia Pinar, who wrote love poems, is the only Spanish woman poet whose work survives as more than a few fragmentary lines.

* **elegy** song or poem that expresses sorrow for one who has died

At the end of the Middle Ages, religious and secular* plays were written and performed at the University of Salamanca and the Toledo Cathedral. These works were the beginning of a tradition of lively Spanish drama that has continued ever since. (*See also* **Arabic Language and Literature; Arthurian Literature; Courtly Love; Hebrew Literature; Historical Writing; Spain, Muslim Kingdoms of; Spanish Art and Architecture; Troubadour, Trouvère; Universities.**)

* **secular** nonreligious; connected with everyday life

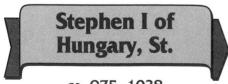

Stephen I of Hungary, St.

ca. 975–1038
King of Hungary

* **pagan** word used by Christians to mean non-Christian and believing in several gods

Stephen I was the founder of the medieval kingdom of Hungary and was its first Christian king. His reign was notable for the development of Christian institutions and for the organization of the Hungarian state.

Stephen was the son of Grand Prince Géza, a noble who had introduced Christianity into Hungary. After Stephen succeeded his father in 997, he spent several years fighting pagan* nobles who claimed the throne. He then sought the pope's permission to be crowned a Christian king. With his coronation, Stephen became the first Christian king in eastern Europe. Strong cultural contacts with the Latin West that followed determined the country's direction for the next thousand years.

Strengthened by the international acceptance of his royal authority and victories over rivals, Stephen turned his attention to organizing his kingdom and the church. He confiscated tribal lands for the crown and established a system of royal counties. He created a ruling class of nobles and knights, and he set up an administration similar to that of other royal courts. To organize the church, Stephen created bishoprics* and monasteries. In his later years, he reopened the old pilgrimage route from western Europe to Jerusalem and established hostels* and way stations along the route.

The last years of Stephen's life were overshadowed by warfare with neighboring states and the issue of succession*. When his son, Prince Imre, was killed in a hunting accident, Stephen named a nephew as his successor. This caused years of internal strife. Plagued by illness and grief over Imre's death, Stephen died in 1038. (*See also* **Hungary.**)

* **bishopric** office of or area governed by a bishop

* **hostel** lodging place or inn

* **succession** the transmission of authority on the death of one ruler to the next

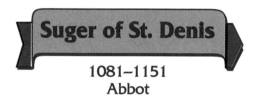

Suger of St. Denis

1081–1151
Abbot

* **patron** person of wealth and influence who supports an artist, writer, or scholar

S uger was a man of many talents. As the abbot of St. Denis, the royal abbey north of PARIS, he undertook various administrative reforms and worked hard to expand the abbey's properties and influence. As a historian, he wrote important chronicles that celebrated the deeds of France's kings. However, his most enduring legacy was as a patron* of architecture. His additions to the abbey church of St. Denis, designed by daring and creative architects, influenced a new GOTHIC ARCHITECTURE that spread from Paris throughout western Europe.

Born into the lesser nobility, Suger entered the monastery of St. Denis at about age ten. While studying there, he formed a lasting friendship with a fellow student, the young prince Louis, who became King LOUIS VI OF FRANCE. As a result of this friendship, Suger later became deeply involved in French politics as well as religion.

Suger became abbot of St. Denis in 1122. Under his direction, the abbey prospered as never before. He increased revenues, improved administration, pursued forgotten claims to lands and rights, and initiated reforms that returned the monks to a strict observance of monastic rule.

In addition to Suger's responsibilities as abbot, he was very involved in politics and the royal court. He accompanied Louis VI on several military expeditions. He was an important and trusted royal adviser who was sent on diplomatic missions to the PAPACY. From 1147 to 1149, when Louis was on the Second Crusade*, Suger served as regent* and governed France in the king's absence. (*See also* **Crusades.**)

* **crusade** holy war declared by the pope against non-Christians. Most were against Muslims, but crusades were also declared against heretics and pagans.

* **regent** person appointed to govern a kingdom when the rightful ruler is too young, absent, or disabled

Sultan

* **caliph** religious and political head of an Islamic state

S ultan was a title for one who held political authority. In Arabic, the word *sultan* originally referred to the concept of political power, might, or authority. However, by the tenth century the word was applied to individuals. In 1051, the Seljuk leader Toghril-Beg was given the title by the caliph* al-Muqtadi as a sign of his position of political power in the Islamic world. Later, the title was used by the AYYUBIDS, MAMLUKS, OTTOMANS, and others. The word was distinctly Islamic, and the title of sultan was used only in Muslim regions. (*See also* **Caliphate.**)

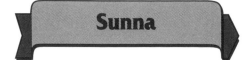

Sunna

* **caliph** religious and political head of an Islamic state

* **Sunnites** Muslim majority who believed that the caliphs should rule the Islamic community

* **predestination** doctrine that God alone determines whether a Muslim goes to paradise or hell

Sunna is an Arab concept that developed during the early history of Islam. It came to mean, in a legal sense, a recommended behavior, especially of the prophet MUHAMMAD.

In pre-Islamic times, the Arabic term *sunna* generally meant way, or manner of acting. With the growth of Islam, various pre-Islamic customs, modeled on the practices of the prophet Muhammad, were incorporated into the new faith. Muslims gradually adopted these as a standard code of behavior and faith.

During the time of the first four caliphs*, the concept of Sunna was applied to their rules and customs, and, in this way, a model was created that later Muslims followed. Since politics and religion were closely linked in the early Islamic period, Sunna emerged as both a religious and a political concept.

As Sunna developed as a political concept, it also evolved with a combined religious and legal meaning. The Sunna of Muhammad eventually became more important than the Sunna of his associates. The great jurist Muhammad ibn Idris al-Shafi'i (who died in 820) established Sunna as a major source of Islamic law, second only to the Qur'an. After al-Shafi'i, the term *sunna* was applied almost exclusively to the deeds and sayings of Muhammad.

Muhammad's Sunna was transmitted through hadith, his recorded sayings and deeds. The Sunna of Muhammad was considered sacred and became identified with orthodox Muslims, the Sunnites*. They believed unconditionally in a number of religious doctrines, including predestination*, and, eventually, the idea that Sunna and Islam are essentially identical. The latter concept implied that any deviations, or changes, from Sunna signify a departure from the truth. Extremely rigid in their observance in the beginning, the Sunnites gradually gained some flexibility. (*See also* **Abu Bakr; Caliphate; Imam; Islam, Conquests of; Islam, Political Organization of; Islam, Religion of; Qur'an.**)

Sunnites

See *Caliphate; Sunna.*

Sutton Hoo

Sutton Hoo is a burial mound near the English town of Woodbridge, about 70 miles northeast of London. In 1939, an 89-foot-long ship that had been ceremonially buried at Sutton Hoo in the 600s was discovered and excavated. Although the ship had almost completely disappeared, the objects that were buried with it made Sutton Hoo the most important European collection of early medieval treasures.

Artifacts found at the site include a helmet ornamented with Swedish designs, a round wooden shield, a 34-inch iron sword, a set of ten silver bowls, a pair of silver spoons, a bronze hanging bowl, a large silver dish with Byzantine markings, a maple-wood lyre, and a pair of drinking horns. The most beautiful objects uncovered at Sutton Hoo were shoulder clasps, a large gold buckle, and a gold-framed purse lid.

Many beautiful artifacts were unearthed at the Sutton Hoo burial site, including this bronze plaque with enamel decorations. Although the wooden ship itself had almost completely disappeared, its size and construction could be seen by the impressions it had left. The objects found here make up the most significant European collection of early medieval treasures.

The purse, probably made of leather or some textile that has long since rotted, contained 37 gold coins. The only coin that could be dated came from the era of Theodebert II, king of the FRANKS, who reigned in the early 600s.

The absence of a body in the grave suggested that the owner of the buried treasures had been a Christian whose corpse had been buried elsewhere, but who had been given a pagan* burial rite by non-Christian followers. However, a recent chemical analysis of the soil in the mound indicates that the mound once held a corpse, but that it has completely decayed. Scientists think that the body in the Sutton Hoo grave may have been that of Raedwald, an East Anglian king who converted to Christianity but returned to his pagan faith before his death in about 625. (*See also* **Anglo-Saxons; Migrations, Germanic.**)

* **pagan** word used by Christians to mean non-Christian and believing in several gods

Sweden

See *Scandinavia.*

See map in Carolingians (vol. 1).

* **dynasty** succession of rulers from the same family or group

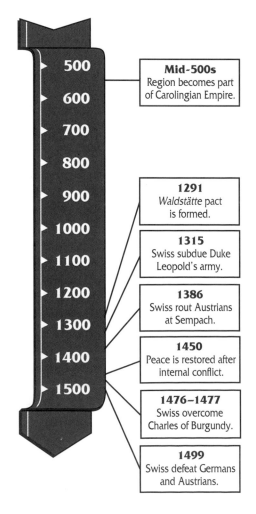

Mid-500s
Region becomes part of Carolingian Empire.

1291
Waldstätte pact is formed.

1315
Swiss subdue Duke Leopold's army.

1386
Swiss rout Austrians at Sempach.

1450
Peace is restored after internal conflict.

1476–1477
Swiss overcome Charles of Burgundy.

1499
Swiss defeat Germans and Austrians.

T he modern nation of Switzerland evolved in the late Middle Ages in a rugged, forested region between Lake Zurich and Lake Lucerne in the Alps Mountains of south-central Europe. The Swiss Confederation was a partnership between mountain people who wanted to protect their independence and growing cities that wanted to remain free of outside control.

Toward the Swiss Confederation. Switzerland has always been at the crossroads of Europe. Sandwiched between France, Germany, and Italy, it is a place where cultures and languages have met and mingled. In the 400s, it was colonized by the Burgundians, ancestors of the French-related western Swiss, and the ALAMANNI, ancestors of the German-related eastern Swiss. By the mid-500s, the FRANKS had defeated the Burgundians and the Alamanni, bringing the various territories of the future Switzerland under the rule of the Frankish CAROLINGIAN Empire. For several centuries, the territories of the future Switzerland were incorporated into the HOLY RO- MAN EMPIRE.

In the late 1100s, the Zähringens, a southern German dynasty*, strengthened their hold over Zurich and the French-speaking regions of Switzerland. In 1197, the archbishop of Cologne offered the German imperial crown to Duke Berchtold V of Zähringen, but the duke refused it. Berchtold died in 1218 without leaving an heir, resulting in an abrupt end to the Zähringen dynasty. By the end of the 1200s, much Swiss territory was controlled by the Austrian HABSBURG DYNASTY, but resistance to Habsburg rule was rising in Switzerland.

The core of the Swiss Confederation that emerged in the late Middle Ages was an isolated, mountainous area called the *Waldstätte* (forest districts). In 1291, as various members of the Habsburg family squabbled over territorial claims, the people of the *Waldstätte* felt war coming. They barricaded their valleys with rock walls and wooden fences, and representatives of three of the forest communities—Uri, Schwyz, and Niwalden— signed a pact to defend each other. This agreement formed the basis for the creation of the Swiss Confederation.

In the early 1300s, the people of Uri and Schwyz proclaimed their independence by invading the local abbeys, which were under Habsburg protection. Duke Leopold of Habsburg led his large army to punish them in 1315. Lying in ambush at the Morgarten Pass, the mountaineers massacred the Austrian knights, who had no time to assemble in battle formation. The duke escaped, but the independence of the *Waldstätte* had been preserved.

Growth of Cities and the Confederation. Although Swiss cities were relatively small (only the cathedral cities of Basel and Geneva had more than 5,000 people), the alliances they formed with the *Waldstätte* played an important part in the creation of the Swiss Confederation. Lucerne joined the alliance in 1332, followed by Zurich (1351) and Bern (1353). The cities provided fresh, dynamic leadership and strengthened the Confederation in its dealings with outsiders, especially the Habsburgs, who still controlled more Swiss territory than the Confederation did. Leadership was provided in turn by Zurich, Lucerne, Schwyz, and Bern. After the mid-1300s, the urban element outweighed the rural element in the Confederation.

Unlike a single, formally organized nation-state, the Confederation was a flexible network of alliances between fairly independent members (the cities and the rural cantons, or districts). Members consulted each other as needs arose. They found ways to avoid confrontations. They sometimes made common resolutions, such as the *Pfaffenbrief* (priest's charter) of 1370, by which legal and criminal cases would be tried in Confederation courts and not in the church's court system.

In the mid-1380s, Zurich and Lucerne seized Austrian strongholds in their areas and welcomed Austrian subjects as burghers (citizens). A Habsburg duke sent troops to attack the rebellious cities. At the Battle of Sempach in 1386, the Swiss defeated and killed the duke. Shortly afterward, the people of Glarus rose up against Habsburg rule, and, with the help of reinforcements from Schwyz, they defeated the Austrians sent to crush their resistance. Glarus became part of the eighth canton of the Confederation.

In the 1400s, the Confederation made further gains against Habsburg control. Bern led the Confederation in the conquest of Austrian Aargau. Part of Aargau was given to Bern. The rest became *Gemeinen Herrschaften* (common domain), territories administered by all of the members of the Confederation.

In the 1440s, a serious rupture occurred in the Confederation, when Zurich and the other Confederates went to war with each other. What began as a territorial dispute between Zurich and Schwyz widened when the Habsburgs entered the conflict on Zurich's side. The other Confederates eventually besieged Zurich until the city received help from French mercenaries* sent by the Habsburgs. Peace was restored in 1450. In the decades that followed, the Swiss gradually gained more territory from the Austrians.

Treaty of Basel.   For centuries, Switzerland had been busy with its own internal politics. Then, in the mid-1470s, at the end of the Middle Ages, the Swiss Confederation dramatically entered the European political scene by attacking Charles the Bold, the duke of Burgundy and the most powerful prince in Europe.

The Swiss attacked Charles because he was trying to extend Burgundy's influence into territories on the border between Switzerland and France. His ambitions were a threat to the independence of French-speaking Switzerland. Duke Charles sent a large army against the Swiss Confederates, but they dealt him crushing defeats in 1476 and 1477. These victories established the military reputation of the Confederate army. Other European states were eager to hire Swiss soldiers as mercenaries.

Switzerland's new military power worried neighboring states and created new tensions with the German Empire, which was still determined to assert its claim to Switzerland. In 1495, the Habsburg emperor MAXIMILIAN I levied taxes on the Confederation, and the imperial court handed down a series of unfavorable decisions against the Swiss towns of St. Gall, Appenzell, and Schaffhausen.

In 1499, a bloody war erupted. On one side were the Germans and the Austrians. On the other were the Swiss Confederation and Grisons, a small republic in the south that later joined the Confederation. Once more, the Swiss demonstrated their military superiority, forcing the emperor to sign a peace treaty in Basel on September 22, 1499. While the Treaty of Basel did not formally state that Switzerland was an independent

William Tell was a Swiss hero and patriot who lived in the 1300s. According to legend, when he refused to pay homage to the hat of a Swiss official, he was arrested. Tell, an expert marksman, was promised his freedom if he successfully shot an apple from his son's head. The event symbolized the struggle of the Swiss people for independence from their Habsburg rulers.

* **mercenary** soldier who fights for payment rather than out of loyalty to a lord or nation

state, it did recognize that Switzerland had separated itself from the German Empire.

The Swiss Confederation continued to expand after the end of the Middle Ages. Basel joined the Confederation in 1501. Geneva, Lausanne, and the western French-speaking territories joined much later, as did several small republics in the south. (*See also* **France; Germany; Migrations, Germanic.**)

Syria

* **dynasty** succession of rulers from the same family or group

* **booty** prizes of war

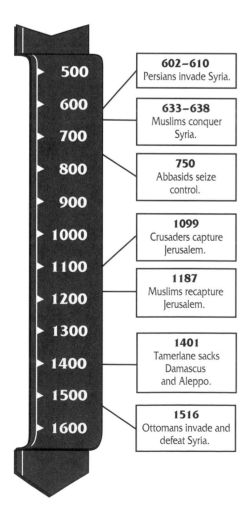

500	**602–610** Persians invade Syria.
600	**633–638** Muslims conquer Syria.
700	**750** Abbasids seize control.
800	
900	
1000	**1099** Crusaders capture Jerusalem.
1100	**1187** Muslims recapture Jerusalem.
1200	
1300	**1401** Tamerlane sacks Damascus and Aleppo.
1400	
1500	**1516** Ottomans invade and defeat Syria.
1600	

Located at the eastern end of the Mediterranean Sea, medieval Syria included the lands that make up present-day Syria, Lebanon, Israel, and Jordan as well as parts of Turkey, Iraq, and Saudi Arabia. In the Middle Ages, the country was the crown jewel of the early Arab Empire and a battleground between Christians and Muslims.

In ancient times, Syria was one of the most important territories of the Roman Empire. Its numerous cities flourished, and an extensive trade in wine, olive oil, silk, glass, and Indian spices brought the region great wealth. Syria was also the birthplace of CHRISTIANITY, and Syrians were among the first converts to the religion. In the early Middle Ages, a large majority of the population were Christian.

When the Roman Empire was divided into eastern and western sections in the 300s, Syria came under Byzantine rule. In the 400s and the 500s, the Christian population of Syria became divided over matters of faith. Some Syrian Christians followed traditional church teachings, while others did not. Religious disunity was followed by political instability. In the early 600s, Syria was invaded by the Persians, but they were pushed back by Byzantine armies. A greater threat soon followed, however. Between 633 and 638, Muslim armies from Arabia invaded Syria and conquered it. The Muslim governor, MU'AWIYA, divided Syria into several military districts, and both Muslim Arab immigrants and Christian Arab Syrians received land in return for constant military preparedness against the Byzantines. Christian Arabs quickly converted to Islam and merged with immigrants to form an Arab ruling class.

Under the first Islamic dynasty* of the UMAYYADS, Syria became the center of a vast Islamic Empire that stretched from Spain in the west to India in the east. The Syrian city of DAMASCUS was the capital of the Umayyad Empire, and taxes and booty* provided the caliphs who lived there with a magnificent royal court. The Umayyad caliphs improved Syrian agriculture and built irrigation works for fields, orchards, and farms. The Umayyad caliph Abd al-Malik built the Dome of the Rock in JERUSALEM, one of the main places of Muslim worship.

Umayyad rule came to an end in 750, when the ABBASIDS seized power. The Abbasid caliphs moved the center of rule to BAGHDAD in Iraq, and Syria was left at the periphery of a new empire centered farther east. Syrians were dropped from the military and ruling classes and replaced with Turkish soldiers and governors. Although they were no longer a part of the ruling elite in Syria, the local populations in cities such as Damascus and Aleppo maintained a degree of self-rule.

In the mid-900s, parts of Syria were taken over by the FATIMIDS. The Fatimid dynasty, which was centered in Egypt, established a separate

During the First Crusade in the late 1090s, Christian armies from Europe invaded Syria. This European illumination shows the siege of the city of Antioch, which yielded to crusaders in 1098. In 1099, the crusaders captured Jerusalem and established crusader states along the Syrian coast.

See map in Islam, Conquests of (vol. 3).

* **Shi'ites** Muslims who believed that Muhammad chose Ali and his descendants as the rulers and spiritual leaders of the Islamic community

* **Sunnites** Muslim majority who believed that the caliphs should rule the Islamic community

* **crusader** person who participated in the holy wars against the Muslims during the Middle Ages

Christian Church in the Middle East

Syria was home to the first Christians and saw the rise of the earliest Christian churches. There were several Christian groups active in the Middle East in the early medieval period: the Nestorians, the Monophysites, the Melchites, and the Maronites. Each had their own doctrines and followed their own traditions. However, they were united in their use of Syriac (the language of the non-Greek-speaking Christians of the Middle East) in the church liturgy. Syriac is still used today in the Christian churches of Turkey, Syria, Iraq, and western Iran.

CALIPHATE opposed to the Abbasids on matters of faith. The Fatimids followed the Shi'ite* branch of Islam, while the Abbasids were Sunnites*. Under these new rulers, urban Arabs in Syria still managed to preserve a degree of self-determination as they had under the Abbasids.

In the mid-1000s, the SELJUKS took control of Syria. This Turkish dynasty of SULTANS succeeded in reducing and eventually ending urban self-rule in Syria. Champions of the Sunnite faith, the Seljuks also drove many Shi'ites from the region. The Seljuks established a large region under control of the sultan that stretched from Iran and Iraq to Syria and Asia Minor. In 1092, this empire broke apart into smaller, independent realms—a situation that made Syria vulnerable to the next challenge it faced.

In the late 1090s, the European armies of the First Crusade invaded Syria. The crusaders* quickly seized Syrian lands, established Christian kingdoms along the Mediterranean coast, and pushed many Muslims to the interior regions of Syria. The final blow was the loss of Jerusalem to the crusaders in 1099. The European hold on Syria did not go unchallenged, however. By 1187, Muslim armies under SALADIN had gathered enough strength to force the invaders from Jerusalem. But Saladin and his successors were unable to force the Christians from other strongholds along the Mediterranean coast.

Syria was overrun by the Mongols in the mid-1200s, and much of Damascus was destroyed. Soon afterward, in 1260, the Mongols were defeated by the MAMLUK DYNASTY of Egypt. The Mamluks took control of Syria and conquered the remaining crusader kingdoms. Their Turkish troops and settlers destroyed many crusader castles, ports, and villages. This destruction had a profound effect on Syria. Agriculture declined, many villages disappeared, and the population shrank. During the 1300s and the 1400s, Syria experienced a period of economic stagnation and political unrest, and its fate once again was decided by foreign rulers. In 1401, the cities of Aleppo and Damascus were sacked by TAMERLANE, but the Mamluks remained in control of Syria.

In 1516, Syria was invaded by the OTTOMANS, and the Mamluk dynasty ended. Syria remained a part of the Ottoman Empire until 1918. For most of the four centuries of Ottoman rule, Syria's economy remained weak and its politics fragmented. (*See also* **Ayyubids; Bohemond I, Prince of Antioch; Byzantine Empire; Castles and Fortifications; Tancred.**)

Tabari, al-

839–923
Muslim scholar

* **chronicle**   record of events in the order in which they occurred

Al-Tabari was considered one of the most learned and productive Islamic scholars of the 800s and the early 900s. Born in northern Iran, al-Tabari studied with various scholars at the leading centers of Islamic learning. He became the foremost authority on the QUR'AN in his time. He was also among the greatest Islamic historians as well as a leading scholar in hadith (traditions of Muhammad's life), Islamic law, and Arabic grammar. His productivity and writing set a standard for medieval Muslim scholarship that was never surpassed.

While al-Tabari wrote numerous works, his reputation is based largely on two works: his 30-volume commentary *(Tafsir)* on the Qur'an, and his "Chronicle of Prophets and Kings." The commentary on the Qur'an represented a major advance in Qur'anic interpretation because of the amount of detailed material presented and the organized way in which individual verses of the Qur'an were treated. The commentary also includes the views of many earlier scholars and lists a wide range of sources. Al-Tabari's chronicle* records events from the Creation to 915, dividing history into pre-Islamic and Islamic times. The material on the pre-Islamic era is loosely organized by dynasties. Beginning with the year 622, the start of the Muslim calendar, events are organized by the year in which they occurred. No other work matched the authoritative scope of this chronicle. It became the most important source for the study of early Islamic history. (*See also* **Arabic Language and Literature; Encyclopedias and Dictionaries; Historical Writing; Islam, Religion of.**)

Talmud

See *Judaism.*

Tamar, Queen of Georgia

Ruled from 1184 to 1212
Medieval ruler of Georgia

Tamar was a medieval queen of Georgia, a country in the Caucasus region between the Black and Caspian Seas. Under Tamar's rule, Georgia reached the height of its power and prestige in the Middle Ages. Independent of the BYZANTINE EMPIRE, the kingdom dominated the Caucasus region.

The daughter of King Giorgi III, Tamar ruled with her father from 1156 until his death in 1184. Opposing families in the royal council then tried to prevent Tamar from exercising full authority. She was forced to appoint a chief adviser acceptable to them and to marry a Russian prince. After the death of her adviser, Tamar began to assert her own authority. She quickly divorced her husband and married someone of her own choice (a prince from another region in the Caucasus). Together, they put down a rebellion of Georgian nobles in 1191.

With the help of other allies, Tamar expanded her kingdom through military might and diplomacy. She also helped her relatives, the KOMNENOS FAMILY, establish the empire of Trebizond along the southern coast of the Black Sea. By the early 1200s, Tamar ruled an empire that extended into neighboring Azerbaijan and ARMENIA. Trade and commerce flourished, and the royal court grew wealthy. This golden age was accompanied by an abundance of literary and artistic creativity. Tamar's flourishing society was depicted in the great Georgian epic poem, *The Man in the Panther's Skin,* written by SHOTA RUSTAVELI. (*See also* **Georgia.**)

See map in Byzantine Empire (vol. 2).

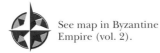

Tamerlane

1336–1405
Central Asian conqueror

See color plate 11, vol. 2.

Tamerlane was a Mongol ruler who tried to reconstruct the empire of Genghis Khan. Considered a great but cruel conqueror, he ended up ruling a vast empire covering central Asia and the Middle East. At his death in 1405, he was making plans to attack China. Tamerlane is shown here in a woodcut made long after his death.

Tamerlane, also called Timur Leng (Timur the Lame), was a military leader who conquered much of central Asia and the Middle East in the 1300s in an attempt to reconstruct the MONGOL EMPIRE of the previous century. A shrewd and able military leader, he led armies into western IRAN, the Caucasus region, ANATOLIA, IRAQ, SYRIA, and India. Known as a fierce and cruel conqueror, Tamerlane and his army fought, massacred, and pillaged with great savagery.

Tamerlane's father was an important commander, and Tamerlane adopted the military techniques developed by GENGHIS KHAN. A cunning

opportunist and political manipulator, Tamerlane maneuvered among various Mongol factions struggling for power in west central Asia, and he became a chieftain in 1361. He quickly gathered power, and by 1370 he had become master of Transoxiana, a region in western Asia. Over the next decade, he extended his control to neighboring regions and began campaigns against western Iran, the Caucasus region, and eastern Anatolia. In the 1380s and the 1390s, Tamerlane's conquests were interrupted several times by military campaigns against the GOLDEN HORDE in Russia, all of which were successful.

In 1398 and 1399, he turned his attention to India, where he campaigned with even greater brutality than usual. He then went to Syria and conquered DAMASCUS, seizing it from the MAMLUK DYNASTY in 1400–1401. His presence in Syria provoked the anger of the Ottoman sultan*, BAYAZID I, whom Tamerlane met in battle and defeated in central Anatolia in 1402. He went on to plunder territories as far as the city of Izmir on the Mediterranean coast of western Anatolia. Three years later, while planning a massive attack on China, Tamerlane died.

Tamerlane's empire was made and governed on horseback. Little was done to establish a government in the conquered areas, although he did establish a capital at SAMARKAND. Conquered regions were simply plundered and left, often to be conquered again at a later time. Because the empire was largely thrown together to satisfy the desire for booty*, it fell apart soon after his death. His vision of restoring the grandeur of the Mongol Empire thus was never achieved.

* **sultan** political and military ruler of a Muslim dynasty or state

* **booty** prizes of war

Tancred

1075–1112
Crusader

 See map in Crusades (vol. 2).

Tancred was a nobleman who played an important role in the success of the First Crusade (1095–1099). The grandson of Robert Guiscard, the Norman conqueror of southern Italy, and nephew of BOHEMOND I, later prince of Antioch, Tancred was well prepared for military life. He became a crusader in 1096 and spent the rest of his life in the Middle East. There, he sought to conquer land from the Greeks, the Turks, the French, and even from his uncle Bohemond.

On the way to the Holy Land, Tancred's first encounter with the Turks and his refusal to take an oath of allegiance to the Byzantine emperor Alexios I Komnenos marked him as a daring fighter and an ambitious young man. While in Byzantine lands, Tancred seized Tarsus, a town in southern ANATOLIA. He was soon forced to abandon it, however, and he returned to the main army of crusaders. After arriving in the Holy Land, Tancred took part in the captures of Antioch and JERUSALEM and seized Bethlehem for himself. While in Jerusalem, he plundered the temple and gained great wealth.

Tancred continued his conquests and was made prince of Galilee. In 1101, he became regent* of Antioch while its prince, his uncle Bohemond, was held captive by the Muslims. During his regency, Tancred defeated the Greeks and the Turks for control of SYRIA. After spending years in the conquests of Syria and PALESTINE, Tancred died in December 1112. His accomplishment in helping expand Christian influence in the Middle East paved the way for the achievements of later crusaders. (*See also* **Crusades; Komnenos Family; Warfare.**)

* **regent** person appointed to govern a kingdom when the rightful ruler is too young, absent, or disabled

Tapestries

See
color plate 5,
vol. 2.

* **patron** person of wealth and influence who
supports an artist, writer, or scholar

Tapestries are decorative fabrics in which a design is woven into cloth, rather than being painted, dyed, embroidered, or otherwise applied to the surface. Often made of wool or silk, tapestries were used as wall hangings or coverings for floors and furniture. During the Middle Ages, they were widely produced by skilled artisans for noble and wealthy patrons*. The tapestries that have survived are considered masterpieces of medieval art and craftsmanship.

Medieval tapestries were practical and ornamental. They helped insulate drafty dwellings and were easily moved from castle to castle. More importantly, they transformed bare stone walls into elegant backdrops for castle life and church ceremonies and were highly prized as elements of a princely way of life. Majestic in scale and brilliantly colored, these woven "paintings" depicted saints' lives, exploits of ancient or contemporary heroes, and scenes of daily life. The transportability of tapestries made them an important means of transferring wealth, and their "stories" provided both entertainment and instruction for medieval audiences.

The creation of a tapestry involved several steps by highly skilled individuals. The imagery began with a compositional sketch, sometimes made by a professional painter or copied from a famous painting. Then, another artist enlarged this model to a full-scale pattern for the weavers to follow. The weavers used their skill to create this design in cloth. The craft of tapestry weaving was regulated by GUILDS, which controlled the colors and the quality of the materials used. English wool was highly prized for its strength and durability, while the use of high-quality dyes ensured that colors would remain strong and vibrant. The most highly skilled weavers were concentrated in certain cities, such as PARIS and BRUGES, where there were many wealthy patrons. By the end of the Middle Ages, Brussels had become the leading tapestry center because of its superior weavers and techniques. (*See also* **Furniture; Saints, Lives of; Textiles; Wool.**)

This 14th-century French tapestry is part of a series called *The Apocalypse of Angers* and depicts a time when Christians in Rome were severely persecuted. In this panel, titled "Worshipping the Image of the Beast," the seven-headed beast represents the seven emperors of Rome. The beast in the center symbolizes the pagan priests. Christ appears at the left with a group of Christian martyrs.

Taxation

Taxation is the process of transferring money or items of value from private individuals to the state or government. The revenues, or income, from taxes are then used for a variety of purposes, such as supporting a government, maintaining armies, and building roads and bridges. During the Middle Ages, taxation varied from region to region and from country to country, and people were subject to many different kinds of taxes.

Taxation in Western Europe

Medieval Europeans were heavily taxed, often in the form of money or crops. Taxes were often given directly to the local lord whose land they farmed and to the king for the support of the realm. Kings levied taxes on exports and imports, various goods (such as wine), the services of knights, and even marriages.

In addition to taxes paid directly to a lord or ruler, people paid indirect taxes, such as tolls for the use of roads, bridges, ports, and market space. Another type of indirect tax was the obligation to provide either special labor in times of need or service in the army during wartime. Villagers might be summoned to build roads or fortresses when the king wished to move or house his troops. Furthermore, townspeople might be asked to maintain roads and local militias.

Jews and Muslims were often taxed heavily in Christian kingdoms. These patterns were common throughout western Europe, but the cases of England and France illustrate some other important aspects of medieval taxation.

Taxation in England. During the period of Anglo-Saxon rule (in the early Middle Ages), taxes in the form of crop payments and military or civil service were common in England. These obligations were assessed on the basis of landholdings. A monetary tax was first devised in 991. Beginning in 1012, taxes known as gelds were collected annually to support the king's armies. The gelds and other revenues were collected by royal officials known as reeves. After 1016, earls* were responsible for tax collection and may have received a portion of the revenue in return. Tolls (fees for privileges, services, or usage) were another form of tax during this period. The most common tolls were those collected on goods sold in the markets and those for passage in and out of seaports or through towns.

When the NORMANS conquered England in 1066, they kept many of the existing taxes and introduced some new ones. These new taxes included scutage (the payment of money in place of military service), feudal aids (money paid to the king in times of special need, such as ransoms and royal marriages), and tallage (gifts or money from towns and boroughs within the king's realm). The Normans also introduced taxes on trade and on Jewish moneylenders.

Under the ANGEVINS, other taxes were imposed on the English people. These included a tax on movable wealth (valuable items that were moved) and a tax on the income of every person in the realm. These taxes originated as a way of financing the CRUSADES, the holy wars that the Christians waged against the Muslims. In the 1200s, import and export taxes were added to the list of taxes in England.

In addition to all these royal taxes, the people of England were taxed by the church, local lords, and boroughs*. Church taxes included the

See map in England (vol. 2).

* **earl** governor of a region in Anglo-Saxon times. The term was later used for a noble title.

* **borough** medieval town with special duties and privileges, such as sending representatives to parliament

Medieval Europeans were heavily taxed by both secular and church governments. The issue of fair taxation was a constant source of conflict. This detail of Masaccio's *Tribute Money* shows a tax payment changing hands. This painting is considered a commentary on a new taxation system begun in Florence, Italy, in the 1400s.

---

* **vassal** person given land by a lord or monarch in return for loyalty and services

* **benefice** church office to which property or income is attached

soul scot (a required offering to a priest at the graveside of a dead person) and the churchscot (a payment of grain or other product to a priest). Eventually, Christians were required to pay the church TITHES, a tenth of their agricultural income in the form of grain or livestock. Another church tax, called Peter's Pence, was collected for the PAPACY in ROME. Lords required both crops and service from those who farmed the manor. Boroughs also taxed their inhabitants in order to pay their lords and for other services.

Taxation in France. Like their English counterparts, French nobility taxed the peasants who worked the land for them and also extracted service in the form of labor. In addition, working-class people had to pay many types of fees for the use of forests, the maintenance of roads, and the operation of mills, ovens, and winepresses. Other payments were owed by vassals* to their lords at the time of the marriage of the lord's daughter or the knighting of his son.

Wars, especially the crusades, required significant payments to the French king. In fact, from 1294 to 1356 a special tax, the war subsidy, was imposed every year to pay the expenses of waging war. After 1356, this tax was replaced by a regular and permanent tax. Taxes known as *aides* were collected on salt, wine, and other commodities. These taxes remained a basic part of the French tax system for four centuries. They were the ancestor of the taille, a regular tax levied by the king on his subjects.

Additional Church Taxes. The church was a major tax collector in medieval Europe. The most common church tax was the tithe, even for kings and emperors, who paid tribute to the papacy in return for favor and protection. The church also received revenues from tolls, fines, fees, and rents. After the mid-1200s, the papacy established taxes on religious benefices*. These taxes became important sources of revenue for the late medieval popes.

Although the church as an institution was a major tax collector, the clergy itself had to pay taxes. Monks secured their monastery's independence from local bishops by paying annual dues to the pope. Bishops, archbishops, and other high clergy members made payments to the papacy when they were appointed to office. In the early 1200s, papal efforts to finance the crusades led to an income tax, in which nearly all clergymen were ordered to pay a part of their income. European monarchs sometimes taxed the clergy with permission from the papacy, usually to help finance crusades. By the early 1300s, monarchs insisted that they were entitled to tax their clergy whether or not they had papal permission. This resulted in serious disagreements between the church and the state. By the end of the Middle Ages, rulers not only taxed their clergy at will but also shared in the profits of papal taxation.

Resistance to Taxation. Taxation was a frequent source of conflict in medieval Europe. Kings resented the papal taxation of churches and lands within their kingdoms. They also resented their inability to tax clergy and churches within their own kingdoms without papal permission. The clergy resisted the heavy taxes required by the papacy, as well as the efforts of secular rulers to impose taxes on them. Other taxpayers resented the high taxes imposed on them by their kings and lords, and the poor felt especially burdened by taxes.

Frontier Economics

Frederick II, one of the most skilled monarchs of the Middle Ages, ruled Germany and parts of Italy. As emperor, he initiated financial reforms in the mid-1200s that elevated his realm to a position of great power in Europe. He eliminated all internal tolls throughout the empire and imposed a state tariff to be levied only at the frontiers. Each frontier in his empire had royal warehouses, to which importers and exporters brought their taxable goods. After the customs duties were paid, the merchandise could be shipped or resold. Through this practice, Frederick gained revenues for his empire and the opportunity to use these goods as leverage in time of war or for diplomatic purposes.

See map in Byzantine Empire (vol. 2).

* **imperial** pertaining to an empire or emperor

Revolts by taxpayers were not uncommon. In 1358, French peasants rose up against their landlords in the Jacquerie, a revolt aimed at the nobility but arising from the burden of taxation. Peasants attacked nobles and the clergy, and they burned houses and churches before being crushed by the army. In England, the Peasants' Revolt of 1381 erupted, partly over the issue of fair taxation. It was quickly suppressed.

Efforts to find new ways of raising money led to important developments in government. Although the earliest European PARLIAMENTS were assembled, in part, to collect taxes, the issue of fair taxation eventually led members to demand the right to consent to taxation.

Taxation in the Byzantine Empire

In the BYZANTINE EMPIRE, the village as a whole was responsible for the tax obligations of each of its inhabitants. If one villager died, for example, other villagers had to pay his share of taxes until the total tax obligation of the village was adjusted. Large landowners were considered separate taxable units.

A direct tax on the land was the main type of tax. Until the 1300s, the tax rates on land varied according to its productivity. Thereafter, the same tax rate was applied to land of all qualities. Each villager was required to pay a tax on the land he farmed. The land tax was paid only by the landowner. Several other taxes, however, were paid by the individuals who cultivated the land, whether they owned it or not. These included a hearth tax on each farmer's household, a tax on the number of oxen he owned, and a tax on the quantity of land he could cultivate efficiently. Special taxes were paid for the use of pasturelands.

Several other taxes were imposed periodically for special needs, such as building roads and bridges, cultivating state-owned lands, and supplying fortresses or feeding armies. In addition, people were obligated to provide lodging for state officials or military troops passing through their area. Certain groups—including large landowners, state officials, and religious institutions—often were granted exemptions from these types of taxes. Farmers who provided military service were exempt unless they failed to perform their military duties when required.

Taxes were collected by special imperial* officials who reported directly to the central financial administration in Constantinople, the capital city of the empire. Taxes for the maintenance of POSTAL SERVICES and roads were controlled by a separate high-ranking official of the emperor's court.

Byzantines also were subject to a number of indirect taxes, including customs duties, sales taxes, and various tolls for crossing bridges, using seaports, and weighing merchandise. Exemptions from such taxes were sometimes granted to certain individuals and institutions, especially monasteries. Foreign merchants from VENICE, GENOA, and other trading cities often obtained important exemptions as well.

Taxation in the Islamic World

In the medieval Islamic world, agriculture formed the basis of most wealth and prosperity. As a result, taxation was based primarily on land and crops. Medieval Muslims distinguished between two types of land: state land captured from non-Muslims and land owned by Muslims. Both

were taxed, but Muslim-owned land was subject to a lower rate of taxation than the other. During the reign of the UMAYYADS, attempts were made in parts of the empire to change the status of Muslim-owned land so that it could be taxed more heavily. This was true in EGYPT, where the change in land status was accompanied by the introduction of direct taxation on individuals.

Muslim rulers taxed land on the basis of its productivity, with irrigated land more heavily taxed than nonirrigated land. Different tax rates also applied to particular crops and to the productive capacity of various types of trees, bushes, and vines. Tax rates generally were reassessed periodically to account for changes in productivity.

Tax payments typically were made in either cash or crops. Under the Umayyads, the governors of provinces* were responsible for collecting tax revenues and ensuring that they were deposited in the royal treasury at DAMASCUS. This proved unsatisfactory, however, so the ABBASIDS appointed special tax collectors to gather a certain portion of provincial taxes. The remaining taxes were raised through a system known as "tax farms." Under this system, powerful individuals in BAGHDAD issued bonds* for the revenue owed by a province, village, or district. These persons were then held liable for the taxes, which they had to collect. (*See also* **Benefice; Cities and Towns; Feudalism; Peasants' Rebellions and Uprisings; Simony; Trade.**)

* **province** Roman term for an area controlled by the empire

* **bond** certificate of ownership of a specified portion of debt that is due to be paid at a certain time

Technology

Technology includes all the ways people manipulate their environment to provide the objects necessary for their life and comfort. The medieval world inherited much technology from the ancients. Medieval craftsmen also developed new technologies of their own. Agriculture, manufacturing, and commerce were all improved during the Middle Ages because of innovations in how various related skills were performed.

Byzantine Technology

Byzantine scholars put great emphasis on theology* and philosophy*. In general, they took little interest in the marketplace and in the mechanical and industrial arts. Byzantine scholars, however, preserved treatises* on mechanics by several early Greek writers. Later, this knowledge found its way to the Islamic world and then to Europe, where it influenced the development of gears, pulleys, and wind-driven machines.

Byzantium had at least two remarkable inventions—Greek fire and the marvelous automata (robotlike devices) of the imperial throne room in CONSTANTINOPLE. Greek fire was a crude oil substance that was sprayed through a bronze pump to set fire to enemy ships. The automata were mechanical models of singing birds, roaring lions, and moving beasts that astonished and delighted visitors to the palace.

The Byzantines were also innovators in the development of counterweights. They developed and manufactured the glass counterweight, which was used to weigh commercial goods. This invention was later adapted and refined by the Arabs.

* **theology** study of the nature of God and of religious truth

* **philosophy** study of ideas, including science

* **treatise** long, detailed essay

Agricultural Technology. The Byzantine Empire was largely rural and agricultural. Illustrated manuscripts depict carts and yokes, threshing tools, plows, and many other farm implements. The *Geoponica,* a Byzantine manual of farming techniques and procedures, appeared in the 900s. It contains a veterinary section that is especially attentive to the health of horses, which were vital to the cavalry units of the Byzantine army.

Alchemy. ALCHEMY was the medieval chemistry that tried to turn base metals into gold. In Byzantium, alchemy, industrial arts, and fine arts became linked, as artisans discovered how to make base metals look like gold or silver. Rings, belt buckles, and pins made of iron, bronze, or lead were coated with silver to create the illusion of the real thing. Tests to confirm the purity of silver and gold were improved, as well as techniques for the care of metals, such as the removal of oxides.

Islamic Technology

The Islamic world is a major link in the chain of the history of technology. Many factors contributed to the high level of technological achievement in Islamic civilization. The Islamic state united a vast number of peoples and cultures under a single government that encouraged the spread of ideas. Intellectual life was stimulated by the fact that Arabic was the universal language of science. Engineers enjoyed great status in society, and artisans were respected for their skill.

The leading industrial technology of the Islamic world was textile manufacturing. English words such as *damask* and *muslin* refer to types of cloth developed in the Islamic world. Other important Arab industries used the principle of distillation* in the manufacture of perfumes, rose water, fats, and oils. Hard soap was first made in the Islamic world, and the manufacture of inks, pigments, and paints reached a high degree of development. Papermaking was introduced to the Islamic world, and eventually to Europe, by Chinese prisoners who started a paper industry at SAMARKAND in the 700s. The earliest Islamic paper factories were established in Baghdad and Syria, and the Islamic world pioneered major innovations in paper technology.

Mechanical Genius. Islamic engineers rarely wrote about ordinary machines. Instead, they recorded only the cleverest and most remarkable inventions. Al-Jazari's *Kitab fi ma'rifat al-hiyal al-handasiya (Book of Knowledge of Ingenious Mechanical Devices),* written in the late 1100s, was the most important document about machines between ancient times and the Renaissance. It discusses water clocks, fountains, water-raising machines, and a piston pump driven by a power wheel.

Waterpower was one of the most important technologies in the Islamic world. Tidal mills were used in IRAQ before the 900s, and later huge mills were built to harness the power of rivers to grind grain. Waterpower was used to drive paper mills in Samarkand and to crush gold ores. Windmill power was also widely used, especially in Egypt in the crushing of sugarcane.

Civil Engineering. Islamic civil engineering endeavors included architectural construction, irrigation canals, dams, and surveying. Engineers and architects held high government offices and were in charge of vast

* **distillation** extracting a pure substance from a mixture

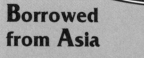

Borrowed from Asia

Many European products, processes, and tools originated in China or elsewhere in Asia and were carried to the West by traders and travelers. Rice, cotton, sugar, and silkworms were all introduced from Asia. The Chinese invented gunpowder and rockets, which were adopted by the Islamic world and then passed on to Europe. The blowgun, for example, originated in Malaysia and reached Europe by the late 1400s. Europeans used blowguns to kill small birds and later adapted the air-pressure principle of the blowgun for devices to load and unload large amounts of liquids and grains.

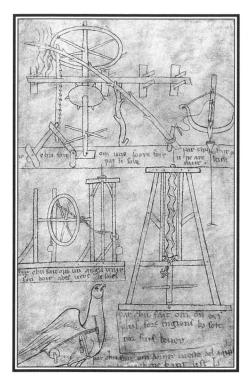

These drawings of various machines are from the sketchbook of Villard de Honnecourt (from the mid-1200s). Shown clockwise from the bottom left are a lectern eagle with a moving head; a device to make a statue turn toward the sun; a self-propelled saw; a crossbow; and an engine for raising weights.

* **vault** section of a three-dimensional arched ceiling of stone

* **flying buttress** stone structure connected to the outer wall of a building by an arch; used to support the vaults

* **relic** object cherished for its association with a martyr or saint

public works with many employees. For example, one superintendent of irrigation had more than 10,000 workers under him. Irrigation was especially important because much of Arabic North Africa and the Middle East was desert or semidesert.

Military Technology. During the 1100s and the 1200s, a number of Islamic authors wrote about military technology. Their works deal with horsemanship, archery, tactics, military organizations, weapons, and technology using iron and steel.

By the late 1200s, there were more than 70 recipes for gunpowder. Rockets and torpedoes carried fire and grenades. Cannon were also used in battle. An Arabic book from this period contains the first illustration of a portable cannon and the formula for its gunpowder.

Western European Technology

Starting around the year 800, western Europe placed an ever-increasing value on technological developments. European inventions in the Middle Ages include the horse collar, the heavy wheeled plow with moldboard, the three-field system of crop rotation, the horizontal-axle windmill, the Gothic vault* and flying buttress*, the mechanical clock, printing with movable type, and the suction pump. By the end of the Middle Ages, such cities as Milan and Augsburg were well on their way to becoming industrial centers, and Europeans possessed the technical skills and equipment to open global sea routes.

Technology and Christian Values. Christianity provided fertile soil for the vigorous growth of technology in western Europe. Like the Jews, Christians believe in a God who is the creator but who is separate from his creation. If, as Christians believe, God has created nature for the use of humans, then nature can be used for any number of purposes. This attitude fits well with the pursuit of technological experimentation.

Trial and Error. Medieval technology was based on the accumulation of skills gained by the practice of crafts. When people observed what worked and what did not work, and then experimented with new methods, inventions were born.

Early European technology advanced by trial and error, rather than by any formal study or application of a scientific method. For example, the invention of eyeglasses in the 13th century was not a product of scientific theories about light. It resulted from a need that arose to display religious relics* under transparent glass. Glass was refined as Italian glassmakers developed a clearer glass and improved ways to cut and polish it. Then, in 1285, some unknown individual balanced two pieces of glass across his or her nose in a wire frame, and a new product was created.

Spirit of Invention. As the Middle Ages progressed, Europeans became fascinated with the idea of inventions. For the first time, people systematically set about inventing solutions to specific problems. The evolution of the mechanical clock is one such example. The water clock, used since ancient times, was not considered satisfactory as a time measurer. Improvements in the design of the water clock, as well as alternative designs—such as the weight-driven clock—were sought throughout Europe, including Muslim Spain. By 1313, someone had invented the hourglass. The hourglass,

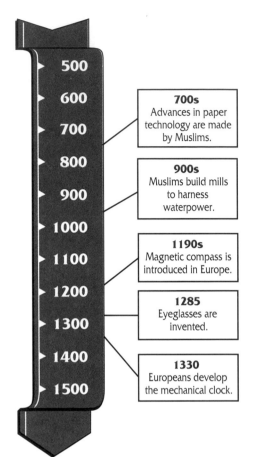

700s
Advances in paper technology are made by Muslims.

900s
Muslims build mills to harness waterpower.

1190s
Magnetic compass is introduced in Europe.

1285
Eyeglasses are invented.

1330
Europeans develop the mechanical clock.

See map in Trade (vol. 4).

however, was chiefly used on board ships, where neither water clocks nor weight-driven clocks would work because of the constant motion. Technicians experimented from the 1260s until close to 1330 before a true mechanical clock was invented. The intensity and extent of this quest for a more accurate clock are shown by the fact that, at about the same time, inventors reached two related solutions to the problem: the verge and the wheel escapement. By the early 14th century, Europe had arrived at a technological attitude toward problem solving that would remain part of its culture.

Exchanges of Ideas.   The best technological improvements by one culture were often adapted by another culture. European improvements in shipbuilding in the Middle Ages included the invention of the sternpost rudder, and the shift from the skin-first to the skeleton-first sequence in constructing the hull of a ship. Northern European shipbuilders borrowed ideas from shipbuilders in southern Europe, and vice versa. Both northern and southern Europeans borrowed the triangular-shaped sail used earlier in the Islamic world.

Another example of technological exchange was the introduction of the magnetic compass into Europe from China (by way of the Muslims) in the 1190s. The magnetic compass was a boon to navigation. The compass could identify the position of the North Star in any weather. Europeans used the compass effectively to extend the number of months a ship could successfully navigate the high seas.

Technological Advances.   Advances in technology in one field also gave rise to advances in other fields. The evolution of the crossbow is an example of how one invention sprang from another. The crossbow, a weapon of war, had been used by ancient Romans. However, the Roman model was ineffective in warfare, and it was used mostly for hunting birds. The crossbow's power depends chiefly on the ability of a trigger to keep tension in a bowstring. As early as the 700s, craftsmen in the West worked to develop a better trigger. The trigger went through five stages of development until it reached its final version in the late 1000s. The new crossbow was considered by the Byzantines and the Muslims to be a horrible device. It usually shot not arrows but square-headed bolts that made terrible wounds.

During the 12th and the 13th centuries, no major changes appeared in the crossbow. It continued to be made of wood or animal horn, or a combination of both. Then, in the early 14th century, craftsmen started to make the crossbow of steel. An extraordinary range of new implements began to appear to make the steel crossbow, including ratchets, cranked gears, screws, levers, and pulleys, in many variations and combinations. The metal parts of these appliances had to be composed of steel or very hard iron, since the pressure in drawing a steel bow would deform a softer metal. Makers of crossbows became experts in shaping metal into complex forms.

The new technology of the steel crossbow was soon used in clock making to produce the coiled steel springs in portable and miniature clocks. The most common form of spring used today in wagons, railway cars, automobiles, and the landing gear of airplanes likewise was a by-product of the technology of the medieval steel crossbow. (*See also* **Agriculture; Arabic Numerals; Bells; Books, Manuscript; Glass; Metals and Metalworking; Printing, Origins of; Roads and Bridges; Ships and Shipbuilding; Textiles; Warfare; Weights and Measures; Writing Materials and Techniques.**)

Teutonic Knights

See *Knights, Orders of.*

Textbooks

* **treatise** long, detailed essay

* **theology** study of the nature of God and of religious truth

* **scribe** person who hand-copies manuscripts to preserve them

Medieval textbooks were the treatises* that UNIVERSITIES used in lectures in the 1200s. Authoritative texts, such as the works of ARISTOTLE, and commentaries on their contents became the foundation of the university curriculum.

Each faculty—liberal arts, theology*, LAW, and MEDICINE—compiled its own list of standard works that lecturers taught and that students were responsible for mastering. As ancient Greek and Arab texts were increasingly translated into Latin, a growing number of treatises became available to Europe's universities for use as textbooks.

The need for standard textbooks led universities such as those in Paris, Oxford, and Bologna to regulate the production and sale of books. At each university, a stationer (combining the roles of publisher and librarian) prepared the official version text (called the exemplar) with the assistance of scribes*, binders, and illustrators. The stationer was the ultimate authority on what material the exemplar contained, and he was in charge of lending it to scholars.

The exemplar was usually divided into 4 to 6 folios, or sections, of 8 to 12 pages (or *peciae*) each. After university masters examined the *peciae* of an exemplar for accuracy, the exemplar's title was added to the official list of authorized university texts the stationer could lend to students. A scholar could rent a *pecia* and either read or copy it. After he returned the original to the stationer, he could rent another. In this way, university scholars read and made copies of important scholarly texts. (*See also* **Books, Manuscript; Law Schools; Medicine; Rhetoric; Writing Materials and Techniques.**)

Textiles

Textiles are woven fabrics of cotton, linen, wool, silk, or a combination of these fibers. During the Middle Ages, the manufacturing of textiles was an important industry in both Europe and the Islamic world.

In Europe, the manufacture of textiles became a major industry that employed many people. In fact, in terms of employment, output, and contributions to international trade, the textile industry became the most important manufacturing industry in Europe in the later Middle Ages. Textiles were valuable trade items, and major textile-producing nations such as Italy, France, Flanders, and England became rich from the export of cloth. Prosperous textile merchants became leaders within their communities.

Various types and qualities of woven fabrics were produced in medieval Europe—from coarse, inexpensive cloths to fine, expensive, luxurious materials. Silks and linens were highly prized. The most valued and expensive textiles were soft, heavy woolens made from the finest wool fibers.

This German woodcut from the late 1400s shows three stages of weaving wool. The weaver at the left is using a loom to weave the yarn into cloth. The man at the right is combing and carding the wool to untangle the fibers and to prepare them for spinning. The woman is spinning the wool fibers into long threads or yarns.

* **comb**   process in which wool is raked back and forth between two metal-toothed combs in order to form fibers

* **card**   process in which wool is passed between two wire brushes several times until the fibers are untangled and aligned

* **spindle**   thin rod used in hand spinning to twist fibers into yarn

* **bobbin**   cylinder or spool on which spun yarn is wound

* **skein**   loosely coiled bundle of yarn

Such woolen cloth was a luxury item valued for its warmth, weight, and durability.

The process of making woolen textiles involved a number of stages. The first steps included shearing, or cutting, the woolen fleece from sheep; washing the wool to remove dirt and grease; drying it in the sun; and then beating it with branches or stones to remove any remaining dirt and to separate the woolen fibers. The cleaned wool was then combed* or carded* to untangle the fibers and to prepare them for spinning. Combing created strong, durable yarns. Carding enabled weavers to blend a variety of wool fibers of different quality or color.

Once combed or carded, the wool fibers were ready for spinning into long threads or yarns. The spinning process involved three stages: pulling fibers from a mass of wool, twisting them together to form a continuous yarn, and winding the yarn onto a spindle* or bobbin*. In the early medieval period, the spinning was done by hand, usually by women. In the 1100s, the spinning wheel was introduced to Europe by way of the Islamic world. This ancient device, invented in Asia, enabled spinners to twist fibers into yarn faster than by hand. However, the yarn produced was often of an inferior quality. As a result, the use of spinning wheels was banned at various times and places to ensure proper quality. By the end of the Middle Ages, improvements in the spinning wheel led to its increased use, even in the production of luxury-grade fabrics. The final stages of spinning were reeling and winding. Reeling involved removing the spun yarn from the spindle, unwinding it by hand, and rewinding it into balls or skeins*. Winding transferred the reeled yarns onto bobbins in preparation for weaving.

The weaving of fibers into fabric was done on a loom. Medieval weavers used two basic types of looms. Before the 1000s, most fabrics were woven on a vertical loom. With this type of loom, the weaver first stretched a series of yarns between beams at the top and bottom of a vertical frame.

* **treadle** foot-operated lever that moves parts of a loom

* **nap** fuzzy surface of cloth

Scottish Tartans: Badge of Identification

Among the most famous examples of the weaver's skill are the Scottish tartans. These woolen cloths of checks and stripes were made into cloaks and kilts. The kilt is a knee-length skirt gathered in pleats around the waist and held in place by a belt. Scottish men wore the kilt as battle dress and for everyday use. Both men and women wore cloaks of tartan.

Tartans were created by village weavers who extracted dyes from local herbs and berries to produce earthy shades of purple, mossy green, and brown. They often repeated the sett, the small check pattern, and added thin bars of color that give the tartan its special look. No one knows for sure when and why tartans became badges of identification for Scottish clans. However, about 2,000 different designs are currently in use.

Another bundle of yarn was then passed back and forth through the vertical yarns, creating a woven cloth of vertical and horizontal threads. The introduction of the horizontal loom in the 11th century revolutionized the textile industry in Europe. This type of loom was a boxlike device with various beams, rollers, straps, and pulleys operated by a foot treadle*. The horizontal loom gave weavers greater control over the weaving process and enabled them to produce cloth more quickly. It also allowed weavers to create cloths of much longer lengths, unlike vertical looms on which cloth length was limited to the loom's height. The main problem with the original horizontal loom was that the width of the cloth was limited. This problem was later resolved by the development of the broadloom, a wider version of the horizontal loom.

Once woven, cloth went through various finishing processes to clean the fabric, remove knots and defects created during weaving, tighten the yarns, stretch the fabric, remove wrinkles and creases, and raise the nap* of the fibers. These processes helped make the fabric stronger and more durable, and they created a smooth, uniform appearance.

In the early Middle Ages, textile making was mostly a rural, family-based craft with little division of labor. Most of the work was done by women. However, as textile manufacturing developed into a large industry, the need for numerous skilled workers increased. As a result, textile workers became highly specialized, with woolsorters, combers, carders, spinners, reelers, weavers, dyers, and others involved in only specific parts of the textile-making process. Men also came to dominate the industry, although women still worked as wage earners in various parts of the process. During the later Middle Ages, some textile workers, including weavers and dyers, organized themselves into GUILDS to protect their interests and to ensure the quality of products. These guilds were dominated by men. In some parts of Europe, textile and other crafts guilds had a prominent role in local government and politics.

In the Islamic world, textiles were very important in both art and the economy. Textile manufacture and trade probably occupied a majority of the working population, and textile centers were located throughout the empire, from Spain in the west to Iran in the east.

A full array of types and qualities of fabrics was available to the inhabitants of the Islamic world. Fabrics were used for clothing, but they also constituted the bulk of household furnishings. In both rural and urban settings, Muslim furnishings consisted mainly of carpets, curtains, covers, and hangings. Instead of chairs, people sat on fabric-covered cushions laid on top of carpets. The quality and richness of textiles reflected their owner's wealth and position. Textiles also played an important political role as diplomatic gifts and rewards to high officials and other persons. The beautifully woven and embroidered carpets and other textiles produced in the Islamic world were much sought after by nobles and rich merchants of Europe.

Certain areas became famous for specific types of textiles and designs. BAGHDAD and Spain, for example, were noted for rich silks. Spanish silks often were woven with scenes of people or animals. In the 1200s, ANATOLIA emerged as a prominent weaving region, and it remained a carpet-producing center for centuries to come. (*See also* **Clothing; Silk; Tapestries; Trade; Wool.**)

Theodora I, Empress

ca. 500–548
Byzantine empress

* **patrician** person of high birth

Byzantine empress Theodora I, wife of Emperor Justinian I, played an active role in government and was influential in the way the empire was run. She was one of the most powerful women in Byzantine history. Theodora is shown here in a mosaic detail from San Vitale church in Ravenna, Italy.

Theodora was the wife and political partner of the Byzantine emperor JUSTINIAN I. Unlike most empresses who stayed in the background, Theodora took an active part in government and exerted a great influence on the way the empire was administered.

Theodora was the daughter of an animal keeper in the amphitheater in CONSTANTINOPLE. A talented actress, she became a performer of comedies and mimes. When Justinian, the nephew and heir of the emperor, fell in love with her, his aunt, the empress Euphemia, was strongly opposed to the match. It was simply unheard of for a person of such a questionable background to marry into the imperial family, much less to become empress. After Euphemia died in 524, the emperor raised Theodora to the rank of patrician* and changed the law that had prohibited such marriages. Justinian and Theodora were married in 525. Two years later, when Justinian succeeded his uncle as emperor, Theodora became empress.

Theodora became more of a public figure than previous empresses. Her name was often included in state documents, in inscriptions on churches and buildings, and in the oath of allegiance required from government officials. Popes addressed letters jointly to Justinian and Theodora, and foreign ambassadors called on her.

Described as a slim, pale brunette, Theodora was intelligent, quick, and some say more decisive than her husband. She was fiercely loyal to her friends and ruthless in the pursuit of her enemies. She was apparently very generous, as evidenced by the many churches, orphanages, and public buildings she had built.

Theodora's moment of greatest personal courage may have come during the Nika Revolt of 532, when a popular uprising seriously threatened the emperor's safety. Justinian's advisers urged him to flee, but Theodora persuaded him to stay, face the rebels, and execute the nephew of a former emperor who was behind the revolt.

Theodora also used her position to protect other women. She had strict laws passed against the sale of young girls. In addition, under her direction, Byzantine divorce laws were changed to give women greater protection and benefits after the termination of their marriages. (*See also* **Byzantine Empire; Women, Role of.**)

Theodoric the Ostrogoth

ca. 454–526
King of the Ostrogoths

Theodoric was king of the OSTROGOTHS, who conquered Italy in the late 400s and brought peace to the region for many decades. He was born in Pannonia, a province in southeastern Europe, where the Ostrogoths had settled with the permission of the Eastern Roman Empire. Theodoric spent ten years of his childhood in the imperial court in CONSTANTINOPLE as a hostage for his people. There he learned much about Roman ways. Following the death of a rival in 481, Theodoric became the undisputed ruler of the Ostrogoths. When Theodoric unified the Gothic tribes and settled them in territory that is now part of BULGARIA, the Eastern Roman emperor, nervous about having so bold a leader so close, encouraged Theodoric to take his people to Italy and to rule there with permission of the Eastern Roman Empire.

After Theodoric led his people to Italy in 488–489, he defeated the barbarian leader ODOACER and set up his government in RAVENNA. He kept much of the Roman administration and established peace and equal justice for both Goths and Romans. Although Theodoric was an Arian Christian, he tolerated Jews and Catholics and even helped Catholics to rebuild their churches.

During his lifetime, the Ostrogoths remained strong and had considerable influence over other tribes in the West. The kingdom weakened rapidly following his death and was soon conquered by the armies of JUSTINIAN I.

Theophano, Empress

died after 976
Byzantine empress

* **regent** person appointed to govern a kingdom when the rightful ruler is too young, absent, or disabled

Theophano was a Byzantine empress with an apparent fondness for court intrigue. She is believed to have been behind the murder of three emperors.

She is accused of having helped poison Constantine VII and later of murdering her husband Romanos II. After Theophano became regent* following Romanos's death in 963, she married Nikephoros II Phokas. She and her lover, John Tzimiskes, then plotted the murder of her new husband. After the murder of Nikephoros, Theophano was banished to a convent. She escaped, only to be caught and exiled to ARMENIA. When her son BASIL II became emperor, Theophano returned to the capital but took no further part in government. (*See also* **Byzantine Empire.**)

Thomas the Slav

died 823
Rebel

See
color plate 8,
vol. 3.

* **depose** to remove from high office

* **iconoclastic** referring to a movement to remove icons (images of Christ and the saints) from all churches

* **caliph** religious and political head of an Islamic state

Thomas was the leader of a large-scale revolt against the BYZANTINE EMPIRE that gained a great deal of support and lasted for several years. The revolt threatened the capital city of CONSTANTINOPLE and seriously weakened the empire before it was finally quelled.

Thomas came from Asia Minor, and, as his name suggests, he was of Slavic origin. He captured the attention of the Byzantine world by claiming to be Emperor Constantine VI, who many years earlier had been illegally removed from the throne in a conspiracy led by his mother.

At the time, Byzantium was in a state of turmoil. Political intrigue and murders had led to frequent changes in the monarchy. After Constantine's mother was deposed* and her successor was killed in battle, the region had four different rulers in the next ten years. The religious controversy over ICONS was also dividing the empire. Moreover, Arabs and Bulgarians were pressing across the empire's frontiers, and the rise of CHARLEMAGNE had put an end to Byzantium's claim to a role in western Europe.

Thomas began his rise by rallying support in his home area of Asia Minor. With support from Arabs, Persians, Armenians, and other groups opposed to Byzantium, the revolt spread across the whole of Asia Minor. Thomas presented himself as the champion of the poor, and he won support from those opposed to the iconoclastic* policy of Emperor Michael II. Under the protection of the ABBASID caliph*, Thomas was crowned

Byzantine emperor in the Muslim city of Antioch. Thomas then led his army across Asia Minor. With naval support from part of the Byzantine fleet, he crossed over into northern Greece, where he picked up further support.

In December 821, Thomas began his siege of Constantinople that was to last for more than a year. The ruler of BULGARIA responded to Michael's call for help, and ships loyal to the empire destroyed Thomas's ships. In the spring of 823, Thomas's revolt collapsed when he was forced to call off the siege and flee. The forces of the emperor pursued him. Thomas was captured, tortured, and finally executed.

The effort to put down the revolt had greatly weakened the empire. The destruction of part of the Byzantine fleet may have contributed to the empire's subsequent loss of Crete and SICILY to the Arabs.

Thousand and One Nights

* **anecdote** short narrative concerning interesting or amusing incidents or events

Thousand and One Nights is the most famous work of medieval Arabic literature in the West. Fragments of manuscript date back as far as the 800s, but the first extended text appeared in the 1400s. The stories show influences from Persia, Baghdad, Egypt, and possibly India. This representation of a monster comes from a late medieval Urdu (Hindustani) edition of the tales.

The popular collection of tales known as the *Thousand and One Nights* (or *The Arabian Nights' Entertainment*) is the most famous work of Arabic literature in the West. The stories are loosely organized within the "frame story" of Shahrazad, a young woman who marries King Shahriyar and then tells him stories every night to prevent her execution the next morning. Out of his mad hatred for all women (because his first wife had been unfaithful), the king marries a young woman every day and then puts her to death the following morning. Shahrazad, daughter of the king's VIZIER, has a plan to tell the king a story every night, but to leave it incomplete so that the king will postpone killing her in order to find out how the story ends. The stories prove so entertaining that, after hearing 1001 tales, the king abandons his cruel plan. Shahrazad is saved, as are other young women.

The frame-story organization allowed for the inclusion of almost any type of story, as long as it was entertaining. The tales are from many places and were passed on by word of mouth for centuries before they were written down. The title of the collection, *Thousand and One Nights*, was intended to indicate a large number. Stories were later added to make up that number, and no two versions contain exactly the same stories. The earliest known written text of the work is a manuscript fragment from the 800s. The first extensive text is from an Egyptian manuscript from the 1400s.

Western readers tend to think of the stories as fairy tales about jinn (spirits) and magic lanterns, but there are many other kinds of stories, including moral tales, stories of gallant gentlemen, historical anecdotes*, romances, legends, fables, parables, humorous stories, and poems. Stories such as *Ala al-Din and the Wonderful Lamp* and *Ali Baba and the Forty Thieves*, for which the work is best known in the West, are not found in any of the Arabic editions.

The stories reflect a mix of Persian, Baghdadian, Egyptian, and Indian origins. The frame-story organization is typical of stories from India, although European writers, such as Geoffrey CHAUCER and Giovanni BOCCACCIO, also used frame stories for their works. The names *Shahrazad* and *Shahriyar* are definitely Persian, and many of the tales are

set in medieval BAGHDAD. The *Thousand and One Nights* did not come to the attention of Europeans until the early 1700s, when a French translation was published. (*See also* **Arabic Language and Literature; Harun al-Rashid; Iran.**)

See color plate 10, vol. 2.

Timbuktu

During the Middle Ages, the fabled city of Timbuktu was a bustling West African trading center. Located on the Niger River on the southern rim of the Sahara desert, Timbuktu connected the Islamic world north of the desert with sub-Saharan West Africa. Medieval Arab merchants and travelers who visited the city were the first to write about its commerce and learning.

The Niger River, which flows through the desert region of the southern Sahara, provided opportunities for settlement and trade in what would otherwise have been an impossibly harsh environment. Local chronicles date the origins of Timbuktu at about 1100, when it served as an exchange place. From Timbuktu, the Niger River flows westward through the desert and then southward through the tropical forest until it reaches Africa's west coast and empties into the Atlantic Ocean.

The fate of Timbuktu was closely tied to the growth and decline of trade across the Sahara in the late Middle Ages. As long as desert caravans made their way across the desert from North Africa to the empires in the southwest, Timbuktu prospered. The city was the chief supplier of goods and the main transit point for their delivery across the desert to Islamic North Africa. Trade included salt from the desert, gold from farther south, cattle from nearby nomadic herders, and grain from the farmers of the Middle Niger Delta. In the 1500s, sea traffic on the Atlantic replaced camel caravans as the best way to reach West Africa.

Three West African empires—Ghana, MALI, and Songhai—contributed to Timbuktu's prosperous years. Ghana was already flourishing when Timbuktu became a major trading center. Timbuktu's first significant commercial transactions may have been conducted with the Ghanaian city of Wagadu in the east. As Ghana declined in importance, the empire of Mali took its place, and Timbuktu became the active hub of this great civilization that extended across the southern Saharan region. In about 1470, Songhai was reorganized by King Askia Muhammad. He created a decentralized empire and allowed Timbuktu to participate as a free city with the authority to direct its own internal and commercial affairs.

Timbuktu combined its rich cultural diversity with Islamic learning to create a unique city of merchant-scholars at the edge of the desert. The population consisted of various African tribes, herders, farmers, and BERBERS and Arabs from the north. Timbuktu was a meeting place of many languages and traditions. The great Muslim traveler IBN BATTUTA, who visited in 1353, wrote an extensive description of the city. That description is the earliest surviving account of medieval Timbuktu.

Timbuktu gained a reputation throughout West Africa as a city of scholars, especially legal scholars. Its most important legal thinker was Ahmad Baba, whose fame spread throughout the Islamic world. The wealthy merchants who controlled Timbuktu gave positions of honor, status, and authority to the city's scholars. (*See also* **Islam, Conquests of; Law; Trade.**)

Tithes

A tithe is a tax of ten percent that the church levied on the revenue from people's occupations during the Middle Ages. Farmers, for instance, were obligated to pay a tenth of their annual harvest to the church. Income from any trade, craft, or commercial transactions was similarly taxed.

The tithe provided revenue for the support of the CLERGY, repairs and maintenance of church buildings, and relief for the poor. Tithes also provided funds for other social services of the church, such as education and medical care.

Although refusal to pay the tithe was rare, underpaying was common. Those who were most reluctant to pay the tithe were often new converts who discovered that their conversion to Christianity came with an unwanted financial obligation. (*See also* **Hospitals and Poor Relief; Law; Parish; Taxation.**)

Toledo

* **archbishop** head bishop in a region or nation

* **Mozarab** Spanish Christian who had adopted some aspects of Arab culture

* **enclave** country or part of a country contained within the boundaries of another country

* **dynasty** succession of rulers from the same family or group

The city of Toledo, located on the Tagus River in central Spain, was an important cultural center during the Middle Ages for Christians, Muslims, and Jews. After the VISIGOTHS gained control of Spain in the 500s, they made Toledo their capital. During the almost two centuries of Visigothic rule, Toledo became an important Christian city with its own archbishop*. Then in 711, Muslims from North Africa invaded Spain and brought Toledo and most of the rest of Spain under their rule.

Under Muslim rule, Toledo became a center of Islamic learning. Some of Toledo's Christians converted to Islam, but others, called Mozarabs*, continued to practice Christianity. A large Jewish community also existed in Toledo at this time. While the Muslims occupied central and southern Spain, the rulers of the small Christian kingdoms in northern Spain dreamed of the day when they could drive the invaders out. Occasionally, Mozarab enclaves* inside Islamic Spain rebelled against their Muslim rulers.

From the late 1020s until the Christians reconquered the city in 1085, Toledo prospered under the rule of the independent Dhu'l-Nunid dynasty*. During the rule of al-MA'MUN, who governed the city from 1043 to 1075, Toledo reached its greatest size with a population of about 37,000. Al-Ma'mun enhanced the city's reputation for learning by his support for the work of scientists, especially in the fields of astronomy and horticulture (the science and art of growing flowers, fruits, vegetables, and ornamental plants). Under his direction, royal horticulturists expanded the city's splendid gardens, which were irrigated by an elaborate system of waterwheels.

See map in Aragon (vol. 1).

In 1085, the Christian ruler of CASTILE, Alfonso VI, conquered the city of Toledo. The capture of this city had great symbolic importance because of the city's history as the Visigothic capital and as the home of an archbishop. Alfonso VI placed the administration of the newly conquered city in the hands of a leader of the city's Mozarab community. However, the nobles and townspeople from Castile, who came to Toledo to seize estates and property abandoned by fleeing Muslims, soon were in charge of the city.

The new Christian rulers of Toledo built on the city's tradition of learning and culture. With support from the Castilian kings, Toledo became an important center for the translation of ancient scholarly texts. Scholars translated Greek and Arabic texts into Latin. These translations facilitated the spread of ancient Greek and Islamic science, mathematics, philosophy, astronomy, and geography to the great European UNIVERSITIES.

* **synagogue** building of worship for Jews

During the first centuries of Christian rule, the Jewish community of Toledo continued to grow and prosper. The city had two Jewish quarters, and many synagogues* were built during this period. However, in the late 1300s, the Christian attitude toward Jews changed, and the persecution of both Jews and Muslims intensified. In 1391, mobs sacked and destroyed one of Toledo's Jewish quarters. A century later, in 1492, all of the Jews of Spain, including what remained of Toledo's once flourishing Jewish community, were expelled from Spain.

During the late Middle Ages, Christians continued to drive Muslims farther south in Spain until they captured the last Muslim city, Granada, in 1492. During the Christian reconquest of Spain, Toledo remained an important symbol and a rallying place for Spanish Christian rulers in their quest to reclaim and unite all of Spain. (*See also* **Islam, Conquests of; Islam, Religion of; Islamic Art and Architecture; Jews, Expulsion of; Spain, Muslim Kingdoms of; Spanish Art and Architecture; Spanish Language and Literature.**)

Tomislav

**early 900s
King of Croatia**

Tomislav was medieval CROATIA's greatest ruler. Croatia is a region in southeastern Europe located between the Adriatic and Black Seas. Tomislav unified Croatia by bringing together its coastal and inland territories, ended Frankish claims in the region, and defended Croatia against Hungarian and Bulgarian invaders.

About 910, Tomislav became the ruler of the coastal part of Croatia, which was called Dalmatian Croatia. The Hungarians, who had recently arrived, were raiding central Europe and the Balkans, and they were threatening the interior of Croatia, known as Pannonian Croatia. Although the FRANKS were in theory overlords of the Pannonians, they offered no help. The Pannonian chiefs then sought assistance from Tomislav, who defeated the Hungarians and created a border between Hungary and Croatia that still exists along the Drava River. Tomislav then took control of the Pannonian region himself and, for the first time, the two Croatias were united. About 925, Tomislav became the first king of united Croatia. (*See also* **Bulgaria; Hungary.**)

Torture

The term *torture* has two meanings: a general one (which changes with the intentions of the torturer) and a specific one that is rooted in legal history. The general meaning is applied to instances of personal assault that range from interrogation to extreme physical pain.

Judicial torture had been part of Roman legal proceedings, and, after the fall of the Western Roman Empire, the practice continued in the BYZANTINE EMPIRE. A digest of laws published by the emperor JUSTINIAN I contained a section on judicial torture, and these cruel procedures were regularly applied to free citizens of low rank.

The Germanic laws that replaced Roman law in western Europe in the early Middle Ages did not provide for the legal torture of free persons, and the practice soon disappeared. Torture came back in the 1100s in response to a tightening of the standards needed to convict people in capital crimes. Since most courts required either two eyewitnesses or a confession by the accused, convictions for serious crimes were hard to obtain. Torture reappeared in medieval courts as a way to elicit confessions in capital cases, which called for the death penalty.

By the 1200s, torture was being used by the INQUISITION and other church courts searching for heretics*. In England and Scandinavia, where jury trials made it easier to obtain convictions, torture was not necessary.

* **heretic** person who disagrees with established church doctrine

Judicial torture was used in some medieval European courts to obtain confessions in capital crimes. Torture was also used by church courts to force heretics to renounce their beliefs. This German painting from the 1400s shows the torture of a suspected heretic.

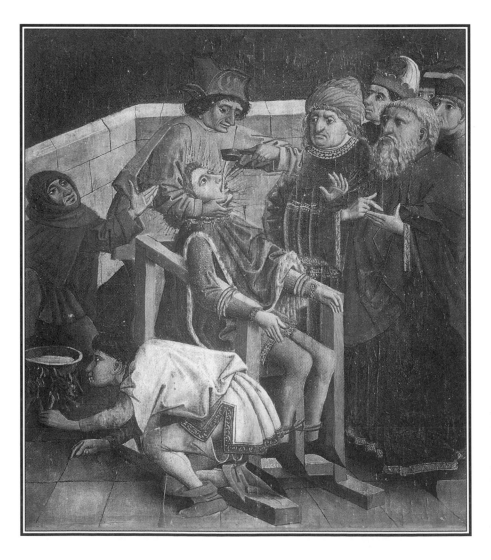

By the end of the Middle Ages, however, judicial torture had become routine procedure in most western European courts. (*See also* **Heresy and Heresies; Law; Trials; Witchcraft, European.**)

* **monarchy** nation ruled by a king or queen

* **Celtic** referring to the ancient inhabitants of Europe, known as Gauls in France and Britons in Britain

See map in Carolingians (vol. 1).

* **militia** army of citizens who may be called into action in a time of emergency

* **crusade** holy wars declared by the pope against non-Christians. Most were against Muslims, but crusades were also declared against heretics and pagans.

Located on the Garonne River in southwestern France, the medieval city of Toulouse was the center of a fiercely independent region. The counts of Toulouse were powerful political figures who played a leading role in resisting the church and the monarchy*. The independence of Toulouse ended in the 1200s, however, when the French kings overcame the rebellious counts and took control of the city.

The city, which was Celtic* in origin, was under Roman authority from the second century B.C. until 413, when the VISIGOTHS conquered the city and their king, Theodoric I, established his court there. In 507, the FRANKS captured Toulouse, but they failed to establish a strong local government. Instead, a family of local nobles took control of the city. From the 700s on, the city under the counts of Toulouse served as a center of Christian defense against Muslim invaders from Spain.

During this period, Toulouse stood entirely inside a wall the Romans had built around it. However, in the 1000s, as the population of the city increased, Toulouse expanded beyond its Roman wall. The townspeople built a bridge over the Garonne River that connected the city with the suburbs that had sprung up on the opposite bank.

In the mid-1100s, the citizens of Toulouse formed a city council with representatives from every quarter of the city. As the council grew in power, Toulouse became a city-state virtually independent of the counts of Toulouse. The city government maintained a militia* that allowed it to gain control over the villages and the nobles in the surrounding countryside for nearly 25 miles.

Toward the end of the 1100s, southern France became a hotbed of HERESY led by the CATHARS, who posed an especially serious threat to the church. They maintained that the God of the Old Testament (the Hebrew Bible) was really the devil and, therefore, that the church was worshiping an evil god. They accused church leaders of corruption and called for more spiritual ways of living. The Cathars gained many followers, particularly in Toulouse and in the nearby city of Albi. The townspeople of Toulouse became deeply divided, some supporting the Cathars and others opposing them.

By 1208, the Cathars were so numerous that Pope INNOCENT III launched the Albigensian crusade* to rid the city and region of them. The counts of Toulouse, who were opposed to foreign intervention, soon found themselves battling the combined forces of the church and the French king. In 1211, the crusader army under Simon de Montfort (the Elder) attacked Toulouse. The city resisted until the following year, when Simon's defeat of Count Raymond VI allowed him to enter the city.

The Treaty of Paris in 1229 settled the fate of Toulouse by arranging the marriage of the daughter of Count Raymond VII to Alphonse of Poitiers, the brother of King LOUIS IX. The marriage assured that the king's family would control Toulouse. The death of Raymond VII, the last count of Toulouse, in 1249, marked the end of independence for Toulouse. Thereafter, Toulouse became an administrative center for the French crown in its campaign to assert the king's control over southern France.

In the early 1300s, the population of the city reached 35,000. However, by 1405, it was down to 22,500, due to warfare and the devastation caused by the BLACK DEATH. A fire that raged for two weeks destroyed most of the city in 1463. (*See also* **Carolingians; Cities and Towns; Inquisition; Islam, Conquests of; Languedoc.**)

Trade

Trade—the exchange of goods for other goods or for money—was a vital part of the economic life of the Middle Ages. Trade between countries varied over time, and the goods shipped ranged from basic necessities, such as salt and grain, to luxury items, such as silk and other fine fabrics. Trade was also important at the local level—for example, when the dairymaid sold her butter at a nearby town market, or when the craftsman traded something he had made for farm produce.

Armenian Trade

Armenia is situated along east-west land routes linking the Mediterranean region to central Asia and the Far East. Because of this central location, Armenia has always played an important role in trade and commerce.

In ancient times, southern Armenia benefited from its closeness to the flourishing cities of Mesopotamia and northern Syria. Under the Roman Empire, and later the BYZANTINE EMPIRE, Armenia was the center of trade for Persia (now known as IRAN), the countries bordering the Black Sea, and Europe. Some of this commerce involved Armenian goods, especially horses, which had been highly prized since ancient times. The most important item, however, was silk from the Far East. Silk was carried over caravan trails to markets, where it was sold to the luxury industries that served the Byzantine court.

Armenian merchants suffered a blow when silkworm cocoons were smuggled into the Byzantine Empire, enabling the Byzantines to make their own silk. A far more serious blow was struck by the Arab invasions of the mid-600s, when constant warfare between Byzantium and the Arabs closed the overland trade routes. Armenian commerce declined in the late 600s and the early 700s, and many Armenian cities and towns were converted into Arab military garrisons*.

A great revival occurred when Armenia became politically stable once again under the Bagratid dynasty* of Armenian kings in the late 800s. A major east-west route was reopened, linking the capital of Dwin with the coastal city of Trebizond. New towns and cities were built. Some of them may have had populations rivaling those of western European cities.

Earlier, Armenian trade had been primarily a transit trade—it involved goods produced elsewhere that simply passed through Armenia. The Bagratid trade revival, however, depended on native industries. Food, timber, and mineral products were important, but manufactured goods

* **garrison** military post

* **dynasty** succession of rulers from the same family or group

dominated the market. The greatest demand was for textiles: cushions, covers, rugs, flowered silks, and the famous "Armenian goods," which were red-dyed fabrics embroidered with silk or gold.

Beginning in the mid-1000s, war with Byzantium and the SELJUK Turks ended the prosperity of the Bagratid era. Armenia's great cities were sacked, and trade became nonexistent. In the early 1200s, peace and economic growth returned to Armenia, and the region once again became the center of a transit trade between the newly created empire of Trebizond and the trading posts maintained on the Black Sea coast by the Italian merchant cities of GENOA and VENICE. When the MONGOL EMPIRE expanded into western Asia, Armenian commerce expanded as well. Armenian merchants obtained special Mongol passes that allowed them to travel as far as central Asia. Gradually, though, rising taxes imposed by the Mongols ruined the Armenian economy, which was further damaged by fighting as the Mongol Empire broke up. The final blow to trade in Armenia came in the late 1400s, when European seafarers discovered new routes to Asia. Traffic on the overland highways through Armenia dwindled. Some Armenian merchants left their homeland to settle in eastern Europe, the Black Sea region, and elsewhere.

Byzantine Trade

Trade in the early Byzantine Empire followed patterns that had been established during the Roman Empire. Spices, pearls, precious stones, and silk from the Far East and the Middle East traveled west to the Byzantine Empire and then farther west to Italy and parts of Europe. Trade within the Byzantine Empire was even more active, for the empire was a single, enormous trading organization, with a common currency and low internal taxes and customs fees.

Interference by the state, however, put a crimp in commercial activity. The government controlled the shipment of grain from EGYPT to CONSTANTINOPLE, it prohibited all but state-owned producers from making silk, and it decreed that all military equipment be manufactured in state factories. Private individuals were unable to operate these enterprises.

Small-scale trade existed at local levels, in the form of exchanges between villages and the surrounding countryside at FAIRS. The major eastern cities manufactured luxury items, such as papyrus (paper made from reeds) and high-quality glass, in small quantities for those who could afford them.

Period of Decline. In the 600s, warfare, PLAGUES, and other catastrophes resulted in a decline in the Byzantine population. The economy became largely agricultural, and people concentrated on producing enough to feed themselves. The empire lost its rich eastern provinces to the Arabs, and the capital city of Constantinople felt the loss of Egypt and its grain. The distribution of free bread to the people of that city, a regular practice since the 300s, ended in the early 600s.

Some long-distance trade did continue, in spite of the difficulties created by the general economic decline, by Arab invasions and conquests, and by the eventual disruption of the sea routes by Muslim pirates. The silk industry grew during the 600s, using raw silk produced within the Byzantine Empire.

Remember: *Words in small capital letters have separate entries, and the index at the end of Volume 4 will guide you to more information on many topics.*

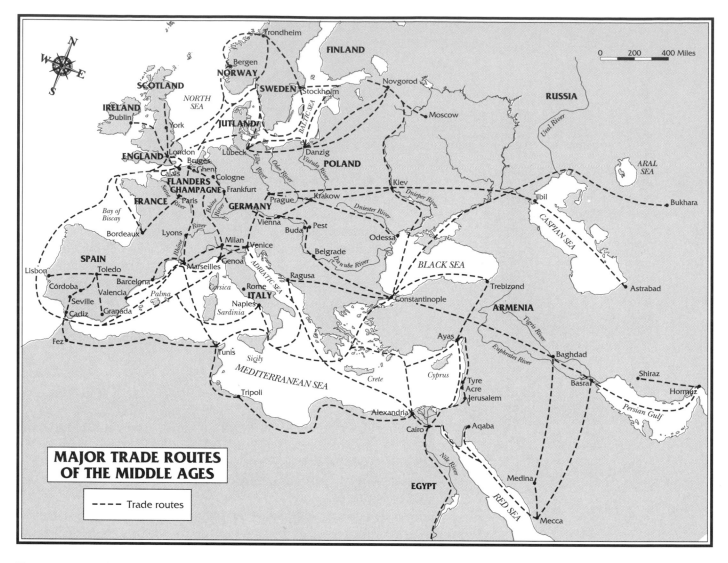

MAJOR TRADE ROUTES OF THE MIDDLE AGES

---- Trade routes

The most successful trading centers of the Middle Ages were situated along river and sea routes. Water was the easiest, least expensive, and safest way to move goods. The busiest trade area was the Mediterranean Sea, which linked the trade routes of Asia, Africa, and Europe. Many trade routes in the Mediterranean, Africa, and the Near East were used successively by different cultures and peoples.

* **aristocrats**   people of the highest social class, often nobility

After the Arab conquests in the east and the south, the economic life of the Byzantine Empire centered on Constantinople and the Black Sea area. Constantinople became a focus of trade and a manufacturing center for silk cloth and luxury products. Although the population and general prosperity increased, the Byzantine economy remained largely rural.

In the late 800s, trade with Italy became important. Byzantine goods sold well in the Italian markets of Amalfi and Venice—cities that had political ties with Byzantium. Merchants from Amalfi were the first Europeans to acquire trade privileges in Constantinople in the 900s, and they set up their own colony there. Byzantine aristocrats* regarded merchants with great suspicion. This attitude changed slowly, as Byzantine merchants and shipmasters became wealthy in the 800s and the 900s. Empress Theodora II herself owned trading ships. Eventually, the Byzantine aristocracy became more involved in commercial activity in Constantinople by renting real estate to merchants.

The Growth of Cities.   During the 1000s, Byzantine society became less rural, as more and larger cities developed. More money was in circulation, and commercial activity increased at home and abroad. With

Constantinople at its center, the empire's sphere of trade extended to Italy, Egypt, Russia, and Turkey. In the 1100s, western Europe became an important market for trade, as Byzantine merchants expanded their trade routes to include Spain and France. Although some Byzantine merchants became wealthy, their political power as a group was limited by an aristocracy whose wealth was land based.

After 1000, Western merchants penetrated the Byzantine economy. In return for Venice's military assistance against the Normans, the Byzantine emperor granted Venetian merchants the right to trade freely in Constantinople and a number of other Byzantine cities. Similar privileges were granted to PISA in 1111 and to Genoa in 1135.

By the late 1100s, the Venetians were deeply involved in the empire's internal trade. Many Westerners lived in Byzantine cities. Perhaps as many as 30,000 Venetians lived in Constantinople in the 1100s. However, there was growing resentment toward them. All Venetians were expelled from Byzantine territories by the emperor Manuel I Komnenos in 1171. Eleven years later, mobs in Constantinople massacred large numbers of Westerners and burned or seized their property.

These events made Westerners eager to obtain firmer control of commercial outposts in the Byzantine Empire, and the CRUSADES offered them an opportunity to do so. During the Fourth Crusade in 1204, Venice captured Constantinople, gaining a dominant position in Byzantine trade. By the time the Byzantines recaptured Constantinople in 1261, the city was again an active commercial center, although Italian merchants dominated the economy.

By the 1300s, Byzantine aristocrats were involved in trade and banking. The Byzantines exported raw materials and agricultural products to western Europe, and they imported cloth, soaps, and weapons. Native Byzantine industries had disappeared. By the 1400s, the Byzantine state had virtually turned over its economy to foreigners, who lived in colonies in Constantinople and other cities and who did not pay taxes or customs fees.

Islamic Trade

Trade had a long history in the Middle East even before the rise of Islam created a large empire. Wherever there were settlements and towns, there was commerce. References to caravan merchants in the BIBLE indicate that, long before the medieval period, there was a well-organized overland trade system in operation in western Asia and the Middle East. Muhammad himself had experience in the caravan trade that crossed the Arabian peninsula and carried spices from southern Arabia to the markets of Byzantium, Syria, and Egypt.

The spread of Islam in the late 600s and the early 700s rearranged political, cultural, and economic boundaries, bringing about a tremendous growth in commerce. Many very diverse areas were joined under a single political and military rule. The world of Islam extended from the Atlantic shores of Spain and Morocco, across North Africa, and east as far as India and central Asia—an expanse that became one gigantic trading area. In the course of their conquests, the Arabs captured large amounts of gold and silver, and these precious metals stimulated economic development.

See map in Crusades (vol. 2).

See color plate 1, vol. 1.

Regulating Trade

In Europe in the Middle Ages, trade was governed by many different authorities at different levels. Local lords or town councils oversaw the daily operation of the marketplaces. Private groups of merchants and tradespeople—such as guilds—determined the amount of goods to be produced and the price of these goods. As the national governments grew stronger and more complex, they began to regulate commerce. Many modern principles of commerce originated in the Middle Ages, including truth in labeling, fair trade, and quality standards.

See color plate 3, vol. 1.

Baghdad in the 800s and the 900s was the center of a great empire. Its markets contained panther skins, rubies, ebony, and coconuts from India; silk, paper, slaves, and marble workers from China; felt and hawks from North Africa; and donkeys, papyrus, and fine cloth from Egypt. The map of the medieval Islamic world, from Morocco in the west to the borders of China in the east, was dotted with cities and towns. Regardless of their size or importance, all towns had a marketplace and some craft workers.

Commercial Arrangements. Long before they existed in the West, mechanisms for extending loans and for transferring and exchanging money over long distances were used by merchants in the Islamic world. Islamic promissory notes (written promises to pay back money owed by a certain time) were probably the origin of modern bank checks. Islamic merchants used a variety of flexible partnership arrangements to pool their money so that they could finance new businesses. Such partnerships also reduced risks and losses by sharing the burden among several parties.

Islamic law had strict rules against USURY, but merchants still found ways to make profits. Trade in the Islamic world was nurtured by Islam, which generally had a positive attitude toward commerce and the honest pursuit of profit.

Mediterranean Trade. Commercial contact between the Middle East and western Europe declined between the 700s and the 900s, but it did not cease altogether. Until the early 1000s, the commercial center of the Islamic world was Baghdad. In the early 1000s, wars in the East and the commercial expansion of western Europe combined to shift the commercial center of the Islamic world to the eastern Mediterranean, especially to Egypt.

During the 1000s and the 1100s, Egypt's major exports were flax (a plant fiber) and linen, which were eagerly sought by European merchants. Egypt also served as a market through which Asian spices, most notably pepper, and other Asian products passed. Egypt imported silk from Spain and Sicily as well as olive oil from North Africa and metals from western Europe. Trade between the Islamic world and western Europe continued through the end of the Middle Ages and beyond.

Western European Trade

Trade in western Europe during the Middle Ages was divided into two great spheres, each centered on an inland sea. The trade of northern Europe was centered on the Baltic and North Seas and the river systems that flow into them. Southern European trade used the Mediterranean as its great highway. The northern trade dealt mainly in bulk goods, such as food and other basic items, and in relatively few luxury goods. The southern trade included bulk goods, but it also was characterized by luxury goods, such as silks and spices imported from Asia. The two trading spheres overlapped in FLANDERS and in CHAMPAGNE, where merchants from all over Europe met at the great international fairs of the Middle Ages. Later, the northern and southern trades met in the markets of BRUGES and Antwerp.

The Romans had developed the large-scale transport of goods from one part of their empire to another, but in the early Middle Ages, after

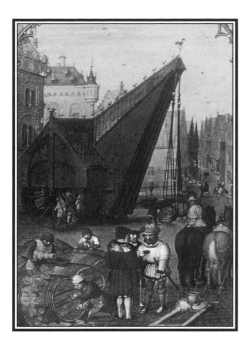

This illumination from the late 1300s shows the port of Bruges, an important trade center in Flanders. Wine merchants are sampling a consignment of wine that has just arrived. The crane used to unload the wine was powered by two human treadmills, one of which can be seen here, and was pivoted on its base. Such a device was considered the latest in modern equipment on European docks.

the fall of the Roman Empire, long-distance trade declined. There was always some trade—in salt, grain, and slaves, for example—but most local regions had very similar economies and had no reason to trade with one another. In the 800s, the Vikings appeared on the European scene, and although their destructive raids have become legendary, their role as traders is less well-known. The Vikings traded eastward from the Baltic Sea to Russia and Byzantium, dealing mainly in furs and in slaves captured in their raids.

Much of the medieval trade in western Europe occurred at fairs. The best known and most important fairs were held in Champagne, a county in France. Fairs were often held in cycles. One of the earliest cycles was organized in Flanders in the 1100s. In Champagne, a cycle of six fairs was held annually in various towns throughout the county. The Champagne fairs drew merchants from all over and were a vital international market during the 12th, 13th, and 14th centuries.

Goods from the East.   The most profitable trade was in exotic goods, including spices and fine fabrics, which were much desired by the nobles who could afford them. These goods traveled from the eastern Mediterranean region through Italy to the Rhine River in Germany. In the early Middle Ages, this trade was largely conducted by eastern Mediterranean peoples, especially Greeks, Jews, and Syrians. Gradually, Italians took advantage of their position in the center of the Mediterranean to acquire a larger share of the trade.

By the beginning of the 1200s, Italy was the commercial leader of western Europe. Venice, Genoa, and Pisa were the most important trading cities, and they were joined later by Milan and Florence. Four major wars between Genoa and Venice were fought before the end of the 1300s. In the end, Venice dominated the luxury trade in Eastern goods. Genoa handled bulk goods and the western Mediterranean trade, finding profit in the markets of Spain and southern France.

The Low Countries and the Hanseatic League.   The Low Countries (present-day Belgium and the Netherlands) also became a major center of trade. Cities in this region were well-known for the high-quality woolen cloth they manufactured. By the 1200s, Bruges and GHENT were busy ports where Italian merchants came to buy cloth and to sell goods that prosperous Flemish people needed or wanted.

The Scandinavians were eventually pushed out of the northern markets by the Germans, who, by the 1100s, had established a string of towns along the southern shore of the Baltic Sea. The merchants from these towns followed the routes that the Vikings had opened eastward into Russia. To organize the northern trade, merchant cities in Germany and on the Baltic formed the HANSEATIC LEAGUE in 1369. They exported Baltic products—such as timber, pitch (used to fill the seams of wooden ships), honey, wax, furs, and, later, grain from Poland and Lithuania. They imported luxury goods and spices. The most important import, however, was salt, which was used in curing fish. Control of the salt trade enabled the Germans to dominate the Scandinavian fish markets.

The BLACK DEATH in the 1300s greatly reduced the population of Europe, which, in turn, led to a decline in trade. After the plague*, people in most areas were able to feed themselves with the products of their

* **plague** disease that swept across the medieval world several times, including the Black Death in the mid-1300s

own countrysides. Political and military events of the late Middle Ages also disrupted commerce. Genoa suffered in the 1400s as its politics sank into chaos, and the Low Countries were battered by the HUNDRED YEARS WAR. By the end of the Middle Ages, trade in western Europe was in a period of deep decline. (*See also* **Agriculture; Banking; Fishing, Fish Trade; Fur Trade; Guilds; Islam, Conquests of; Markets; Roads and Bridges; Scandinavia; Silk; Slavery; Travel and Transportation; Weights and Measures.**)

* **pilgrimage** journey to a shrine or sacred place

See map in Islam, Conquests of (vol. 2).

* **imperial** pertaining to an empire or emperor

* **feudal** referring to the social, economic, and political system that flourished in western Europe during the Middle Ages

* **siege** long and persistent effort to force a surrender by surrounding a fortress with armed troops, cutting it off from aid

D uring the Middle Ages, in both Europe and the Islamic world, people traveled for a variety of reasons, including trade and pilgrimages*. They traveled under many different circumstances and by several different means.

The Arab conquests of the 600s and the 700s created an immense Islamic Empire that made travel and transportation necessary for reasons of government, defense, and cultural and religious unity. A common language and religion made travel across the vast empire both convenient and more common than elsewhere in the medieval world. As Muslims expanded their empire and trade routes west to Europe, European interest in the East and other faraway places increased considerably in the late Middle Ages.

Western European Travel

During the early Middle Ages, western Europeans traveled very little. Following the Germanic migrations and the collapse of the Roman Empire in the West, Europe was in a state of social disorder and economic depression that discouraged people from leaving home. As political and economic conditions improved later in the Middle Ages, travel and trade within and beyond western Europe increased.

The Early Years. The system of roads built by the Romans had given Europeans the means of relatively easy travel and communication. From the eastern Mediterranean all the way to Britain, travelers and imperial* messengers could journey with a high degree of safety along the highly advanced Roman network of roads. By easing travel and communication, the network helped trade to flourish and CHRISTIANITY to spread after its legalization in the 300s.

However, with the fall of the Roman Empire, travel and transportation decreased sharply, as Europe's economy declined and trade diminished and became more localized. In many places where people struggled to feed themselves and their families, they had neither the money nor the leisure time for travel. Furthermore, travel was illegal for SERFS, who were not permitted to leave their work on the lord's land.

Travel could also be dangerous. Travelers risked being robbed, killed, or kidnapped by bandits. Many of those who were kidnapped were sold into slavery. The frequent battles that occurred during the feudal* period posed another threat to travelers. Travelers could be caught up in the fighting or prevented from reaching their destinations by blockades or sieges*.

 See map in Trade (vol. 4).

Of course, some people did travel during the early Middle Ages. Those who traveled in the service of kings, nobles, or the pope were given food, lodging, and horses by designated families in each region whose duty it was to take care of official travelers. Royal and noble households also traveled. Great lords moved their entire households—including family members and servants—from estate to estate, living off the food and provisions that had been gathered before the move.

Moreover, medieval government was of a highly personal nature. Kings and lords traveled through their realms to show themselves to their people, thus reaffirming the bonds of loyalty and protection that were so much a part of FEUDALISM. Many kings spent the greater part of each year traveling through their kingdoms to oversee the operations of their royal governments. In addition, rulers and nobles traveled in the course of military campaigns.

Many Europeans who traveled during the early Middle Ages did so for religious reasons. The spread of Christianity increased the number of people who traveled as pilgrims, as officials on church business, and as MISSIONARIES. Pilgrims traveled to JERUSALEM, ROME, and hundreds of other religious shrines*, most of which drew pilgrims because they contained the relics* of SAINTS. As early as the 600s, pilgrims from as far away as England traveled to Rome. Not only was Rome the city where the pope lived, but it was the burial site of the two most famous martyrs* of early Christianity— Peter and Paul. Another popular pilgrimage destination of the early Middle Ages was the shrine of St. Martin in Tours in France, which was believed to have the power to cure disease. Pilgrimages were also considered a way in which people could atone, or make amends, for their sins. Many a sinner, burdened by the past, believed that his or her sins would be forgiven by a pilgrimage to the shrine of a martyr or a saint. For religious pilgrims, the dangers and difficulties of travel only added to the merit of the pilgrimage.

Other people traveled for reasons of church business and politics. Bishops and archbishops made the journey to Rome to see the pope, and some popes traveled in western Europe, especially in Italy and France. Many CLERGY members and lesser church officials traveled constantly, carrying out their duties within the provinces, dioceses*, and PARISHES.

In the early medieval period, Christian missionaries were active in Gaul (present-day France), Germany, and the British Isles. Accounts of some missionary journeys in Gaul suggest that the missionaries traveled by riverboat. During the 500s and the 600s, many travelers used waterways because the Roman roads were falling into disrepair and new roads and bridges had not been built. Missionaries from IRELAND were among the greatest travelers of the early Middle Ages. They carried Christianity to SCOTLAND and northern England and founded MONASTERIES in England, Scotland, France, Italy, and SWITZERLAND.

The monks of the British Isles, especially Ireland, were famous for their learning. They traveled through Christendom as welcome guests in monasteries and courts. One chronicler* recorded the story of two Irish monks who arrived in Gaul with a shipload of merchants. They went with the merchants to the marketplace, where they announced that they had wisdom to sell. When CHARLEMAGNE heard about them, he invited them to his court.

* **shrine** place that is considered sacred because of its history or the relics it contains

* **relic** object cherished for its association with a martyr or saint

* **martyr** person who suffers and dies rather than renounce a religious faith

* **diocese** church district under a bishop's authority

* **chronicler** person who records events in the order in which they occurred

See color plate 8, vol. 3.

During the Middle Ages, several inventions allowed for more efficient use of animals for pulling vehicles. This German miniature from around the 800s is considered by many to be the first image to depict a modern horse collar.

Other travelers who used the roads in the early Middle Ages included MINSTRELS, who provided entertainment and news of other places, and artists and craftspeople, who sometimes traveled great distances to work for kings and nobles. Charlemagne, for example, hired artists from the BYZANTINE EMPIRE and Italy to decorate his palace in AACHEN. Vagrants, or homeless people, also traveled the roads. Some were beggars, while others were criminals or fugitive serfs who had run away from their lords.

Trade increased in Europe during the CAROLINGIAN era of the late 700s and the 800s. Rivers became important trade routes, and many cargo boats traveled the inland waterways of France and southern Germany. The city of PARIS on the Seine River was an important trading center for grain and French wines. VENICE traded with the Islamic world and Asia. Italian merchants brought spices, silks, and other goods from the East to Europe. Slaves were also traded. European dealers sold slaves from eastern Europe and Russia to customers in Islamic Spain and the East.

In the 800s and the 900s, Europe was beset by a new wave of raids and invasions. After the Muslims conquered Spain, they invaded southern France and seized SICILY. Magyars from HUNGARY attacked the German, French, and Italian countrysides. The most dreaded invaders of all were the VIKINGS, who plundered and destroyed towns, ports, and monasteries in England, Ireland, and France. The disorder, looting, and fighting that lasted until the mid-900s brought travel and transportation to a near standstill for many Europeans.

Later Middle Ages.   About 1000, several new developments in Europe greatly increased travel. As a result of an improvement in the economy, more land was cleared, more crops were grown, and more food was produced. As more communities produced food surpluses, individuals and entire regions devoted their energies to other industries. FLANDERS, for example, became noted for its textiles. As towns and cities grew and became centers of industry and trade in the 1100s and the 1200s, commercial travel increased.

Transportation increased as merchants spent much of their time each year traveling between FAIRS to buy and sell goods and to arrange

for the transport of these goods. These fairs and markets attracted many people, some of whom came from great distances. Since fairs brought prosperity to the regions where they were held, efforts were made to promote them and to attract more sellers. The counts of CHAMPAGNE, the site of one of Europe's largest and best-known fairs, offered safe conduct through their realm and protection for merchants on their way to or from the fairs.

Toward the end of the Middle Ages, merchants hired agents in distant places to buy and sell goods for them. Instead of traveling themselves, the merchants assigned carriers to transport goods on packhorses or in carts or riverboats. This practice gave birth to a new professional class of brokers and movers.

Religious travel continued to increase in the late Middle Ages, as the church and the PAPACY expanded. As its administrative bureaucracy* grew more complex, more officials traveled on church business, inspecting monasteries and enforcing regulations. There was also a steady stream of travelers bound for the church's headquarters in Rome on religious business.

An interest in relics remained relatively constant throughout the medieval period. During the 11th century, a new practice arose—taking the relics on tour. When funds were needed to repair or rebuild a monastery, convent, church, or cathedral, the relics housed there were taken to remote parts of the country where people were willing to pay money to view the sacred objects. The clergy members who accompanied the relics traveled extensively for this purpose.

Pilgrimages became so popular that roads leading to certain shrines were often congested with travelers. In 1400, the French royal council forbade the king's subjects from making pilgrimages to Rome for fear that so many Frenchmen out of the country at one time would leave the kingdom defenseless.

Although a religious motivation seems to have been strong among most pilgrims, there is some evidence to suggest that, for some people, pilgrimages were an escape from the boredom of their lives, or simply a chance to travel and to satisfy their curiosity about the world. Evidence from the late 1300s suggests that while on the journey pilgrims generally enjoyed themselves. The pilgrims in Geoffrey CHAUCER's great poem, the *Canterbury Tales,* for example, are clearly in a holiday mood as they make their way to CANTERBURY to visit the shrine of St. Thomas BECKET.

By the late Middle Ages, pilgrimages had formed the foundation of a major industry—the travel business. Pilgrims provided financial support for the inns, vendors, and other services in the villages and towns that lined the pilgrimage routes. Some of the earliest known guidebooks were essentially descriptions of pilgrimages, complete with maps of the routes and notes about inns, ferryboats, and other useful travel information.

ROYAL HOUSEHOLDS traveled extensively during the late Middle Ages since kings and nobles spent much of their time on the road. In fact, from the 900s on, German emperors did not have permanent capitals. Instead, they traveled widely throughout their domain, setting up court at their various estates or taking quarters in religious houses. The kings of

* **bureaucracy** large departmental organization such as a government

 See map in Crusades (vol. 2).

England also traveled extensively. An account of King HENRY II OF ENGLAND reported that "he was always traveling about on intolerable daily journeys which seemed twice the normal length, and he was merciless in this to his household which followed him." Likewise, the kings of France traveled so often that, in 1319, Philip V changed his residence 81 times. All this travel allowed monarchs to inspect their realms, to show themselves to the people in order to strengthen their loyalty, and to find new places where they could indulge themselves in their favorite sports, HUNTING AND FOWLING.

Royal officials joined the kings in their travels. They took along the royal ARCHIVES, which were packed in special barrels and transported by packhorses. Until the 13th century, people who had business at the English or the French court first had to find out where the king was and then to travel with him until their business was finished. Judges, tax collectors, and other government officials also traveled more widely as their duties increased and became more complex.

Many craftspeople traveled to practice their crafts. English stoneworkers, for example, journeyed from place to place to work on the king's various building projects. Artists, entertainers, and minstrels traveled from place to place, and poets traveled in search of wealthy patrons*. In the 1100s and the 1200s, TROUBADOURS visited the courts of France, Spain, and Italy, and some even ventured as far as Hungary and the Middle East.

With the growth of UNIVERSITIES, increased numbers of students were willing to travel to study with certain greatly respected scholars. The universities of Bologna (in Italy) and Paris (in France) attracted teachers and students from all over Europe. Poor, wandering students barely able to afford food and books became familiar figures in the Middle Ages. In England in the 1300s, traveling students who did not have papers from their teachers attesting to their good standing were regarded as beggars and could be sent to jail.

The CRUSADES, which were called to liberate Jerusalem and the rest of the Holy Land from Muslim control, involved all social classes—from the rootless and "masterless" men and women who followed PETER THE HERMIT on the First Crusade, to the sons of kings and nobles who organized their own expeditions. The crusades and the subsequent establishment of crusader kingdoms in the Holy Land opened up travel to the East.

In the 13th and the 14th centuries, merchants and missionaries pushed well into the central Asian steppes* along the silk routes, which had been made secure by the conquests of the MONGOLS. Missions to the Mongol kingdom in the 13th century and the travels of Marco POLO to the East stimulated interest in travel beyond Europe to India, China, and other distant places. The knowledge of China and the East encouraged Portuguese and Spanish sailors to travel to the Azores, the Canary Islands, and Africa in the 15th century in search of an alternate route to the East that would bypass Muslim-held territories.

Islamic Travel

Freedom of movement was an important feature of medieval life in the Islamic world, since the conquests of Arab armies created a far-flung empire that stretched from Persia (IRAN) in the east to Spain in the west and

* **patron** person of wealth and influence who supports an artist, writer, or scholar

See color plate 9, vol. 1.

* **steppe** vast treeless plain of southeastern Europe and Asia

included ARABIA, the rest of the Middle East, and North Africa. Throughout the Middle Ages, government officials, merchants, Islamic scholars, and pilgrims traveled widely across this huge region. Of the many journals, diaries, geography books, and writings of travelers about their journeys, the best known is the autobiography of IBN BATTUTA. While most of these medieval Islamic travelers belonged to the middle or upper levels of society, travel also touched the lives of poor peasants, whose culture was influenced by travelers and goods from faraway places.

Reasons for Travel.   People in the medieval Islamic world traveled for many reasons—for trade opportunities, for religious pilgrimages, for military campaigns, for the administration of conquered territories, or as part of the large population shifts that occurred when nomadic* tribes migrated or when the government relocated groups of people from one part of the empire to another.

* **nomadic** wandering from place to place to find food and pasture

Most Muslims traveled for economic or religious reasons, and often they combined the two. For example, a merchant might buy or sell goods on his way to visit MECCA or another holy shrine. The quest for religious knowledge was one of the leading reasons for travel in the Islamic world. Muslims believed that the best way to learn the traditional lore of their faith was to hear it recited by a scholar who had heard it from an earlier scholar. For this reason, students who were deeply dedicated to the study of Islam sometimes spent years traveling throughout the Islamic world for a chance to sit at the feet of renowned scholars.

Travel Conditions.   Long-distance travel was fairly commonplace in the medieval Islamic world. Unhindered travel appears to have been a goal of Islamic governments, and there were few political barriers to travel, even between hostile states.

However, travel was expensive, tiring, and sometimes dangerous. While goods and passengers traveled by sea between Mediterranean ports and between Arabia and India, ships were subject to piracy and shipwreck. Most Muslims depended on overland travel, which had its own difficulties.

During the early Middle Ages, wheeled vehicles disappeared from the Middle East almost entirely. Transportation was by foot or by animal, with pack animals carrying belongings. The military used horses for battle and for rapid communications. Strong governments maintained a system of horse relays to carry official messengers swiftly across the empire. Ordinary travelers, however, were limited to donkeys, mules, and camels. Most freight was carried by camels, which could be fitted with covered litters to transport women and sick people. Travelers banded together in large caravans for reasons of security. These caravans averaged about 20 miles a day, spending each night at a caravansary*.

* **caravansary** lodging in the East where caravans stopped to rest, usually surrounding a spacious courtyard

The ideas and information that travelers spread across the Islamic world helped create and maintain the cultural unity that characterized the Islamic world. In turn, travel was made easier for Muslims because many features of life, such as the Arabic language and the Islamic faith, were the same from Spain to Persia. A student, merchant, or pilgrim who traveled from one part of the Islamic world to another could expect to find a familiar and comfortable welcome at every stage of the journey. (*See also* **Cities and Towns; Islam, Conquests of; Migrations, Germanic; Pilgrimage; Relics; Roads and Bridges; Slavery; Trade.**)

Trials

Methods for determining guilt or innocence, or trials, changed greatly during the Middle Ages. In the early medieval period, Europeans used oaths and physical ordeals to determine the fate of an accused person. Ordeals continued until the 1100s, when European courts developed new ways of making decisions that relied on witnesses, judges, and juries.

Oaths. In most ordinary and many serious crimes, the parties swore oaths as to their innocence, and they brought others to court to swear to the worthiness of their oaths. The elders presiding over the case then determined the guilt or innocence of the parties and an appropriate punishment, if any.

Ordeals. The ordeal courts were used to determine whether an accused person was innocent or guilty of a serious crime. Ordeals were based on the belief that God actively takes part in human events to reward the good and to punish the wicked. The ordeal was used as a way to focus God's attention on a specific case. The outcome of the ordeal was in God's hands, and it was thought that God would not allow an innocent person to suffer or a guilty one to escape punishment. A priest usually blessed the proceedings, and the results were accepted without question.

There were various kinds of ordeals. In the ordeal of cold water, accused criminals were tied up and submerged in water. If they floated to the surface, they were considered to be guilty. In the ordeal of boiling water and the ordeal of hot iron, the accused person's hands were scalded or burned. If the wounded hands became infected within three days, the person was considered guilty.

Another form of ordeal was called trial by combat. The accuser and the accused, each swearing to the truth of his claim, fought until one was victorious. The winner was considered truthful and the loser untruthful. The loser lost more than the case in question. He could be further punished for making a false claim.

Confidence in physical ordeals gradually declined. In the late 1100s, the English king HENRY II enacted legal reforms that reduced the reliance of courts on ordeals. The Fourth Lateran Council in 1215 forbade priests from participating in ordeals, and these trials slowly disappeared from most parts of Europe in the 1200s.

Inquests. Ordeals were replaced by inquests, in which judges heard witnesses on both sides of a dispute. In criminal cases, the suspect was publicly accused at the beginning of the inquest. Then, the testimony of the witnesses was heard. After the questioning of witnesses (and, sometimes, the judicial TORTURE of the accused) was completed, the court issued its judgment. Inquests became widely used in England, France, and Italy. Church courts also held inquests. Commonly used for such crimes as robbery, murder, arson, and forgery, inquests were also used to settle land disputes.

One of the most significant of King Henry's reforms was the requirement that a jury be present at inquests. (A jury is a group of people summoned by the court to hear evidence and sworn to hand down a decision based on that evidence.) In England, two types of juries emerged for criminal cases—the grand jury, which was used to indict, or accuse, a suspect;

and the trial jury, which was used to hear the evidence and then to determine guilt or innocence. Early trial juries consisted of 12 men from the area who were familiar with the parties in the case. However, by the end of the Middle Ages, jury members were expected to make their decisions on the basis of the presentations made in court, rather than on their own opinions about the people involved.

heretic person who disagrees with established church doctrine

Inquisitions. The inquisition was a special type of inquest that church courts, and sometimes royal courts, used to try cases of HERESY. In the 1230s, Pope Gregory IX appointed investigators called inquisitors to seek out heretics*, such as CATHARS and WALDENSIANS, and to bring them to trial. After the inquisitors collected evidence, they assembled a tribunal, or court of justice, in which they questioned the suspected heretics. Since heresy was a crime punishable by death (heretics were burned at the stake), a conviction could be obtained from the testimony of two eyewitnesses or a confession by the accused. Finding eyewitnesses was not always easy. However, judicial torture was already an accepted practice. Inquisitors often ordered the torture of accused people so that they would confess. Some did confess just to stop the pain. (*See also* **Inquisition; Law; Oaths and Compurgations; Torture; Witchcraft, European.**)

Tristan, Legend of

romance in medieval literature, a narrative (often in verse) telling of the adventures of a knight or a group of knights

The legend of Tristan inspired some of the greatest literary works of the Middle Ages. Based on a Celtic legend, the story was retold mostly by French and German poets, and its characters appeared in works about King Arthur's court. The most outstanding version of the legend, the German romance* poem *Tristan and Isolde* by Gottfried von Strassburg, is widely regarded as one of the literary masterpieces of the medieval period.

According to the legend, Tristan's uncle, King Mark of Cornwall, asks for his aid in winning the love of a woman named Isolde. Tristan persuades Isolde to marry the king. However, Tristan and Isolde unknowingly drink a love potion that causes them to betray the king's trust by falling in love with each other. Their enemies at court tell the king that Tristan and Isolde are in love, and they are banished to the forest. There, they face many dangers and tragically die.

These illuminations are from a 13th-century manuscript of Gottfried von Strassburg's *Tristan and Isolde.* King Mark is shown banishing Tristan and Isolde from court. They escape to a forest, where they face many dangers. Considered the most outstanding version of the Tristan legend, Gottfried's story is regarded as a literary masterpiece of the Middle Ages.

The story circulated among storytellers in WALES as early as the 800s. Eventually, it came to France, where a version known as the *Estoire* appeared about 1150. This version is now lost, but most of the other medieval versions were based on it.

Several poets who produced new versions of the Tristan story in the late 1100s added their own interpretations. For example, Eilhart and Beroul emphasized the lovers' cleverness in escaping detection, while Thomas of BRITTANY and Gottfried von Strassburg stressed the ideals of CHIVALRY and COURTLY LOVE.

Thomas's version was the source for Gottfried von Strassburg's romance, which he wrote about 1210. He followed Thomas's example by focusing on Tristan's loyalty and devotion, which were two principles of courtly love. Gottfried explored the powerful nature of love and its effect on Tristan's behavior. He described Tristan's love as an almost mystical* experience and even used religious symbols to describe it.

Gottfried's work and other Tristan poems were widely read and translated both during and after the Middle Ages. The story of Tristan continues to this day to fascinate readers and to challenge writers to create ever new versions of the legend. (*See also* **Arthurian Literature; Celtic Languages and Literature; French Language and Literature; German Language and Literature.**)

* **mystical** referring to the belief that divine truths or direct knowledge of God can be experienced through meditation and contemplation as much as through logical thought

---

Trota and Trotula

According to legend, Trota was a respected woman physician in the Italian city of Salerno in the 1100s. She was credited with the authorship of a handbook of general medical care, called the *Practica,* based on her practical knowledge. She was also considered to be the author of the *Trotula,* an immensely popular work on women's medicine that was named after her.

The *Trotula,* which first appeared about 1200, consisted of three treatises*. The most widely read treatise was the first one, which concentrated on gynecology* and obstetrics*. The second one was also about women's medicine, but it included advice on cosmetics and beauty aids as well. The third treatise dealt with cosmetics and care of the body. Translated into many languages, including Irish, English, French, German, Flemish, and Catalan, the *Trotula* was the most popular work on women's medicine in the later Middle Ages. (*See also* **Handbooks (Fachschrifttum); Medicine; Women, Roles of.**)

* **treatise** long, detailed essay
* **gynecology** branch of medicine that deals with diseases and care of the female reproductive system
* **obstetrics** branch of medicine that deals with childbirth

---

Troubadour, Trouvère

Troubadours and trouvères were composers of poetic songs in medieval France. The troubadours, who lived in southern France and began composing first, were popular in the late 1100s. The trouvères, based in the north, became active in the 1200s. The poetry of both groups, written in the local vernacular* rather than in Latin, represented a new style of literature.

Troubadour poetry was meant to be sung, and the poet usually composed both the words and the melody. In the south, the poems were

* **vernacular** language or dialect native to a region; everyday, informal speech

performed at the courts of the NOBILITY for audiences that were educated and of the highest social class. Often the poets themselves were aristocrats*. (One of the earliest troubadours was Duke WILLIAM IX OF AQUITAINE.) The poems were usually performed by professional singers rather than by the composer.

Great nobles became patrons of the poets, supporting and encouraging their work. The counts of TOULOUSE and Marseilles and the viscountess of Narbonne were leading patrons of troubadours. The nobility in nearby Italy and Spain also actively supported the poets. In the 1100s, ELEANOR OF AQUITAINE, who married the king of France and later the king of England, frequently invited troubadours to her court to perform. She was greatly loved and admired for her support of the arts.

Troubadour poems followed a standard form: short lines grouped into rhyming stanzas that were usually about eight lines long. The entire song was rarely more than 60 lines and generally ended with one or two short stanzas.

The most common subject of troubadour songs was COURTLY LOVE, in which the poet sings of his love for a lady and describes her beauty and virtues and his own passionate feelings toward her. The devotion of the poet toward his beloved is often compared to that of a knight toward his lord. The poet sings of trying to win the lady's love, and she sometimes rewards him with signs of encouragement. Depending on his success at winning her favor, the lover may sing about his sense of hope or despair. The concept of the beloved lady controlling the fate of her suitor became a standard theme in medieval poetry, as troubadour poetry spread from southern France to northern France, Italy, and Spain.

A few troubadour poems dealt with subjects other than love. They involved moral and political themes or were in praise of a patron or a lord. Troubadours also composed songs for dancing.

* **aristocrats** people of the highest social class, often nobility

See color plate 9, vol. 1.

Troubadours and trouvères, such as the ones in this illumination, usually composed music to their own poems. Written in the local dialect, their poetry represented a new style of literature. They enjoyed their greatest popularity in the 1100s and the 1200s.

In northern France, one of the first trouvères to write in the troubadour style was CHRÈTIEN DE TROYES, who later became famous for his longer romance poetry. Like the southern troubadours, the trouvères sang about the romantic ideals of courtly love, although the trouvères developed different rhyming patterns and refrains and wrote in their own local dialect. Some trouvères formed poetry GUILDS and organized poetry competitions. The most popular of these guilds was called the Puy d'Arras. The trouvères helped spread the idea of courtly love to other parts of northern Europe. (*See also* **Chivalry; French Language and Literature; Italian Language and Literature; Provence; Spanish Language and Literature.**)

Troy, Story of

The story of the fall of Troy was one of the most popular tales of the Middle Ages. While modern readers know the story from the works of the ancient Greek poet Homer, who described the fall of Troy in his epic poem, the *Iliad,* medieval readers learned about Troy in the works of medieval authors, especially Benoît de Sainte-Maure.

Benoît, a French clerk who worked in the court of King HENRY II OF ENGLAND, wrote his 30,000-verse *Roman de Troie (Romance of Troy)* about 1165. Based on the work of authors from the 300s and the 400s, Benoît's poem tells the story of the Greek adventurers Jason and his companions, the Argonauts, their search for the Golden Fleece (the wool of a flying ram), and the long siege of Troy by the Greeks. Benoît also told the story of the Trojan Horse, the large wooden horse with Greek warriors hidden inside it that the Greeks used to fool the Trojans and to bring about Troy's defeat.

Like other medieval authors who wrote about the ancient world, Benoît filled his poem with details from medieval life—people, architecture, ARMOR, and CLOTHING of the Middle Ages. Benoît displayed extensive knowledge of ancient history and geography and stressed the importance of learning from the ancient world. Written in Old French, his poem was enormously popular and was widely copied, imitated, and translated into other languages. The poem influenced the English writers John LYDGATE and Geoffrey CHAUCER and the Italian writer Giovanni BOCCACCIO, all of whom wrote their own versions of the story of Troy. (*See also* **Classical Tradition in the Middle Ages; French Language and Literature.**)

Turmeda, Anselm

ca. 1352–ca. 1423
Catalan author

Anselm Turmeda was a colorful late medieval writer who examined religion and human nature from a unique blend of Christian and Muslim perspectives. Born in the Spanish province of CATALONIA, Turmeda became a FRANCISCAN monk at the age of 20 and later studied theology in Paris and Bologna. About 1387, he converted to Islam in the North African city of Tunis and took the Arabic name Abdallah el Tarjumi. However, he continued to write in Catalan and to maintain contact with his homeland.

Turmeda's best-known work is *La disputa de l'ase (Debate with a Donkey),* in which he debates a donkey and seven insects about human

nature, the soul, wisdom, and immortality. The *Disputa* also includes tales about the seven deadly sins, criticisms of religious orders, and prophecies about the future. Turmeda's autobiography in Arabic, *Tuhfa,* which criticizes Christianity, became well-known throughout the Islamic world and remains in print in Arabic. Turmeda's tomb in Tunis is a Muslim holy site. (*See also* **Encyclopedias and Dictionaries; Islam, Religion of; Virtues and Vices.**)

Tuscany

See map in Italy (vol. 3).

* **siege** long and persistent effort to force a surrender by surrounding a fortress with armed troops, cutting it off from aid

Tuscany is a province in western ITALY, north of Rome, that was fought over in the early Middle Ages. After the cities of Tuscany achieved self-government in the 1100s, the region continued to experience conflict, as cities and factions within cities engaged in intense political struggles. In the late Middle Ages, after the city of FLORENCE achieved superiority over the region, Tuscany became a center of art and culture.

Tuscany had been under Roman control until 489, when THEODORIC THE OSTROGOTH invaded Italy. The Goths routed the Byzantines at Mugello in 542, but ten years later the Byzantines defeated the Goths to win control of Tuscany. Because the people resented the Byzantines for imposing heavy taxes on them, the massive LOMBARD invasion of Italy in 569 met little resistance in Tuscany.

After years of disorder and destruction in the 500s and the 600s, Tuscan cities revived during the reign of the Lombard king Liutprand from 712 to 744. After CHARLEMAGNE's invasion from 773 to 774 ended Lombard rule in northern Italy, he sent some of his forces to Florence to place the city under the control of his supporters.

From about 810, Boniface I (a supporter of Charlemagne from BAVARIA) and his family governed Tuscany for 150 years. In 845, Boniface's grandson, Adalbert I, gained control of the most important route through the Apennine Mountains, which controlled communications between Rome and northern Italy. In doing so, he became master of Tuscany and one of the most powerful men in Italy.

In the 900s, after the rulers of Tuscany allied themselves with the HOLY ROMAN EMPIRE, Tuscany was ruled by noble families with political ties to the empire. However, in the 1000s, the cities of Tuscany became divided. Some cities supported the German emperor, while others allied themselves with rebellious factions. Tuscan cities fought against one another, and their disagreements were further complicated by bitter feuds between noble families.

In 1028, Emperor Conrad II made Boniface, the count of CANOSSA, the ruler of Tuscany. However, after Boniface's death, his daughter Matilda (the marquess of Tuscany) defied Emperor Henry IV, and the emperor laid siege* to Florence to break Matilda's resistance. When the city survived his attack and forced him to leave, Matilda extended her control over the surrounding Tuscan countryside.

In the 1100s, after Florence and other Tuscan cities became independent communities governed by city councils, they continued to be divided by internal conflicts. After fierce fighting between the GUELPHS

AND GHIBELLINES had gripped Florence for years, Florence passed into the hands of the city's GUILDS in the mid-1300s. During this time, Florence gained control of the rest of Tuscany and became a powerful Italian city-state.

In the 1400s, Florence was dominated by the wealthy MEDICI FAMILY. Under the patronage* of Cosimo de' Medici, Florence became the leading city in Italy in art and culture. At the height of its power and splendor, Florence under Lorenzo the Magnificent was the center of art and culture that helped launch the Italian Renaissance. (*See also* **Italian Language and Literature; Migrations, Germanic.**)

* **patronage**   the support of an artist, writer, or scholar by a person of wealth and influence

Ulama

*U*lama is the term used to refer to Islamic religious scholars who have had a great influence on Islamic history. Over the centuries, the ulama have transmitted Islamic knowledge and interpreted the QUR'AN, the holy book of Islam. They have also been state officials with civil and judicial responsibilities.

The ulama never formed a distinct social class, although they played an important role in the establishment of religious, political, legal, and economic institutions throughout the Islamic world. They were theologians*, lawyers, judges, legal consultants, prayer leaders, preachers, teachers, scribes, secretaries, agents, market inspectors, and tax collectors. The influence of the ulama shaped public opinion in many areas. They could rally public support for a ruler or rally the public against a regime they opposed.

The rise of the ulama was connected to the need of the early Islamic communities to preserve and transmit knowledge of the Qur'an and hadith*. They played a major role in the development and elaboration of Islamic law.

Despite their great influence, the ulama did not have a formal system of education until the late 11th century, when a SELJUK leader introduced the idea of colleges for training ulama. The ulama remained an important force in public life until the 1800s, when some parts of the Islamic world adopted modern bureaucracies* and secular* education. (*See also* **Caliphate; Damascus; Islam, Political Organization of; Islam, Religion of.**)

* **theologian**   person who studies religious faith and practice

* **hadith**   collected traditions of the words and deeds of Muhammad

* **bureaucracy**   large departmental organization such as a government

* **secular**   nonreligious; connected with everyday life

Umar I ibn al-Khattab

ca. 592–644
Founder of the Islamic state

* **caliph**   religious and political head of an Islamic state

*U*mar I ibn al-Khattab was the second caliph* and the real founder of the Islamic state that rose to greatness during the Middle Ages. A member of an influential clan, Umar at first opposed MUHAMMAD. After converting to Islam, however, Umar urged Muhammad to make his teachings public. He was not only Muhammad's father-in-law, but he became the prophet's adviser and close friend.

Umar was among the first 50 people to join Islam. He was the first person to urge that Muhammad's teachings be collected in a holy book of Islam, the QUR'AN. It was he who decided that the Islamic calendar should begin with the hegira, Muhammad's move to Medina in 622.

After Muhammad's death, ABU BAKR was elected the first caliph. In 634, Umar succeeded Abu Bakr and began an active campaign to spread Islam through expansion and conquest. During his ten-year reign as caliph, Muslims created the core area of what eventually became a large Islamic empire. In well-planned campaigns, Umar's forces conquered IRAQ, SYRIA, and EGYPT. This Arab-Islamic expansion brought about large population shifts, as Arab Muslims colonized the newly conquered lands. Urban growth increased dramatically. The most important new cities were Basra and KUFA in Iraq and al-Fustat in Egypt. Built to house troops and their families, these cities eventually became provincial* capitals. Basra grew into a cosmopolitan* port where merchants traded with China and East Africa.

Umar argued against turning the conquered lands into booty* to be plundered by the invading Muslims. Instead he imagined an expanding, unified Islamic state. Non-Muslims were free to remain in this state if they accepted Islamic rule and agreed to pay taxes. Umar created an administrative and fiscal structure for the newly formed Islamic state. He started the practice of setting salaries for state officials, including the office of caliph. The state established a system of taxes and collected its share of each area's produce, which was distributed to the soldiers. Soldiers who had participated in the conquests and their families were also given salaries and other benefits.

As the state grew larger and more complex, so did the caliph's duties. Umar delegated some of his responsibilities, including the leading of prayer and the judging of disputes, to other officials. He kept a tight grip on all state officials to ensure that they did not steal from the public treasury.

Umar died of wounds inflicted by an assassin's dagger on November 3, 644. He left behind a well-established and organized state. (*See also* **Caliphate; Islam, Conquests of; Islam, Political Organization of; Islam, Religion of.**)

* **provincial** referring to a province or an area controlled by an empire

* **cosmopolitan** having an international outlook, a broad worldview

* **booty** prizes of war

Umar Khayyam

**1048–1131
Persian poet
and mathematician**

During his lifetime, Umar Khayyam was widely respected as a leading mathematician and astronomer in his native Persia (present-day IRAN). To later generations, he was better known as a poet. His best-known work is a set of melancholy poems called the *Rubaiyat* (a ruba'i was a quatrain, or verse of four lines).

During 18 years at the sultan's court in Isfahan, Umar Khayyam created a new solar calendar and drew up plans for a large, new observatory. His poems were not mentioned in any source from his own lifetime. Following his death, however, other writers began to quote them. By the mid-1300s, some 60 quatrains had appeared; by the 1800s, more than 1,200 quatrains were attributed to Umar Khayyam. His work achieved vast international fame after Edward FitzGerald of Britain translated them into English in 1859. Some quatrains were widely quoted, especially this one: "The moving finger writes, and having writ/Moves on, nor all your piety nor wit/Shall lure it back to cancel half a line/Nor all your tears wash out a word of it." Modern scholars, however, believe that only about 100 of the quatrains were actually written by Umar Khayyam.

* **dynasty** succession of rulers from the same family or group

* **Shi'ites** Muslims who believed that Muhammad chose Ali and his descendants as the rulers and spiritual leaders of the Islamic community

* **Sunnites** Muslim majority who believed that the caliphs should rule the Islamic community

* **caliphate** office and government of the caliph, religious and political head of the Islamic state

* **provincial** referring to a province or an area controlled by an empire

* **autocratic** ruling with absolute power and authority

The Great Mosque at Córdoba

One of the largest mosques in the world, the Great Mosque of Córdoba, was built during the Middle Ages. Begun in 785 during the caliphate of Abd al-Rahman I, the mosque is surrounded by an outer wall and set inside a courtyard. The interior of the mosque is notable for its 856 columns, linked by red and white horseshoe-shaped arches. This forest of columns creates an ever-shifting perspective for the eye of the viewer. Some of these columns were taken from older Christian and Visigothic buildings. Mihrabs, or prayer niches, in the walls of the building face in the direction of the holy city of Mecca. Enlarged in the 800s and the 900s, the mosque became a Christian church after the conquest of Córdoba in 1236.

The Umayyads were the first Islamic dynasty*. They ruled over a vast empire stretching from Spain in the west to central Asia and India in the east. It was during the early days of the Umayyad rise to power that Islam split into Shi'ite* and Sunnite* factions, a division that has continued to the present.

Foundations of Umayyad Power. The Arabian city of MECCA was home to the powerful Umayyad clan. The Umayyads played an important role in Arabian trade, and they became major landholders in the western Arabian peninsula. Their economic importance was matched by social and political influence. By the time Islam emerged in the early 600s, the Umayyads enjoyed a dominant position in Mecca, and they also had significant contacts and influence among the Arab tribes in SYRIA.

When MUHAMMAD's forces occupied Mecca in 630, the Umayyads at first opposed the Prophet. Yet, they soon were participating in the early Arab conquests, and their chieftains played important roles as military leaders. Umayyad fortunes in the early caliphate* centered on the rise of two of the clan's leading figures, Uthman ibn Affan and MU'AWIYA ibn Abi Sufyan. Uthman, an early convert to Islam and a son-in-law of Muhammad, was appointed caliph in 644 and became the founder of the dynasty. As caliph, Uthman appointed Umayyad kinsmen to important provincial* posts and took major steps toward centralizing power. Meanwhile, Mu'awiya, who was governor of Syria, did much to strengthen Umayyad power there.

Uthman's autocratic* policies and the favored position of the Umayyads throughout the empire eventually provoked a mounting tide of discontent and then open opposition. Rising tensions resulted in the murder of Uthman in 656, and this was followed by a period of great turmoil and civil war. The only leader acceptable to the various opposition groups was ALI IBN ABI TALIB, Muhammad's cousin and son-in-law. Ali had strong support from a faction that came to be known as the Shi'ites. (In time, the Shi'ites became a general movement within Islam that opposed the ruling dynasty, while Orthodox Muslims, or Sunnites, supported the caliph as the rightful representative of the Islamic community.) Ali was named caliph by Arab leaders from the city of Medina, but he never enjoyed general support within the empire. In addition, Mu'awiya refused to acknowledge Ali's claim to the caliphate. When Ali was assassinated in 661, Mu'awiya became caliph. With his succession, the Sufyanid branch of the Umayyad dynasty began.

As caliph, Mu'awiya governed on a grand scale. He shifted the caliphate to DAMASCUS, and the city became the Umayyad capital and the administrative center of the Islamic world. Lavish palaces and administrative buildings were built, and court life and ceremonies were based on practices borrowed from the Byzantines and the SASANIANS of Iran. Mu'awiya skillfully increased his power and gained the support of various tribal groups, and he continued the development of a centralized, authoritarian regime. When Mu'awiya died in 680, his son Yazid succeeded him as caliph. This established a precedent of hereditary succession to the caliphate.

Early Umayyads. The greatest achievement of the early Umayyads was the devising of a system that unified their domains and laid the

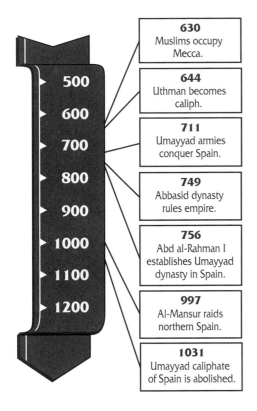

630	Muslims occupy Mecca.
644	Uthman becomes caliph.
711	Umayyad armies conquer Spain.
749	Abbasid dynasty rules empire.
756	Abd al-Rahman I establishes Umayyad dynasty in Spain.
997	Al-Mansur raids northern Spain.
1031	Umayyad caliphate of Spain is abolished.

* **garrison** military post

See map in Byzantine Empire (vol. 2).

* **patron** person of wealth and influence who supports an artist, writer, or scholar

* **booty** prizes of war

foundations for the development of other governmental institutions. Under Mu'awiya and Yazid, the caliphate developed a strong imperial government with various bureaucratic departments. In the provinces, authority was delegated to a small circle of trusted commanders, or emirs. The emirs exercised full executive, military, and economic powers. They supervised their own provincial bureaucracies and reported directly to the caliph. Their provincial capitals became military garrisons* from which the armies of the caliph could carry Islam into neighboring territories.

At the same time, early Umayyad rule was also characterized by internal rivalries among various Islamic factions. Many Arabs, particularly in IRAQ, the heartland of the empire, resented what they considered to be unfair use of their land and an invasion of their rights. In addition, many newly converted Muslims were rapidly becoming resentful of their second-class status within Umayyad society. After the deaths of Yazid and his successor, Mu'awiya II, the enemies of the Umayyads took advantage of the mounting chaos. Rebellions erupted in the late 600s, and a different branch of the Umayyad dynasty gained control. This branch of the dynasty, the Marwanids, produced all the remaining Umayyad caliphs.

During the late 600s and the early 700s, the Umayyads continued to face internal strife and challenges to their authority. The caliphs of this period thus sought to strengthen their base of power. Steps were taken to regularize the system of dynastic succession. Authority in the provinces was concentrated in the hands of a small group of trusted professional officers rather than tribal allies. Lastly, the caliphs sought to unify the various parts of the empire by promoting Arabic as the common language of government and religion.

High Point of Umayyad Rule. The first half of the 700s marked the peak of Umayyad political power and expansion. In the west, Umayyad troops quickly conquered North Africa and swept into Spain in 711. In the Middle East, the armies of the caliph besieged CONSTANTINOPLE (unsuccessfully) and then pressed on into central Asia. In the east and the south, Arab forces reached as far as the Indus River valley. This vigorous period of conquest was accompanied by the growth of large trading cities and a large-scale migration of Arabs throughout the empire. Canals and irrigation systems were repaired and extended, large tracts of unexploited land were reclaimed, and roads were built. Charitable services for the poor and disabled were established, and mosques were rebuilt or enlarged. Islamic culture and scholarship increased, as the Umayyad caliphs became patrons* of poets, artists, and scholars. This era marked the emergence of a distinctly Islamic culture and political system, which helped to unite the vast empire.

Collapse of the Umayyad Regime. Umayyad rule depended on the loyalty of a small Arab ruling class who served as the military leaders, administrators, and officials of the empire. This ruling class had great privileges, such as not having to pay taxes on conquered lands and having the first access to booty*. Meanwhile, the lands conquered by the Umayyads contained many non-Arabs who had converted to Islam. Many of these converts had cultures far older and more advanced than that of the Arabs. However, since they were not Arab by birth, they were treated as

See map in Islam, Conquests of (vol. 2).

See color plate 11, vol. 2.

* **vizier** Muslim minister of state

second-class citizens. This led to resentment against the Umayyads and eventually gave rise to rebellion. In the 740s, anti-Umayyads took control of towns in IRAN and Iraq, and the Umayyads were defeated in several major battles. In 749, Abul-Abbas of the ABBASID clan was named caliph. This marked the beginning of the Abbasid dynasty. In 750, the last Umayyad ruler, Marwan ibn Muhammad, fled from Syria to Egypt, where he was killed.

Although Umayyad rule of the Islamic Empire was ended, the Umayyad story was far from over. One family member, Abd al-Rahman, escaped the slaughter of his family and fled to Spain, where he founded a new Umayyad dynasty. Abd al-Rahman I declared Islamic Spain independent of the Abbasid caliphate, and he ruled as emir from 756 to 788. His court at CÓRDOBA consisted of a small circle of relatives and family friends who had moved to Spain on hearing of his success. By the early 800s, Spain (known as al-Andalus in Arabic) was an independent state within the Muslim world, and its emir held all civil and religious power.

In 929, Abd al-Rahman III was confident enough in his power to proclaim himself caliph of al-Andalus. Abd al-Rahman III waged war on the Christian kingdoms of northern Spain and sought to undermine the Muslim rulers of North Africa. His rule marked the high point of Islamic culture in Spain, and he built beautiful mosques, gardens, libraries, and palaces throughout the realm. Umayyad rule in Spain continued to grow under al-MANSUR, a powerful vizier* who waged constant war against the Christian kingdoms in the late 900s. By the mid-1000s, however, internal dissension threatened the power of the Umayyads of Spain. The caliphate was abolished in 1031, and the Umayyad kingdom was divided into a number of small kingdoms ruled by Arab, BERBER, or MAMLUK leaders. (*See also* **Arabia; Caliphate; Islam, Conquests of; Spain, Muslim Kingdoms of.**)

Universities

* **charter** written grant from a ruler conferring certain rights and privileges

Universities and colleges began in the Middle Ages. While schools and academies of various kinds had existed throughout the ancient world, organized institutions of higher learning were not established until the late medieval period. The first use of the term *university* was in reference to a group of scholars and their students in PARIS in 1221.

The university was a legally recognized group of people with an identity who were organized for a purpose, similar to a modern corporation. This independent legal standing is what made the university different from other schools. For example, many cathedrals and monasteries had schools, but these schools did not have separate, distinct existences under the law.

Universities generally were formed in one of two ways. A university could develop from an already existing school (or group of students and teachers), or it could be founded with a charter* from the pope or from a king. Once a university was incorporated, it became an independent legal entity, although medieval universities maintained close ties with the church, and university officials often held church positions as well.

Originally, colleges were residences for students that were funded by charitable donations. They later developed into institutions of higher learning where students could reside as well as attend lectures. In the Middle Ages, colleges usually were associated with universities. For example, Oxford University in England was, and is to this day, made up of a number of colleges.

European Colleges and Universities. The first colleges in Europe were founded in France and in Italy in the late 1100s. English and Spanish colleges began in the mid-1200s, and these were followed by German colleges in the 1300s and Scottish and Polish ones in the 1400s. European colleges evolved from student residences into self-governing academic communities where students and scholars learned together, usually as part of a university.

Several developments paved the way for the emergence of universities in the 1200s. Schools that were connected to cathedrals and monasteries produced a pool of scholars and an atmosphere favorable to learning. Interest in learning was also stimulated by increased contact with Islamic scholars and by new translations of Arabic works and the works of ancient Greek thinkers—especially ARISTOTLE, whose works on logic and the sciences became an important part of the curriculum of medieval universities. Furthermore, the incorporation of many towns and GUILDS established a legal model for the incorporation of universities.

Europe's first university grew out of the community of scholars and teachers who lived in Paris and who were making that city an important center of higher learning. By the mid-1200s, the University of Paris (later and currently referred to as the Sorbonne) had been organized as a self-governing corporation, licensed to grant degrees in theology*, church law, medicine, and arts.

At about the same time, another kind of university was emerging in Bologna, Italy, a city that was becoming Europe's center for legal studies. In addition to teaching LAW, faculty members in Bologna delivered lectures on such practical subjects as composition, for training civil servants in the preparation of documents. Around 1200, the students of Bologna, who had organized themselves into two groups—one for Italians and one for foreign students—formed the University of Bologna. The students ran the university themselves. They elected their own administrators and directed the teachers by having the power to withhold their fees.

The first university in the British Isles, Oxford University, also originated in the 1200s. Like Bologna, Oxford was a student-run university with assemblies of students in charge of establishing its rules and managing its operations. By the end of the Middle Ages, Europe had dozens of universities, both large and small, from SCOTLAND and SCANDINAVIA in the north to PORTUGAL in the west and HUNGARY in the east.

European universities offered similar courses of study and had similar requirements. Students could begin their academic training at about 14 years of age in a section of the university called the faculty of arts. There they studied grammar, logic, history, MATHEMATICS, and philosophy. These young arts students generally attended lectures for six years and spent the next two years conducting disputations*. Students who

* **theology** study of the nature of God and of religious truth

* **disputation** debate; exercise in the oral defense of a thesis by the principles of logic

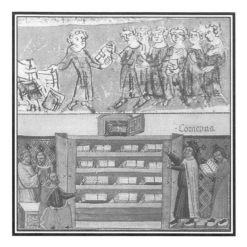

Contact with Islamic scholars and new translations of the works of Greek philosophers rekindled the desire for higher learning in Europe in the later Middle Ages. Europe's first university was chartered in Paris in the mid-1200s. This illumination shows students in the library at the University of Paris.

See map in Byzantine Empire (vol. 2).

* **patronage** the support of an artist, writer, or scholar by a person of wealth and influence

* **mosque** Muslim place of worship

passed their examinations and conducted successful disputations received the bachelor of arts degree. Another year or so of study was needed to earn the master of arts degree. With a master of arts degree, a graduate could teach the arts or enroll in one of the higher faculties of law, MEDICINE, or theology.

These higher faculties offered more demanding programs. No one could become a master of theology before the age of 35, for example, because such a degree required at least 12 years of study beyond a master of arts degree. However, an individual could become a master of medicine in much less time. In Paris, a degree in medicine required about four years of study beyond the master of arts degree.

The two main teaching methods in European universities were lectures, which usually began at around six or seven in the morning, and disputations. In disputations, students argued for or against a statement made by the instructor. Many disputations involved the fine points of interpreting scholarly texts, while others ranged widely over the social, economic, and political issues of the day. These exercises gave medieval students a chance to discuss and to think critically about important religious and political questions.

Since the earliest universities did not have their own buildings, classes were held in churches, monasteries, convents, and even palaces. As colleges were absorbed into universities, the universities acquired the buildings of the colleges, which they used for classrooms and lecture halls. Some universities raised funds to construct their own buildings and meeting places—the forerunners of today's campuses.

Byzantine Higher Education.   The BYZANTINE EMPIRE did not have independent, self-contained universities like those that emerged in Europe in the late Middle Ages. Higher education was provided by private teachers, by members of professional groups, or by officially appointed teachers paid by the state.

CONSTANTINOPLE, which surpassed Rome, Athens, and Alexandria as the main center of Byzantine learning, was the empire's only center of higher study after the 600s. The purpose of Byzantine higher education was to train civil servants, church officials, doctors, and lawyers. In 863, chairs of grammar, RHETORIC, and philosophy (including astronomy and MUSIC) were established in the imperial palace. However, the emperor's patronage* of higher education and funding by the state were irregular. Private teachers bore the main responsibility for providing higher education.

Only a very small percentage of people in the empire benefited from higher education. Yet those who received such an education were the shapers of Byzantine culture. They helped preserve and make popular the heritage of the ancient Greek world, and they were instrumental in eventually passing it on to Europe during the Renaissance.

Islamic Colleges.   Colleges in the Muslim world began in the 600s and the 700s—long before they appeared in Europe—and they reached their full development in the 900s.

Students who attended certain mosques* to study Islamic law and theology received encouragement and support. Generous Muslim patrons provided funds for the lodging of poor students and for the expenses of students who came from far away. One provincial governor, Badr ibn

Hasanawaih (who died around 1014) funded 3,000 colleges over the 30-year period of his governorship. Since Islamic law was the most important subject, other college members were subordinate to the professor of law, who was usually also the college's director.

Students began their higher studies at the age of 15 and finished their undergraduate studies in four years. The graduate could then teach young children or go on to higher-level studies, which could take up to 20 years. A graduate degree made him eligible to receive a license to teach college and to issue legal opinions. (*See also* **Books, Manuscript; Law; Libraries.**)

Urban II, Pope

ca. 1035–1099
Pope and reformer

* **crusades** holy wars declared by the pope against non-Christians. Most were against Muslims, but crusades were also declared against heretics and pagans.

See map in Holy Roman Empire (vol. 2).

See map in Crusades (vol. 2).

Urban II, best remembered as the pope who called for the First Crusade*, was a church reformer who helped the PAPACY recover from one of its most difficult periods. The final split between the Byzantine and Roman branches of the church had been followed by a struggle between the papacy and the HOLY ROMAN EMPIRE that had threatened to divide the Western Church.

Before becoming pope, Urban was a French cleric known as Odo. In 1084, Pope GREGORY VII sent him to Germany. The German king Henry IV had just conquered ROME, had installed Clement III as the new pope, and had had himself crowned emperor. During Easter Week in 1085, Urban held a meeting inside Germany on behalf of Pope Gregory. At that meeting, Urban urged that all the acts and followers of Clement III be condemned. Urban's action was in bold defiance of the emperor, and it was done within the emperor's own territory.

In 1088, Urban was elected the new pope, but his position was so insecure that he dared not enter Rome, where Clement III was still in residence and claimed to be pope. Urban spent the first five years of his papacy outside Rome gathering support against Clement. By 1093, he felt strong enough to enter Rome and to take charge of the papacy. As pope, Urban implemented many of the reforms that Gregory VII had favored. He also established diplomatic contact with the Byzantine emperor Alexios I KOMNENOS in the hope of healing the rift between the Eastern and Western Churches.

In 1095, at the Council of Clermont in France, Urban called for the First Crusade to liberate JERUSALEM. He is probably best known for this act. The titanic struggle that followed between Europe's crusaders and the Muslim Turks lasted for two centuries and changed the course of medieval history. (*See also* **Christianity; Church-State Relations; Crusades; Pilgrimage.**)

Usury

Usury refers to the practice of charging interest on loans. While today the practice is widely accepted (with the term *usury* generally reserved for interest rates that are excessively high), in the Middle Ages usury meant the payment of any interest at all.

Medieval Christian, Jewish, and Islamic law all forbade the repayment of any amount of money greater than the original amount of the loan. On the other hand, the ancient Romans had had no such objections to charging interest on loans, although later Roman law codes had set limits on the interest rates that could be charged.

Nevertheless, the success of the church in portraying usurers as wrong-doers who deserved punishment in heaven as well as on earth is reflected in the *Divine Comedy,* the great medieval poem of DANTE ALIGHIERI. The *Divine Comedy* describes in vivid detail the tortures inflicted on the souls of usurers in the seventh circle of hell. (*See also* **Excommunication; Law; Trade.**)

Valencia

See map in Aragon (vol. 1).

* **parliament** meeting or assembly of elected or appointed representatives

* **viceroy** person appointed to rule a country or province as the official deputy, or representative, of the ruler

* **charter** written grant from a ruler conferring certain rights and privileges

* **feudal** referring to the social, economic, and political system that flourished in western Europe during the Middle Ages

Valencia is both a province and a city on the Mediterranean coast of SPAIN. During the early Middle Ages, Valencia was controlled at different times by the VISIGOTHS, the Byzantines, and the Muslims. In the 1200s, it became a separate Christian kingdom within the kingdom of ARAGON. The region's many active seaports helped Valencia become a major trading power in the Mediterranean. By the 1400s, the city of Valencia had become the most important city of Spain, rivaling other European trading giants, such as VENICE.

When the Muslims conquered Spain in the 700s, Valencia became part of the region of Arabic Spain known as al-Andalus. In 1094, Valencia was briefly reconquered from the Muslims by the Spanish soldier and hero known as the CID. The province was taken back by the Muslims in 1102. Finally, between 1232 and 1245, Valencia was captured from the Muslims by James I, the king of Aragon and count of BARCELONA.

James I established Valencia as a separate kingdom within Aragon and allowed it to have its own parliament*, currency, and laws. In James's day, the region prospered with many large castles and walled towns. Heavily irrigated plains dotted its coastal regions, and bustling port cities linked it in trade with North Africa, the Balearic Islands, and southern France. Despite the Christian conquest and efforts to colonize the region with Christians, Muslims remained in the majority for many years, and they maintained their own laws, language, and religion.

James I organized his new kingdom with an administration headed by a viceroy*, who was assisted by other officials. The parliament, or cortes, initially met only during crises but later evolved into a permanent representative group. Each town in the kingdom elected executive officers, a legislative council, and a court. Local customs were codified into law by charters*. The crown controlled most of the cities and a great amount of land. However, the nobility and the church dominated other areas, and their rights were protected by feudal* privileges. As a result, Valencia was a mixture of land and interests of the king, the nobility, and the church and semi-independent territories.

Valencia developed a rich history and culture in the later Middle Ages. It was home to many religious orders and provided the church with several popes. A university was founded in 1245, and higher education flourished. Europe's first psychiatric hospital was established in the city of Valencia in 1409. The kingdom became a bridge for the exchange of medical knowledge from the Islamic world to Europe. Valencia's celebrated paper industry, founded by the Muslims, helped to spread the use of paper in Europe.

When printing came into use in the 1400s, the city of Valencia became Spain's most important publication center.

The 1400s were, in many ways, the golden age in Valencia. The city was a prosperous commercial and cultural center. Literature flourished with many remarkable poets, writers, and musicians. This period was also a time of great unwillingness to accept others of different religious views, including Muslims, and especially Jews. The INQUISITION began its activity in Valencia in 1484. This intolerance—combined with internal strife, corruption, commercial crises, piracy, and PLAGUE in the 1500s—marked the end of the medieval period in Valencia. (*See also* **Castellan; Jews, Expulsion of; Spain, Muslim Kingdoms of.**)

Vandals

See map in Migrations, Germanic (vol. 3).

* **booty** prizes of war

The Vandals were a Germanic people who entered the Roman Empire in the early 400s. They settled first in Spain and then in North Africa, where they lived for about a century until their defeat by the BYZANTINE EMPIRE. The region of Andalusia in southern Spain is named after them.

The Vandals originated in SCANDINAVIA or the Baltic region. In the first century, they began migrating south and settled in eastern Europe. Pressure from the HUNS in the late 300s forced the Vandals and other Germanic peoples westward into the Roman Empire. The Vandals moved into Spain in 409, but within a few years they were driven farther south by the VISIGOTHS.

Under the leadership of King Genseric, the Vandals left Spain in 429 and migrated to the Roman provinces of North Africa. As a result of several treaties with the Romans, the Vandals took control of the richest parts of that region. In 455, the Vandals captured ROME and pillaged the city for two weeks. They carried off booty* and took many captives, including the widow and two daughters of the emperor, Valentinian III. The Vandals also raided Sicily and other islands, virtually paralyzing Mediterranean commerce.

Vandal power slowly declined after 477 as a result of internal and external pressures. Their rule in North Africa ended in 533 when Byzantine forces sent by Emperor JUSTINIAN I easily defeated the Vandal army. Within a short time, all traces of Vandal occupation had disappeared. The actions of the Vandals, however, are remembered in the English word *vandalism*, which means malicious or wanton destruction of property. (*See also* **Migrations, Germanic.**)

Venice

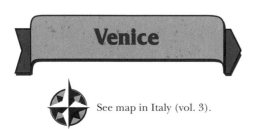

See map in Italy (vol. 3).

The Italian city-state of Venice was one of the leading powers of medieval Europe. Rising on mudbanks and little islands in lagoons along the northern Adriatic Sea, the city and its history were greatly influenced by geography. Situated between the BYZANTINE EMPIRE to the east and European states to the north and west, Venice became a great center of commerce and trade. Its wealth came from shipping goods from one corner of the world to another. In a world that was largely rural

Venice was one of the largest cities in medieval Europe and was an important center of international commerce. It is located in northern Italy at the center of a shallow lagoon on the Adriatic Sea. This late medieval map shows Venice with its system of canals, including the Grand Canal near the center, which cuts the city in half. Venice had few economic rivals during the Middle Ages.

* **feudal**   referring to the social, economic, and political system that flourished in western Europe during the Middle Ages

* **apostle**   early follower of Jesus who traveled and spread his teachings

* **relic**   object cherished for its association with a martyr or saint

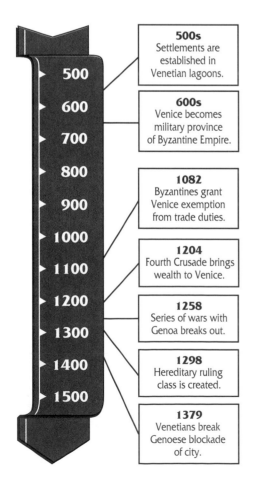

500s
Settlements are established in Venetian lagoons.

600s
Venice becomes military province of Byzantine Empire.

1082
Byzantines grant Venice exemption from trade duties.

1204
Fourth Crusade brings wealth to Venice.

1258
Series of wars with Genoa breaks out.

1298
Hereditary ruling class is created.

1379
Venetians break Genoese blockade of city.

and feudal*, and dominated by warriors and religious officials, Venice was almost unique: an urban commercial center ruled by wealthy merchants and their families.

Early History.   According to local legend, Venice was founded in the early Christian era by the apostle* Mark while he was preaching Christianity in the region. In reality, the area was largely uninhabited until the late 300s, when its isolated mud flats and islands became a refuge for Romans fleeing the mainland during the Germanic invasions. The destruction on the mainland caused by successive waves of invaders, particularly the Lombards, convinced many Romans to remain in the lagoons. By the late 500s, a dozen settlements existed in the area. One of these, the Rialto, would later became the heart of the city of Venice.

The lagoon settlements became a sanctuary for Roman culture. For the Byzantines, the area was an important link with the West and a base of operations to extend their control along the western Adriatic coast. By the end of the 600s, the lagoon area had become a military province of the Byzantine Empire, ruled by a dux. In time, the dux, or doge, became the chief executive of Venice.

In the late 700s and the early 800s, the CAROLINGIANS attempted to gain control of the lagoon communities. Their failure to conquer the Rialto marked the beginning of that community as the center of Venice. In 810, Venice gained important rights from the Byzantines, including the right to trade in Carolingian territory in the West. About this same time, the remains of the apostle Mark were brought to Venice from Egypt. A chapel was built to house the saint's relics*, and this eventually evolved into the magnificent cathedral of San Marco. These events were important steps toward greater independence and wealth.

Emerging Independence.   In the 800s and the 900s, as Byzantine influence in the West weakened, Venice aggressively extended its control over the northern Adriatic. It defeated neighboring towns, set up connections in conquered regions, destroyed pirate strongholds, and established a naval presence to keep the seas open and to prevent Muslim forces from advancing up the coast. As a reward for military aid against the Muslims, the Byzantine emperor granted the Venetians various privileges, including a reduction in taxes on imports and other trade advantages. In 1082, the emperor granted Venetians other special rights, including not having

How Venice Prospered

Venetian power rested on a government-controlled navy and privately run businesses. Venetian ships were built by private builders to standards set by the government. The city's fleets were organized, led, and protected by the state, and each voyage was under government control.

In contrast, the raising of money for business ventures was private and was restricted to Venetian citizens. Money for commercial ventures was raised in a variety of ways: the sea loan, a straight loan at a high rate of interest; the cambio, a bill of exchange; and the *colleganza*. The *colleganza* involved two investors: one who invested money, and another who invested time and effort and actually took the physical risks of a trading voyage. The partners split the profits. For the partner who made the voyage, it was possible to gain profits with very little money. For the money investor, a successful venture usually provided a good return on the investment.

* **crusades** holy wars declared by the pope against non-Christians. Most were against Muslims, but crusades were also declared against heretics and pagans.

* **booty** prizes of war

* **hereditary** passed on from parent to child

See color plate 7, vol. 1.

to pay taxes on trade within the empire, the right to live under their own laws, and the right to establish commercial districts in other cities. These privileges assured Venice a leading role in the trade of the empire and the Mediterranean region. Venice soon became one of the richest cities in Europe.

During the 1100s, Venice faced problems at home and elsewhere. At home, power struggles among different groups led to a number of political reforms, including limitations on the power of the doge and the establishment of a group of advisers to him. Yet, political power remained in the hands of wealthy merchants, whose commitment to commercial growth helped produce more wealth for the city. Abroad, Venice faced increasing resentment and hostility from its economic competitors, especially the Byzantine Empire and the city of GENOA. In the 1100s, popular uprisings and incidents of violence threatened Venetian traders and communities in the empire, and steps were taken to limit Venetian privileges. In 1171, the Byzantine emperor ordered the arrest of all Venetians in the empire and seized their property. The Venetians responded by sending a large, but unsuccessful, naval force against the Byzantine Empire. Despite such problems, Venice continued to flourish.

New Power and Wealth.   Venice entered a new phase of power and wealth during the crusades*. During the Fourth Crusade, Venice was assigned to transport European crusaders to the Holy Land. As partial payment for this service, Venice received a large share of booty* when the crusaders attacked and plundered CONSTANTINOPLE in 1203 and 1204. The immense wealth gained from this crusade solidified Venice's position as a leading European power.

Once again, success brought problems. Increased wealth led to renewed internal tensions, as new merchant families competed with old established families for political power and social status. The city also endured a long series of wars with Genoa. War broke out between the two powers in 1258, with the first victory going to Venice. Triumph was short-lived, however, and Venice suffered a series of major defeats in the late 1200s. This period of war was just the beginning of a conflict that continued until the late 1300s.

Venetian dominance in the East began to wane in the late 1200s and the 1300s as a result of growing competition, a slowing of economic growth, and shrinking markets. Continuing losses in the war with Genoa, plus the burden of its cost, created new tensions in the city, and these led to further changes in government. In 1298, a hereditary* ruling class was created, and political participation was limited to about 200 wealthy families. A large, centralized government emerged in the early 1300s, with power in the hands of two groups: the Council of Forty, which was concerned mainly with criminal and internal matters, and the Senate, which was concerned with diplomatic and commercial concerns.

The last phase of the war with Genoa began in the 1370s, when the Genoese sailed up the Adriatic and threatened the lagoon cities. In 1379, the Genoese navy approached Venice and tried to starve the city and force it to surrender. The Venetians, however, blockaded the Genoese ships in the lagoon and starved them into submission instead. This was a great victory for Venice. Early in the 1400s, Venice conquered a number of territories in northeastern Italy. This expansion broadened Venetian economic interests and laid the foundation for its continued power and prosperity. With its triumph over Genoa and its move onto the mainland, Venice consolidated the rule of a merchant nobility over a commercial empire connecting East and West. It also created a territorial state that dominated some of the richest lands in Italy. (*See also* **Commune; Crusades; Italy; Lombards, Kingdom of; Trade.**)

Vikings

The term *Vikings* refers to the Scandinavians who sailed out of their northern homelands of Norway, Sweden, and Denmark in the 800s, 900s, and early 1000s. Propelled by a need for more land and the rapid growth of population, Vikings raided, plundered, settled, and traded from the North Atlantic in the west to Russia in the east. Their warriors made their presence felt in Europe and the Mediterranean and struck fear into the hearts of all who experienced their onslaught. The period of Viking expansion took place from about 800 to about 1050. This era is called the Viking Age.

In Scotland and Ireland.   The first Viking raids were accomplished by warriors from Norway and occurred in the British Isles around 793. Sharing a North Sea location with the Norsemen (Vikings from Norway), the British Isles presented an accessible target. Setting out from the fjords (deep sea inlets) of Norway's coast, the Norse sailed south to the Orkney and Shetland Islands off Scotland's north coast. After raiding the islands and both the Irish and Scottish coasts of the Irish Sea, the Vikings settled Orkney and Shetland. Both islands remained under Scandinavian control for the rest of the Middle Ages.

In the early 800s, the Norse began raiding along the coasts of Ireland. By the 830s, they had established permanent settlements there. Some of these grew into such towns as Dublin, Limerick, Wexford, Wicklow, and Cork. During the 900s, the Norse made political connections with the Vikings at York, a town in the north of England. When Ireland's Vikings converted to Christianity and intermarried with the native Irish, their absorption into Irish culture became inevitable.

Nevertheless, the Viking destruction greatly disrupted the culture of Ireland. Viking attacks put an end to the Irish production of illustrated manuscripts, which had achieved a high level of sophistication. The production of metalwork and stonework also suffered. The anonymous Irish author of *The War Against the Foreigners* recalled the era of destruction with bitterness: "If each tongue shouted incessantly in a hundred thousand voices, they could never list the sufferings which the Irish—men and women, laity and clergy, young and old—endured from these warlike, savage people."

In the North Atlantic.   The excellent ships and navigational skills of the Vikings allowed them to sail west into the stormy North Atlantic from Shetland. They explored and settled the Faeroe Islands, Iceland, Greenland, and eventually North America.

A Famous Forgery

A map of the world showing Vinland appeared in 1965 and was immediately hailed as the only pre-Columbian map to show North America. However, the unusually accurate depiction of Greenland and some other features raised doubts about the map's authenticity. In 1972, analysis of the map using modern techniques revealed that the ink on the map contained a chemical compound unavailable before 1920. Even the map's strongest defenders were forced to admit that it was a forgery.

Iceland was the major achievement of Viking overseas settlement. With the exception of a few Irish monks, the island had no native population when the Vikings arrived. Thus, there was no need for conquest and there were no people to absorb. Once Iceland was sighted by the Vikings in the 860s, a period of intense settlement followed. Between 870 and 930, the population of the island grew to between 15,000 and 25,000. The Icelandic Vikings adopted Christianity around 1000, when two Icelandic chieftains returned from Norway, where they had been converted by King Olaf Tryggvason. They convinced the other chieftains to accept Christianity.

For the Vikings, Iceland was a stepping-stone into the North Atlantic. Eric the Red reached Greenland in the 980s and returned to Iceland to organize a colonizing party. Twenty-five ships set out for the new land, but only 14 arrived. The surviving settlers established towns on the southwestern coast. Christian missionaries soon followed, and religious communities and dioceses* were founded. By the 1400s, however, the Greenland settlements ended, probably as a result of the harsh climate.

The North American continent was within easy reach of Greenland, and the Vikings landed and settled there briefly about 1000. One of the Icelandic sagas, called *Greenlanders' Saga,* tells how Bjarni Herjolfsson was thrown off his course in 985. The Viking was on his way from Iceland to Greenland when a violent storm broke out. Sailing west, Herjolfsson sighted land in three different places before he returned to Greenland. Years later, Leif, son of Eric the Red, retraced Herjolfsson's route and landed in all three places. Farther south, Leif sighted another land. He called this place Vinland. Later expeditions by Leif's relatives to this site led to settlements. However, none of the settlements on Vinland lasted more than three years. The Vikings' hostile contact with native peoples, called Skraelings by the Vikings, may have been the reason for the failure of the settlements.

In the 1960s, excavations at L'Anse aux Meadows in Newfoundland uncovered the remains of a medieval Viking settlement. Archaeologists estimate that it may have been inhabited for 20 or 30 years. However, there is no evidence to link this site with Vinland.

Danes in Frankish Lands and Beyond. Vikings from the Danish peninsula made major raids on the lands of the FRANKS beginning in 834. At first, these raids were seasonal. Between spring and autumn, Viking raiding parties attacked randomly along the French coast and up rivers. However, after 850, the Vikings spent the winter in Frankish lands as well. Monks fled their monasteries, and people living along the coasts and rivers moved inland. Some communities paid ransom (later called DANEGELD) to avoid attack, but the Vikings simply took the silver and attacked elsewhere.

Some Vikings sailed all the way to Spain and the Mediterranean. From 859 to 862, a fleet of 60 Viking ships raided the eastern shores of Spain and the Balearic Islands, sailed up the Rhône River to Valence, and attacked Italy.

The greatest period of Viking destruction lasted from 879 to 892. During this time, a great Viking army plundered unchecked between the Seine and the Rhine Rivers, while other Vikings raided the Loire region.

* **diocese** church district under a bishop's authority

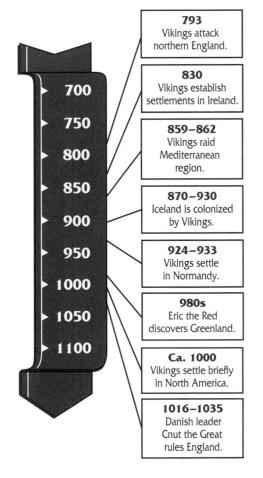

793
Vikings attack northern England.

830
Vikings establish settlements in Ireland.

859–862
Vikings raid Mediterranean region.

870–930
Iceland is colonized by Vikings.

924–933
Vikings settle in Normandy.

980s
Eric the Red discovers Greenland.

Ca. 1000
Vikings settle briefly in North America.

1016–1035
Danish leader Cnut the Great rules England.

700
750
800
850
900
950
1000
1050
1100

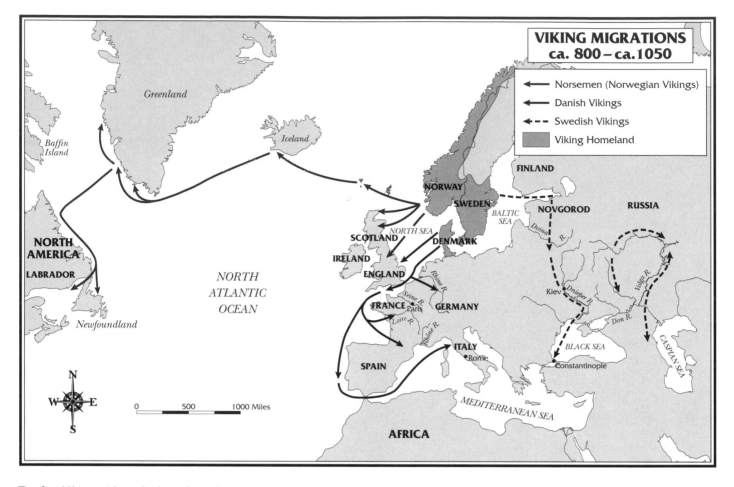

Viking migrations map caption:

VIKING MIGRATIONS ca. 800 – ca. 1050

→ Norsemen (Norwegian Vikings)
→ Danish Vikings
⇢ Swedish Vikings
▨ Viking Homeland

The first Viking raids took place along the northern English coast in 793. For the next two and a half centuries, Vikings migrated east throughout Europe and into Russia. To the west, they reached as far as North America.

* **duchy** territory ruled by a duke or a duchess

* **chronicle** record of events in the order in which they occurred

In the Seine region, the Viking army spent a year besieging PARIS and pillaging the countryside. In 892, Francia was beset by famine and disease, possibly as a result of an exceptionally bad harvest. The Vikings left for more fruitful lands, many of them sailing to England.

The final phase of Viking history in Francia began after 900. At this time, the Vikings attempted to settle in the land of the Franks. King Charles the Simple and the Viking leader, Rollo, reached an agreement by which the Vikings were allowed to settle in the lower Seine in return for defending the region. The original area of Viking settlement expanded in 924 and again in 933. The Viking settlers became known to the Frankish people as NORMANS, and the land they settled became the medieval duchy* of Normandy. Soon other Viking settlers came from Denmark, northeastern England, and Ireland. They quickly adopted French customs and the Christian religion. These Normans abandoned their language and left behind few traces of their Viking past.

Danes in England.   Danish Vikings settled in England in two waves. The first period of settlement took place between 835 and 954. The second one took place between 980 and 1035. Viking raids had been occurring along the southern coast of England before the arrival of a great Danish army in East Anglia in 865. As noted in an Anglo-Saxon chronicle*, the Vikings took horses in East Anglia and went north to seize York. The Danes controlled East Anglia, Mercia, and Northumberland until 878,

See color plate 12, vol. 2.

when King Alfred the Great defeated them. The Danish leader Guthrum converted to Christianity and left Wessex, and he and Alfred agreed on a boundary between their lands.

York became the center of a Viking kingdom from which the Danes exercised power as far west as Dublin. Large numbers of Danes settled in northern England during the late 900s, as evidenced by the many Scandinavian words in the English language. Some of these include *happy, call, law,* and *ill.* Danish control of York ended in 954, but Viking power in England continued.

The second wave of Danish attacks were national campaigns led by the Danish royal family and its generals. From 991 to 1009, the English king Ethelred II the Unready was forced to pay more than 100,000 pounds of silver in danegeld to the Danish invaders. However, tribute was not enough. The Danes seized the English crown, first in 1014 and then in 1016, when Cnut the Great became king of England. Cnut ruled England until 1035. He also became the Danish king in 1019 and king of Norway in 1028.

Swedes in Russia. In the early 800s, Vikings from Sweden crossed the Baltic Sea and penetrated the river systems of Russia. They settled first at Novgorod, then farther south. There, under the leadership of Rurik, they founded Kievan Rus. In the years immediately after 989, the conversion to Christianity of Vladimir I, the leader of Kievan Rus, resulted in the baptism of much of the population, as well as closer commercial ties with Byzantium*. Intermarriage between the Vikings and the native population created a new group of Slavic people—the Russians. (*See also* **Exploration; Historical Writing; Navigation; Scandinavia; Scandinavia, Culture of; Ships and Shipbuilding.**)

 See map in Kievan Rus (vol. 3).

* **Byzantium** ancient city that became Constantinople; also refers to the Byzantine Empire

Villages

Villages, rural communities surrounded by fields, were the principal environment in which people lived until the 1800s, when the Industrial Revolution drove people to the cities.

Origins of Villages. Before the Middle Ages, Europe did not have many settled communities that could be called villages. Rural life was usually organized around the single household. People lived on isolated farms or in hamlets of two or three households. People identified themselves with a family, clan, or tribe, rather than with a geographical location. Their sense of community came from kinship ties, not from where they lived.

The Romans organized the countryside of their empire around individual farmsteads, called villas. These farmsteads were located near trading posts along the roads. Some of the villages that later emerged on lands belonging to the Roman Empire—from Italy to England—were probably located on the sites of old Roman villas.

Historians and archaeologists* are still studying the history of villages to determine when people first began to gather together in large numbers of villages. Some have suggested that village settlement originated as early as the 500s. These early villages, however, were often not permanent. Archaeologists who have uncovered and examined traces of early medieval

* **archaeologist** scientist who studies past human cultures, usually by excavating ruins

communities in England, Germany, and elsewhere have discovered that many villages formed and were abandoned after a few generations. Other villages were inhabited very briefly, perhaps only for a few years, and then their inhabitants moved on. New villages were later built on the sites of some of these early settlements. Other early village sites remained abandoned forever.

The rural settlement patterns of the middle medieval period emerged over several centuries. The individual farmsteads that the Romans had built across Europe were mostly abandoned between the 200s and the 600s. However, this period was not necessarily the time when the villages were first settled. During the early Middle Ages, much of the European countryside was uninhabited.

The growth of villages took place in two stages. The first stage is difficult to date because it occurred at different times in different parts of Europe. This initial stage was hastened as people felt a weakening of the ties that linked them to their clans or tribes. Instead of identifying themselves in terms of kinship, individuals and families started to identify themselves by where they lived. People who lived in the same area began to see that they were linked by a shared neighborhood, even though they did not yet live in a central place but remained scattered across the countryside. This stage in the history of villages has been called the territorial community. People living within a territorial community worked together to enforce and to maintain local law and order, and to decide how public resources—such as timber, water, and grazing pastures—could best be shared.

Certain settlements existed side by side with the territorial communities. These were the great manors of the nobles. Manors were much like the old Roman villas. They included slaves and peasants who were dependent on the lord for their livelihood.

Beginning in the 800s and continuing through the 900s, the territorial communities and the lordly households entered the second stage in the history of villages. During this stage, people living in a territorial community drifted toward a population center, which eventually became a village. The term *village* comes from the Latin word *villa*.

Rural dwellers moved into villages for many reasons. In places where the countryside was lawless or dangerous, people sought safety in numbers. They also realized that living close together made it easier to cooperate on community projects, such as building a bridge or clearing a field. Lords and nobles supported the growth of villages too. During this period, the lords gained much authority and built castles for themselves and their families. Country folk found themselves increasingly under the authority of these powerful individuals. Landowners wanted the peasants who worked their land to live in one place so that the landlord's agent—called a reeve—could more easily collect rents or taxes from the peasants. Some villages grew up around castles or manor houses. Others sprang up along well-traveled roads. Christianity also helped many villages get started. As churches were built across the countryside, villages grew up around them. The church could serve as a meeting hall, a warehouse, or a place of refuge as well as a place of worship.

By the year 1000, stable villages had formed across Europe, especially in areas where most people made their living from the land.

Remember: Consult the index at the end of Volume 4 to find more information on many topics.

Village Justice

In many parts of Europe, the final say in matters of guilt and punishment lay with the local lord, but villagers also took much responsibility for maintaining law and order. Communities invented ways to keep the peace. They fined people for violent, drunken, or insulting behavior. Serious offenders could be punished with mockery or even banishment. Villagers appointed constables to patrol the lanes and roads and chose officials to round up stray animals. Some villages had fire prevention rules, since a single fire could destroy an entire community of thatch-roofed houses.

See color plate 3, vol. 1.

See map in Black Death (vol. 2).

Villages dotted central England, the grain-growing regions of northern Europe, the Mediterranean plains of southern France and Italy, and the open lands of Spain and of central and eastern Europe. In other parts of Europe, where the growing of grain was less important, there were fewer villages. In rugged or mountainous regions—such as the Alps, the highlands of central Europe, and the Pyrenees Mountains of northern Spain—isolated individual homesteads remained scattered over the countryside.

Village Life. Villages consisted of households, which included a married couple, their children, and perhaps a few elderly or unmarried relatives. The head of the household was the husband or father, who spoke for all members of the household in village affairs. Most records of medieval villages contain information only about the heads of households. Villages were not assemblies of equals. People living in a medieval village were very much aware of which households were the most prosperous, and the heads of these households generally had the greatest influence in the village councils.

Villages ranged in size from 10 households with a total of about 50 people (anything smaller was a hamlet) to well over 200 households with more than 1,000 people. Unlike the larger, busier settlements called market towns, villages did not have major markets to attract buyers from the surrounding area. Instead, several villages would send produce and other wares to the nearest market town to be traded or sold.

The history of the village is a history of fields as well as of houses. The center of the village was an area of houses, built near a castle, manor house, or church. Around this core were vegetable gardens, orchards, and outbuildings, such as stables. Beyond lay the fields from which the villagers drew their livelihood.

By the 1200s, three kinds of field systems had been developed by villagers. Each system reflected a specific landscape. The open-field system, which probably dates from the 700s or the 800s, was common in central England and across the fertile plain that stretched from France to Poland. In this system, farmland was made up of long, narrow strips that were grouped together in blocks. The holdings of individual peasants or of landlords consisted of strips scattered among various blocks. Crops were raised on different strips each year, and animals could graze on the strips that were not planted with crops. In the infield-outfield system, used in northern Europe, grain fields near the village were farmed intensively, while fields farther away were used as pastures for grazing animals. The Mediterranean system continued the Roman practice of mixing vegetable gardens, olive and chestnut groves, and vineyards with small grain fields. In each case, peasants spread out from the residential core of the village in the morning to work their fields and the fields belonging to their landlords, and they returned to their homes in the center of the village at night.

Much of Europe was ravaged by PLAGUES and war during the middle and the late 1300s. During this time, most villages lost large segments of their population, and some villages disappeared entirely. In one area of southern France, for example, a tax record from 1471 lists 577 villages, but 157 of them had no inhabitants. When villages were resettled in the 1400s and the 1500s, people tended to build solid, long-lasting homes. Village houses built before about 1459 seldom lasted for more than one or two generations, but some of those built around 1500 still survive. Even where villages were completely rebuilt after the Middle Ages, however, the villagers continued to use the fields that had been laid out by earlier medieval farmers. Fields, rather than buildings, are the best surviving traces of medieval villages. (*See also* **Agriculture; Castles and Fortifications; Family; Feudalism; Nobility and Nobles; Serfs and Serfdom.**)

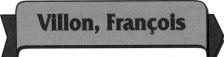

Villon, François

ca. 1431–ca. 1463
Poet

François Villon was one of the best-known poets of the Middle Ages. His adventurous life made him a popular hero in romantic tales set in medieval PARIS. Although his taste for autobiographical poetry puts him very much in the spirit of poets of the 20th century, his life was a good deal more exciting than that of most modern poets.

François Villon was born in poverty in Paris, where he was adopted by a priest. He served for a time in the minor ranks of the CLERGY and studied at the University of Paris. Unable or unwilling to take up a career, Villon spent the rest of his life living by his wits.

In 1455, he was charged with theft and the murder of a priest and was sent to prison. Released by authorities when they issued a pardon of prisoners in honor of a celebration, he was then received at the court of Charles of Orleans. However, before long he was sent away and was reduced to tramping the highways. He was sentenced to death for a minor crime, but he was released on appeal and was exiled from Paris. What happened to Villon after 1463 is not known. What is certain, however, is that he found the time, perhaps while in hiding or in prison, to create some of the greatest poems ever written in the French language.

His surviving works include two mock wills, the *Lais* (1456) and the *Testament* (1461), and various BALLADS and other poems. Two of his most admired poems are the "Debate Between Villon and His Heart" and the "Ballad of Hanged Men." Villon's writings capture the sights, sounds, people, and folklore of Paris in the 1400s. The energy of his language and the complexity of his emotions have kept his work alive for more than five centuries. (*See also* **French Language and Literature.**)

Vincent Ferrer, St.

1350–1419
Preacher

For 20 years, the DOMINICAN preacher Vincent Ferrer traveled across Europe preaching to thousands of people. Bands of flagellants (followers who whipped themselves in penance for their sins) assisted him in his travels. In his SERMONS, Vincent urged his listeners to confess their sins, renounce their evil ways, and prepare themselves for the Last Judgment, which he said was approaching. During a troubled time, brought on by the BLACK DEATH and the Great SCHISM, he sometimes preached to as many as 20,000 people at a time. His preaching was said to have moved even those who did not understand Spanish.

Born in VALENCIA, Vincent entered the Dominican Order at age 17 and was ordained* 12 years later. He served as confessor to Queen Yolanda

* **ordain** to bless, dedicate, and appoint to a particular level of the clergy. Ordination is performed by a bishop in the Roman Catholic and Eastern Orthodox Churches.

of ARAGON for four years before moving to AVIGNON to be the confessor and chaplain of the newly elected pope Benedict XIII. On October 3, 1398, during a serious illness, Vincent had a vision of Jesus standing between St. DOMINIC and St. FRANCIS OF ASSISI and urging him to "go forth and preach."

For the rest of his life, Vincent did exactly that. He preached throughout Europe, at first walking, but then, when his health began to fade, riding a donkey. In 1418, close to the end of his life, he preached before King HENRY V OF ENGLAND in Normandy.

Vincent helped end the Great Schism by persuading King Ferdinand I of CASTILE to withdraw Spain's support for the antipope* in Avignon. The Parisian theologian John GERSON wrote to Vincent, "But for you, this union [of the papacy] could never have been accomplished." (*See also* **Papacy.**)

* **antipope** one who claims the pope's title but is not recognized in modern lists as a legitimate pope

Vincent of Beauvais

ca. 1190–ca. 1264
Friar and encyclopedia writer

* **priory** small monastery or convent headed by a prior or prioress

The largest and most comprehensive encyclopedia of the Middle Ages may have been the work of a DOMINICAN friar whose life and identity are buried in shadows. Vincent was born in Beauvais around 1190. He studied at the University of Paris and was one of the first to join the newly founded Dominican house of St. Jacques in Paris. In about 1230, he was transferred to a new priory* in his hometown of Beauvais, where he pursued his scholarly interests and served as assistant to the prior in the 1240s. The turning point for his scholarly work came when King LOUIS IX OF FRANCE learned of his collection of quotations and passages from the works of great authors. The king requested a copy for himself and provided the money Vincent needed to finish the project.

Vincent's three-part work, *Speculum maius*, summarized all the knowledge from ancient and Christian thinkers that was available at the time. The first part, *Speculum naturale*, was a survey of all SCIENCE and learning. It covered scientific topics from ALCHEMY to zoology and praised the scholarship of the ancients. The second part, *Speculum historiale*, traced the history of the world from the Garden of Eden to the year 1254. The third part, *Speculum doctrinale*, presented intellectual theories about language, MATHEMATICS, economics, and education. Some manuscripts also contained a fourth part, *Speculum morale*, but that was added in the 1300s by an unknown source. The great encyclopedia, which cited more than 400 sources and contained more than 3,000,000 words, was quickly translated into many languages and served as a major reference work for nearly 400 years. (*See also* **Bible; Encyclopedias and Dictionaries.**)

Virtues and Vices

Virtues and Vices are the qualities of good and evil in human thought and conduct. They played a significant role in medieval religion and art.

In ancient Greece, the philosopher Plato discussed the concept of Virtues in his famous work the *Republic*. Plato considered various Virtues to be necessary traits for the ideal citizen. During the Middle Ages, the Christian church adopted and promoted these traits to the faithful. The

* **theological** pertaining to the nature of God, the study of religion, and religious beliefs

* **cardinal** of primary importance

* **fresco** method of painting in which color is applied to moist plaster and becomes chemically bonded to the plaster as it dries; also refers to a painting done in this manner

main Christian Virtues included the three theological* virtues of faith, hope, and charity and the four cardinal* virtues of prudence, justice, temperance, and fortitude. The opposing Vices were idolatry (worshiping false gods), despair, avarice (greed), cowardice, and the Seven Deadly Sins of pride, covetousness, lust, anger, gluttony, envy, and sloth.

In the Middle Ages, the Virtues and Vices often were represented in art by human figures. Considered to belong to a category of angels, the Virtues usually were represented by female figures wearing armor and carrying objects of symbolic meaning. The depiction of Virtues and Vices was popular in medieval frescoes*, sculpture, and illuminated manuscripts. CHARTRES CATHEDRAL, for example, contains sculptures of the Virtues and Vices. In Gothic art, the Virtues often were depicted as walking on their corresponding Vices. The conflict between the Virtues and Vices was also a common theme in medieval literature. For the church, the Virtues and Vices served as a way to teach and spread ideas of morality and righteousness. (*See also* **Allegory; Angels; Cathedrals and Churches; Christianity.**)

Visigoths

* **Moors** Spanish Muslims descended from the Arab conquerors

See map in Migrations, Germanic (vol. 3).

The Visigoths were part of a larger group of Germanic peoples known as the Goths, who migrated from SCANDINAVIA to the Black Sea region during the early Christian era. In the early Middle Ages, the Visigoths migrated into the Roman Empire and finally settled in SPAIN, where they ruled until they were conquered by the Moors* in 711.

In the late 200s, the Visigoths raided eastern parts of the Roman Empire and settled in the Roman province of Dacia. For about 100 years, they lived in relative peace with the Romans, adopting many Roman ideas and customs. Relations between the Visigoths and the Romans began to deteriorate in the late 360s. Even so, when the HUNS defeated the OSTROGOTHS and pushed toward Visigothic territory, the Visigoths asked and received permission to enter the Roman Empire in 376. Tensions soon increased again between the Romans and the Visigoths, and in 378 the Visigoths defeated the Roman army at the Battle of Adrianople.

In 401, under the leadership of King Alaric I, the Visigoths tried to move into Italy, but they were stopped by the VANDALS. In 410, they returned, entered Italy, and sacked ROME. From Italy, the Visigoths entered Gaul (modern-day France) and signed a treaty with the Romans that allowed them to settle in the province of Aquitanica Secunda (AQUITAINE). Under the leadership of King Theodoric I, the Visigoths increased their power, expanded their territory, and helped the Romans fight the Vandals and the Huns.

By the late 400s, the Visigoths controlled a large territory in southern Gaul. However, after their defeat by the FRANKS in 507, they withdrew from Gaul and based their kingdom in Spain. During the late 500s, the Visigoths in Spain accepted Catholic CHRISTIANITY. In the 600s, they adopted laws that helped unite the Roman and Visigothic parts of the population.

Rebellions and civil wars in the late 600s left the Visigothic kingdom badly divided and disorganized. When the Moors invaded Spain in 711, the Visigoths were easily defeated, and their kingdom came to an end. As

the Moors advanced, parts of the Visigothic population retreated to the northwestern part of Spain and eventually created a separate Christian state known as the kingdom of ASTURIAS. (*See also* **Asturias-León; Law; Migrations, Germanic; Spanish Art and Architecture; Spanish Language and Literature; Toledo.**)

Visions

The rich, and sometimes mystical, imagination of the Middle Ages found expression in the literature of visions that appeared all over western Europe in the 1100s and reached a high point in the 1300s.

Medieval CHRISTIANITY encouraged followers to look beyond this world to another. As a result, people perceived reality on different levels. For example, a rose might be a rose, but it also might be something more—a spiritual symbol or the manifestation of an invisible spirit. For the medieval mind, various levels of reality—natural, symbolic, mystical, and moral—sometimes overlapped and merged.

In the 1100s, medieval artists and writers developed an extensive visionary literature to express this many-layered reality. They composed stories about dreams, visions, and mystical experiences. Often the work involved a person falling asleep and having a dream that taught him or her some important lesson about truth. However, some works, such as the *Divine Comedy* of DANTE ALIGHIERI and the *Confessio Amantis* of John GOWER, were not cast explicitly as dreams or visions even though they were clearly visionary writings.

* **vernacular** language or dialect native to a region; everyday, informal speech

Visionary literature was often written in the vernacular*, although some very important works were written in Latin. Those who wrote in Latin include HILDEGARD OF BINGEN, Elizabeth of Schönau, Gertrude the Great, Richard of St. Victor, and St. BONAVENTURE.

Some works were light, while others explored profound philosophical and religious issues. As a whole, they covered the wide range of medieval experience, thought, and imagination. Visionary literature was also one realm of medieval Christianity where women participated in an important way. (*See also* **Allegory; Beguines and Beghards; Boccaccio, Giovanni; Chaucer, Geoffrey; English Language and Literature; French Language and Literature; German Language and Literature; Italian Language and Literature; Latin Language; Petrarch; Roman de la Rose; Spanish Language and Literature.**)

Vizier

Beginning in the late 700s, the chief administrator of the Muslim caliphate* was called the vizier (*wazir* in Arabic). Originally a financial officer who shared power with the chief secretary, the vizier during the time of the ABBASIDS rose to be the caliph's chief executive agent. Today we might call such a person a prime minister.

* **caliphate** office and government of the caliph, religious and political head of the Islamic state

The title originally comes from the QUR'AN, the Islamic holy book, which describes Aaron, the brother of Moses, as his *wazir,* or aide. The role

* **bureaucracy** large departmental organization such as a government

of the vizier was primarily political and administrative. The vizier was not directly concerned with administering justice or with religious matters. Rather, he supervised the operation of the state bureaucracy*. Much of the vizier's work involved receiving communications from administrators and coordinating the operation of different government departments (called *diwans* in Arabic). Later, when many caliphs chose to withdraw from the day-to-day management of state affairs, the vizier became the power behind the throne. Although the office began as the creation of the Abbasid caliphs, other Islamic chief administrators adopted the title. (*See also* **Caliphate; Islam, Political Organization of.**)

Vlad Tepes

ca. 1431–1476
Prince of Walachia

* **depose** to remove from high office

Vlad Tepes fought for Romanian independence from the Turks in the 1400s. His reputation, however, rests on his extreme cruelty. The name *Tepes,* or Impaler, was given to him shortly after his death, and it refers to a particularly brutal method of execution.

Vlad III Tepes (the Impaler)—also known as Dracula, a diminutive form of his father's name Dracul—was a controversial leader in the late Middle Ages. He was regarded as a fighter for Romanian freedom and independence and as a monster who brutally slaughtered thousands of people.

Vlad II Dracul, was the voivode (prince) of WALACHIA, a region in the heart of present-day Romania. He was overthrown by Hungarian forces in 1447. The following year his son, Vlad III, supported by a large Turkish army, returned to Walachia and proclaimed himself voivode. Vlad III's reign lasted only a few months before pro-Hungarian forces drove him into exile.

After 8 years in exile, Vlad changed sides. On September 6, 1456, he swore allegiance to the king of Hungary and then for the next 6 years pursued a policy marked by ferocious cruelty. In the Transylvanian region, he brutalized German merchants, looted and burned villages, and murdered men, women, and children by hoisting them onto long, sharp stakes that ran through the length of their bodies. This method of execution, known as impalement, became his trademark. After Walachian nobles deposed* him in 1462, Vlad fled to Hungary, where for 12 years he was kept under house arrest. In 1476, he returned and soon after was killed in battle by a combined Turkish-Walachian force.

In the years that followed, Vlad's legacy of cruelty vastly overshadowed his reputation as a freedom fighter against the Turks. The enduring image of Vlad Tepes as a bloodthirsty monster paved the way for his later identification with the vampire Count Dracula immortalized in Bram Stoker's novel, *Dracula,* which was published in 1897. (*See also* **Hungary.**)

Walachia and Moldavia

Walachia and Moldavia are neighboring regions on the Balkan peninsula of eastern Europe. Walachia is bordered by the rugged peaks of Hungary's Transylvanian Alps on the north and by the Danube River on the south. Moldavia lies to the northeast of Walachia, between the Carpathian Mountains and the Black Sea. Today, Walachia is part of the country of Romania. Moldavia was part of the Soviet Union from the 1940s, but in the early 1990s it became the independent republic of Moldova.

The Social Pyramid

Society in Walachia and Moldavia was shaped like a pyramid. At the top was a small but powerful class of voivodes and their families. Below them were the officers of the court and the principal landowners. Lower on the social scale—but still members of the privileged classes—were the clergy and the wealthy merchants. Below them were the free peasants, artisans or craftspeople, and miners. Lower still were the serfs, and at the bottom of the pyramid were the slaves. These were mostly Gypsies or prisoners of war. Gypsies often worked for princes as artisans or in wealthy households. Usually they had no rights, and, like prisoners of war, they were treated as property to be disposed of at their master's whim.

 See map in Ottomans and Ottoman Empire (vol. 3).

* **principality** region that is ruled by a prince

By the 1200s, Walachia and Moldavia had been settled by a people called the Vlachs. Although the Vlachs spoke the Romanian language, which is related to Latin, their origins are the subject of intense debate among scholars. Some experts claim that the Vlachs were descended from the Romans who colonized the area during the height of the Roman Empire in the 200s, and that people of Roman origin lived continuously in the region from that time. Other historians argue that the early Roman inhabitants of the eastern Balkans were wiped out by invaders during the early Middle Ages, and that the Vlachs came into Walachia and Moldavia from south of the Danube in the 1200s. Whatever the Vlachs' origin, by the 1200s they overwhelmingly outnumbered the other ethnic groups that lived in Walachia and Moldavia.

In the late Middle Ages, Walachia and Moldavia were semi-independent states ruled by princes called voivodes (from the Slavic word for governor). Because medieval Walachia and Moldavia were frontier states—situated between Latin Western Europe and the BYZANTINE EMPIRE, and later between Christianity and Islam—they were often drawn into wars started by their larger, more powerful neighbors.

History of Walachia.   In the early 1200s, the Hungarian kings treated Walachia as a district of southern Hungary. They built a fortress, called Severin, from which to oversee lands that had been ruled by Vlach voivodes. A century later, a Vlach voivode named Basarab I (1310–1352) defeated a Hungarian army in battle in 1330 and won Walachia's political independence. He was succeeded as voivode by his son, Nicholae Alexandru. The Basarab family ruled Walachia until the 1600s.

The third Basarab voivode, Vladislav I, who ruled from 1364 to 1377, forged an agreement with Hungary. In return for recognizing the king of Hungary as Walachia's overlord, Vladislav was given the fortress of Severin and part of Transylvania. The greatest of the Basarab voivodes was Mircea the Old, who ruled from 1386 until 1418. Mircea expanded Walachian territory to the mouth of the Danube, encouraged the growth of mining and trade, and kept peace with Moldavia, HUNGARY, BULGARIA, and POLAND. Mircea also founded churches and monasteries. During his reign, the greatest threat to Walachia came from the south. The southern Balkan peninsula had been occupied since the late 1300s by the OTTOMANS, an Islamic Turkish people who were at war with the Byzantine Empire. Walachia became the front line of Christian resistance against the Muslim advance into Europe.

After Mircea's death, two branches of the Basarab family fought for control of Walachia. One side was supported by the Ottoman Turks and the other by Hungary. Throughout the middle and late 1400s, Walachia was in turmoil, alternately controlled by Hungary and the Turks. The most notorious voivode of this era was VLAD TEPES, also known as Dracula. When the Ottomans defeated Hungary in 1526, Walachia passed into the hands of the Ottoman Empire.

History of Moldavia.   In the mid-1300s, a Hungarian king sent one of his warlords east across the Carpathians to extend Hungary's borders into the region called Moldavia. Instead, this warlord and his successors set up an independent principality* in Moldavia, attracting Vlach migrants to settle there. Hungary kept trying to gain control of Moldavia, however,

From the late 1300s to the early 1500s, the religious and cultural life of Walachia and Moldavia was largely shaped by the Eastern Orthodox faith. Many Orthodox monasteries, including this one, were built in Moldavia. After Byzantium fell to the Turks in 1453, Moldavia's rulers gave money to the Turks to enable Moldavians to keep their religious traditions.

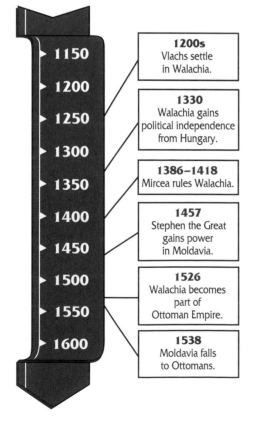

1150		**1200s** Vlachs settle in Walachia.
1200		
1250		**1330** Walachia gains political independence from Hungary.
1300		
1350		**1386–1418** Mircea rules Walachia.
1400		
		1457 Stephen the Great gains power in Moldavia.
1450		
1500		**1526** Walachia becomes part of Ottoman Empire.
1550		
1600		**1538** Moldavia falls to Ottomans.

and in 1387 the Moldavian voivode Petru I Musat accepted Polish overlordship in return for Poland's help against Hungary. In the years that followed, Moldavia made many treaties and alliances with Poland. The contact with the Latin Christian Poles helped introduce Latin CHRISTIANITY to Moldavia.

Alexander the Good was voivode of Moldavia from 1400 until 1432. His reign was marked by religious toleration, increased trade, and the region's participation in the international affairs of eastern Europe. Alexander's death was followed by a fierce power struggle among his sons and grandsons, but in 1457 a voivode called Stephen III the Great came to the throne. During his rule, Moldavia became a major eastern European power. Stephen managed to defend his land against Hungary, Poland, and the Turks. To fend off a Turkish invasion, he rebuilt Moldavia's forts along the lower Danube. Several times Stephen sent troops into neighboring Walachia to topple pro-Turkish voivodes from the Walachian throne, and in 1475 he led a combined force of Moldavian, Hungarian, and Polish troops to victory against a Turkish army. To honor Stephen's victories over the Turks, Pope Sixtus IV called the voivode "the Athlete of Christ."

Stephen was followed by less capable rulers, and gradually Moldavia grew weaker. The principality's strength was drained by disputes with Walachia, by uprisings among the nobility, by the Turkish conquest of Hungary, and by a long war with Poland. In 1538, the Ottoman sultan Süleyman I the Magnificent succeeded in making Moldavia part of the Ottoman Empire. Like Walachia, Moldavia would remain in Ottoman hands until the 1800s.

Cultural and Economic Life.   The religious and cultural life of Walachia and Moldavia was shaped by the Eastern Orthodox faith, the form of Christianity practiced in the Byzantine Empire. Between the late 1300s and the early 1500s, many great Orthodox monasteries were founded in Walachia and Moldavia. During the late 1400s, after the Byzantine Empire fell to the Turks, Moldavia's rulers gave money to Orthodox monasteries in Turkish territory to keep their religious traditions

alive. Latin Christian communities existed (often uneasily) side by side with Orthodox communities in the principalities. Hungary, Poland, and the PAPACY all sent missionaries into the region.

Most books written in Walachia and Moldavia before the mid-1400s were religious texts. The most interesting is a history called *Chronicle of the Days When the Land of Moldavia Was Founded by the Will of God.* It was written under the command of Stephen the Great of Moldavia. The artworks of Walachia and Moldavia were modeled on those of the Byzantines. The most elaborate of these were paintings of religious scenes that covered the outer walls of churches.

The Vlachs were originally migrating herders who lived by raising sheep, cattle, and goats. During the late Middle Ages, they entered enthusiastically into trade with other regions. Wheat, wine, wax, cattle, and honey from Walachia and Moldavia were shipped south along the Black Sea coast and on to Italy, where they were exchanged for cloth and other manufactured items. The Vlachs continued to live mostly in the countryside, while the towns that grew up along trade routes in Walachia and Moldavia were inhabited by a mix of Germans, Poles, Armenians, Jews, Greeks, and Italians.

Waldensians

* **heresy** belief that is contrary to church doctrine

* **lay** not linked to the church by clerical office or monks' and nuns' vows

* **excommunicate** to exclude from the rites of the church

The Waldensians were a group of Christians who lived in western Europe from the late 1100s to the end of the Middle Ages. Waldensianism was the longest-lived, and probably the largest, of all medieval movements called heresies*.

The Waldensian movement was begun by Waldes, a wealthy French merchant from the town of Lyons. About 1173, Waldes had a deeply religious experience that convinced him to give away his wealth and to devote his life to begging and preaching. Waldes quickly gained many followers in and around Lyons.

As Waldensianism grew, church officials became hostile to the movement because it put the CLERGY in a bad light. The Waldensians were ordered to stop begging in public, but they refused. In 1179, Waldes and some followers went to Rome to bring their case before a church council presided over by Pope Alexander III. The officials at the council resented the way that the Waldensians' poverty reflected badly on the great wealth of the church and the clergy. More importantly, however, the church officials strongly condemned the lay* preaching of the Waldensians and ruled that they could preach only if authorized to do so by their local priests. Back in Lyons, the local priests refused to give the Waldensians permission to preach. When the Waldensians disobeyed and preached anyway, they were excommunicated* and expelled from the city. The movement soon spread to other cities in southern France and northern Italy.

At first, the Waldensians were only a troublesome sect, but they soon adopted more heretical ideas and established their own church with their own priests and rituals. The Waldensians considered the Church of Rome to be corrupt, and they condemned its power. They urged that the priests of the Roman Church be ignored and disobeyed and that worthy followers, including women, become the new priests of the Waldensian church. The Waldensians refused to accept the concept of PURGATORY, and they believed that people went directly to either heaven or hell after death. Without Purgatory, there was no need for prayers for the dead or INDULGENCES. The practice of selling prayers for the dead and indulgences was a major source of income for the church, and without it the very existence of the church was threatened. The Waldensians also believed in a literal interpretation of the Bible's moral teachings, urged the reading of the Bible in the vernacular*, and denied the cult of saints.

* **vernacular** language or dialect native to a region; everyday, informal speech

By the time Waldes died, sometime between 1205 and 1218, Waldensianism had spread from its base in southern France and northern Italy and had become firmly established in many areas of western Europe. In some areas of BOHEMIA, MORAVIA, and Germany, entire villages adopted the heretical faith. The reaction of the church to the Waldensians remained mostly hostile. At first, the Waldensians were excommunicated and banished from their towns. Occasionally, INQUISITIONS forced some of them to repent or be burned. Large-scale inquisitions, begun around the 1230s, stopped the spread of Waldensianism in some areas. By about 1300, the movement had been wiped out in urban areas of the Mediterranean region, but it survived in mountainous rural areas. Inquisitions against Waldensians in Bohemia were especially ruthless. Elsewhere in Europe, however, the Waldensians were left alone for long periods until the end of the Middle Ages or longer. They exist in northern Italy and southern France even today. (*See also* **Bible; Christianity; Heresy and Heresies.**)

Wales

* **Briton** person who inhabited Britain before the Anglo-Saxon invasions

See map in England (vol. 2).

In the Middle Ages, Wales was a fiercely independent land located on a wide peninsula in the western part of the British Isles, where Welsh princes fought to preserve their freedom from English rule. Despite pressures from the outside, the Welsh maintained their language and culture and celebrated the heroes of their history in song and poem.

The medieval Welsh were a Celtic-speaking people who, like the neighboring Britons*, had been ruled by the Romans during their occupation of Britain. As the Romans withdrew from the British Isles in the early 400s, other peoples moved into Wales—Britons from the north, Irish from the west, and ANGLO-SAXONS from the east—to create what became the Welsh people. By the early 500s, several Welsh kingdoms began to take shape. These were Gwynedd in the northwest, Powys in the east midlands, Dyfed in the southwest, and Gwent in the southeast. Out of this patchwork of small domains emerged several strong rulers who eventually dominated the other princes and laid the foundation for a united kingdom of Wales.

The most powerful Welsh kingdom in the early medieval period was Gwynedd, located on the island stronghold of Anglesey and ruled by Cadwallon. After the king of Northumbria defeated him in battle in the 600s, Cadwallon fled across the Irish Sea to IRELAND. He later returned to Wales and expanded his kingdom eastward at the expense of the English. Cadwallon's dream of further conquests ended when he was killed in battle by

As England extended political control over Wales, new castles were built in the region. Harlech castle, on the northwest coast of Wales, was built by King Edward I in 1285. Sitting high atop a cliff guarding the approach to Tremadoc Bay, Harlech became an important Lancastrian stronghold during the Wars of the Roses.

the new king of Northumbria. By this time, Wales had become a military frontier subject to attacks by the English. In the 700s, King Offa began construction of a great earth wall, called Offa's Dyke, that stretches about 120 miles along the border between England and Wales.

Failure to Unify.   Although several of the early Welsh kings tried to unite the region, none succeeded. One Welsh leader—Hywel the Good (the only Welsh king ever granted this title)—came close. He ruled over much of Wales for more than 40 years. He issued his own coinage, codified the laws, and made St. David's (a town on the southwestern coast of Wales) a bishop's seat. After Hywel's death in 950, most of what he had accomplished was undone, and a period of disorder followed. According to *Brut y Tywysogion (Chronicle of the Princes),* a valuable source of information about Welsh history in the Middle Ages, about 35 rulers met violent deaths between 950 and 1066 (the Norman conquest). Destructive raids by the VIKINGS no doubt contributed to much of the disorder of these years. Attacks from the east by the Anglo-Saxons also added to the problems of Welsh rulers.

Then, a new hope appeared for the Welsh people. In 1039, Gruffydd ap Llywelyn became the ruler of Gwynedd and Powys. He conducted raids across the border into England and forced the English king, ED-WARD THE CONFESSOR, to make peace. According to *Brut y Tywysogion,* Gruffydd was killed "through the treachery of his own men," indicating the dangers that faced any Welsh ruler who tried to bring other princes under his rule.

The inability of the Welsh to achieve political unification was exploited by the new Norman rulers of England. Soon after he conquered England and became its king, WILLIAM I THE CONQUEROR installed Norman earls in the border area between Wales and England. These marcher lords (from the French word *marche* meaning border or frontier) built castles from which they policed and defended the region.

During the late 1000s, new settlers were attracted to the border area. They worked on the Norman manors and established themselves in the

Lords of the Border

The Norman lords that William the Conqueror installed in the border area between Wales and England used their military skill to expand Norman rule into Wales. From their castle strongholds, the lords exercised kinglike authority over the people under their rule. Unlike their English counterparts, they could wage war on their own, raise armies, and build castles without the king's permission. They were free to exploit the people in their area by collecting rents, confiscating crops, and levying tolls and fines.

* **manor** farming estate, usually with a house for the lord and a village for the local farmworkers

* **homage** formal public declaration of loyalty to the king or overlord

See color plate 7, vol. 3.

* **annex** to add a territory to an existing state

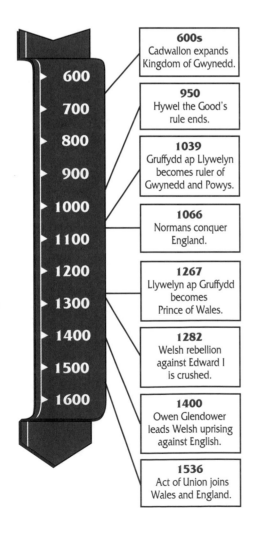

600s
Cadwallon expands Kingdom of Gwynedd.

950
Hywel the Good's rule ends.

1039
Gruffydd ap Llywelyn becomes ruler of Gwynedd and Powys.

1066
Normans conquer England.

1267
Llywelyn ap Gruffydd becomes Prince of Wales.

1282
Welsh rebellion against Edward I is crushed.

1400
Owen Glendower leads Welsh uprising against English.

1536
Act of Union joins Wales and England.

towns that were springing up. Welsh people living on the manors* and in the towns gradually absorbed Norman customs into their native culture. However, the Welsh in the highland regions of the north continued their traditional customs. Two distinct cultures appeared in Wales: Norman, located mainly in the south and border areas, and Welsh, located firmly in the north.

Welsh princes regarded the Norman kings of England as their overlords and paid them homage*, believing that doing so would make them more secure against future Norman aggression. However, the English kings wanted more than Welsh homage; they wanted to rule Wales. King HENRY II tried to conquer Wales but failed and never tried again. Welsh princes such as Owain Gwynedd and Rhys ap Gruffydd frustrated further English attempts at conquest. Their defiance inspired the further growth of Welsh identity. In 1176, Rhys ap Gruffydd invited Welsh poets to Cardigan castle for an eisteddfod, or congress, during which they competed in the performance of songs and poems in praise of ancient Welsh traditions.

In the early 1200s, Llywelyn the Great tried to gain for Wales the same kind of independent status enjoyed by SCOTLAND in relation to the English crown. As Prince of Wales, he paid homage to the king of England on behalf of all other Welsh lords. They, in turn, paid homage to him. In this way, Llywelyn hoped to unify Wales under his rule. As a result of the truce he made with King HENRY III in 1233, he succeeded in achieving his aims. LLYWELYN AP GRUFFYDD also assumed the title of Prince of Wales and gained the homage of important Welsh lords. His undoing was his failure to pay homage to Henry's ambitious and unforgiving successor, EDWARD I. Edward attacked Wales, annexed* Welsh lands, and forced Llywelyn to pay homage. The Welsh were momentarily subdued, but they rose up against Edward in 1282. One year later, the English crushed the Welsh rebellion and executed its leaders.

English Control Strengthened.   The English then extended their political control and the rule of English law over Wales. They divided the land into counties called SHIRES and embarked on an intensive program of castle building. These huge fortresses, bustling with arms and soldiers, supported English rule in a hostile environment and prevented further Welsh uprisings. In 1303, Edward I installed his son, the future EDWARD II, as Prince of Wales in order to make peace with the rebellious Welsh. Many Welsh became supporters of the new English order and served as SHERIFFS and military leaders in the English army.

The last rebel to fight for Welsh independence was Owen Glendower, who led a revolt across Wales in 1400. Students from Oxford University and Welsh laborers in England rushed home to join the revolt. Even Charles VI of France gave his support to Glendower. The English king, Henry IV, quelled the rebellion and forced Glendower to retreat. Frightened by the Glendower uprising, the English joined Wales to England once and for all in 1536. Union came only after Wales served as a battleground between English royal factions—the Lancastrians and the Yorkists—competing for the crown of England. (*See also* **British Isles, Art and Architecture; Celtic Languages and Literature; England; Wars of the Roses.**)

Walter, Hubert

**ca. 1150–1205
Justiciar, chancellor,
and archbishop**

* **crusades** holy wars declared by the pope against non-Christians. Most were against Muslims, but crusades were also declared against heretics and pagans.

* **archbishop** head bishop of a region or nation

* **chancellor** official who handles the records and archives of a monarch

Hubert Walter's service to two English kings made him one of the most powerful administrators of the medieval period in western Europe. In 1190, Walter accompanied RICHARD I THE LION-HEARTED on a crusade* to the Holy Land, where his diplomatic skills impressed the king. After deciding to return home, Richard placed Walter in charge of organizing and supervising the return of his knights while he went on ahead. On Richard's return trip to England, however, he was captured and held for a very large ransom by the emperor HENRY VI OF GERMANY.

Walter eventually reached England, and he took charge of the government as its JUSTICIAR, or administrator, for Richard during the king's absence. In 1193, Walter also became the archbishop* of CANTERBURY. As head of both church and state, Walter demonstrated extraordinary administrative ability. His first task was to raise the money for Richard's ransom. He did so by levying heavy taxes. The English CLERGY were not used to paying taxes, but when Walter insisted that they must, they were in no position to argue with the archbishop. The money was raised and Richard was freed in 1194. The king, however, spent only a few months in England before departing for territorial wars in FRANCE. He never returned.

Walter governed England until Richard's death in 1199. As archbishop of Canterbury, he then crowned King John, who recognized Walter's ability by making him chancellor* of England, a position he held until his death in 1205. (*See also* **Angevins; Church-State Relations; Crusades.**)

Walther von der Vogelweide

**ca. 1170–ca. 1230
Singer and composer**

* **notation** system for recording music using written notes or symbols

* **patronage** the support of an artist, writer, or scholar by a person of wealth and influence

Walther von der Vogelweide was medieval Germany's greatest singer and composer. He was greatly admired in his time for the beauty of his singing voice and the melodies he composed. Unfortunately, there was no reliable musical notation* in his day, and his music has long since been lost. Based on his lyrics that survived, he is now remembered as a poet. It was, however, his ability as a minstrel and creator of musical entertainments that provided him with his living.

Musicians of the medieval period depended on the patronage* of the nobility for their living. During Walther's years (more than 30) as a professional musician, he had many patrons. Some songs praise one potential emperor, while others express admiration for another who also claimed the throne. These political shifts probably reflect a change in patronage.

Walther composed other kinds of songs as well. His love songs were especially popular. He wrote songs about COURTLY LOVE in which he presented the romantic ideal, and he composed love songs in which he celebrated the joys of physical love. Walther also composed religious songs and hymns to be sung in church and by people making PILGRIMAGES.

One of his most popular songs, *Unter der linden,* is about love under a linden tree. Another of his famous songs contemplates the difficulties of obtaining wealth, honor, and God's grace at the same time. One of his final songs, called his *Elegy,* asks, "Where have they vanished, all my many years?" Although Walther was paid to compose great melodies, his memory has endured because of his exceptional lyrics. (*See also* **German Language and Literature; Goliards; Music; Troubadour, Trouvère.**)

See map in Migrations, Germanic (vol. 3).

* **feudalism** social, economic, and political system of western Europe in the Middle Ages in which vassals gave service to their lord in return for his protection and the use of the land

* **mercenary** soldier who fights for payment rather than out of loyalty to a lord or nation

* **provincial** referring to a province or an area controlled by an empire

* **steppe** vast treeless plain of southeastern Europe and Asia

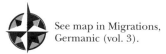

* **Frankish** referring to the Germanic tribe called the Franks, who dominated western Europe in the early Middle Ages

* **chain mail** flexible armor made of small metal rings linked together

The Middle Ages saw significant changes in the way wars were fought. In western Europe, the military tradition under feudalism* gave way to the use of mercenaries* and gunpowder weapons. Both of these changes prepared the way for the advent of modern warfare. Significant changes also took place in Byzantine and Islamic warfare.

Western European Warfare

The history of medieval warfare in western Europe can be divided into three periods: tribal warfare (500–ca. 730), feudal warfare (ca. 730–ca. 1200), and late medieval warfare (ca. 1200–1500).

Tribal Warfare.   Little is known about the warfare of the Germanic peoples who established themselves in the western provinces of the Roman Empire. In the army of the VISIGOTHS, the king was the supreme commander. Under him were the commanders of the provincial* armies and their divisions. The field army consisted of officers and slaves. Both served as the regular fighting troops and were provided with full military equipment. Apparently, the Visigoths learned how to fight on horseback during their years on the Ukrainian steppes*, as they showed by their victory over the Roman legions at Adrianople in 378.

In the kingdom of the LOMBARDS in Italy, military service was required of all freemen. Members of the upper classes served as warriors on horseback (cavalry), while the lower classes made up the foot soldiers (infantry). They all were required to supply their own weapons and armor. The ANGLO-SAXONS in England had a similar system. All able-bodied freemen were obliged to serve in the infantry when summoned.

The FRANKS also required every freeman to be available for military service. Like other Germanic tribes whose original homeland was the forest—where cavalry was of little use—the Franks fought as infantry. After their defeat in 554 at the hands of Byzantine horse archers, however, the Franks began using body armor. By the early 700s, the Frankish* king and great lords and their households rode to battle on horses. However, their main method of fighting was carried out on foot.

Military Feudalism.   Military feudalism developed in the early Middle Ages in response to the collapse of Roman government in western Europe and the threat from the Arabs, who had conquered North Africa and Spain. The decline of trade and the economic slowdown that followed deprived European rulers and lesser lords of the resources they needed to maintain an army.

The Muslim conquest of Visigothic Spain in the early 700s created a crisis for the Franks. This crisis became especially acute after the Arabs pushed across the Pyrenees into southern France. The Arab advance was finally stopped by CHARLES MARTEL near Poitiers in 732, but the Franks were unable to follow up on their victory because they could not chase after the mounted Arabs. As a result, the Franks decided to train troops to fight on horseback.

The introduction of the stirrup in the early 700s gave mounted warriors distinct advantages over the infantry. The horseman—protected by shield, iron cap, and chain mail* shirt—could rise in his stirrups and brace himself to strike the enemy with his lance or sword. A bit and bridle enabled him to maneuver his horse. Until the late Middle Ages, no infantryman was a match for a mounted knight at close quarters.

The arms and armor for mounted service were expensive, however, and the training and the practice needed to control a horse while holding a shield and using a sword or lance were demanding. Trained knights had to be supported financially, since anyone who had land to farm had neither the time for training nor the resources to purchase the necessary equipment. Charles Martel solved the problem by providing his warriors with land grants called fiefs* and peasants to work the land. Other Frankish landowners, lay and church, followed Martel's example. They had at their disposal private armies of mounted knights who could be called to battle at a moment's notice. The collapse of the CAROLINGIAN Empire in the 800s and the VIKING raids that followed accelerated the spread of military feudalism, as those who needed protection sought to join up with lords who could defend them.

Feudalism spread rapidly, reaching its peak in the 1000s, when knights became more interested in developing their land than in military service. By the 1100s, knights in western Europe had to contribute only 40 days of unpaid service to their lord. In England, a knight could even escape that obligation by paying a fine instead of doing military service. Also, the practice of using mercenaries reduced the need for the service of knights. In places where military feudalism was firmly established, such as northern France, warfare was constant. This was true even in such well-run feudal states as Flanders, Normandy, and Anjou.

Norman Warfare.   The military skills of the NORMANS (Vikings who settled in northwestern France) were dramatically displayed in the 1000s when Norman warriors simultaneously established the Kingdom of SICILY, which included southern Italy and Sicily, and conquered England.

When Normans began crossing the Alps and invading southern Italy in the early 1000s, they were hired as mercenaries by Lombard dukes and local Byzantine rulers. However, as more Normans arrived, they seized the land and established themselves as local rulers. In 1071, Normans captured Bari, the last Byzantine stronghold in southern Italy. By 1076, the Normans were in control of most of southern Italy and the island of Sicily, which they had seized from the Muslims in stages. The Normans were able to achieve their military successes with small but highly effective cavalry units. By the early 1100s, the Norman Kingdom of Sicily was the most powerful military state in western Europe.

Norman military skill was demonstrated in the British Isles at the Battle of HASTINGS, when the Norman army of WILLIAM I THE CONQUEROR invaded England and defeated the army of King Harold II. The Norman victory began a new era of English history.

Late Medieval Warfare.   Warfare in western Europe changed after 1200. The improved economy enabled monarchs to hire mercenary troops. Also, vassals* were allowed to fulfill their obligation to their lord by paying others to perform their military service for them. Another change in warfare was that the once powerful infantry again became an important factor in success on the battlefield.

During the Hundred Years War (from 1337 to 1453), the use of the longbow by English infantrymen allowed them to dominate the early

In the history of medieval warfare, few groups struck as much fear into people as the Vikings. With sturdy ships and superior navigational skills, the Vikings attacked and plundered Europe from about 800 to 1050, in a period that has come to be known as the Viking Age. This manuscript illumination from around the 1100s shows a Danish attack on the English town of Thetford.

* **fief** under feudalism, property of value (usually land) that a person held under obligations of loyalty to an overlord

* **vassal** person given land by a lord or monarch in return for loyalty and services

phases of the war. A packed flight of arrows disrupted French knights before they could reach the battle. When the French learned to refrain from fighting pitched battles and switched to tactics of raiding and skirmishing, the tide of battle began to turn in their favor. By switching tactics, and with increased artillery power near the end of the war, the French recaptured all the land they had lost (except Calais).

In the late Middle Ages, the Swiss established themselves as formidable fighters. The Swiss troops could be organized rapidly because universal military service was the rule. In very short order, units from each valley and district, under their own officers and colors, marched to the gathering place to take their positions in the national army. From there, the army marched off to battle. The basic Swiss weapons were the halberd* and a 15-foot-long pike. The Swiss army advanced toward the enemy in three columns, armed with pikes. The halberdiers were situated in the center of the formation. They were ready to advance on the flanks if and when the advancing columns were halted.

The Swiss established themselves as a fierce fighting force when they defeated the powerful army of Charles the Bold, duke of BURGUNDY. The Burgundians consisted of heavily armed cavalry aided by foreign troops with special fighting skills—archers, pikemen, and light cavalry from England, Flanders, and Germany. However, the Swiss army was more cohesive and flexible. It was hard to outflank, and it never waited to be attacked. The Swiss defeated the Burgundians twice—in 1476 and again in 1477 at the Battle of Nancy. Duke Charles was killed at that final clash.

In the late Middle Ages, the history of warfare was forever changed by the invention of gunpowder and the development of firearms. After the first mention of firearms in the early 1300s, references to them appeared with increasing frequency in official documents, chronicles*, and manuscript illuminations.

By the 1400s, large guns, capable of firing stone cannonballs that weighed up to 600 pounds, were in use. In the final phases of the Hundred Years War, Charles VII of France used heavy guns to reduce more than 60 English-held fortresses within the period of little more than a year. By the end of the Middle Ages, the use of cannons and large guns made the castle obsolete as a fortress. Stone battlements and thick walls were no match for artillery.

Byzantine Warfare

After the seventh century, Byzantine warfare was primarily defensive. The Byzantine Empire was more interested in protecting its territory than in conquering new lands. The Byzantines regarded war as a necessity forced on them by hostile and aggressive neighbors. This attitude shaped Byzantine military strategy and foreign policy.

Military Strategy. For most of its history, Byzantium employed a military strategy that sought to reduce military risk and to keep dangerous gambles to a minimum. Instead of striving for a decisive, pitched battle, Byzantine generals tended to rely on cleverness and deception. In battle, they put a premium on timing, creativity, and surprise.

Byzantine military success was greatest when the emperor and his officials in CONSTANTINOPLE allowed their field commanders to act quickly and

* **halberd** weapon with an axlike cutting blade and a sharp, pointed spike

* **chronicles** record of events in the order in which they occurred

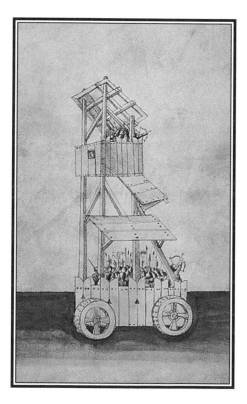

In siege warfare, enemy troops set up a blockade against a walled fortification and attempted to capture it. Special tactics and equipment were used on both sides during a siege. The siege tower, seen in this illumination from the mid-1400s, was moved to where it overlooked the walls of the besieged castle or town. Archers fired down on the defenders, while other soldiers scaled the walls.

decisively when they needed to. Also, during times of long, drawn-out warfare, the Byzantine military did best when a steady and efficient flow of supplies and money was maintained.

Byzantine armies tended to be small, and most campaigns rarely exceeded 20,000 troops. The Byzantines relied on tactics that involved ambushes, ruses, and sudden cavalry charges rather than masses of men fighting in fixed positions. The Byzantines did not station huge armies on their borders to defend their lengthy frontiers. Instead, they kept mobile field armies farther back ready to engage foreign invaders once they had moved into the interior.

Often Byzantine troops tried to cut off and destroy smaller units of an army. Sometimes, they blocked mountain passes needed by foreign invaders to return to their own territory. They engaged in a pitched battle only when they were sure that they possessed overwhelming superiority and that the odds for a victory were good.

Byzantine warfare relied on cavalry and mounted archers more than on infantry. The arrows required by the mounted archers were supplied by districts that specialized in the production of arrows. They were carried to the army on a train that might also transport other supplies for the army, such as shields, javelins, siege machines, chain mail sleeves, metals, timber, leather, cloaks, cloth, containers, carpentry materials, tools, jars, food, and wine.

After the 1000s, the Byzantine Empire depended increasingly on outsiders to maintain its military effectiveness. In its last years, the empire had to hire foreigners who were familiar with the new firearms and artillery.

In lengthy wars that lacked a decisive outcome, the Byzantines often sought peace through negotiation. Sometimes, the military leaders launched campaigns that were designed to create a more favorable bargaining position or to give a boost to peace talks already underway. Throughout the long history of the empire, Byzantine diplomats and generals learned how to negotiate and fight simultaneously in the hope of winning a reasonable settlement.

Islamic Warfare

In the Middle Ages, Muslim armies consisted of warriors from the highest social class, volunteers, conscripts*, and mercenaries. The duty to fight for Islam provided a strong motivation, and warriors were rewarded with wealth and prestige. After the initial wave of Islamic conquests in the 600s and the 700s, most Muslim rulers resorted to the services of paid foreign troops and slaves.

Infantry and Garrison Cities.   Infantry played a central role in early Islamic warfare. In the earliest days of Muslim conquests in the 600s, armies consisted of foot soldiers armed with bows and spears. Their commanders were wealthy nobles on horseback. Camels were used in the Middle East and North Africa for riding and for transporting baggage. The animals were usually placed around the camp to help warn the Muslims of the approach of invaders. Muslims also used ditches to fortify encampments or battlefield positions.

Early Muslim warriors built garrison cities called *amsar* to help them dominate each new territory they conquered. These were usually tents and

---

* **conscripts** men drafted for military service

Better Alive than Dead

Medieval warfare was not destructive by modern standards, especially for members of the aristocracy. Commanders did more maneuvering than fighting, and politics and diplomacy were often more important than battles. During the Hundred Years War, the total amount of actual fighting was only a few weeks.

By the late 1300s, the armor worn by knights in battle had become so heavy that knights rarely engaged in heavy battle or were seriously injured. Also, if a prisoner could afford to, he might buy his freedom by paying a ransom. Thus, a captured enemy soldier might be more valuable alive than dead.

huts surrounding a central area that consisted of the commander's residence and a place for meetings, prayer, and drills. The central area also served as an inner fortress in time of attack. The garrison city as a whole was a base for the launching of the next wave of military conquest.

Cavalry and Infantry. While infantry continued to form the bulk of Islamic fighting forces, the number of horsemen grew with the wealth of the empire and the development of an aristocracy. IRAN, Central Asia, and other places in the eastern part of the empire provided troops trained for cavalry warfare.

A military tradition of the coordinated use of infantry and cavalry developed in Egypt, North Africa, and Spain. Slaves from Europe and Africa provided the manpower for the regiments of foot guards who were used in the center of the battle line. Armed with swords, spears, and round shields, these slave troops stabilized the center of the battle formation and protected the commander and his armored mounted escort, as well as the archers and javelin throwers. A lightly armed cavalry was placed on the wings of the battle formation to harass the enemy. This latter group also might be held in reserve until released to rout the broken ranks of the enemy.

On the frontiers of the empire in Spain and central Asia, Muslim warfare consisted of cavalry raids against non-Muslims. The raids were designed to frighten, confuse, and keep the enemy off balance. The SELJUK Turks, who emerged on the central Asian frontier of the Islamic Empire in the 1000s, conquered Iran by using the Turkoman nomads* who followed them into the Middle East as mounted warriors. The army of SALADIN, who confronted the crusaders* in the Holy Land, employed horsemen trained to charge and retreat, concentrate or scatter, until they formed as one unit for the final attack.

This kind of warfare relied on the speed and mobility of cavalry. Cavalry warfare reached the height of its effectiveness in the 1200s during the rule of the MAMLUKS in Egypt. The OTTOMANS' use of artillery and heavy siege guns toward the end of the Middle Ages anticipated the more destructive weaponry of modern warfare. (*See also* **Armor; Castles and Fortifications; Chivalry; Crusades; Islam, Conquests of; Islam, Religion of; Knighthood; Knights, Orders of; Migrations, Germanic; Slavery; Weapons.**)

* **nomad** person who wanders from place to place to find food and pasture

* **crusader** person who participated in the holy wars against the Muslims during the Middle Ages

Wars of the Roses

The Wars of the Roses consisted of a series of battles fought in England between 1455 and 1487 by the two rival houses of Lancaster and York. Several historical plays by William Shakespeare made the Wars of the Roses a famous part of English history. Shakespeare treated the three decades of battles and intrigues as a dramatic duel for the throne of England between the two noble houses. However, the struggle was more complex than that because many participants switched sides in their pursuit of self-interest, and many nobles avoided participation altogether. By the end of the wars, the ability of English nobles to disrupt national life had been checked, and the authority of PARLIAMENT had been strengthened.

This illumination shows the capture of King Henry VI by the earl of Warwick after the Battle of Northampton in 1460. The name *Wars of the Roses* was not used to describe these dynastic disputes until long after they took place. The badge of the Lancastrians included a red rose; the badge of the Yorkists included a white rose. These symbols, however, probably were not used by the combatants. Writers later used the roses as emblems of the conflict.

First Phase (1455–1461).

HENRY VI OF ENGLAND was the boy king who was on the throne when France finally emerged victorious in the HUNDRED YEARS WAR. This disastrous defeat for England ended that nation's ambitions in Europe and resulted in many strained relationships in English politics.

Since Henry VI was a weak leader and subject to bouts of madness, various nobles were eager to step forward. The most ambitious of these was Richard of York, who confronted the king's supporters on the battlefield at St. Albans on May 22, 1455. The battle lasted only about half an hour and settled nothing (although two important noble supporters of the king were slain).

Henry's wife, Margaret of Anjou, was determined that her young son, Edward, become king. She rallied nobles to her side, raised an army, and, in 1459, persuaded parliament to charge the Yorkists with rebellion. On the battlefield, however, neither side was able to win a decisive victory. The nobles finally arranged a compromise that recognized Henry as king and Richard of York as his heir.

Richard was not satisfied and pursued his claim, until he was killed in battle at Wakefield in 1460. However, his son, Edward, pressed on and had himself crowned Edward IV. In a showdown on March 29, 1461, he defeated Margaret's army at Towton in what proved to be the bloodiest battle of the wars. The first phase of the Wars of the Roses ended with the Lancastrian king Henry VI a prisoner in the Tower of London and the son of Richard of York on the throne.

Second Phase (1469–1471).

The ambitious brother of the Yorkist king (Edward IV) allied himself with Queen Margaret, who had fled into exile. When Margaret sent her army to fight Edward IV at Tewkesbury on May 4,

1471, her troops were defeated. The Yorkists killed Margaret's son in the battle and had her husband murdered in the Tower of London. The Wars of the Roses seemed over, and it appeared that Edward IV and the Yorkists had won.

Third Phase (1483–1487).   After Edward IV died in 1483 and his 12-year-old son was crowned Edward V, the young king's ambitious uncle, Richard of Gloucester (the boy's protector) proclaimed himself King RICHARD III. He placed the young king and his brother in the Tower of London, where they were subsequently murdered. Richard III himself was killed in battle at Bosworth on August 22, 1485, by the forces of young Henry Tudor, representing the Lancastrian line. He became King Henry VII, the first Tudor king. Two years later, the Wars of the Roses ended when a Yorkist challenger was killed trying to win back the crown from the Lancastrians. This was the last time an English king and a rival claimant met on a battlefield. (*See also* **Cade's Rebellion; Prisons; Warfare.**)

Waterworks

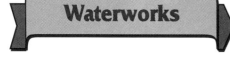

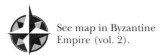

See map in Byzantine Empire (vol. 2).

See color plate 8, vol. 3.

During the Middle Ages, water was a very important resource, as it is today. It was needed to maintain health and agricultural production, and also to support industry and to enhance transportation. As beneficial and necessary as water was to medieval communities, it could also be extremely destructive in times of flooding. The increase in the construction of waterworks during the Middle Ages had as much to do with production as it did with protection.

Early medieval leaders in both the East and the West understood the need to regulate water flow. The Byzantine emperor Justinian, who reigned from 527 to 565, built several underground cisterns, or tanks, to store a water supply for the city of CONSTANTINOPLE. In Italy, St. Frediano, the bishop of Lucca (in Italy) from 561 to 589, successfully drained the Lucchese plain by redirecting the course of the Serchio River from the eastern to the western side of his city so that it emptied directly into the sea instead of into the Arno River. In this way, the land was made suitable for farming.

Efforts to control flooding and to develop water systems were made by local people who had little knowledge of the types of systems that were successful elsewhere. The most urgent water issue of the early medieval period was flooding. Flooded plains made the cultivation of fields difficult. Furthermore, flooding impeded the construction of effective canal projects. For example, in the late 700s, CHARLEMAGNE tried to construct a canal to link the Rhine and the Danube Rivers in order to ease the transport of military equipment, but rains kept washing away the canal's foundations.

Western Europeans responded to the population growth of the 11th century with an increase in waterworks projects. Perhaps the most spectacular of these were in the Low Countries (the Netherlands) along the North Sea. Much of this coastal region was marshland and peat bogs. People of the region reclaimed the wetlands. They did this by building dikes* and sluices* around a marshy area and then removing the water. The reclaimed tract of land was known as a polder. Between the 12th and the 14th centuries,

* **dike** earthen bank constructed to prevent flooding of low-lying land

* **sluice** structure with gates for controlling the flow of water from a canal or river

hundreds of windmills were built to remove the water. By the early 1300s, the reclaimed lands supported more than 3,000 households, or about 13,000 people.

In the medieval cities of western Europe, water was often supplied through pipes that ran into the city from water sources beyond the city walls. The cathedral and priory* of Canterbury were supplied with water by lead pipes that fed into water tanks and a fishpond. Medieval Nuremberg had water mains made of hollow logs and special machines for drilling them.

Increased trade during the Middle Ages led to the construction of many bridges. As larger and more rapidly flowing rivers were spanned, stone replaced wood as the preferred building material. Some medieval bridges were built on artificial islands called starlings, but this method had problems. The piers on which the bridges were constructed were close together, increasing the water flow through the remaining passages. The rapidly flowing water eroded the base material of the starlings on which the piers rested. By the 1300s, this problem was solved by the invention of the cofferdam, a watertight enclosure that enabled bridge builders to construct piers below the riverbed.

Canal construction also increased during the Middle Ages. Between 1391 and 1398, a canal was built that connected the North and the Baltic Seas and that eliminated the need to sail around Denmark to reach Prussia. The canal's system of locks and gates allowed ships to be raised and lowered in keeping with changing elevation levels of the land along the canal. The canal was an impressive demonstration of how far medieval engineering and waterworks construction had advanced. (*See also* **Agriculture; Castles and Fortifications; Flanders and the Low Countries; Land Use; Roads and Bridges; Travel and Transportation.**)

* **priory** small monastery or convent headed by a prior or prioress

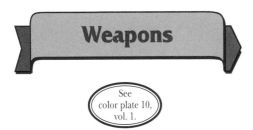

Weapons

See color plate 10, vol. 1.

Throughout the medieval world, various types of weapons were used to defend land and people and to attack enemies. There were several classes of medieval weapons: edged weapons, such as swords and daggers; shafted weapons, such as lances and axes; and missile weapons, which included arrows and cannon. During the Middle Ages, technological advances in ARMOR led to changes in weaponry and weapon design. Moreover, the development of cannon dramatically changed the nature of warfare.

Edged Weapons.   Swords and daggers were the most common weapons used in hand-to-hand combat. The sword was the only weapon that was designed solely for killing people and that did not develop from hunting weapons, such as bows and arrows, or from tools, such as knives and axes. The sword was universally regarded as the most noble of weapons, and many medieval epics celebrated the sword because of the awe, and even magic, associated with it.

The medieval sword was a straight cut-and-thrust weapon, usually with a double-edged blade more than two feet in length. Sword making was a specialized art. Blacksmiths had to laboriously hammer and weld together thin strips of steel and iron of varying hardnesses to form the core of the

This illumination shows the siege of a French city in the 1300s. Various types of weapons are being used for both offense and defense. Soldiers are using spears, swords, pike axes, longbows, and cross-bows. A small cannon sits in the foreground. The soldiers are wearing armor and using shields for their defense.

Murderous Weapon

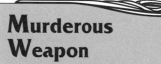

The medieval crossbow, a short bow mounted crosswise on a wooden stock, shot arrows and stones with deadly force. Invented by the Chinese in 1200 B.C. and in use in Europe since Roman times, the crossbow had undergone im-provements by the 12th century that greatly increased its effective-ness as a weapon. In 1139, a church council declared the crossbow "too murderous" and tried unsuccessfully to ban its use against Christians—although against heretics and infi-dels it was highly recommended. The crossbow remained popular throughout the Middle Ages.

blade and then add sharp edges of very hard steel. Good swords were rare and, therefore, very expensive. Three medieval centers of sword making were especially renowned: TOLEDO in Spain and two cities in Germany—Passau and Solingen.

Each sword was specially designed for its owner, and thus no two swords were exactly alike. The shapes of blades as well as the weight, length, and handle design all varied. Moreover, certain types and styles of swords were more common in different regions and at different times. From the 1000s to the 1300s, for example, most swords had parallel edges designed for slashing blows. From about 1350 to the mid-1500s, swords generally were tapered to a sharp point, which made them more suitable for thrusting blows.

Daggers were once an everyday accessory of a man's clothing. One of the most common types of dagger had a single-edged, sharply pointed blade that could be used both as a household tool and as a handy weapon. Like swords, the designs and styles of daggers also varied according to place and time.

Shafted Weapons.   The most common shafted weapon was the lance. The typical medieval lance consisted of two parts: the shaft, usually made of wood, and a steel head or point. The shape and design of lances varied according to their purpose and the period. Up to the 1000s, Byzantine cavalry had 12-foot lances, while western European knights carried much

* **pole arms**   shafted weapons with axlike
cutting blades

* **halberd**   weapon with an axlike cutting blade
and a sharp, pointed spike

* **poleax**   weapon with a blade combining ax,
hammer, and spike

* **partisan**   weapon with a long spear blade and
a pair of curved projections at the base

* **longbow**   archer's weapon about five to six
feet in length for the rapid shooting of
arrows

* **chain mail**   flexible armor made of small
metal rings linked together

shorter lances, 8 to 10 feet in length. Battle lances had sharp points, while tournament lances were tipped with blunt projections that helped prevent them from piercing armor. Other shafted weapons included various types of spears and pole arms*, including the halberd*, poleax*, and partisan*.

Missile Weapons.   During the early Middle Ages, the most common projectile weapons were the crossbow and the longbow*. The arrows fired by these weapons could be very deadly. By the early 1300s, for example, improvements in the crossbow allowed its arrows to pierce the meshes of a chain mail* shirt. Many improvements in armor were made to overcome the danger of improved bows.

The most revolutionary development in medieval weaponry was the introduction of cannon. In the Islamic world, cannon were first used in the mid-1200s. The earliest recorded use of cannon in western Europe was in the early 1300s. The early cannon often were dangerous to those using them, since structural weaknesses could produce fatal explosions. As cannon became heavier, problems arose in moving them and aiming them accurately. By the late 1300s, cannon with barrels weighing up to 600 pounds were in use, and by the 1400s cannon could fire projectiles weighing hundreds of pounds.

The development and improvement of cannon reversed the centuries-old dominance of defense over offense. Since large cannon projectiles could destroy the defensive walls of castles or towns, fortifications had to be redesigned and strengthened. The most famous medieval victory involving cannon was the defeat of the city of CONSTANTINOPLE by the OTTOMANS in 1453, when cannonballs as heavy as 800 pounds made holes in city walls that had withstood attack for more than one thousand years. (*See also* **Armor**; **Chivalry**; **Crusades**; **Knighthood**; **Metals and Metalworking**; **Technology**; **Warfare**.)

Weights and Measures

See
color plate 1,
vol. 1.

In the Middle Ages, systems of weights and measures often varied from place to place. Some measurements of Roman origin continued to be used, while many other regional standards of measurement arose.

The Romans had maintained a system of measures across their empire, and the system survived in the BYZANTINE EMPIRE. In medieval Europe, the basic Roman unit of weight, the *libra,* continued to be used. The French *livre,* the Italian *lira,* and the English pound (abbreviated *lb.*) all have a common Roman origin. The Roman mile continued to be used as well, but it became based on the northern European units of feet instead of on the Roman standard of 1,000 paces. Liquid measurement was based on the *pinte,* or pint, which was about equal to the modern quart. The medieval quart was a unit of dry measurement, about equal to the modern quart.

In medieval Europe, however, people created measures as they needed them. To understand the medieval system, think about a recipe that calls for "a heaping spoonful" or "large eggs." How much is "heaping"? How small can a "large" egg be before it becomes a medium-sized

Animals are being weighed in this European game market. Through much of the Middle Ages, weights and measures were imprecise and varied from place to place. More consistent standards became important in the later Middle Ages as commerce expanded and goods were traded over greater distances.

See color plate 3, vol. 1.

egg? Such a recipe is based on approximations and depends on the judgment and experience of the cook. In that respect, it is like the medieval system of weights and measures.

For example, in Lincolnshire, England, a particular measure of land was called a *bescia*. A *bescia* referred to the amount of land a man could dig with a spade between May 1 and August 1. However, people in Herefordshire, England, had a land measure called a math, which meant the amount of land a man could mow in a single day.

Even when the methods of measurement were the same, the standards against which things were measured might vary. In the English counties of Sussex and Suffolk, milk was measured in units called meals, one meal being the amount of milk taken from a single cow during one milking. A cubit, which was used to measure length, was the distance from a person's elbow to the tip of the middle finger.

The local nature of weights and measures often made business transactions extremely complicated. Some medieval monarchs, including the Frankish emperor CHARLEMAGNE in the ninth century, were aware that problems existed with their system of weights and measures. They issued decrees and laws that attempted to establish clear standards, but these decrees were too vague and often merely added to the confusion.

For most rural people, these differences did not matter much. However, standard weights and measures became important as commerce and trade expanded in the late Middle Ages and goods were traded over greater distances. In the 12th and the 13th centuries, the use of standard measurements was strictly enforced within the fairgrounds at the great medieval FAIRS, such as the one in the county of CHAMPAGNE in France. One of the most widely traded European goods—woolen cloth—was measured by the ell. The ell was defined in Champagne as two feet, six inches, and it was accepted as a standard measurement in many of the major cloth manufacturing centers of northwestern Europe.

In the late medieval period, some places also developed consistent standards for wholesale shipments of goods. For example, Bordeaux and several other French cities produced wine in units called *pièces*. A merchant in a distant city who ordered 10 *pièces* of wine from Bordeaux knew exactly how much wine he was buying.

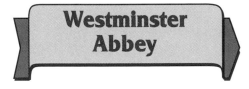

Westminster Abbey

* **abbey** monastery under the rule of an abbot or abbess

* **nave** main part of a church or cathedral between the side aisles

Westminster Abbey is the magnificent church in London that is the traditional site for the coronations and burials of the kings and queens of England. For more than 900 years, it has been an English national shrine. Westminster Abbey is also one of England's most important Gothic structures.

The last Saxon king, EDWARD THE CONFESSOR, began building an abbey* church near his palace in Westminster around 1050. After Edward's death in 1066, he was buried in the abbey. Shortly thereafter, the new king of England, WILLIAM I THE CONQUEROR, was crowned there, beginning its tradition as the site of royal burials and coronations.

King HENRY III ordered construction of the present building in 1245, but the nave* was not finished until the 1400s. Henry wanted to copy the royal churches of France and may have sent his architect, Henry of Reynes, to study the latest French styles of the cathedrals at Rheims and Amiens. Although the architecture of Westminster Abbey is English in most respects, it has many French Gothic features, especially its soaring height and its flying buttresses. Westminster Abbey has been called "the most French of all English Gothic churches." (*See also* **Gothic Architecture.**)

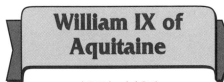

William IX of Aquitaine

1071–1126
Aristocrat and troubadour

William of Aquitaine was a nobleman and poet. Also known as Guillaume de Poitiers, he was the seventh count of Poitiers and ninth duke of Aquitaine. However, he was also a TROUBADOUR who loved worldly pleasures and scorned religious leaders who took a more somber view of worldly joys. In the eyes of many of his medieval contemporaries, he was a scandalous, mocking, but fascinating fool, who made a joke of everything, even his own soul.

Although William was an important and active member of the French aristocracy, he is remembered today primarily for his poetry. He was the earliest of the troubadours whose works are known to have survived, and he was the first poet whose verse expressed the tradition of COURTLY LOVE that soon came to be so important in European literature. Of the 11 of his poems that are in existence, 6 are burlesques (witty, mocking poems) and 5 are serious. Of the last group, 4 are about love and the remaining one is a farewell to CHIVALRY.

The burlesques are obscene, blasphemous, and full of insults designed to offend religious feelings. One poem was considered so shocking that, many years later, a translator refused to render it into English. William offended the church in other ways too. In 1097, while the lord of TOULOUSE

* **excommunicate**   to exclude from the rites of the church

was away during the First Crusade, William seized Toulouse, even though all lands belonging to crusaders were protected by the church. When the bishop excommunicated* him, William had the bishop arrested. William went on two crusades himself. The first ended in disaster in 1101, when the Turks slaughtered his army as it was crossing ANATOLIA. His second crusade in Spain in 1120 was much more successful. (*See also* **Crusades; French Language and Literature.**)

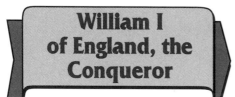

William I of England, the Conqueror

ca. 1027–1087
Duke of Normandy
and king of England

William I, better known as William the Conqueror, was the first NORMAN ruler of England. His invasion and conquest of England, in 1066, ushered in an era that changed forever the course of English history, culture, and language.

Born in Normandy (a region of present-day France), William was the illegitimate son of the duke of Normandy, Robert I. When Robert died on a pilgrimage to the Holy Land, young William was designated as his successor. For about ten years, however, Normandy fell into great disorder, as various members of the duke's family struggled for positions of power. The crisis erupted in 1046/1047 when William's cousin, Guy of Burgundy, attempted to seize power with the support of several other Norman lords. William defeated his opponents with help from the French king, Henry I, and established his authority to rule.

* **duchy**   territory ruled by a duke or a duchess

As duke of Normandy, William maintained a very strong relationship with the nobility and assumed an authority over the church that was exceptional. William strengthened his duchy* against external threats from the count of Anjou and the king of France by defeating several invasion attempts and gaining control of the region of Maine to the south. To protect his western frontier, he maintained the traditional Norman dominance in BRITTANY. He strengthened his position to the east by marrying Matilda, the daughter of the count of FLANDERS, and establishing feudal* lordships over several counts in the area. By the 1060s, William had unified Normandy, brought new lands into his domain, established unquestioned control over the nobility, and developed a good relationship with the church. The duchy was now sufficiently strong and at peace for William to direct his attention toward England.

* **feudal**   referring to the social, economic, and political system that flourished in western Europe during the Middle Ages

One of William's uncles was the childless king EDWARD THE CONFESSOR of England. Edward had invited William to England in 1051 (and may have named him his heir). In 1064, the English earl, Harold of Wessex, visited Normandy. Harold was another potential heir to the English throne, but William claimed that Harold's visit to Normandy signified a recognition of William's claim to the throne. When King Edward died in 1066, Harold took the throne. William protested Harold's assumption of power and invaded England. At the Battle of HASTINGS on October 14, 1066, William's Norman army defeated Harold's forces. William was crowned king of England in WESTMINSTER ABBEY on December 25, 1066.

See color plate 4, vol. 2.

William spent the rest of his life ruling both England and Normandy, moving frequently between the two areas. In England, he launched military campaigns against WALES and SCOTLAND that strengthened English

control over those regions. In France, he defended Normandy against the French king and seized more territory. His ability to adapt the institutions of both realms to his rule reflected his skill as a statesman. His control over the colonization of England by the Norman nobility was evidence of his great authority. The creation of the DOMESDAY BOOK was proof of the abilities of his administration. The close relationship between England and France that William established greatly influenced the later development of both countries. William was killed in 1087 during a military campaign in France, and he was buried in a Norman abbey in the town of Caen in northern France. (*See also* **Bayeux Tapestry; England; Lanfranc of Bec.**)

William Marshal

ca. 1146–1219
Knight, baron, and
guardian of England

* **dynasty** succession of rulers from the same family or group

* **squire** aide to a knight

* **duchy** territory ruled by a duke or a duchess

* **feudal** referring to the social, economic, and political system that flourished in western Europe during the Middle Ages

William Marshal played a leading role in English history during the reigns of several kings from the Plantagenet dynasty*. During his long and full life, William served his royal masters as knight, trusted counselor, tutor, and guardian of the realm. When he died at the age of 73, William Marshal was remembered as "the best knight who ever lived."

Taking his last name from his grandfather, who was marshal at the court of HENRY I OF ENGLAND, the young William was sent to Normandy to serve as squire* to the CHAMBERLAIN of the duchy*. There, he became skilled in tournaments and received his training for battle.

He also came to the attention of Henry II's wife, Eleanor of Aquitaine. Through her influence, William became the military tutor and leading knight in the household of Henry's oldest son. William quickly established himself as a trusted military and political adviser and a knight of the highest order.

King RICHARD I THE LIONHEARTED rewarded William's loyalty by bestowing on him a wife, Isabel, and vast estates, both in England and in Normandy. In a short time, William became one of the major landed BARONS of the realm. During Richard's reign in the 1190s, William was at the center of English political life. He served in a series of administrative and military positions in England and in several border areas. In addition, he went to war for Richard against the French king, PHILIP II AUGUSTUS. When King JOHN came to the throne in 1199, he rewarded William with more land and various important positions.

However, William's relationship with John was an uneasy one much of the time. John was suspicious of William's divided loyalties, since William was a feudal* lord in France as well as in England. The two were reconciled at a crucial time in John's troubled reign, and William may have played a vital role in the drafting and the acceptance of MAGNA CARTA in 1215.

On his deathbed, John appointed Marshal the guardian of his young son, HENRY III, and of the kingdom itself until Henry was old enough to assume power. During his guardianship, Marshal took the first steps toward the restoration of political stability and royal authority within the kingdom. (*See also* **Chivalry; Crusades; England; Feudalism; Nobility and Nobles; Warfare.**)

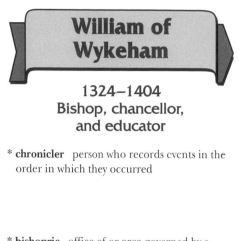

William of Wykeham

1324–1404
Bishop, chancellor, and educator

* **chronicler**   person who records events in the order in which they occurred

* **bishopric**   office of or area governed by a bishop

* **chancellor**   official who handles the records and archives of a monarch

Born to an English peasant family in Wickham (in Hampshire, England), William rose to a position of power in the court of King EDWARD III. So important was William's influence as Edward's chief minister that the French chronicler* Jehan FROISSART reported that at the English court "all things were done by him and without him nothing was done."

When William entered the king's service about 1347, he began as a clerk and keeper of the king's dogs. He rose steadily in the ROYAL HOUSEHOLD, and in 1356 he was given the responsibility for enlarging Windsor Castle, the king's favorite residence. His building success gained him the confidence of the king and the respect of the court. After his ordination as a priest in 1362, he was quickly rewarded with major church offices. In 1366, he became the bishop of Winchester, one of the wealthiest bishoprics* in Europe. One year later, the king appointed William chancellor* of England.

William amassed a great fortune, which he used in the service of education and religion. In 1387, he founded a school in Winchester for poor students. By the time construction was completed on Winchester College School, as it was called, it was the largest school in England. William also founded New College, Oxford, and enlarged Winchester Cathedral, one of the largest churches in England.

During the reign of King RICHARD II, from 1367 to 1400, William was criticized for mismanaging the royal finances. PARLIAMENT dismissed him in 1371, but William soon returned to favor at court and remained active in English politics until his death. (*See also* **England; Gothic Architecture; Schools; Universities.**)

Witchcraft, European

* **heresy**   belief that is contrary to church doctrine

* **incantation**   magical chant

In medieval Europe, what began as simple sorcery or magic developed into the practice of witchcraft. Church leaders condemned witchcraft as devil worship and as a dangerous heresy* and ruthlessly persecuted anyone suspected of being a witch. The European witch trials and burnings that began in the late Middle Ages resulted in the deaths of between 100,000 and 200,000 people (mostly women) and the torture, harassment, and intimidation of millions more.

Origins.   European magic developed out of the tradition of sorcery. In fact, the Old English word *wicca* (pronounced witcha) means sorcerer. Sorcery used simple charms and spells to achieve practical results, such as curing a headache or putting a curse on an enemy. Sorcerers used herbs, folk medicine, and wax figures to heal and to cast spells. One Anglo-Saxon magical formula to get rid of warts advised individuals to "take the water of a dog and the blood of a mouse, mix together, smear the warts with this; they will soon disappear." To shrink an enemy into insignificance, a person was advised to recite the following curse: "May you become as small as a linseed grain, and much smaller than the hipbone of an itch mite, and may you become so small that you become nothing."

Some magic incantations* included religious (usually Christian) elements, such as in the following recommendation for a heart ailment: "If a man is troubled by tumors near the heart, let a girl go to a spring that runs due east, and let her draw a cupful of water moving with the current, and let her sing on it the Creed and an Our Father."

Pagan* religion and folklore from the pre-Christian period in Europe also contributed to the development of medieval witchcraft. Early European folklore often included stories of a band of spirits, which was believed to roam the countryside and to gather in deserted places on the moors and in the forests. These spirits or ghosts, described as part human and part animal, went on rampages of destruction, killing any living creature that crossed their path.

The leader of this wild band of spirits was usually female. The Germans called her Hilda or Berta, but by the end of the 800s she had merged with the Roman goddess Diana. Those who traveled with her and followed her commands were considered witches. The first important European legal text to refer to witchcraft, *Canon episcopi*, condemned those who believed that "they ride out at night on beasts with Diana and a horde of women."

Witchcraft as Heresy.   When the church began to condemn this mixture of sorcery and pagan folklore as heresy, a new, dark chapter in the history of European witchcraft began. Originally, a sorcerer was someone who practiced magic without the help of spirits. By the 400s, however, St. AUGUSTINE's argument that magic was the work of evil spirits, or demons, had become the accepted view within the church. With this change in philosophy, the attitude toward sorcerers also changed. Since demons were agents of Satan, or the devil, the sorcerer was therefore regarded as a servant of Satan. Priests hearing confessions were advised to condemn magic and the use of curses and spells. Many of the charges brought against suspected witches concerned their supposed ability to cause storms or to inflict disease or death on animals or human beings.

Witches were increasingly seen not just as magicians or sorcerers but as heretics in league with the devil. The church, as defender of godliness, committed itself to search out and destroy all witches. By defining sorcerers as heretics (persons who were against the established beliefs of the church), the church made it much easier to prosecute them.

In the 12th century, the beliefs of a group of Christian heretics, known as CATHARS, gave increased importance to the devil. The Cathars emphasized Satan's great powers as lord of the entire world, including all matter, the body, and all pleasures and satisfactions. Although the Cathars did not intend to glorify Satan, their portrayal of him as an omnipotent figure made him the object of worship for some people.

Inside the church, interest in the devil increased. SCHOLASTICISM, which dominated medieval thought from the 1100s on, emphasized the pact that witches supposedly made with Satan and promoted the idea that heretics and witches were part of Satan's army. Scholastic thinkers called the gatherings of witches "sabbats," thus making it clear that they believed witches, heretics, and Jews were joined together in the service of the devil. Scholastic thinkers also established that, with rare exceptions, witches were women, since they were accused of having sexual intercourse with the devil, who was always pictured as male.

The INQUISITION (a medieval court established to investigate heresy) and other church courts targeted witchcraft by separating it from sorcery

Two witches are making rain in this woodcut from the late 1400s. European witchcraft was a mixture of ancient sorcery and pagan folklore, involving the use of simple spells, the practice of folk medicine, and the belief in spirits. The church believed that witches were in league with the devil, and it ruthlessly persecuted suspected witches.

* **pagan** word used by Christians to mean non-Christian and believing in several gods

* **excommunicate** to exclude from the rites of the church

and making it a heresy, punishable by burning at the stake. After the first execution of heretics at Orleans (in France) in 1022, the church's war against heresy intensified. In 1198, Pope INNOCENT III ordered that anyone continuing to hold heretical beliefs after having been convicted and excommunicated* should be arrested again and burned at the stake.

Between 1227 and 1235, Pope Gregory IX established the papal Inquisition. In 1252, Pope INNOCENT IV issued a decree that authorized the imprisonment, torture, and execution of heretics. Since witchcraft was increasingly defined as a heresy that involved a pact with the devil and sorcery was regarded as another form of witchcraft, the conviction rates of people accused of witchcraft skyrocketed.

The Inquisition presumed that everybody accused of witchcraft must be guilty. Suspects, therefore, were interrogated and tortured until they confessed. These confessions were then used as evidence to support a conviction.

Witch Craze.   The European witch hunts gained momentum when a DOMINICAN friar, Heinrich Institoris, became the inquisitor for southern Germany in 1474. In 1486, Institoris published his *Malleus maleficarum* (called the "hammer against witchcraft"). It quickly became one of the most widely read books of the time, and it was published in 14 editions by 1520. This work helped fan the flames of the witch craze that engulfed Europe during the Renaissance and the Reformation—and later America—and destroyed many thousands of innocent women. (*See also* **Alchemy; Astrology and Astronomy; Devils and Demons; Joan of Arc; Magic and Folklore; Torture; Trials.**)

Forced Confession

In 1438, in La Tour du Pin in southern France, the Inquisition arrested an old man named Pierre Vallin and had him tortured until he confessed to having served the devil for 63 years.

Vallin was also forced to confess that he offered his own baby daughter up as a human sacrifice, attended witches' meetings, and ate the flesh of murdered children. After his conviction, Vallin was tortured again and was forced to name other witches. Following his confessions, Vallin was burned at the stake.

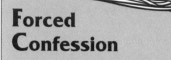

Wolfram von Eschenbach

ca. 1170–1217
German poet

Wolfram von Eschenbach was one of the most popular poets of medieval Germany. His literary output was enormous. It is estimated that he wrote more than 40,000 verses. Today, he is remembered for his major work, *Parzival.* Little is known about Wolfram's life except that he was probably a knight in the service of a German lord who supported his writing.

Wolfram's reputation rests on *Parzival,* his epic poem about a knight's quest for the Holy Grail, the cup Jesus drank from during the Last Supper. The story is similar to the story told by the French poet CHRÉTIEN DE TROYES. The young hero Parzival travels to the court of King Arthur and has many adventures while serving the king. When he becomes lost in a forest, a mysterious stranger directs him to the Grail Castle. There, King Amfortas suffers from a crippling illness, which Parzival fails to inquire about. His failure to ask a question of the king seals Parzival's fate because asking would have cured Amfortas. Shamed by his seeming lack of compassion, the knight renounces God and sets off in search of the Grail. After numerous adventures and encounters with other knights and maidens, Parzival returns to the Grail Castle. He asks the redeeming question of Amfortas, he becomes the Grail King, and his sons inherit the Grail Kingdom.

Parzival is filled with religious symbolism. The Grail is a symbol of salvation, and the Grail Kingdom is a symbol of heaven. Parzival's failure to ask Amfortas the cause of his pain symbolizes human sinfulness. In addition,

many scholars point to the story's political meaning. Wolfram lived during the time of the HOLY ROMAN EMPIRE, and from that perspective the Grail Kingdom may be seen as a training ground for potential rulers. Parzival's rule over the kingdom may be his birthright, but he must demonstrate maturity in order to claim it. (*See also* **Arthurian Literature; Chansons de Geste; Chivalry; German Language and Literature.**)

Women, Roles of

See color plate 2, vol. 1.

D uring the Middle Ages, the primary role of women was to maintain family life. Men became warriors, merchants, and artisans, while women generally became wives, mothers, and housekeepers. Nevertheless, some medieval women found ways to develop their talents within and beyond the functions sanctioned by both society and religion.

Women in Europe.   In medieval Europe, young girls did not have as much personal or legal freedom as boys. While unmarried, they were under the authority of their fathers. After marriage, they answered to their husbands. Unmarried women generally were looked on with suspicion and were seen as burdens on their families. Among the upper classes, however, women could choose the convent as an acceptable alternative to marriage. Some of these women, including HROTSWITHA VON GANDERSHEIM and HILDEGARD OF BINGEN, made great contributions to literature and to learning.

The role of women in the medieval period depended on social class. Upper-class women and queens often knew how to read, write, and calculate with numbers, and they were often well versed in many subjects. Many were responsible for taking care of household accounts and managing estates while their husbands were at war or conducting business at court. Noble ladies left some household tasks to servants while they supervised the running of the manor.

Among the middle class in medieval towns, women often helped in their husbands' businesses or practiced a trade of their own. Many middle-class women developed skill in business, led fairly independent lives, and were treated with respect by their husbands because of their contributions.

In peasant families, women had full responsibility for household activities and often shared in agricultural labors as well. In addition to cooking, cleaning, sewing, tending gardens, and caring for domestic animals, they also helped plow and harvest crops.

By far the most important responsibility of the majority of medieval women was the management of the household. The manufacture of clothing and the preparation of food were entirely in the hands of women. They also made candles, soap, and dyes, and they prepared medicines and cosmetics from herbal recipes. Women were responsible for raising the children and teaching their daughters household skills. The many responsibilities of women in the household gave them a position of significant influence in the family.

Under FEUDALISM, the role of women changed somewhat. Legally, their position worsened. Their right to inherit property was restricted in favor of male heirs (although a daughter could inherit an estate if there were no sons). A wife's duty was to produce a male heir, and, if she did not, her husband could seek to have the marriage annulled. Widows had to relinquish

The Education of Young Ladies

Aristocratic parents in the Middle Ages often did not raise their own children. It was customary for them to send their children to the homes of other nobles for education and training. Young girls generally were trained as ladies-in-waiting. Under the supervision of the lady of the manor, girls were taught to spin, weave, embroider, sew, and prepare medicines and cosmetics. They also learned to sing, dance, play music, and read and write in their own language and possibly in a foreign language. Since mealtime rituals were very important, girls learned proper table manners. During leisure hours, they might sit in the garden and listen to music, read romances, or engage in flirtatious conversation with young boys in training as pages and squires. Their exposure to the company of young men was important, since part of the reason for sending young girls to other households was to find suitable marriage partners for them.

The primary role of women in the Middle Ages was caring for the family. A woman learned household skills—weaving, spinning, sewing, baking, and brewing. She also learned to prepare household items, such as candles, medicines, and cosmetics. In upper-class families, the woman supervised servants who performed these household tasks.

See color plate 11, vol. 1.

guardianship of their children to their overlord, and they had to obtain the consent of the overlord to remarry. Yet, while the legal position of women worsened, among the upper and middle classes life probably became more civilized and comfortable for women. Whether the code of honor known as chivalry influenced this development is in dispute.

Women in the Islamic World.   The family was recognized as the foundation of Islamic society, and among its most important functions were to perpetuate and to increase the Muslim population. Marriage was seen as a union of a man and a woman who were attracted to each other by their basic differences: male toughness, harshness, and aggressiveness tempered by female gentleness, softness, and acceptance. Women thus had a somewhat equal, though different, role in the family.

In the Islamic world, the husband was the head of the family. A good wife respected her husband and obeyed his wishes. Meanwhile, the husband was expected to make sure that his wife's needs were served at his expense, although, in practice, wives often volunteered to take care of the household chores themselves. They stayed at home to care for their children and to look after other domestic responsibilities. However, ordinary women ventured out when necessary to obtain items that the family needed. Upper-class women, on the other hand, tended to remain at home, deliberately keeping themselves away from the public eye. When they went out, they covered their faces with veils. (Ordinary women dressed modestly but went about their work with their faces uncovered.)

Divorce was rare in Islamic society. Islamic law provided full legal rights for women. For example, a woman could have the right to divorce written into her marriage contract. Even if she had not done so, she could still apply for divorce on the grounds of cruelty or the failure of her husband to provide for her well-being. Despite such laws, it was often easier for men to obtain a divorce than it was for women.

Women in Jewish Society.   The role of the Jewish woman in medieval society was also defined by her position as wife and mother. Jewish girls generally were restricted to home instruction in practical matters in preparation for their family responsibilities. Marriage was valued very highly, and having children was a basic commandment of the Jewish religion. Mutual rights and duties of spouses were written into a marriage contract, and women had the same right to divorce as men. If childless, widows were sometimes obligated to marry a brother of their husband.

See color plate 4, vol. 1.

Jewish women often enjoyed a higher status in practice than in the law. For instance, although Jewish widows had no right of inheritance, it was not uncommon for them to participate in the economic life of the community. A few Jewish women even studied religious law and became scholars. (*See also* **Courtly Love; Family; Inheritance Laws and Practices; Islam, Religion of; Women's Religious Orders.**)

Women's Religious Orders

D uring the Middle Ages, monastic houses for women were the only alternative to marriage for daughters of the nobility. The religious life had important benefits for women of the Middle Ages since it provided the opportunity for women to receive an education, to apply their skills, and to pursue a career. Ordinarily, these paths were closed to women in medieval society. It is important to remember that most women who became nuns in the Middle Ages were from the upper classes. Poor women and peasant women had fewer alternatives.

Many of the medieval religious houses for women were subject to supervision and control by the MONASTERIES with which they were associated. However, some of the nuns governed themselves, and sometimes even the monks. The legacy of these medieval women—as reflected in their writings, their artwork and handicrafts, and their spirituality—has made a rich and enduring contribution to history.

Early Female Monasticism.   As MONASTICISM spread in western Europe in the early medieval period (500s–800s), several religious houses for women were founded. Most of these were located in the region that later became France. Double monasteries, consisting of two houses—one male, one female—were common at this time.

Inspired by Frankish double monasteries, the English established 12 double houses of their own. Several of these were founded by a noblewoman and abbess*, Hilda of Whitby, in the late 600s. The VIKING invasions that began in the mid-800s ended the growing monastic culture in England. On the European continent, however, new monasteries for women continued to be founded. In northern Italy, for example, there were approximately 45 monasteries for women by 1100.

After 1000, the women's monastic movement underwent a change. Women wanted their own communities, to be based on the Benedictine Rule, especially as it was followed by the monks at Cluny in France. The members of some of the new houses elected their own abbess, usually in the presence of the founder and the founder's family. The abbess was then consecrated* by the bishop, although, beginning in the mid-1000s, that privilege was frequently claimed by the pope.

* **abbess** female head of an abbey or monastery. The male equivalent is an abbot.

* **consecrated** declared sacred during a church ceremony

This French illumination shows Franciscan nuns attending a mass in their convent. The Order of St. Clare, or the Poor Ladies, was established by St. Francis of Assisi in 1212. In 1298, the pope gave the sisters of the Franciscan order rights equal to those of the Franciscan brothers. By 1400, the order had about 15,000 sisters in about 400 convents.

* **priory** small monastery or convent headed by a prior or prioress

In Germany, monastic houses for women were generally started by women on their own or in cooperation with their husbands or relatives who were members of the CLERGY. Some members of the nobility established monastic houses for their daughters. To be an abbess in these monasteries was an honor. Several princesses held that position.

New Religious Houses. In the 1100s, several religious orders created new monasteries for women. In the double abbey of Prémontré in northern France, men and women lived separately, with only the church building used in common. However, the sisters were completely subordinate to the monks and were forbidden to sing or to talk except in church. The order of the Premonstratensians lasted from 1120 to 1137. By the late 1200s, the women's order had died out, except in Belgium.

The order of Fontevrault, on the other hand, was headed by women. Founded around 1100 in France by ROBERT D'ARBRISSEL, the order was placed under an abbess in 1115. It had 33 priories* under its supervision, including one in England. The abbess had full powers over both the female and male religious communities. She chose which young men would become priests when they reached the age of 18, and she supervised the management of all properties belonging to the order—including woods, farmland, vineyards, fisheries, and mills.

The CISTERCIANS and the Carthusians were other religious orders that established communities for women. Cistercian nuns were cloistered (shut away), wore white robes, and ate no meat. They spent their time praying, reading, sewing and embroidering vestments, teaching young girls, and copying manuscripts.

Dominicans and Franciscans. The famous religious orders that emerged in the 1200s—the DOMINICANS and the FRANCISCANS—established houses (called convents) for men and women. The first house founded by St. DOMINIC was a women's institution.

Separate Lives

In the 1100s, the English cleric Gilbert of Sempringham organized a religious order for men and women. The brothers and sisters lived in the same monastery but in separate houses. They could talk through a small hole in the wall of the women's house, but they could not see each other. There was only one church, but the men and women were separated by a heavy curtain. They could hear each other pray and sing, but they still could not see each other.

* **prioress**   head of a convent; rank below abbess

In 1207, the local bishop gave Dominic permission to establish a convent for 12 women who wanted to devote their lives to prayer. He connected it to a nearby house of Dominican men, and he took personal responsibility for the convent's spiritual direction. Dominic assigned the day-to-day management of the convent to Guillelmine Fanjeux, who served as its prioress* until her death in 1225. In 1218, the convent at Prouille (France) received papal recognition as an independent religious community belonging to the Dominican order.

In 1218 and 1219, two more Dominican houses for women were established in Madrid and Rome. In 1224, however, the order suspended the establishment of any additional ones. Several years later, a shift in papal attitude toward monastic houses for women led to the creation of more houses. By 1303, there were 42 Dominican convents in Italy, 74 in Germany, 13 in France, 8 in Spain, and others in Bohemia, Poland, Hungary, Scandinavia, and England (where the Dominicans founded their first convent in 1356).

The Franciscan Second Order, known as the Order of St. Clare or Poor Ladies, was established in 1212 by St. FRANCIS OF ASSISI, when a house for a young woman named Clare who wanted to join the Franciscans was built at the church of San Damiano in Assisi, Italy. As later houses for the order were built, they were supplied with a new rule by Hugolino, a cardinal who served as protector of the order. The new rule did not include the principle of poverty as set down by St. Francis, and it greatly displeased Clare.

When Hugolino ascended to the papacy as Pope Gregory IX, he offered property and income to the Poor Ladies. This was a tempting offer since most women's houses were poor and always in need. However, Clare refused. She then obtained papal permission for the sisters of San Damiano to live a life of complete poverty. Although Hugolino's rule remained in effect for other houses of the Poor Ladies, some stayed loyal to the ideal of poverty. One such house was established in Prague by Agnes, daughter of the king of BOHEMIA. Pope INNOCENT IV tried to place the Poor Ladies under the supervision of the Franciscan brothers, but both sides objected. In 1298, Pope BONIFACE VIII gave the sisters of the Order of St. Clare rights equal to those of the Franciscan brothers.

By 1400, there were about 15,000 sisters of the Order of St. Clare and 400 convents in Europe. About 250 of these were in Italy and the rest mostly in France, Spain, and Germany. The convents of the Order of St. Clare ranged in size from as few as 3 members to as many as 250 in NAPLES and Krakow (in Poland). Most of the larger houses had between 50 and 80 members. (*See also* **Beguines and Beghards; Christianity; Clergy; Family; Mysticism; Women, Role of.**)

Wool

Wool was one of the most important products of medieval economies. In England and Flanders, it was the leading export product. Wool merchants amassed great fortunes, and those involved in the processing of wool, from its raw state into finished cloth, were important workers in a prosperous industry.

The cool and damp climate of the British Isles was ideal for raising thick-coated sheep, and most landowners in England kept flocks. In the

The manufacture of wool was one of the most important industries in Europe in the later Middle Ages. Weaving, which began as a family craft, became a major industry controlled by the guilds. This Venetian merchant of the late 1300s is weighing wool, the single most important material used to make woven fabric.

early 1200s, the bishop of Winchester owned more than 15,000 sheep. However, most flocks were smaller, and the sheep farmers with small flocks supplied most of England's wool for export. In the 1300s, the most highly prized English wool came from the Welsh border area and from the West Midlands. Such towns as Lincoln, Beverly, and Stamford became centers of cloth making. On the Continent, Spanish merino wool and French wool were also prized, but none equaled English wool for its strength and luxuriousness.

The production of cloth from raw wool involved several operations. The raw wool had to be combed to remove knots and dirt. Next it was spun into thread, which was woven on a loom. After the wool was woven into a loose cloth, it was shrunk and thickened in vats of water, making a tighter weave. The finished cloth was then dyed. In the 1200s, the English used three major dyes—a deep blue dye called woad, a tomato red dye called madder, and a rare scarlet dye called grain. Scarlet-colored wool was used to make clothing for royalty and people of high social standing. English monarchs wore scarlet robes trimmed with ermine (white fur). (*See also* **Agriculture; Clothing; England; Flanders and the Low Countries; Silk; Textiles.**)

Writing Materials and Techniques

* **papyrus** writing material made by pressing together thin strips of the inner stem of the papyrus plant

During the Middle Ages, writing materials and techniques varied, depending on the cost and availability of materials and on the purposes for the written texts. Writing materials ranged from stone, glass, and textiles to papyrus*, parchment*, and paper. The techniques of writing ranged from simple graffiti-type markings to elaborate, highly ornamented scripts. With the development of printing toward the end of the Middle Ages, writing materials and techniques became somewhat more standardized.

This Byzantine scribe is using a stylus to write on parchment. Parchment was a durable and flexible material produced from the hides of goats and sheep. It was the predominant material used for books until about the year 1000, when paper was introduced. By 1500, paper had replaced parchment as the primary writing material.

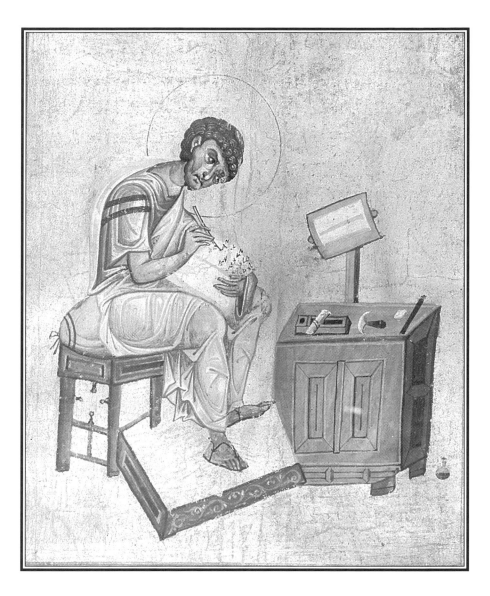

* **parchment** writing material made from the skin of sheep or goats

Writing in the Islamic World.   The early Muslims used both parchment and papyrus. In the mid-700s, the Chinese art of papermaking was introduced to the Islamic world from the eastern part of the empire. The manufacture and use of paper then gradually spread westward. Paper factories were established in BAGHDAD in the late 700s, in Egypt in the 800s, and in Spain by the end of the 1100s. During the 900s, parchment, papyrus, and paper were all used in the Islamic world, but the use of papyrus quickly died out.

The paper of the Islamic world generally was made of linen and flax. The liquefied pulp of these materials first was poured into molds. As this mixture hardened, it was pressed, sized, and polished to form paper. From the earliest days of papermaking, the Muslims produced several grades of paper. All were expensive, and the use of paper was therefore probably restricted to the ruling, administrative, and religious classes. Certain places, such as SAMARKAND and DAMASCUS, gained a reputation for the high quality of their paper. As early as the 800s, colored papers were in use; blue, yellow, red, olive green, and violet were especially popular. Good-quality papers were sometimes used as gifts or as currency.

* **lampblack** carbon compound made from the soot of burning oil and used as a pigment in paints and inks

* **tannin** compound derived from oak bark and other plant materials

* **vitriol** type of metallic compound that has a glassy appearance

* **scribe** person who hand-copies manuscripts

See color plate 8, vol. 2.

* **pumice** volcanic material used for smoothing and polishing

Inks were made from lampblack*, soot, tannin*, vitriol*, and nuts. The inks favored by scribes usually were dark and heavy, and they required paper with a glazed surface. Reed pens were considered better when working with thick inks and glazed papers. Scribes generally owned expensive writing sets that consisted of a container for reeds, an inkpot, and possibly an ink pad—an implement made of wool or flax that helped spread ink evenly on writing materials.

The development of European papermaking in the 1200s led to a decline in Islamic papermaking in later centuries. By the 1300s and the 1400s, less expensive European-made papers poured into the Islamic world, and the local papermaking industry vanished.

Writing in Western Europe. Medieval writing in western Europe was done on a wide variety of materials. The expense and scarcity of manufactured writing materials, such as paper and parchment, sometimes encouraged the use of readily available natural materials. In Sweden and Russia, for example, writing often was done on birch bark, and in Spain and Ireland various types of documents were scratched on pieces of slate. Wax tablets were used quite extensively by scribes* throughout Europe. Because wax tablets were easy to erase, they were particularly favored for writing rough drafts and other texts that were frequently revised.

While a variety of materials might be used for ordinary texts, important texts that were meant to be more permanent were usually written on either parchment or papyrus. Papyrus was imported primarily from Egypt. When the Islamic conquests disrupted Mediterranean commerce in the 600s, the supply of papyrus was reduced, and parchment became the most important writing material. Early medieval parchment was thick and stiff. In the later Middle Ages, technological advances produced parchment that was unsurpassed for its thinness, flexibility, whiteness, ink retention, and durability.

The craft of papermaking was first introduced in western Europe in the 1000s by Muslims in Spain and Sicily. At first, Europeans imported paper from Muslim producers in the Mediterranean region, but, by the late 1200s, paper mills in Italy were also manufacturing paper. By the 1300s, paper overtook parchment as the preferred writing material in western Europe, and as technologies advanced, manufacturers could produce large quantities of paper more cheaply.

The two most common types of pens used in medieval Europe were the calamus, made from a carved reed, and the quill, or penna. Early medieval scribes also used a hard-pointed, pen-shaped instrument, called a stylus, for making line rules on wax tablets or parchment or for sketching illustrations. The stylus was eventually replaced by black lead in the 1100s and then by ink in the 1200s. A variety of different-colored inks was used. Text usually was written in black or brown ink, while titles, initial letters, and other marks were written in red or other colors.

Medieval scribes used pumice* stones and razors to smooth out rough places in the parchment and to erase mistakes. They often used compasses for designing page layouts and illustrations and a straightedge to help keep text running along a straight line. During the late Middle Ages, scribes often used wooden pattern boards that had slots cut into them to guide the drawing of the lines used as line rules. (*See also* **Books, Manuscript; Printing, Origins of.**)

Wulfstan of York

died 1023
Church leader and scholar

* **archbishop** head bishop in a region or nation

W
ulfstan of York was an important figure in England during the late 900s and the early 1000s. However, we know little of his life before 996, when he became bishop of London. In 1003, he was made archbishop* of York, a post he held until his death.

Wulfstan was probably a BENEDICTINE monk before his rise to prominence. He was a noted scholar, especially interested in law, and he may have been a member of the royal council. He drew up a code of laws aimed at ending lawlessness in northern England. The code is considered noteworthy because it provided that 12 leading citizens in each community should seize habitual lawbreakers and force them to come to court. This may have been the forerunner of the jury system that was later established by King HENRY II. He may also have written some laws that were later passed by CNUT THE GREAT, the Danish king who ruled England from 1016 to 1035. In his writings, Wulfstan outlined the public duties of each class of society, urged Cnut to govern as a Christian king, and promoted the blending of the Danish and Anglo-Saxon cultures.

Wulfstan's reputation, however, rests on his power as a preacher of forceful and eloquent sermons about the basics of the Christian faith. He often wrote under the pen name of Lupus (Wolf), and in his most famous sermon—*Sermon of the Wolf to the English*—he paints a grim picture of English society in the early 1000s. It was a time when priests and monks often strayed from their vows and duties and the king had difficulty enforcing Christian values on new Danish settlers. (*See also* **England.**)

Wyclif, John

ca. 1335–1384
**English theologian
and reformer**

* **philosophy** study of ideas, including science

* **theology** study of the nature of God and of religious truth

* **heretic** person who disagrees with established church doctrine

* **rector** priest in charge of a parish

* **secular** nonreligious; connected with everyday life

* **Eucharist** Christian ritual commemorating Christ's Last Supper on earth; also called Communion

* **excommunicate** to exclude from the rites of the church

J
ohn Wyclif was a controversial English theologian who wrote many influential works on philosophy* and theology*. Wyclif was critical of the church, and he was denounced as a heretic* for some of his views on church doctrine. His writings and ideas influenced the LOLLARDS in England, Jan HUS in BOHEMIA, and other religious reformers.

Wyclif was educated at Oxford University, and from 1356 to 1381 he spent much of his time there as a respected teacher. He was also a rector* at several PARISHES (local communities served by the church), including one in Lutterworth (in Leicestershire), where he lived during the last years of his life. In 1371, Wyclif became active and outspoken on political issues. He attended a meeting of PARLIAMENT that year at which the status of church property was discussed. Wyclif sided with those who argued that secular* authorities could seize church property in times of emergency. During the next few years, Wyclif became active in the anticlerical movement, and his interests turned towards church doctrine.

Several of Wyclif's views on church doctrine were condemned in 1377 by Pope Gregory XI, who called for his arrest. Attempts to condemn Wyclif in England failed at first, in part because he was protected by powerful individuals. In 1380, however, a commission at Oxford declared Wyclif's teaching on the Eucharist* heretical. The following year, Wyclif retired to Lutterworth, where he continued to write his controversial views. No attempt was made to excommunicate* him—no doubt because of continued support by powerful people.

An idea found in many of Wyclif's writings is the differentiation between the "actual church," with its hierarchy of church officials, and the "true

John Wyclif was an English theologian and reformer whose views on church doctrine were condemned by the pope. Wyclif insisted that the Bible was the sole authority on church doctrine, and that laws made by the church were valid only if they conformed to Scripture. He denounced the wealth and power of the clergy because it did not reflect the teachings of the Bible.

* **canon law** body of church law

The Wyclif Bible

The Wyclif Bible was one of the great landmarks in the history of the Bible and of the English language. The Wyclif Bible was the first translation of the Latin Bible into the English vernacular. It is unclear whether Wyclif himself initiated this Bible, although his emphasis on the importance of Scripture certainly inspired the work. It is also doubtful that Wyclif took part in the immense task of the actual translation and its revisions. Most of the work on the Bible was done by his followers, notably Nicholas Hereford.

church," which consisted of a community of righteous believers. Wyclif believed that all people were predestined for either heaven or hell, and only those predestined for heaven were members of the true church. As a result, Wyclif questioned the authority of all church officials, even the pope. He argued that religious authority was not automatically connected to church office and that only the truly righteous could exercise authority.

In matters of church doctrine, Wyclif insisted that the Bible was the sole and ultimate source of authority. Canon law* and the writings of early church fathers and theologians were valid only when they conformed to Scripture. He condemned the wealth and power of the CLERGY because they did not reflect the teachings of the Bible. He also condemned monastic life because its separation of the individual from the ordinary life of the church was not found in Scripture. The subject that most angered the church, and that led to Wyclif's final condemnation, was his view on the Eucharist. Wyclif denied the doctrine of transubstantiation, which claims that bread and wine turn into the body and blood of Christ during the Mass. He argued that nothing in the Bible supports this view.

Through his own teaching and that of his followers, Wyclif's ideas were spread throughout England and into other parts of Europe. After his death, the church continued to condemn his views and to persecute his followers.

Yet, his ideas took root among many religious reformers, and Wyclif became a forerunner of the great church reform of the 1500s known as the Protestant Reformation. (*See also* **Christianity; English Language and Literature; Excommunication; Heresy and Heresies; Mass, Liturgy of; Universities.**)

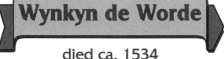

Wynkyn de Worde

died ca. 1534
Printer and bookseller
in London

* **duchy**   territory ruled by a duke or a duchess

Although Wynkyn de Worde was the most important English printer and bookseller of the late Middle Ages, little is known about his early years. He came from the duchy* of Lorraine (part of present-day France), and by 1479 he had settled in London as assistant to printer William CAXTON. He later owned several print shops, where he produced religious works, dictionaries, Latin grammars, sermons, almanacs, practical manuals, and poems and plays. De Worde published more than 700 volumes, which included the works of many authors. Some of these works were illustrated by his own woodcuts. De Worde introduced new styles of printing into England, and he also helped to modernize and simplify the English language. (*See also* **Books, Manuscript; Latin Language; Printing, Origins of.**)

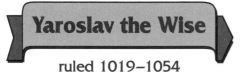

Yaroslav the Wise

ruled 1019–1054
Russian ruler

* **steppe**   vast treeless plain of southeastern Europe and Asia

   See map in Byzantine Empire (vol. 2).

* **metropolitan**   in the Eastern Church, a high-ranking bishop of a large city

In 1019, after a long war with his half brother, Yaroslav became grand prince of the Russian state called KIEVAN RUS. At first, he had to divide the state with another half brother, Mstislav, but after Mstislav died in 1036, Yaroslav was the sole ruler of united Rus. Brave in battle, although he was lame since childhood, Yaroslav waged war on the Poles, the Baltic peoples, the BYZANTINE EMPIRE, and the Turkic peoples of the steppes*, extending the Russian borders in all directions. He also used diplomacy and marriage to link his family to several royal families in Europe.

Yaroslav's reign was the golden age of medieval Russian culture. He founded schools and libraries, paid scholars to translate Greek and Latin works into the Slavic language of the Russian people, and beautified his capital city of Kiev with many monasteries and churches, including a splendid cathedral called Hagia Sophia. He also built new city walls that had a famous gate called the Golden Gate. According to the metropolitan* who was the head of the Russian church at that time, Yaroslav gave "the famous city of Kiev a crown of glory." (*See also* **Dmitrii Ivanovich Donskoi; Ivan III of Muscovy; Muscovy, Rise of; Novgorod.**)

Yazid I ibn Mu'awiya

ruled 680–683
Early Islamic ruler

* **caliph**   religious and political head of an Islamic state

Yazid I, the most controversial ruler of early Islamic times, was the second caliph* of the UMAYYAD dynasty*. Raised in Syria, Yazid inherited the CALIPHATE from his father, MU'AWIYA. Unfortunately, Yazid was unable to hold together the fragile alliances that Mu'awiya had forged among rival Arab tribes. Yazid's brief reign was a time of turmoil and disaster for the young Islamic state.

Trouble erupted when al-Husayn ibn Ali refused to accept Yazid as caliph. As the grandson of the prophet MUHAMMAD, the founder of Islam, al-Husayn had many followers who supported his own campaign to become caliph. In 680, Yazid's Umayyad forces trapped al-Husayn in the city

* **dynasty** succession of rulers from the same family or group

* **martyr** person who suffers and dies rather than renounce a religious faith

of Karbala, in present-day Iraq. Al-Husayn refused to surrender and was killed. This intensified the split between Shi'ites and other early Muslims. Al-Husayn became a martyr* of the Shi'ites, who still form a small but powerful minority within Islam.

For several years, Yazid struggled to keep rival tribes and sects in line. The final explosion came in 683, when one of al-Husayn's comrades led a revolt in Mecca. Umayyad forces besieged the holy city. Yazid remained in Syria, where he died two months into the siege. His death threw the Islamic Empire into confusion, as factions broke away or fought for power. Yazid entered Islamic history as the caliph responsible for the murder of the Prophet's grandson and the violation of Mecca. (*See also* **Husayn ibn Ali, al-; Islam, Conquests of.**)

Ypres

See map in Trade (vol. 4).

Ypres, a town in the southwestern part of present-day Belgium, was an important center of cloth production during the Middle Ages. The town was part of the county of FLANDERS, a nearly independent state whose strong counts had loose ties to their overlords, the kings of France. Ypres and other Flemish towns gradually won their independence during the later Middle Ages.

Ypres (called Ieper in the Flemish language) is located on the Iperleet, a tributary of the Yser River. In the 800s, the count of Flanders built a castle on the Iperleet to defend the region against VIKING invaders. The castle was administered by the CASTELLAN, a representative of the count. The fortification and its outbuildings were all that comprised Ypres for a period of 100 years.

When western Europe entered an economic revival in the 900s, Ypres benefited from its location near two important trade routes: the Yser River and the road that linked the Flemish city of BRUGES with France. A community of merchants settled on the banks of the Iperleet across from the castle. Here, in an area called the forum, they built homes, warehouses, and a market. Later, a large hall that became the center of the wool trade was added. Until the 1100s, the forum was governed by the castellan. The townspeople who lived in the forum of Ypres were legally free, whereas the peasants of the countryside were not.

Golden Age of Prosperity.   As Ypres and nearby towns grew in size and economic importance, they began to demand greater independence from the counts of Flanders. After one count, Charles the Good, was assassinated in Bruges in 1127, independence came quickly. Charles left no heirs, and a war broke out among nobles for his title. To win their support, these nobles granted charters* to various towns, turning them into self-governing COMMUNES. Ypres received such a charter and became independent of the castellan's authority. The merchants of the forum were responsible for the town's finances, justice system, security, defense, and GUILDS. They governed Ypres through a council of 13 magistrates. At first, the magistrates were appointed for life by the count, but after 1209 they were elected by the inhabitants of Ypres for terms of one year.

The 1200s were a golden age of economic and political power for Ypres. The city was already known as the foremost Flemish center of wool

* **charter** written grant from a ruler conferring certain rights and privileges

Wool and Good Works

Ypres was run by its leading merchant families, whose wealth from wool enabled them to adopt the manners and lifestyle of nobility. These prosperous families also had a strong sense of civic pride, and they did much to improve the quality of life in Ypres. They built churches, funded public works, established hospitals, and organized schools. Their pride and wealth were reflected in the hall they built to house the cloth guilds. It was the largest and most magnificent guild hall in western Europe—a symbol of the prosperity the merchants enjoyed during the Middle Ages.

cloth production. The craftspeople of Ypres imported raw wool from England and made it into fine cloth. Merchants from all over western Europe sought Ypres's product. By the 1200s, Ypres, together with the Flemish cities of GHENT and Bruges, controlled the political and economic life of Flanders. Wealthy merchants forced the counts to follow practices that benefited the interests of these cities.

Commerce in Ypres during the mid-1200s included not only the wholesale wool trade but also a system of banking and credit. Wool from Ypres was bought and sold at the large medieval FAIRS, one of which was held near Ypres. Merchants came from France, Italy, and Germany to attend the fair, and the economy of the region boomed as a result of this interaction. Ypres was also part of the powerful federation of merchant cities called the HANSEATIC LEAGUE. At its peak, Ypres had a population of about 28,000.

Misfortune and Decline. Many factors brought about the decline of Ypres, which began in the late 1200s. There were bitter conflicts among the craftspeople who made the wool and the merchants who sold it. One issue was the demand of the craftspeople for a role in local government. Wars between France and Flanders in the 1300s disrupted industry and trade, bringing strife to the countryside and higher taxes to pay for the wars. In 1316, Europe entered a period of severe famine. During this time, nearly 3,000 people died in Ypres from starvation and disease. Thirty years later, the PLAGUE devastated the region again. At one point, the population of Ypres fell to as low as 8,000.

In 1384, Flanders came under the rule of the powerful dukes of BURGUNDY, who tried to restore the region's prosperity. By that time, however, the economy of Ypres was in ruins. Cheaper wool cloth made in England was sweeping Flemish cloth from the European markets. In the centuries that followed, trade shifted to Europe's seaports and industrial centers, and Ypres's fortune declined. (*See also* **Textiles; Trade; Wool.**)

Zanj

See map in Islam, Conquests of (vol. 2).

Zanj was a medieval Arabic term for the peoples of East Africa. The Zanj were known in the Middle East in pre-Islamic times, but the first recorded use of the word was in 680 in a reference to Zanj slaves. Muslims regarded the Zanj as socially inferior, and this attitude was reinforced by racial and cultural hostility reflected in Arabic literature and folklore. Medieval Arabic writers considered the Zanj to be lazy and dishonest, and descriptions of Zanj slaves usually emphasized their blackness. The Zanj were also thought to possess magical powers.

Fear and distrust of the Zanj were reinforced for centuries by a great slave revolt that occurred in southern IRAQ between 868 and 883. Most of the rebels were Zanj slaves who had been subjected to the harshest and cruelest of conditions. The rebels succeeded in taking control of much of southern Iraq, and it was not until 882 that the ABBASIDS were able to capture the rebel capital and end the revolt. The memory of this slave revolt discouraged the further use of large concentrations of slave labor for agriculture in Islamic countries. However, black slaves continued to be popular as soldiers and domestic servants.

Information in Arabic sources about the Zanj was limited to the coastal areas of East Africa. Nevertheless, this information was important because it was the only written evidence about East Africa before the Portuguese arrived there in the 1400s. The first Islamic mention of Zanj land dates from the 700s, and more extensive accounts come from the works of Arab geographers of the 900s and the 1100s.

Islamic sources describe the land of Zanj as a place of rivers, harbors, islands, mountains, volcanoes, and cities. The Zanj were divided into different ethnic groups and kingdoms that were constantly at war. They had no horses, so their soldiers rode cattle. Zanj kings ruled according to custom, and if a king ruled unjustly, he could be killed and his children denied succession to the throne. The Zanj engaged in trade, farming, gold mining, fishing, and hunting, especially for leopards and elephants. They wore iron jewelry, filed their teeth, and loved music and dancing. They greatly admired the Arabs and were easily kidnapped by slave merchants. The Zanj worshiped idols and natural forces and had medicine men, but they also believed in a supreme being. By the late Middle Ages, many Zanj rulers had converted to Islam, which became firmly established in Zanj cities and coastal regions. (*See also* **Maps and Mapmaking; Nubia; Slavery.**)

Suggested Readings

Atlases and Encyclopedias
History and Society
Daily Life
Biography
Women in the Middle Ages
Christianity
The Islamic World
The Jewish World
Literature
Art and Architecture
Science and Technology
Wars and Warfare

Atlases and Encyclopedias

The Atlas of the Crusades. Edited by Jonathan Riley-Smith. New York: Facts on File, 1990.

Atlas of the Islamic World Since 1500. Edited by Francis Robinson. New York: Facts on File, 1987.

Atlas of the Jewish World. Edited by Nicholas De Lange. New York: Facts on File, 1992.

Atlas of Medieval Europe. Edited by Donald Matthew. New York: Facts on File, 1989.

The Cultural Atlas of Islam. Edited by Isma'il Faruqi and Lois L. al Faruqi. New York: Macmillan, 1986.

Cultural Atlas of the Viking World. Edited by James Graham-Campbell. New York: Facts on File, 1994.

Dictionary of the Middle Ages. Edited by Joseph R. Strayer. 13 volumes, including index. New York: Charles Scribner's Sons, 1989.

A Historical Atlas of the Jewish People. Edited by Eli Barnavi. New York: Schocken Books, 1992.

The Illustrated Encyclopedia of Arthurian Legends. Edited by Ronan Coghlan. Rockport, Md.: Element, 1993.

History and Society

Barber, Richard. *The Reign of Chivalry.* New York: St. Martin's Press, 1980. Illustrated survey of knighthood and the laws of war.

Barlow, Frank. *The Feudal Kingdom of England, 1042–1216.* New York: Longman, 1968.

Barraclough, Geoffrey. *The Crucible of Europe: The Ninth and Tenth Centuries in European History.* London: Thames & Hudson, 1976. Guide to the period from Charlemagne to the end of the Viking migrations.

Bendiner, Elmer. *The Rise and Fall of Paradise: When Arabs and Jews Built a Kingdom in Spain.* New York: Dorset Press, 1990.

Brown, R. Allen. *The Normans and the Norman Conquest.* Rochester, N.Y.: Boydell Press, 1995.

Burrow, J. A. *The Ages of Man: A Study in Medieval Writing and Thought.* New York: Oxford University Press, 1989.

Campbell, James, ed. *The Anglo-Saxons.* Ithaca, N.Y.: Cornell University Press, 1982.

* Asterisk denotes book for young readers.

Cantor, Norman. *The Civilization of the Middle Ages.* New York: HarperCollins, 1994.

Chamberlain, E. R. *Florence in the Time of the Medici.* New York: Longman, 1982.

Claiborne, Robert. *Our Marvelous Native Tongue: The Life and Times of the English Language.* New York: Random House, 1987.

Collins, Roger. *Early Medieval Europe, 300–1000.* New York: St. Martin's Press, 1991.

Duckett, Eleanor S. *Carolingian Portraits: A Study in the Ninth Century.* Ann Arbor: University of Michigan Press, 1988.

Eco, Umberto. *The Name of the Rose.* New York: Harcourt, 1980. Mystery novel, with rich historical background, involving murders in a monastery and the Franciscan sleuth who helps solve the crimes.

Edge, David, and John M. Paddock. *Arms and Armor of the Medieval Knight.* New York: Crescent Books, 1988.

Evans, Joan, ed. *The Flowering of the Middle Ages.* New York: McGraw-Hill, 1966.

Foster, R. F. *The Oxford Illustrated History of Ireland.* New York: Oxford University Press, 1989.

Fumagalli, Vito. *Landscapes of Fear: Perceptions of Nature and the City in the Middle Ages.* Cambridge, Mass.: Blackwell, 1994.

Gary, Dorothy H. *The Splendor of Byzantium.* New York: Viking, 1967.

Gendel, Milton, ed. *An Illustrated History of Italy.* New York: McGraw-Hill, 1966.

Gies, Frances. *The Knight in History.* New York: Harper-Collins, 1987.

Gray, Robert. *A History of London.* New York: Dorset, 1986.

Guy, Jan. *The Horizon History of Russia.* New York: American Heritage, 1970.

Haskins, Charles H. *The Renaissance of the Twelfth Century.* 1927. Reprint. Cleveland, Ohio: Meridian Books, 1957.

Haverkamp, Alfred. *Medieval Germany, 1056–1273.* New York: Oxford University Press, 1992.

Hearder, Harry. *Italy: A Short History.* New York: Cambridge University Press, 1991.

Herm, Gerhard. *The Celts: The People Who Came Out of the Darkness.* New York: St. Martin's Press, 1975. History of the Celts from 400 B.C. to the court of King Arthur.

Hetherington, Paul. *Byzantium: City of Gold, City of Faith.* London: Orbis Publishing, 1983.

Hollister, C. Warren. *Medieval Europe: A Short History.* New York: McGraw-Hill, 1993.

Hopkins, Andrea. *Knights.* New York: Artabras, 1990.

Howarth, David. *1066—Year of the Conquest.* New York: Viking, Penguin, 1981.

Huizinga, Johan. *The Waning of the Middle Ages.* 1924. Reprint. New York: St. Martin's Press, 1949. Cultural history of the later Middle Ages in France and the Netherlands.

James, Edward. *The Franks.* Cambridge, Mass.: Blackwell, 1991.

Jones, Gwyn. *A History of the Vikings.* New York: Oxford University Press, 1984.

Keen, Maurice. *Chivalry.* New Haven, Conn.: Yale University Press, 1986.

Lewis, C. S. *The Discarded Image.* New York: Cambridge University Press, 1994. Introduction to the medieval world view.

Loomis, Roger Sherman. *A Mirror of Chaucer's World.* Princeton, N.J.: Princeton University Press, 1965. Pictures of the people, places, and things described by Chaucer.

Maclean, Fitzroy. *Scotland: A Concise History.* New York: Thames & Hudson, 1993.

Manchester, William. *A World Lit Only by Fire.* Boston: Little, 1993.

Markale, Jean. *The Celts.* Rochester, Vt.: Inner Traditions International, 1993.

McCrum, Robert, William Cran, and Robert MacNeil. *The Story of English.* New York: Viking, Penguin, 1993. Companion to the acclaimed public television series.

Morgan, David O. *The Mongols.* Cambridge, Mass.: Blackwell, 1987.

Morgan, Kenneth. *The Oxford Illustrated History of Britain.* New York: Oxford University Press, 1992.

Parry, J. H. *The Discovery of the Sea.* Berkeley and Los Angeles: University of California Press, 1981.

Phillips, J. R. S. *The Medieval Expansion of Europe.* New York: Oxford University Press, 1988. Revealing account of European encounters with the Near East and Asia long before Columbus.

Southern, R. W. *The Making of the Middle Ages.* New Haven, Conn.: Yale University Press, 1961.

Strayer, Joseph R. *On the Medieval Origins of the Modern State.* Princeton, N.J.: Princeton University Press, 1970. Classic study of medieval statecraft—royal power, the struggle of church and state, and feudalism.

Tuchman, Barbara. *A Distant Mirror: The Calamitous Fourteenth Century.* New York: Ballantine Books, 1978. Narrative of wars, plagues, and unrest in a troubled age.

Vasiliev, A. A. *History of the Byzantine Empire, 324–1453.* Madison: University of Wisconsin Press, 1980.

White, Lynn, Jr. *Medieval Technology and Social Change.* New York: Oxford University Press, 1966.

Wright, Esmond. *The Medieval and Renaissance World*. Secaucus, N.J.: Chartwell Books, 1979. Covers European, Islamic, Jewish, and Asian cultures.

Zacour, Norman. *An Introduction to Medieval Institutions*. 2d ed. New York: St. Martin's Press, 1976. Includes such topics as feudal manors and villages, commerce and industry, towns, vassals, law, and schools.

Ziegler, Philip. *The Black Death*. Dover, N.H.: Alan Sutton Publishing, 1991.

Daily Life

*Biesty, Stephen. *Cross-sections: Castle*. New York: Dorling Kindersley, 1994. Cleverly illustrated book that shows detailed drawings of many aspects of castle life.

*Cherry, John. *Goldsmiths*. Medieval Craftsmen series. Toronto: University of Toronto Press, 1991.

Gies, Frances, and Joseph Gies. *Life in a Medieval Village*. New York: HarperCollins, 1991.

Gies, Joseph, and Frances Gies. *Life in a Medieval Castle*. New York: HarperCollins, 1979.

———. *Life in a Medieval City*. New York: HarperCollins, 1981.

Hanawalt, Barbara A. *The Ties That Bound: Peasant Families in Medieval England*. New York: Oxford University Press, 1989.

*Pfaffenbichler, M. *Armourers*. Medieval Craftsmen series. Toronto: University of Toronto Press, 1991.

Power, Eileen. *Medieval People*. 1924. Reprint. New York: HarperCollins, 1992. Classic study of medieval society through the stories of six diverse individuals.

Riché, Pierre. *Daily Life in the World of Charlemagne*. New York: Oxford University Press, 1992.

Rowling, Marjorie. *Life in Medieval Times*. New York: Dorset, 1987.

*Staniland, K. *Embroiderers*. Medieval Craftsmen series. Toronto: University of Toronto Press, 1991.

Biography

Barlow, Frank. *Thomas Becket*. Berkeley and Los Angeles: University of California Press, 1990.

Browning, Robert. *Justinian and Theodora*. New York: Praeger, 1971.

Cantor, Norman F. *Medieval Lives: Eight Charismatic Men and Women of the Middle Ages*. New York: HarperCollins, 1995. Portraits of Alcuin of York, Eleanor of Aquitaine, Robert Grosseteste, Hildegard von Bingen, and several others are revealed through imagined conversations.

Dahmus, Joseph. *Seven Medieval Historians*. New York: Nelson Hall, 1981.

———. *Seven Medieval Kings*. New York: Barnes & Noble, 1967. Includes Harun al-Rashid, Charlemagne, Henry II, and Louis IX.

Dunn, Ross. *The Adventures of Ibn Battuta, A Muslim Traveler of the 14th Century*. Berkeley and Los Angeles: University of California Press, 1986. A book based on Ibn Battuta's own writings about his travels on three continents and a source for the history and culture of the medieval Islamic world.

Flanagan, Sabina. *Hildegard of Bingen: A Visionary Life*. New York: Routledge, 1989.

Florescu, Radu R., and Raymond T. McNally. *Dracula: Prince of Many Faces*. Boston: Little, Brown, 1990.

Gardner, John C. *The Life and Times of Chaucer*. New York: Knopf, 1978. Portrait of Chaucer's life and works.

Gillingham, John. *Richard the Lionheart*. New York: New Amsterdam Books, 1994.

Hindley, Geoffrey. *Saladin*. New York: Barnes & Noble, 1976.

Kelly, Amy. *Eleanor of Aquitaine and the Four Kings*. Cambridge, Mass.: Harvard University Press, 1974.

Labarge, Margaret Wade. *Saint Louis: Louis IX, Most Christian King of France*. Boston: Little, Brown, 1968.

Painter, Sidney. *William Marshal*. New York: Barnes & Noble, 1995.

Pernoud, Regine. *Joan of Arc by Herself and Witnesses*. Lanham, Md.: Madison Books UPA, 1982.

Warren, W. L. *Henry II*. Berkeley and Los Angeles: University of California Press, 1973.

Women in the Middle Ages

Anderson, Bonnie, and Judith P. Zinsser. *A History of Their Own: Women in Europe from Prehistory to the Present*. New York: Harper & Row, 1988.

Echols, Anne, and Marty Williams. *An Annotated Index of Medieval Women*. Princeton, N.J.: Marcus Wiener, 1992.

———. *Between Pit and Pedestal: Women in the Middle Ages*. Princeton, N.J.: Marcus Wiener, 1994.

Labarge, Margaret Wade. *A Small Sound of the Trumpet: Women in Medieval Life*. Boston: Beacon, 1988.

Petroff, Elizabeth A. *Medieval Women's Visionary Literature*. New York: Oxford University Press, 1986.

Shahar, Shulamith. *The Fourth Estate: A History of Women in the Middle Ages*. New York: Routledge, 1984.

Uitz, Erica. *The Legend of Good Women: Medieval Women in Towns and Cities*. Mt. Kisco, N.Y.: Moyer Bell, 1994.

Christianity

Barraclough, Geoffrey. *The Medieval Papacy*. New York: Norton, 1979. Illustrated survey of one of the most important medieval institutions.

Fremantle, Anne. *The Age of Belief: The Medieval Philosophers*. Boston: Houghton Mifflin, 1977. Introduction to medieval philosophy; contains several excerpts from the writings of St. Augustine, Boethius, Abelard, St. Bernard, and others.

Gordon, Anne. *A Book of Saints*. New York: Bantam, 1994.

Leclercq, Jean. *The Love of Learning and the Desire for God: A Study of Monastic Culture*. New York: Fordham University Press, 1985.

Lehane, Brendan. *Early Celtic Christianity*. New York: Barnes & Noble, 1993.

McManners, John, ed. *The Oxford Illustrated History of Christianity*. New York: Oxford University Press, 1992.

Oakley, Francis. *The Western Church in the Later Middle Ages*. Ithaca, N.Y.: Cornell University Press, 1985.

The Islamic World

Denny, Frederick. *An Introduction to Islam*. New York: Macmillan, 1994. Introduction to the Islamic religion; gives clear explanations of basic concepts and practices.

Hayes, John R. *The Genius of Arab Civilization: Source of Renaissance*. 3d ed. New York: New York University Press, 1992. Covers all aspects of classical Arab culture in many parts of the Islamic world.

Hourani, Albert. *A History of the Arab Peoples*. Cambridge, Mass.: Harvard University Press, 1991. A scholarly work that provides many new insights.

Landay, Jerry M. *The Dome of the Rock*. New York: Newsweek, 1972.

Leacroft, Helen, and Richard Leacroft. *The Building of Early Islam*. London: Hodder and Stoughton, 1976.

Lewis, Bernard. *The Arabs in History*. 6th ed. New York: Oxford University Press, 1993.

———. *Istanbul and the Civilization of the Ottoman Empire*. Norman: University of Oklahoma Press, 1972. Study of Ottoman culture from the 13th to the 19th century.

Maalouf, Amin. *The Crusades Through Arab Eyes*. New York: Schocken, 1989. Narrative based on Arab accounts.

*Mantin, Peter, and Ruth Mantin. *The Islamic World: Beliefs and Civilization, 600–1600*. New York: Cambridge University Press, 1993.

*Moktefi, Mokhtar. *The Arabs in the Golden Age*. Brookfield, Conn.: Millbrook Press, 1992.

Payne, Robert. *The History of Islam*. New York: Barnes & Noble, 1959.

Pickthall, Mohammed. *The Meaning of the Glorious Koran*. New York: NAL/Dutton, 1993. Standard, readable translation of the Qur'an.

Saunders, J. J. *A History of Medieval Islam*. New York: Routledge, 1978. Basic introduction to medieval Islamic history up to the 11th century.

Schacht, Joseph, and C. E. Bosworth, eds. *The Legacy of Islam*. 2d ed. New York: Oxford University Press, 1974. Classic work; covers many aspects of Islamic culture and relates them to world history.

Stewart, Desmond. *Mecca*. New York: Newsweek, 1980. Oversized, illustrated book; provides much information on the past and present of this historic city.

*Townson, Duncan. *Muslim Spain*. Minneapolis, Minn.: Lerner, 1979.

The Jewish World

Cohen, Mark R. *Under Crescent and Cross: The Jews in the Middle Ages*. Princeton, N.J.: Princeton University Press, 1994.

Gerber, Jane S. *The Jews of Spain*. New York: Free Press, 1992.

Lewis, Bernard. *The Jews of Islam*. Princeton, N.J.: Princeton University Press, 1987. Introduction to minorities in medieval Islam.

Wigoder, Geoffrey W., ed. *Jewish Art and Civilization*. New York: Walker, 1972.

Literature

Collections

Adler, Elkan N., ed. *Jewish Travellers in the Middle Ages: Nineteen Firsthand Accounts*. New York: Dover, 1987. Firsthand accounts by ambassadors, pilgrims, scholars, and merchants—a Jewish perspective on medieval life.

Bogin, Meg. *The Women Troubadours*. New York: Norton, 1980. An introduction to the women poets of 12th-century Provence with a collection of their poems.

Bullfinch, Thomas. *The Age of Chivalry and the Legends of Charlemagne*. New York: Marboro Books, 1992.

Burrow, J. A., and T. Turville-Petre, eds. *A Book of Middle English*. Cambridge, Mass.: Blackwell, 1996.

Carola, Leslie C., ed. *The Irish: A Treasury of Art and Literature*. Southport, Conn.: H. L. Levin, 1994. Illustrated anthology of Irish art and literature from prehistoric to modern times.

Delaney, Frank. *Legends of the Celts*. New York: Sterling, 1994.

Goodrich, Norma L. *Medieval Myths: Recreations of Great Myths of the Middle Ages*. New York: NAL/Dutton, 1994.

Hieatt, Constance B., ed. *Beowulf and Other Old English Poems*. New York: Bantam, 1988.

Kvideland, Reimund, and Henning K. Sehmsdorf, eds. *Scandinavian Folk Belief and Legend.* Minneapolis: University of Minnesota Press, 1988.

Ross, James B., and Mary M. McLaughlin, eds. *The Portable Medieval Reader.* New York: Viking, Penguin, 1977. Selections from the works of outstanding medieval writers, representing many aspects of medieval life.

Sherley-Price, Leo, trans. *Bede: Ecclesiastical History of the English People.* New York: Viking, Penguin, 1991.

*Yeats, William Butler. *Fairy and Folk Tales of Ireland.* New York: Collier (Macmillan), 1983. A famous Irish poet retells stories from his country's lore.

Works of Individual Authors

Alighieri, Dante. *Inferno.* Translated by John Ciardi. 1954. Reprint. New York: NAL/Dutton, 1982.

——. *Paradiso.* Translated by John Ciardi. 1961. Reprint. New York: Mentor, 1970.

——. *Purgatorio.* Tranlated by John Ciardi. 1961. Reprint. New York: NAL/Dutton, 1989.

Andreas Capellanus. *The Art of Courtly Love.* Translated by John Jay Parry. New York: Columbia University Press, 1960.

Anglo-Saxon Chronicle. Edited and translated by G. N. Garmonsway. New York: Everyman's, 1994.

The Arabian Nights. Translated by Husain Haddawy. New York: Norton, 1995. Translation based on an authentic medieval manuscript.

Béroul. *The Romance of Tristan.* Translated by Alan S. Fedrick. New York: Penguin, 1980.

Boccaccio, Giovanni. *The Decameron.* New York: Penguin, 1972.

Boethius. *The Consolation of Philosophy.* Edited by Richard H. Green. New York: Macmillan, 1962.

Chaucer, Geoffrey. *The Canterbury Tales.* Edited by Nevill Coghill. New York: Penguin, 1977. A modern English version.

——. *Troilus and Crisedye.* Edited by Nevill Coghill. New York: Viking, Penguin, 1971. A modern English version.

——. *The Canterbury Tales.* Edited by Kent A. Hieatt and Constance B. Hieatt. New York: Bantam, 1982. Selections of the tales in Middle English, with modern English translations.

Chrétien de Troyes. *The Complete Romances of Chrétien de Troyes.* Edited by David Staines. Bloomington and Indianapolis: University of Indiana Press, 1993.

Christine de Pizan. *A Medieval Woman's Mirror of Honor: The Treasury of the City of Ladies.* Translated by Charity Willard. Tenafly, N.J.: Bard Hall Press, 1989.

Comnena, Anna. *The Alexiad of Anna Comnena.* Translated by E. R. Sewter. New York: Viking, Penguin, 1979.

Froissart, Jean. *Chronicles.* Translated by Geoffrey Brereton. New York: Viking, Penguin, 1978.

Goodrich, Norma L. *King Arthur.* New York: HarperCollins, 1989.

Gregory of Tours: *A History of the Franks.* Translated by Louis Thorpe. New York: Penguin, 1974.

Guillaume de Lorris and Jean de Meun. *The Romance of the Rose.* Translated by Frances Hogan. New York: Oxford University Press, 1994.

Joinville and Villehardouin: Chronicles of the Crusades. Edited by M. R. B. Shaw. New York: Penguin, 1963.

*Kamen, Gloria. *The Ringdoves.* New York: Atheneum, 1988. From the Fables of Bidpai; retold and illustrated by Gloria Kamen.

Kempe, Margery. *The Book of Margery Kempe.* New York: Penguin, 1985.

Malory's Le Morte D'Arthur. Edited by Keith Baines. New York: Mentor (Penguin), 1962.

Marie de France: Fables. Edited and translated by Harriet Spiegel. Toronto: University of Toronto Press, 1987.

Petrarch's Lyric Poems. Edited by Robert M. Durling. Cambridge, Mass.: Harvard University Press, 1976. Original Italian text of poems with modern English prose translation.

Polo, Marco. *The Travels of Marco Polo.* Translated by Ronald Latham. New York: Penguin, 1958.

The Rubaiyat of Omar Khayyam. Translated by Edward FitzGerald. New York: Viking, Penguin, 1981.

Sir Gawain and the Green Knight. Edited by J. A. Burrow. New York: Penguin, 1987.

Song of Roland. Translated by Dorothy L. Sayers. New York: Penguin, 1957.

Villon, François. *The Poems of François Villon.* Edited by Galway Kinnell. New York: New American Library, 1965. Bilingual edition with medieval French and modern English prose translation.

Wolfram von Eschenbach. *Parzival.* Translated by A. T. Hatto. New York: Penguin, 1980.

Art and Architecture

Beckwith, John. *Early Medieval Art.* New York: Thames & Hudson, 1985. Covers Carolingian, Ottonian, and Romanesque periods.

*Binski, Paul. *Painters.* Medieval Craftsmen series. Toronto: University of Toronto Press, 1991.

Blair, Sheila, and Jonathan Bloom. *The Art and Architecture of Islam, 1250–1800.* New Haven, Conn.: Yale University Press, 1994. The art of the Islamic period, discussed against its historical background.

*Brown, S., and D. O'Connor. *Glass-Painters*. Medieval Craftsmen series. Toronto: University of Toronto Press, 1991.

*Coldstream, Nicola. *Masons and Sculptors*. Medieval Craftsmen series. Toronto: University of Toronto Press, 1991.

De Hamel, Christopher. *A History of Illuminated Manuscripts*. San Francisco: Chronicle Books, 1994.

———. *Scribes and Illuminators*. Medieval Craftsmen series. Toronto: University of Toronto Press, 1991.

Dodds, Jerrilyn D., ed. *Al-Andalus: The Islamic Arts of Spain*. New York: Metropolitan Museum of Art, 1992. Articles about the art of Islamic Spain, illustrated with numerous color photographs.

Janson, H. W. *History of Art*. 5th ed. New York: Abrams, 1995.

Kinross, Patrick B. *Hagia Sophia*. New York: Newsweek, 1972.

Kostop, Spiro. *A History of Architecture*. New York: Oxford University Press, 1995.

Krautheimer, Richard. *Early Christian and Byzantine Architecture*. New Haven, Conn.: Yale University Press, 1986.

Laing, Lloyd, and Jennifer Laing. *Art of the Celts*. New York: Thames & Hudson, 1992.

*Macauley, David. *Castle*. Boston: Houghton-Mifflin, 1977. An account of the building of a castle by a famous technical illustrator.

———. *Cathedral: The Story of Its Construction*. Boston: Houghton-Mifflin, 1981.

Martindale, Andrew. *Gothic Art*. New York: Thames & Hudson, 1985.

Meehan, Bernard. *The Book of Kells*. New York: Thames & Hudson, 1994.

Nuttgens, Patrick. *The Story of Architecture*. London: Phaidon, 1995.

Rice, David Talbot. *Art of the Byzantine Era*. New York: Thames & Hudson, 1985.

———. *Islamic Art*. New York: Oxford University Press, 1975.

Rodley, Lyn. *Byzantine Art and Architecture: An Introduction*. New York: Cambridge University Press, 1994.

Snyder, James C. *Medieval Art: Painting, Sculpture, Architecture, 4th–14th Centuries*. New York: Abrams, 1989.

Stokstad, Marilyn. *Medieval Art*. New York: Harper-Collins, 1986.

Swaan, Wim. *The Gothic Cathedral*. New York: Doubleday, 1969.

White, John. *Art and Architecture in Italy, 1250–1400*. New Haven, Conn.: Yale University Press, 1973.

Science and Technology

*Beshore, George. *Science in Early Islamic Culture*. New York: Franklin Watts, 1988.

Gimpel, Jean. *The Medieval Machine: The Industrial Revolution of the Middle Ages*. New York: Viking, Penguin, 1977.

Hoyt, Edwin. *Arab Science: Discoveries and Contributions*. New York: Nelson, 1975. The scientific achievements of the Arabs within the context of their history.

Lindberg, David C. *The Beginnings of Western Science: The European Scientific Tradition in Philosophical, Religious, and Institutional Context, 600 B.C. to A.D. 1450*. Chicago: University of Chicago Press, 1992. Narrative account of the development of science in the West from antiquity to the early Renaissance.

Lindberg, David C., ed. *Science in the Middle Ages*. Chicago: University of Chicago Press, 1978. Introductory essays on various aspects of medieval science and technology.

Murdoch, John E. *Album of Science*. Volume I: *Antiquity and the Middle Ages*. New York: Charles Scribner's Sons, 1984.

Wars and Warfare

Billings, Malcolm. *The Cross and the Crescent: A History of the Crusades*. New York: Sterling, 1990.

Dahmus, Joseph. *Seven Decisive Battles of the Middle Ages*. New York: Nelson-Hall, 1983.

Jarman, Rosemary H. *Crispin's Day: The Glory of Agincourt*. Boston: Little, Brown, 1979. A portrait of medieval warfare.

Seward, Desmond. *The Hundred Years War: The English in France, 1337–1453*. New York: Macmillan, 1982.

———. *The Wars of the Roses: Through the Lives of Five Men and Women of the Fifteenth Century*. New York: Viking, Penguin, 1995.

Riley-Smith, Jonathan, ed. *The Oxford Illustrated History of the Crusades*. New York: Oxford University Press, 1995.

Warner, Philip. *Sieges of the Middle Ages*. New York: Barnes & Noble, 1968.

* Asterisk denotes book for young readers.

Photo Credits

Volume 1

Color Plates

for *Daily Life* between pages 116 and 117:

1: Scala/Art Resource; 2: The Pierpont Morgan Library/M.399, f.2v/Art Resource; 3: E. T. Archive; 4: The Granger Collection; 5: Superstock; 6: Superstock; 7: Erich Lessing/Art Resource; 8: Superstock; 9: Superstock; 10: The Pierpont Morgan Library/M.775, f.122v/Art Resource; 11: Superstock; 12: Superstock; 13: Giraudon/Art Resource; 14: Superstock; 15: Scala/Art Resource

Black-and-White Photographs:

2: Foto Marburg/Art Resource; 4: Giraudon/Art Resource; 6: The Granger Collection; 8: Ruth Dixon/Stock Boston; Peter Menzel/Stock Boston; Jean Claude Lejeune/Stock Boston; 10: Giraudon/Art Resource; 16: Alinari/Art Resource; 20: Alinari/Art Resource; 24: Alinari/Art Resource; 28: Alinari/Art Resource; 29: Giraudon/Art Resource; 30: Paris, Bibliothèque Nationale/Superstock; 46: The Bettmann Archive; 51: Snark/Art Resource; 55: Superstock; 57: Foto Marburg/Art Resource; 59: British Library; 61: Paris, Bibliothèque Nationale/Bridgeman; 64: Erich Lessing/Art Resource; 66: Giraudon/Art Resource; 69: The Bettmann Archive; 74: Alain Keler/Art Resource; 77: Giraudon/Art Resource; 78: V&A/Art Resource; 83: Scala/Art Resource; 87: Foto Marburg/Art Resource; 88: Foto Marburg/Art Resource; 92: Giraudon/Art Resource; 95: Giraudon/Art Resource; 99: Giraudon/Art Resource; 103: The Granger Collection; 109: Scala/Art Resource; 112: Alinari/Art Resource; 114: Lauros-Giraudon/Art Resource; 116: Giraudon/Art Resource; 120: Alinari/Art Resource; 122: Josephine Powell; 131: Foto Marburg/Art Resource; 133: Metropolitan Museum of Art/The Cloisters Collection, 1954; 139: Foto Marburg/Art Resource; 140: Giraudon/Art Resource; 141: Bridgeman/Art Resource; 149: Giraudon/Art Resource; 155: Giraudon/Art Resource; 159: Gian Berto Vanni/Art Resource; 162: Giraudon/Art Resource; 171: Scala/Art Resource; 173: Alinari/Art Resource; 174: Foto Marburg/Art Resource; 176: Bridgeman/Art Resource; 178: Hulton Deutsch Collection, Ltd.; 180: SEF/Art Resource; 184: Giraudon/Art Resource; 188: Giraudon/Art Resource; 193: Giraudon/Art Resource; 205: Bridgeman/Art Resource; 212: Bridgeman/Art Resource; 215: Scala/Art Resource; 219: Alinari/Art Resource; 221: The Granger Collection; 223: Lauros-Giraudon/Art Resource; 226: Alinari/Art Resource

Volume 2

Color Plates

for *Art and Architecture* between pages 126 and 127:

1: Scala/Art Resource; 2: Scala/Art Resource; 3: Erich Lessing/Art Resource; 4: Scala/Art Resource; 5: Superstock; 6: Art Resource; 7: Scala/Art Resource; 8: Superstock; 9: Bridgeman/Art Resource; 10: The Pierpont Morgan Library/M.500, f.11/Art Resource; 11: Giraudon/Art Resource; 12: Werner Forman Archive/Art Resource; 13: Giraudon/Art Resource; 14: The Granger Collection; 15: Scala/Art Resource

Black-and-White Photographs:

1: Paris, Bibliothèque Nationale/Art Resource; 3: Giraudon/Art Resource; 6: Giraudon/Art Resource; 13: Giraudon/Art Resource; 18: Giraudon/Art Resource; 20: Giraudon/Art Resource; 23: Alinari/Art Resource; 25: The Pierpont Morgan Library/M.917, f.206/Art Resource; 27: Alinari/Art Resource; 29: Snark/Art Resource; 34: The Bettmann Archive; 36: Alinari/Art Resource; 39: The Granger Collection; 44: Giraudon/Art Resource; 47: Bridgeman/Art Resource; 48: The Granger Collection; 50: The Granger Collection; 63: E. T. Archive; 64: Werner Forman Archive/Art Resource; 68: The Granger Collection; 72: Giraudon/Art Resource; 80: Giraudon/Art Resource; 85: Foto Marburg/Art Resource; 91: Giraudon/Art Resource; 95: Giraudon/Art Resource; 100: Giraudon/Art Resource; 103: Art Resource; 109: Giraudon/Art Resource; 113: Giraudon/Art Resource; 121: Giraudon/Art Resource; 123: Alinari/Art Resource; 127: Alinari/Art Resource; 132: Giraudon/Art Resource; 135: Erich Lessing/Art Resource; 137: Giraudon/Art Resource; 142: Giraudon/Art Resource; 145: Bridgeman/Art Resource; 146: Foto Marburg/Art Resource; 148: Giraudon/Art Resource; 149: Scala/Art Resource; 154: Foto Marburg/Art Resource;

164: Alinari/Art Resource; 169: Giraudon/Art Resource; 172: Alinari/Art Resource; 175: Giraudon/Art Resource; 178: E. T. Archive; 184: Scala/Art Resource; 186: Erich Lessing/Art Resource; 187: The Granger Collection; 190: G. E. Kidder Smith; 191: E. T. Archive; 193: Giraudon/Art Resource; 195: British Library;

201: Snark/Art Resource; 203: Giraudon/Art Resource; 204: Foto Marburg/Art Resource; 209: D. Y./Art Resource; 219: Giraudon/Art Resource; 223: Snark/Art Resource; 225: Giraudon/Art Resource; 228: Giraudon/Art Resource; 229: Snark/Art Resource; 233: Scala/Art Resource; 234: Giraudon/Art Resource; 236: Giraudon/Art Resource

Volume 3

Color Plates
for *People of the Middle Ages* between pages 126 and 127:

1: E. T. Archive; 2: Scala/Art Resource; 3: Scala/Art Resource; 4: The Granger Collection; 5: Scala/Art Resource; 6: Giraudon/Art Resource; 7: Bridgeman/Art Resource; 8: Giraudon/Art Resource; 9: Scala/Art Resource; 10: Bridgeman/Art Resource; 11: The Granger Collection; 12: Giraudon/Art Resource; 13: The Granger Collection; 14: E. T. Archive; 15: E. T. Archive

Black-and-White Photographs:
4: Giraudon/Art Resource; 8: Art Resource; 10: Giraudon/Art Resource; 12: Giraudon/Art Resource; 14: Foto Marburg/Art Resource; 21: The Pierpont Morgan Library/M.500, f.4v/Art Resource; 24: Giraudon/Art Resource; 28: Erich Lessing/Art Resource; 31: Alinari/Art Resource; 39: Werner Forman Archive/Art Resource; 41: Giraudon/Art Resource; 44: Yale University Art Gallery; 49: Foto Marburg/Art Resource; 54: Giraudon/Art Resource; 55: Bridgeman/Art Resource; 58: Bridgeman/Art Resource; 61: Alinari/Art Resource; 68: Giraudon/Art Resource; 74: Giraudon/Art Resource;

76: Erich Lessing/Art Resource; 82: E. T. Archive; 88: Giraudon/Art Resource; 91: Paris, Bibliothèque Nationale; 92: British Museum; 100: The Granger Collection; 102: The Granger Collection; 103: The Granger Collection; 111: Giraudon/Art Resource; 112: Giraudon/Art Resource; 117: Giraudon/Art Resource; 120: Giraudon/Art Resource; 122: The Bettmann Archive; 128: Giraudon/Art Resource; 131: Giraudon/Art Resource; 134: Giraudon/Art Resource; 136: Giraudon/Art Resource; 140: Alinari/Art Resource; 143: Giraudon/Art Resource; 150: E. T. Archive; 153: Giraudon/Art Resource; 157: Art Resource; 161: Giraudon/Art Resource; 171: The Granger Collection; 174: Giraudon/Art Resource; 178: The Granger Collection; 188: Erich Lessing/Art Resource; 191: The Granger Collection; 193: Alinari/Art Resource; 199: Giraudon/Art Resource; 202: The Granger Collection; 206: British Library; 207: Nimatallah/Art Resource; 208: The Granger Collection; 210: Giraudon/Art Resource; 215: E. T. Archive; 218: Alinari/Art Resource; 220: British Museum; 225: The Granger Collection; 227: Alinari/Art Resource; 230: Giraudon/Art Resource; 233: Erich Lessing/Art Resource; 234: The Granger Collection; 237: Giraudon/Art Resource

Volume 4

Black-and-White Photographs:
2: Giraudon/Art Resource; 3: Giraudon/Art Resource; 5: Alinari/Art Resource; 6: Foto Marburg/Art Resource; 9: Foto Marburg/Art Resource; 12: Giraudon/Art Resource; 17: Giraudon/Art Resource; 19: Foto Marburg/Art Resource; 22: Foto Marburg/Art Resource; 25: Scala/Art Resource; 27: E. T. Archive; 30: Art Resource; 32: Foto Marburg/Art Resource; 34: Giraudon/Art Resource; 40: Art Resource; 46: Alinari/Art Resource; 48: Alinari/Art Resource; 53: The Granger Collection; 55: E. T. Archive; 57: The Bettmann Archive; 59: The Granger Collection; 61: Foto Marburg/Art Resource; 66: Giraudon/Art Resource; 67: SEF/Art Resource; 68: Alinari/Art Resource; 71: Alinari/Art Resource; 74: Alinari/Art Resource; 80: Foto Marburg/Art Resource; 84: Scala/Art Resource; 88: Lauros-Giraudon/Art Resource; 90: Art Resource; 92: Giraudon/Art Resource; 97: Bridgeman/Art Resource;

99: Foto Marburg/Art Resource; 101: Scala/Art Resource; 103: Giraudon/Art Resource; 105: Giraudon/Art Resource; 107: Alinari/Art Resource; 111: Foto Marburg/Art Resource; 114: Foto Marburg/Art Resource; 116: Alinari/Art Resource; 118: The Granger Collection; 122: Foto Marburg/Art Resource; 129: The Granger Collection; 132: Foto Marburg/Art Resource; 137: Foto Marburg/Art Resource; 139: E. T. Archive; 148: The Granger Collection; 152: Alinari/Art Resource; 164: Erich Lessing/Art Resource; 166: The Granger Collection; 169: Bridgeman/Art Resource; 173: The Pierpont Morgan Library/M.736, f.10/Art Resource; 174: E. T. Archive; 177: Bridgeman/Art Resource; 180: Giraudon/Art Resource; 182: E. T. Archive; 187: The Granger Collection; 190: Giraudon/Art Resource; 192: The Granger Collection; 194: E. T. Archive; 195: Scala/Art Resource; 198: The Granger Collection

Index

Aachen, **1:1,** 1:17, 3:90
Abacus, 1:34, 3:125
Abbasids, **1:1–3** *(illus.),* 1:31
　art and architecture under, 3:24–25
　Baghdad, capital city of, 1:60–62 *(illus.),* 137,
　　197, 3:12
　Cairo under, 1:131
　caliphate under, 1:2–3, 137–38, 3:10
　caliphs of, 2:192–93, 3:113–15, 164
　clothing styles under, 1:207
　Damascus under, 2:18
　diplomacy under, 2:30
　hospitals and poor relief under, 2:220
　hunting under, 2:228
　in Iraq, 3:12, 13
　Islamic administration under, 3:18
　Jews under, 3:50
　libraries under, 3:90
　Palestine under, 3:191
　Samarra as capital city of, 4:35–36
　scientific texts translated under, 4:51
　Syria under, 4:100, 101
　taxation under, 4:109
　Umayyads, defeat of, 4:146
Abbey, 3:145–46
Abd Allah ibn Ali, 3:114
Abd al-Malik, 1:138–39, 3:191, 4:100
Abd al-Rahman I, 1:227, 4:87, 89, 144, 146
Abd al-Rahman III, 1:227, 4:87, 89, 146
Abelard and Heloise, **1:3–4** *(illus.),* 1:40, 86,
　2:214, 3:209
Abraham bar Hiyya, 4:52, 65
Abraham ben Meïr ibn Ezra, 2:197
Abu Abd Allah Muhammad XI (Boabdil), 2:178
Abu Bakr, **1:5,** 1:13–14, 135, 3:15, 153
Abu Nuwas, 1:33
Abu'l-Abbas, 1:2, 3:114, 4:146
Abu'l-Ala al-Ma'arri, 1:33
Abu'l-Atahiya, 1:33
Abu-l-Fadl Bayhaqi, 2:215
Abyssinia. *See* Ethiopia
Acolyte, 1:202
Acre, port of, 3:191 *(illus.)*
Actons, 1:42
Adab (type of book), 1:33–34
Adalbert of Prague, St., 4:80 *(illus.)*
Adalbert I of Tuscany, 4:141
Adam de la Halle, 2:132–33
Adam of Bremen, 4:39
Adamnan (biographer), 1:166
Adelaide, daughter of king of Burgundy, 2:157
Adelaide of Savoy, 3:100
Adelard of Bath, 3:125, 4:73
Adil, al-, 1:58
Adolf II of Holstein, count, 3:102
Adrian II, pope, 2:16, 3:173
Adrian IV, pope, **1:5–6** *(illus.),* 2:126, 3:14
Adrianople, 3:187, 188
Adrianople, Battle of (378), 4:162
Aelfric, abbot of Eynsham, 2:61
Aelius Donatus (Latin grammarian), 3:78
Aetios of Amida, 3:130

Afanasii Nitikin, 4:82
Afonso I of Portugal, 3:229
Afonso II of Portugal, 3:230
Afonso III of Portugal, 3:230
Aghlabids, 4:70
Agilulf of Turin, king, 3:96–97
Agincourt, Battle of (1415), 2:201 *(illus.),* 202
Agriculture, **1:6–13** *(illus.)*
　climate and, 1:202, 203
　famine and crop failure, 2:83–85, 86
　field systems in, 4:159, 160
　food and, 2:103–10
　gardens and, 2:144
　land used for, 3:73, 74
　serfs and serfdom and, 4:60–63 *(illus.)*
　slash-and-burn technique, 3:63, 73–74
　technology in, 4:110
　villages and, 4:157–60
　waterworks and, 4:178
　in western Europe, 1:10–13, 150, 151, 2:54,
　　3:223, 224
Ahai of Shabha, 4:65
Ahmad Baba, 4:119
Ahmad ibn Tulun, 1:131
Aidan, St., 3:144
Aigues-Mortes, France, 2:118, 3:76 *(illus.),* 77
Ain Jalut, Battle of (1260), 1:77
A'isha, **1:13–14,** 1:21, 3:153
Aksum, Ethiopia, 2:64–65
Ala al-Dawla (ruler of Isfahan), 2:235
Alamanni, **1:14–15,** 1:74–75, 211, 3:137, 138 *(map)*
Alaric I, 3:138, 4:162
Alaric II, 3:80
Albert II of Germany, 2:160
Albert V of Germany, 1:56
Albertus Magnus, **1:15,** 1:16, 27, 40, 54, 4:46
　(illus.)
Albigensian crusade, 1:161, 2:211, 3:4, 76–77,
　237, 4:123
Albigensians. *See* Cathars
Albrecht (Habsburg), 2:188
Alchemy, **1:15–17** *(illus.),* 1:50, 3:109, 4:5, 110
Alcuin of York, **1:17,** 2:221, 3:65, 90, 4:49
Alexander II, pope, 3:48
Alexander III, pope, 2:65, 126, 127, 3:177, 4:167
Alexander V, pope, 4:45
Alexander III of Scotland, 3:202 *(illus.),* 4:54
Alexander of Tralles, 3:130
Alexander the Good of Moldavia, 4:166
Alexandria, Egypt, 1:182, 199, 2:47, 3:89
Alexandru, Nicholae, prince of Walachia, 4:165
Alexiad (Anna Komnena), 2:214, 3:70–71
Alexios I Komnenos, 1:96–97, 124, 2:8–10, 75,
　3:70, 71, 4:149
Alexios II Komnenos, 3:71
Alexios IV, emperor, 2:11
Alfonso I the Battler of Aragon, 1:36, 160
Alfonso IV of Aragon, 1:37
Alfonso V of Aragon, 3:169, 4:72–73
Alfonso III of Asturias/Portugal, 1:53, 2:28
Alfonso VI of Castile and León, 1:36, 190–91,
　4:87, 88 *(illus.),* 121

Alfonso VII of Castile, 1:150
Alfonso X el Sabio, **1:18,** 1:149 *(illus.),* 2:28,
　143, 159
　Castilian language and, 1:151, 4:92 *(illus.),* 93
　conquest of Muslim Spain, 4:87
　political hermandades against, 2:212
Alfonso XI of Castile, 1:151
Alfred the Great, **1:18–19,** 2:21, 53–54, 61,
　3:97, 4:69, 157
Algebra, 3:62, 125–26
Algirdas (ruler of Vilnius), 3:95
Alhambra, **1:19–20** *(illus.),* 1:225, 2:177, 3:28,
　4:89, 90
Ali ibn Abi Talib, **1:20–21,** 2:212, 4:144, 145
　A'isha and, 1:14
　caliphate of, 1:135, 136
　Islamic theology and, 1:31, 3:21
　Kufa as capital of, 3:73
　Mu'awiya's defeat of, 1:21, 3:152, 4:75
Alids, 3:128
Aljubarrota, Battle of (1385), 3:231
Allegory, **1:21–22,** 2:151
　in bestiaries, 1:87–88
　biblical exegesis and, 1:89
　drama and, 2:40
　Fortune, 2:113–14 *(illus.)*
　in French romances, 2:131, 4:17–18
　German, 2:151–52
　in Italian literature, 3:31
Almohad dynasty, 2:177, 197, 3:27, 51, 52, 4:87,
　90
Almoravids, 1:150, 191, 3:27, 52, 4:87, 90
Almshouses, 3:100
Alp Arslan (Seljuk leader), 4:57
Alphabets, 2:16, 4:30, 81–82
Alphonse of Poitiers, 2:118, 4:123
Alsace-Lorraine, 1:147
Althing (assembly), 4:42
Altneuschul (Prague), 3:233 *(illus.)*
Alvaro de Luna, 1:152
Amalarius of Metz, 2:38
Amalfi, Byzantine trade with, 4:126
Aman (passport), 2:32
Ambos (reading desks), 2:138–39
Ambrosian liturgy, Gregorian chant of, 2:179
Ambrosius Aurelianus, 1:45
Ambry, 2:136
Amulets, 3:109
Anastasius IV, pope, 1:5
Anatolia, **1:22–23,** 1:114
　Byzantine Empire and, 1:22–23, 124, 126
　Empire of Nicaea in, 3:172
　Islamic conquest of, 3:17
　Ottoman rule in, 1:76, 3:183, 186
　Seljuks of Rum in, 4:58
Anchorites, 3:59
Andalus, al-. *See* Spain, Muslim kingdoms of
Andrea da Barberino (writer), 3:32
Andrew II of Hungary, 2:11, 225
Andronikos I Komnenos, 3:71, 72
Andronikos II Palaiologos, 3:190
Angels, **1:23–24** *(illus.),* 4:162

Angelus bell, 1:81
Angevins, **1:24–25,** 2:200
achievements of, 2:57–58
Boccaccio's early works and, 1:93
in England, 2:55–58, 3:176, 4:106
in France, 1:25, 4:72
Kingdom of Sicily under, 4:72
Naples under, 3:169
Papal States and, 3:196
Philip II Augustus's victory over, 2:117
Provence under, 3:236
Anglo-Norman art and architecture, 1:109–10
Anglo-Saxon Chronicle, 2:61
Anglo-Saxons, **1:25,** 1:183, 2:52–55, 3:139
achievements of, 2:54–55
Alfred the Great and, 1:18–19
art and architecture of, 1:108–9
Battle of Hastings ending rule of, 2:193
Bretwaldas and supremacy of Wessex, 2:53–54
early kingdoms, 2:53
English common law and, 3:81–82
family life among, 2:78
language and literature of, 2:59, 60–61
London and, 3:97–98
military service among, 4:172
taxation under, 4:106
Anjou, English rule over, 2:55–57, 58
Annals, 1:189
Anne of Bohemia, 4:10
Anne of Brittany, duchess, 1:111
Anno II, archbishop of Cologne, 1:213
Annunciation Cathedral in Kremlin, 4:28
Anointing, **1:25–26,** 3:65–66
Ansano, St., 4:73
Anselm of Canterbury, **1:26,** 1:141, 2:199
Ansgar, St., 4:44
Anthemios of Tralles (architect), 2:189
Anthony of Egypt, St., 2:212
Antioch, 1:97, 182, 2:9–10
Antipopes, 1:58
Anti-Semitism, **1:26–27,** 1:67, 3:45
during Black Death, 1:91, 200–201, 3:49
conversos and, 1:225–26
expulsion of Jews and, 1:27, 3:48–49
Antwerp, 1:112, 2:188
Appanage system, 2:118
Apprentice system, 2:184
Apse, 1:161
Aquinas, Thomas, St., **1:27–28** (illus.), 1:40
Albertus Magnus and, 1:15
on angels, 1:24
Augustine's ideas challenged by, 1:54
Dominicans and, 2:37
heresy defined by, 2:210
on Ibn Rushd, 2:234
Aquitaine, **1:28–29** (illus.), 1:73, 74, 2:50 (illus.)
English rule in, 2:45, 46, 47
Arabia, **1:30–31** (illus.)
Abu Bakr's uniting of, 1:5
Berbers as allies of Arabs, 1:85
defeat of Sasanians, 4:38
Jewish communities in, 3:50
Mecca, 3:127–28 (illus.)
Muhammad and, 3:153
under Umayyads, 4:144–46
Arabian Nights. See Thousand and One Nights
Arabic language and literature, **1:32–34**
classical tradition preserved in, 1:199
courtly love adapted from, 2:7
Hebrew literature and, 2:198

in Iran, 3:9–10
Islamic libraries and, 3:90
Islamic literacy and, 3:93
literature
encyclopedias and dictionaries, 2:51
by Hafiz, 2:189
Ibn Sina and, 2:235
by al-Jahiz, 3:38
by al-Ma'arri, 3:105
on mathematics, 3:124
on medicine, 3:132
in Sicily, 4:73
Thousand and One Nights, 4:118–19 (illus.)
rhetoric, 4:8
Spanish literature and, 4:91, 92
Arabic numerals, **1:34** (illus.), 3:125, 4:18
Arabic script, 1:138–39
Aragon, **1:35–38** (map), 1:150
Aragonese rule over Sicily, 4:72–73
Barcelona as capital of, 1:70–71, 158
Catalonia's union with, 1:159–60
Granada and, 2:178
James I the Conqueror, ruler of, 3:38–39 (illus.)
Louis IX and peace between France and, 3:102
Navarre and, 3:169, 170
Pedro IV, ruler of, 3:207
Arama, Isaac, 4:65
Archbishops of Canterbury. See under Canterbury
Archery, 2:141
Archimedes, 3:125, 126
Architecture. See British Isles, art and architecture; Byzantine architecture; Gothic architecture; Islamic art and architecture; Romanesque architecture; Spanish art and architecture
Archives, **1:38–39,** 4:134
Archpoet, 1:143, 2:168
Ard plow, 1:7, 9, 11–12
Ardesir I, 4:37
Arian heretics and Arianism, 1:182, 183, 227, 3:183
Aristotle in the Middle Ages, 1:15, **1:39–40**
Aquinas and, 1:27, 28
Augustine's philosophy and, 1:54
Bacon on, 1:59
Grosseteste's promotion of, 2:181
Ibn Rushd's commentaries on, 2:233
medicine in Europe and, 3:130
Oresme's translation of, 3:182
Scholasticism and, 4:46
Arius (Christian teacher), 1:182
Armenia, **1:40–41,** 3:17, 4:37
culture of, 2:215, 3:109, 161
trade and, 4:124–25
Armillary sphere, 4:52
Armoire, 2:136, 137 (illus.)
Armor, **1:41–45** (illus.), 3:68
heraldry and, 2:206–8 (illus.)
metals and metalworking for, 3:136
warfare and, 4:172, 173, 175
weaponry and, 4:179
Armorica, 1:110
Arnold of Brescia, 1:5
Arnold of Guines, 1:156
Arnulf (Carolingian), 1:144
Arnulf of Carinthia, 1:147, 2:155, 156
Árpád (Magyar leader), 2:224
Art. See British Isles, art and architecture; Byzantine art; Gothic painting; Gothic sculpture; Islamic art and architecture;

Romanesque art; Spanish art and architecture
Artevelde, Jacques van, 2:101
Artevelde, Philip van, 2:101
Arthur of Brittany, 1:110–11, 2:50
Arthurian literature, **1:45–47** (illus.)
Brittany's oral tradition popularizing, 1:165
English, 2:61, 3:111–12
French romances, 1:180–81, 2:131
German, 2:153, 154–55, 4:188–89
Holy Grail and, 2:131, 155
Italian, 3:32
prestige of knights and, 3:67
tournaments and acting out of, 2:142
Tristan, legend of, 2:131, 155, 4:137–38 (illus.)
Artillery, **1:47–48,** 1:154. See also Weapons
Ashura, Islamic fast day of, 2:93
Asia Minor. See Anatolia
Askia Muhammad, King of Songhai, 4:119
Asot I of Armenia, 1:41
Astrarium of de' Dondi, 2:37, 38
Astrolabe, **1:48,** 1:51, 204, 3:118, 171, 4:52, 53 (illus.)
Astrology and astronomy, **1:49–52** (illus.)
calendars and, 1:132–34
Chaucer's writings on, 1:177
de' Dondi and, 2:37–38
Jewish, 4:52
magic and folklore and, 3:106–8, 109
Pedro IV's support of, 3:207
scientific instruments for, 1:48, 4:52–53
Asturias-León, **1:52–53,** 1:149, 3:229, 4:163
Athanasius of Alexandria, 2:212
Athos, Mount, 3:216
Attachment courts, 2:112
Attila the Hun, 2:226, 227, 3:139, 198
Augustine, 1:25, **1:53–54,** 1:182, 3:186
Augustinianism, 1:54, 2:133
Austrasia, 1:144, 3:135
Austria, **1:54–56** (illus.), 1:75, 2:187–88, 4:98–99
Automata, 4:109
Avars, 1:54, 55, 3:72
Averroës. See Ibn Rushd
Avianus (writer), 2:72
Avicenna. See Ibn Sina
Avignon, **1:57–58**
culture in, 2:172, 3:238
papacy based in, 2:119, 4:26
Great Schism and, 1:57–58, 186–87, 4:44–45
Philip IV the Fair and, 3:212–13
St. Catherine of Siena and, 1:164
Awza, al- (scholar), 2:17
Aybak, sultan, 3:112
Ayyub ibn Shadhi, 1:58, 4:33
Ayyubids, **1:58–59,** 2:48
in Arabia, 1:31
Cairo under, 1:132
Damascus under, 2:19
Jerusalem under, 3:42
Palestine under, 3:191
Saladin and, 1:58, 2:48, 4:33, 34
Aziz, al- (Fatimid ruler), 2:89
Azores, 2:70
Azriel, Rabbi, 1:130

Babenbergs, Austria under, 1:55–56
Babylonian Jews, 3:50–51, 57–58
Bacon, Roger, 1:16, 52, **1:59–60,** 3:87, 119

Badr, Battle of (624), **1:60,** 3:153
Badr ibn Hasanawaih, 4:148–49
Baghdad, **1:60–62** *(illus.),* 3:13
    Abbasid founding of, 1:137, 197, 3:12, 114, 115
    central administration of, 3:18
    Ibn Khurdadhbih of post office in, 2:232
    Islamic architecture in, 3:24
    libraries in, 3:90
    Mongol sacking of (1258), 1:138
    population at its height, 1:194
    Round City, 1:61, 3:24, 115
    trade in, 4:128
Bagrat III, 2:150
Bagratids, 1:41, 2:150, 4:124–25
Bahriya corps, 1:77, 3:112
Bail or bailey, 1:154
Bailiff, **1:62,** 2:112
Bailli, **1:62,** 2:116
Baiuvarii (Germanic tribe), 1:74–75
Bakers, regulation of, 2:107–8
Baldwin of Jerusalem, king, 2:14
Baldwin II of Jerusalem, king, 3:69
Baldwin of Boulogne, 2:9
Baldwin I Iron-arm of Flanders, count, 2:98
Baldwin V of Flanders, count, 2:99
Baldwin VII of Flanders, count, 2:99
Baldwin VIII of Flanders, count, 2:99
Baldwin IX of Flanders, count, 2:11, 99
Baldwin of Hainaut, 2:69
Balearic Islands, James I's conquest of, 3:39 *(illus.)*
Balkhi, al- (scholar), 3:116–17
Ball, John, 3:206 *(illus.)*
Ballads, **1:63,** 2:19, 133, 4:15
Balliol, John (Scottish king), 4:14
Ballistas, 1:47
Baltic countries, **1:63–65** *(illus.),* 2:14, 191, 3:94–95
Ban, Jewish, 3:46, 84
Banking, **1:65–69** *(illus.),* 3:45, 49, 129, 4:74, 128
Baphaeon, Battle of (1301), 3:183
Baptism, 4:31
Barbarian invasions. *See* Migrations, Germanic
Barber-surgeons, **1:69–70** *(illus.),* 2:205–6, 3:132, 133
Barcelona, 1:68, **1:70–71,** 1:158, 2:105
Bard, **1:71,** 1:164, 165, 166, 3:161
Barmakids, 2:192
Baron, **1:71**
Barrow houses, 2:108
Bartholomaeus Anglicus, 2:52
Bartolo da Sassoferrato, **1:72**
Basarab I, prince of Walachia, 4:165
Basel, Council of (1433), 1:96
Basel, Treaty of (1499), 4:99–100
Bashshar ibn Burd, 1:33
Basil I the Macedonian, **1:72,** 1:123
Basil II "Killer of Bulgars," **1:73,** 1:114, 124, 3:64
Basil the Great, St. (bishop of Caesarea), 2:218, 3:147
Basilica churches, 1:118, 161, 2:168
Basques, 3:169, 170
Basra, 3:12
Bastide, **1:73–74** *(illus.),* 1:216
Bastions, 1:157
Batu (Mongol ruler), 2:167, 3:151
Baude Cordier, 3:161 *(illus.)*
Bavaria, 1:55, **1:74–76,** 1:95
Bavarians, 1:54–55
Bayazid I, Yildirim, **1:76,** 3:188, 4:76, 104

Baybars al-Bunduqdari, **1:77,** 2:13, 3:112, 4:2
Bayeux Tapestry, **1:77,** 2:44 *(illus.),* 193 *(illus.)*
Bayt al-Hikma (House of Wisdom), 1:61
Bayt al-Mal (treasury) in Damascus, 2:18 *(illus.)*
Beatrice (mother of Ferdinand III), 1:18
Beatrice Portinari, 2:22–23
Beatus of Liébana, 4:90
Becket, Thomas, St., 1:26, **1:78–79,** 1:142, 168, 190
    Henry II and, 1:78–79, 2:200
    tomb as shrine, 1:141, 3:215–16 *(illus.)*
Bede, **1:79,** 2:214
Bedouins, 1:30, 32–34, 3:179
Beguinages, 1:80
Beguines and Beghards, **1:80–81,** 2:43, 188, 3:128–29
Béla III of Hungary, 2:225
Belgium, 1:111–12
Belisarios (general), 3:60
Bell Tower of Ivan the Great, 3:157 *(illus.)*
Bells, **1:81–82**
Benedict III, pope, 3:172
Benedict XI, pope, 2:119, 3:37
Benedict XIII, pope, 4:45
Benedict Biscop, 3:90
Benedict of Nursia, St., **1:82,** 1:83 *(illus.),* 3:90, 146, 147
Benedictine Rule, 1:82, 3:147–48, 4:191
Benedictines, 1:81, **1:82–84** *(illus.),* 3:90, 128–29
Benefice, **1:84**
Benoît de Sainte-Maure, 4:140
Beowulf, **1:84–85,** 2:60
Berbers, **1:85,** 3:17, 4:86, 87
Berchtold V of Zähringen, duke, 4:98
Berengar of Tours, 2:210
Berengaria of Navarre, 4:9–10
Berenguer Ramon, 1:37
Berke (Mongol ruler), 2:167
Berkyaruq (Seljuk sultan), 4:58
Bern, Switzerland, 4:99
Bernard of Clairvaux, St., 1:4, **1:85–86,** 1:192, 2:10, 21, 3:123, 4:23
Berry, Agnes, 3:203
Berserks, **1:86**
Berthold von Henneberg, 3:127
Bertran de Born, **1:86–87**
Bestiary, **1:87–88** *(illus.),* 3:38, 108
Bible, **1:88–89** *(illus.),* 1:181
    Alcuin Bibles, 1:17
    angels in, 1:23
    Gutenberg, 2:185, 186
    Hebrew, 1:88
    Hebrew literature on, 2:197
    Jewish sermons to explain, 4:64–65
    Judaism and, 3:58
    in Middle English, 2:62
    midrashim, commentaries on, 3:108
    millenialism based on, 3:141
    Rashi's commentaries on, 4:4
    rhetoric to examine, 4:8–9
    Scholasticism and, 4:46
    Waldensians' literal interpretation of, 4:168
    Wyclif, 4:198
Birger Magnusson of Sweden, 4:43
Birgitta, St., **1:89–90**
Biruni, al- (geographer), 3:117
Bishops, 1:139, 182, 207, 3:200, 201. *See also* Clergy
Bjarni Herjolfsson, 4:155

Black Death, **1:90–92** *(map),* 3:221
    Clement VI and, 1:200
    Decameron set against background of, 1:94
    in Egypt, 1:132, 2:49
    famine crisis ended by, 2:86
    in Florence, 2:102–3
    in France, 2:120, 3:200
    guilds after, decline in, 2:184
    Jacquerie and pressures of, 3:205
    Jews during, 1:91, 200–201, 3:49
    in Languedoc, 3:77
    in London, 3:100
    Mamluk dynasty and, 3:112–13
    medicine and, 3:132
    population decrease and, 3:227–28 *(illus.)*
    trade and, 1:90, 91 *(map),* 4:129–30
    urban decline during, 1:196
Black magic, 3:107
Black Stone (relic), 3:128 *(illus.)*
Blacks. *See* Ethiopia (Abyssinia); Mali; Slavery
Blacksmiths, 3:136, 137
Blanche of Castile, **1:92–93** *(illus.),* 2:50, 117, 3:101, 102
Blanche of Navarre, 1:168
Blue Tomb of Maragha, 3:26
Bobbio, monastery at, 1:214
Boccaccio, Giovanni, **1:93–95,** 1:175–76, 3:7, 30–31 *(illus.),* 32
Bodel, Jean, 2:39
Boethius, 1:22, 40, 176, 2:113, 3:124
Bogoliubskii, Andrei, 3:155
Bogomils, 1:160, 2:211
Bohemia-Moravia, **1:95–96** *(illus.)*
    Cyril and Methodios in, 2:16–17
    Gothic painting of, 2:173
    Henry III of Germany's control of, 2:203
    Hus as leader and hero of Bohemia, 2:229–30
    Sigismund's struggles with Hussites in, 4:76
    Slavic alphabet and literature in, 4:81–82
Bohemond I, prince of Antioch, **1:96–97,** 1:124, 2:10, 3:71, 4:104
Boleslaw I the Brave of Poland, 2:158, 3:185, 223, 4:80 *(illus.)*
Boleslaw III of Poland, 3:224
Bologna, Italy, 3:122 *(illus.),* 133, 4:48 *(illus.)*
Bologna, University of, 3:79, 81, 84–85, 4:147
Bonaventure, St., **1:97,** 2:124–25
Boniface VIII, pope, **1:98**
    church-state relations and, 1:98, 190
    Dante and, 2:23
    Great Schism and, 1:186
    Holy Year proclaimed by, 2:217–18
    Jacopone da Todi excommunicated by, 3:37
    jubilee indulgence issued by, 3:1
    Order of St. Clare and, 4:193
    Philip IV the Fair and, conflict between, 1:98, 2:119, 3:66, 212–13
    rites of death and burial and, 2:26
Boniface IX, pope, 4:26
Boniface of Montferrat, 2:11
Boniface I of Tuscany, 4:141
Boniface, St., 1:75, 83, **1:98,** 3:144, 207, 208
Bonne, queen of France, 3:106
Bonsignori family, 4:74
Book of hours, **1:99,** 1:104, 2:25 *(illus.),* 26, 172
Bookbinding, 1:100–101
Books
    calligraphy, 1:139
    courtesy, 2:4–6
    encyclopedias and dictionaries, 2:50–52

handbooks, 2:143, 190–91, 4:138
herbals, 2:208–10 (*illus.*)
libraries, 3:89–91 (*illus.*)
of magic, 3:107
Books, manuscript, **1:99–104** (*illus.*)
  Book of Kells, 1:108, 3:13, 61
  classical tradition preserved in, 1:199–200
  death and burial depicted in, 2:25 (*illus.*), 26
  gardens in, 2:146
  Gothic style in illumination, 2:171–72
  Hätzlerin, scribe of, 2:194
  Hebrew, 2:197
  hunting and fowling depicted in, 2:228 (*illus.*)
  Irish-Saxon, 1:108
  Islamic, 1:100, 101–2, 104, 3:24 (*illus.*)
  Jewish, 1:101, 3:43–44
  literacy and, 3:93, 94
  printing development and, 3:234–35
  Romanesque style in, 4:21, 24
  Spanish, 4:90
  textbooks, 4:113
Boris of Bulgaria, king, 1:114
Börjigin clan of Mongols, 3:150
Borough, **1:104–5,** 2:54
Bosnia, **1:105–6**
Bosworth Field, Battle of (1485), 2:59, 4:178
Bourges Cathedral, 2:169 (*illus.*)
Bouvines, Battle of (1214), 2:100, 116–17, 3:212
Boyars, Bulgarian, 1:113, 114, 2:42, 3:178
Bracteates, 4:43
Bradwardine, Thomas, 3:126
Braga, Portugal, 3:229
Brailes, William de, 1:104
Braziers, 2:195
Breaking of the fast, festival of, 2:92–93
Breath deodorizers, 2:3
Brendan, St., 2:68 (*illus.*)
Brethren of Purity, 2:51
Brethren of the Common Life, **1:106–7**
Brétigny, Treaty of (1360), 1:172
Bretons, 1:110–11
Bretwaldas, 2:53–54
Breviary, **1:107**
Breviary of Alaric, 3:80
Brian Boru (king of the Irish), 3:14
Brid, John, 2:107–8
Bridges, 1:22, 4:13, 179
Brigit, St., **1:107–8**
Britain, 3:139, 142, 173. *See also* England;
  Ireland; Scotland; Wales
British Isles, art and architecture, **1:108–10**
  (*illus.*), 4:24
Brittany, duchy of, **1:110–11,** 1:165
Brothers of the Sword, 1:64
Bruce family, 4:14
Bruce, Robert, 4:54
Bruges, **1:111–12**
Brunelleschi, Filippo, **1:112–13** (*illus.*)
Brunhilde of Austrasia, queen, 1:14, 144, 3:135
Bruno I, archbishop of Cologne, 1:213, 3:185
Brythonic language and literature, 1:165
Bubonic plague, 1:90, 3:219–22
Builders, 1:222–23
Building construction. *See* Construction, building
Bulgaria, 1:73, **1:113–15** (*illus.*), 3:72, 155, 188,
  4:59, 82
Bulgars, 1:113, 3:72
Buonelmonti, Cristoforo, 1:221 (*illus.*)
Bureaucracy, Byzantine, 1:126–27
Burgh, Hubert de, 2:200

Burgundy, **1:115–17** (*illus.*), 1:146, 214, 2:157,
  3:54, 135, 4:22
Burial. *See* Death and burial in Europe
Bursa, Ottoman capital city of, 3:29
Bury St. Edmunds, abbey of, 1:204
Buscheto (architect), 3:218
Butchers, 2:108
Buttresses, 1:224, 4:19
  flying, 1:174 (*illus.*), 175, 224, 2:169, 3:177
Buyids, 1:138, 3:12–13, 4:57
Byrnie (chain mail tunic), 1:42
Byzantine architecture, **1:117–19**
  building construction and, 1:224–25
  cathedrals and churches, 1:118–19, 161–62,
    163, 2:189–90 (*illus.*)
  in Ravenna, 4:4, 5 (*illus.*)
Byzantine art, **1:119–21** (*illus.*)
  Anglo-Saxon art and, 1:109
  early Italian painters and style of, 2:164
  icons in, 1:120, 123, 2:236 (*illus.*), 237
  jewelry, 2:146
  in Jewish synagogues, 3:43
  lighting devices, 3:91–92
  mosaics, 1:119, 3:151–52
  in Ravenna, 4:4, 5 (*illus.*)
Byzantine Church, 1:64, 123, 124, 183–184, 185
  architecture of, 1:118, 119
  in Constantinople, 1:220–21
  Cyril and Methodios and spread of, 2:16–17
  Hagia Sophia as seat of, 2:190
  icons in, 1:120, 123, 2:235–37
  mysticism and, 3:165
  in Serbia, 4:59, 60
  in Walachia and Moldavia, 4:166
Byzantine Empire, **1:121–28** (*illus.*) (*map*)
  agriculture in, 1:6–8, 127
  Anatolia and, 1:22–23, 124, 126
  Anna Komnena's history of, 3:70–71
  archives of, 1:38
  Armenia and, 1:40, 41
  astrology and astronomy in, 1:49
  Basil II "Killer of Bulgars" and, 1:73
  Bulgaria and, 1:113, 114–15
  Christianity in. *See* Byzantine Church
  church-state relations in, 1:189
  cities and towns of, 1:128, 192–94, 4:126–27
  clothing in, 1:206–7, 208 (*illus.*)
  crusades and, 1:114–15, 124–25, 154, 4:127
  diplomacy in, 2:28–29, 32
  fairs in, 2:73, 4:125
  fall of Ostrogoths to, 3:183–84
  family in, 2:75–76
  government and social structure, 1:126–28
  Greek language in, 2:178–79
  guilds in, 2:183, 184
  heresies in, 2:211
  higher education in, 4:148
  history, 1:21–26
  hospitals in, 2:218–19, 3:130
  Kievan Rus and, 3:64
  Krum of Bulgaria's war against, 3:72
  law in, 1:72, 2:76, 3:79
    inheritance, 3:3
  libraries in, 3:89
  literacy in, 3:92–93
  Lombards and, 1:122, 3:96
  Macedonian dynasty, 1:23, 72, 123–24
  medicine in, 3:130
  Mehmed II's conquest of, 3:134
  monasteries in, 1:119, 128, 3:146

  monasticism in, 3:147
  al-Mu'tasim's defeat of, 3:164
  Naples as part of, 3:168
  Nicene Empire and preservation of culture
    of, 3:172
  Ottoman conquest of, 3:183, 188
  Palaiologos family, 1:194, 3:188, 190
  Palestine under, 3:190
  Papal States under, 3:195
  Plato in, 3:222
  postal services in, 3:231
  restoration of (1261), 3:172
  roads in, 4:11–12
  Sasanian campaigns against, 4:38
  Serbia and, 4:59–60
  silk industry in, 4:77
  slavery in, 4:79
  social classes in, 1:127–28, 4:85–86
  taxation in, 4:108
  technology in, 1:7–8, 4:109–10
  Theodora I, empress of, 1:122, 4:1, 116 (*illus.*)
  Theophano, empress of, 4:117
  Thomas the Slav and revolt against, 4:117–18
  trade and, 1:221, 4:125–27
  Venice and, 4:126, 127, 152, 153
  warfare in, 4:174–75
Byzantine literature, **1:128–29**
  classical tradition preserved in, 1:199
  historical writing, 2:214–15
  magic and folklore in, 3:108
  by Psellos, 3:130, 222, 4:1
  rhetoric, 4:8
Byzantium, 1:121, 220

Cabala, **1:130,** 2:197–98, 3:58–59, 166, 167
Cade's Rebellion, **1:130,** 2:59
Cadwallon of Wales, 4:168–69
Caedmon (poet), 2:60
Caesar, Julius, 2:114
Caesarius of Arles, St., 3:237
Cairo, **1:131–32** (*illus.*), 1:194, 197, 2:89, 4:51
Calais, English siege of (1346–1347), 2:223
Cale, Guillaume, 3:205
Calendars, 1:52, 79, **1:132–34** (*illus.*), 2:93. *See
  also* Clocks and reckoning of time
Caliphate, **1:135–38**
  under Abbasids, 1:2–3, 137–38, 3:10
  Abu Bakr and, 1:5
  Ayyubid dynasty and, 1:58
  Battle of Siffin and succession to, 4:75
  Fatimids and, 2:88–90 (*map*)
  historical writing at courts of caliphs, 2:215
  in Iran, 3:10
  Islamic political organization and, 3:18
  Jews' role in Islamic, 3:50
  Spanish Muslim, 4:87
  under Umayyads, 1:136–37, 4:144–46
Calixtus II, pope, 1:217, 3:49
Calixtus III, pope, 3:38, 55
Calligraphy, Islamic, 1:101, **1:138–39** (*illus.*),
  4:3 (*illus.*)
Camel, Battle of the (656), 1:14, 21
Campania, 3:168
Can Grande della Scala, 2:24
Canal construction, 4:178, 179
Canary Islands, 2:70
Cannibalism, famine and, 2:85, 86, 87
Cannons, introduction of, 1:47, 48, 81, 157,
  222, 4:174, 181
Canon law, 3:2, 78, 79, 81, 85

Canonical hours, 1:203
Canonization, **1:139,** 2:124, 4:32
Canons (groups of priests), 1:163
Canossa, **1:140** *(illus.),* 1:186, 190, 2:181
Canterbury, **1:140–42** *(illus.)*
    archbishops of, 1:141, 2:54
        Becket, 1:26, 78–79, 142, 168, 190, 2:200
        Lanfranc, 1:26, 141, 3:60, 75
        Langton, 1:141, 3:56, 75, 110
        Walter, 3:60, 4:10, 171
      Becket's tomb as shrine in, 1:141,
        3:215–16 *(illus.)*
Canterbury Cathedral, 1:141 *(illus.),* 142
Canterbury Tales (Chaucer), 1:141, 175, 176
    (illus.), 177, 2:63, 72, 3:7, 4:133
Capellanus, 1:146
Capet, Hugh, 1:116–17, **1:142,** 147, 2:114, 115
Capet, Robert, 1:116–17
Capetian dynasty, 1:142, 147, 2:97, 114, 115–20,
    3:198
Capua, Raymond, 1:164
Caravan travel and trade, 4:127, 135
Carcassonne dynasty in Catalonia, 1:158
Carcassonne, France, 1:74 *(illus.)*
Cardinals, College of, **1:142–43,** 1:186, 3:195
Carinthia, 1:56, 75
Carloman (Charlemagne's brother), 1:170
Carloman (son of Charles Martel), 1:144, 174
Carloman (son of Charles the Bald), 1:147
Carloman (son of Pepin III), 1:145
Carmelites, 2:133
Carmina Burana, **1:143,** 3:7
Carnival, tradition of, 3:107
Caroline minuscule, 3:93
Carolingians, **1:144–47** *(map),* 1:184
    Aachen under, 1:1
    Alamanni under, 1:14–15
    under Charlemagne, 1:145–46, 170–71
    diplomatic missions of, 2:31
    dukes under, 2:42
    forests under, restrictions on use of, 2:111
    Gaul and, 2:114
    Germany and, 2:155–57
    Jewish communities under, 3:48
    Languedoc under, 3:76
    legal traditions under, 3:80
    palace school of, 4:49
    Provence under, 3:236
    Switzerland under, 4:98
    Venice and, 4:152
Carthusians, 3:90, 4:192
Cartography. *See* Maps and mapmaking
Casimir III of Poland, 3:224
Cassian, John, 3:237
Cassino Depositions, 3:29
Cassiodorus, **1:148,** 2:52
Castellan, **1:148,** 1:158, 159, 2:115
Castellanies, 2:95
Castile, **1:149–52** *(illus.),* 1:160
    Alfonso X el Sabio and, 1:18, 151
    Aragon and, 1:37–38
    Asturias-León and, 1:52, 53
    Blanche of, 1:92–93 *(illus.),* 2:50, 117, 3:101, 102
    Granada and, 2:177, 178
    Navarre and, 3:170
    Portugal and, 3:229, 231
Castles and fortifications, **1:152–57** *(illus.)*
    cannons and, introduction of, 4:181
    castellans as commanders of, 1:148, 158,
      159, 2:115

constable of royal castle, 1:218
construction of, 1:152–57, 224, 2:14
    family life in, 2:79
    furniture in, 2:136, 137
    in late Middle Ages, 1:157
    in Syria, 4:101
    urban growth and development and, 1:197
    vassals living in lord's, 2:95
    villages formed around, 4:158
    in Wales, 4:169, 170
    warfare against, 2:224
Catalan Atlas, 3:117 *(illus.)*
Catalan language and literature, 3:104, 207
Catalonia, **1:158–60** *(illus.)*
    Aragon and, 1:37, 159–60
    Barcelona as capital of, 1:70–71
    Romanesque painting in, 4:23
Catechumens, Mass of the, 3:124
Cathars, 1:80, **1:160–61,** 2:14
    Albigensian crusade against, 1:161, 2:211,
      3:4, 76–77, 237, 4:123
    Dominic's mission to, 1:161, 2:35, 36
    heresy of, 2:211
    importance given to devil by, 4:187
    Inquisition and, 3:8 *(illus.)*
    Louis VIII's success against, 2:117
    in Provence, 3:237
    in Toulouse, 4:123
Cathedra (chair), 2:138
Cathedral schools, 3:131, 4:46–48
Cathedrals and churches, **1:161–63** *(illus.)*
    Byzantine, 1:118–19, 161–62, 163
    chapters of, 1:163, 170
    cities and towns and, influence on, 1:195
    construction of, 1:161–63, 224–25, 2:170
    Gothic sculpture in, 2:174–76 *(illus.)*
    Gothic style, 2:168–71 *(illus.)*
    grammar schools in, 4:49
    libraries at, 3:90
    Notre Dame, 2:170, 3:160, 176–77, 199
    paradise expressed through, 3:198
    parish and, 3:200–201
    proprietary (private) churches, 3:201
    right of sanctuary in, 1:218, 4:36
    Romanesque style, 4:19–21 *(illus.),* 37
    stained glass windows, 2:113, 146, 166–67,
      169–70, 171, 3:198
    villages formed around, 4:158
    See also specific cathedrals
Catherine of Alexandria, St., 2:92
Catherine of Siena, St., **1:163–64,** 2:37
Catherine of Valois, 2:223
Catherning (St. Catherine's Day), 2:92
Cavallini, Pietro, 2:172
Cavalry warfare, 4:172–73, 174, 175, 176
Caxton, William, **1:164,** 2:63
Celestine I, pope, 3:204
Celestine III, pope, 3:4
Celestine V, pope, 1:98
Celibacy of clergy, 1:201
Celtic art, 1:108
Celtic languages and literature, **1:164–66**
    bards and, 1:71, 164, 165, 166, 3:161
    German romances based on, 2:155
    in Ireland, 3:14
    on Llywelyn ap Gruffydd, 3:96
    Marie de France's stories based on, 3:120–21
    replacement in Gaul by Vulgar Latin, 2:129
    Tristan, legend of, 4:137–38
    See also Minstrels; Troubadour, trouvère

Celts, 1:25, 110, 211, 3:97
Cemeteries, 4:6
Cemetery cities, 1:132
Cenobitic monasticism, 3:147
Central Asia, Islamic art and architecture in,
    3:25–26
Central-heating systems, 2:194
Ceramics, 3:25, 26, 29, 4:89
Ceremonies of diplomacy, 2:32–33
Chain mail, 1:41, 42
Chalcedon, Council of (451), 2:211
Chamberlain, **1:166–67,** 2:57, 115–16, 4:27
Chamois, 3:86
Champagne, County of, **1:167–68,** 2:120
    fairs in, 1:68, 167, 195, 2:74, 4:128, 129
    Jean de Joinville, seneschal of, 2:132, 214, 3:40
    Marie de Champagne, 1:181, 3:119–20
Chancellor, 1:168, 2:57, 115–16
Chancery, **1:168–69**
Chandos, Sir John, 2:224
Chansons de geste, **1:169,** 2:130–31, 3:170,
    4:16–17 *(illus.)*
Chapels, 3:201
Chaplain, **1:169**
Chapter, 1:163, **1:170**
Charity to the poor. *See* Hospitals and poor relief
Charlemagne, **1:170–71** *(illus.)*
    Aachen as capital under, 1:1
    Alcuin of York and, 1:17
    Bavaria and, 1:55
    book production encouraged by, 1:102–3
    Carolingian rule under, 1:145–46, 170–71
    Catalonia, conquests in, 1:158
    cathedral schools under, 4:47
    Christianity, promotion of, 1:184
    in Dalmatia and Pannonia, 2:7
    diplomatic missions of, 2:31
    drama revival under, 2:38–39
    Einhard's biography of, 2:49
    father of, 3:207–8 *(illus.)*
    France and, 2:114
    Holy Roman Empire and, 2:216
    Italy, invasion of, 3:33
    Leo III's coronation of, 1:170–71, 184,
      189–90, 2:1 *(illus.),* 216, 3:87, 193, 4:25
    Lombards, defeat of, 3:97
    money standardized by, 3:149
    Rome under, 4:25
    Song of Roland about, 1:169, 2:130, 3:170,
      4:16–17 *(illus.)*
    successors of, 1:146
    weights and measures standards and, 4:182
Charles III, Holy Roman Emperor, 2:155
Charles IV, Holy Roman Emperor, 1:95 *(illus.),*
    96, 116, 2:160, 3:180, 4:57 *(illus.)*
Charles IV of Bohemia, 2:229
Charles IV of Czechoslovakia, 3:232
Charles III the Simple, king of France, 1:147,
    3:175, 4:156
Charles IV of France, 2:120
Charles V of France, **1:171–72,** 2:30, 91, 121
Charles VI of France, 1:172, 173, 2:101, 121,
    4:170
Charles VII of France, **1:172–73** *(illus.),*
    2:121–22, 202, 223, 3:37–38, 54–55
Charles VIII of France, 1:111, 3:127
Charles V, Habsburg ruler, 2:188
Charles Martel, 1:144, **1:173–74,** 3:17, 4:172, 173
Charles II the Bad of Navarre, 3:205
Charles of Anjou, 1:25, 116, 126, 2:13, 14–15, 4:72

Charles of Orleans, 3:100 (*illus.*)
Charles the Bald, 1:116, 146, 147, 2:98, 129
Charles the Bold, duke of Burgundy, 4:99, 174
Charles the Fat, 1:147
Charles the Good, count of Flanders, 2:99, 4:200
Charles University (Prague), 3:232
Charonton, Enguerrard, 3:238
Charters, 4:56
Chartres Cathedral, 1:163, **1:174–75** (*illus.*),
    2:167, 170, 4:22
Chaucer, Geoffrey, **1:175–77**, 2:63, 72
    Canterbury Tales by, 1:141, 175, 176 (*illus.*),
    177, 2:63, 72, 3:7, 4:133
Chausses, mail, 1:42
Cheese mongers, 2:109
Chess, 2:143, 152
Chests (furniture), 2:136
Chichele, Henry, 1:141
Child, Francis J., 1:63
Childeric I, 3:134
Childeric III, 1:144, 3:135, 207
Children, 2:6, 75, 76, 77, 78–81, 3:2, 228.
    See also Family
Children's Crusade, **1:177–78** (*illus.*)
Chimney systems, 2:195–96
Chin of China, 3:150
China, 2:70–71, 147, 4:76–77, 110
Chivalric orders, 1:179–80, 186, 2:10, 3:70.
    See also Knights, orders of
Chivalry, 1:41, **1:178–80** (*illus.*)
    Arthurian literature and, 1:45
    courtesy books and, 2:4, 5
    Edward III of England and, 2:46
    in English literature, 2:63, 3:111
    in French literature, 2:130, 133, 134
    German lyrics and, 2:153
    during Hundred Years War, 2:224
    knighthood and, 1:178–80 (*illus.*), 3:67
    women's position and, 2:82
Chorny, Daniel, 4:28
Chothar II of Neustria, king, 1:144, 3:135
Chrétien de Troyes, 1:46–47, **1:180–81**, 2:131,
    154, 3:120, 4:140
Christian art, 2:26, 4:90. *See also specific countries'
    art and architecture*
Christian calendar, 1:134
Christianity, **1:181–87** (*illus.*)
    on astrology and astronomy, 1:51–52
    Augustine and philosophy of, 1:53–54
    in Baltic countries, 1:64–65
    Basil I the Macedonian and spread of, 1:72
    Bible and, 1:88–89 (*illus.*)
    Black Death and weakening of church, 1:91
    in Bosnia, 1:105–6
    in Bulgarian Empire, 1:114, 115
    Byzantine and Orthodox Churches. *See*
        Byzantine Church
    canon law and, 3:78, 79
    Charlemagne's reforms of church, 1:146
    cities and towns and, influence on, 1:195
    College of Cardinals, 1:142–43, 186, 3:195
    Constantine I and legalization of, 1:181, 219
    conversos to, 1:225–26
    Coptic, 1:131, 2:48 (*illus.*), 3:179
    in Croatia, 2:7
    cult of Mary, 3:122–23
    devil in, 2:27–28
    Divine Office, 1:107, 2:26, 33, 179
    division in church, 1:183–85
    early Carolingian kings and, 1:144–45

early church, 1:118, 181–83
    in England, 1:140–42, 4:54–55
    in Ethiopia, 2:64–65
    feasts and festivals of, 2:90–92, 94
    Great Schism. *See* Schism, Great
    Gregory I the Great's writings and, 2:180
    heresy. *See* Heresy and heresies
    hermits and, 2:212–13, 3:59, 147, 4:14–15
    historical writing on, 2:214
    hospitals and poor relief and, 2:218–21,
        3:69, 88–89, 130, 4:120
    in Hungary, 2:225
    icons in, 1:119, 120, 123, 2:235–37 (*illus.*),
        3:152, 4:28–29
    Irish, 1:107–8, 3:13, 144, 204, 4:131
    Jerusalem and, 3:40–41
    Jews in Europe and, status of, 3:48–49, 51
    in Kievan Rus, 1:73, 3:64
    Leo III and, 3:87
    in Lithuania, 3:95
    liturgy of the Mass, 3:123–24
    millenialism in, 3:141–42
    monasteries. *See* Monasteries
    monasticism. *See* Monasticism
    mysticism and, 3:165–66
    Palestine and, 3:190, 191
    pilgrimages in, 3:213–16
    Platonic studies and, 3:222–23
    in Poland, 3:223
    in Portugal, 3:228, 229, 230
    in Provence, 3:237
    reform and schism in, 1:184–85
    religious archives of, 1:38
    religious instruction in, 4:6–7
    Roman Church, 1:182–83, 185–87, 189
    Russian Orthodox Church, 1:185, 3:156
    sacraments in, 4:31
    Sts. Cyril and Methodios and, 1:89, 184,
        2:16–17, 3:145, 4:81–82
    in Scandinavia, 3:144–45, 4:39, 40, 42, 44
    slavery and, 4:61, 79
    technology and values in, 4:111
    veneration of saints in, 1:139, 4:32–33 (*illus.*)
    Virtues and Vices in, 4:161–62
    visions in, 4:163
    Waldensian sect, 3:76, 4:167–68
    women's religious orders, 1:80–81, 2:124,
        3:165–66, 4:191–93 (*illus.*)
    Wyclif and church reform, 1:187, 4:197–99
        (*illus.*)
    See also Cathedrals and churches; Clergy;
        Missions and missionaries, Christian;
        Papacy, origins and development
Christine de Pizan, **1:187–88** (*illus.*), 2:5–6
Chronicles, **1:188–89**
    Byzantine, 2:214
    about famine, 2:85, 86
    French, 2:132, 134, 223 (*illus.*)
    Italian, 3:32
    Middle English, 2:61
    by Pedro IV, 3:207
    Russian, 3:64
    Scandinavian rhymed, 4:43–44
    by al-Tabari, 4:102
Church taxes, 4:106–7
Churches. *See* Cathedrals and churches
Church-state relations, **1:189–90**
    benefices and, 1:84
    Boniface VIII and, 1:98, 190
    Canossa as victory for church in, 1:140

concordats and, 1:217
    Dante and, 2:23–24
    in England, 1:190, 4:171
    in France, 1:190, 3:194–95, 212–13
    Gregory VII and, 1:186
    Innocent III on, 3:4
    Innocent IV and, 3:5
    kingship theories and, 3:65–67
    Matilda of Tuscany and, 3:126–27
    papacy and, development of, 3:192–95
        (*illus.*)
    simony and, 4:78
Cicero, Marcus Tullius, 1:49, 200, 2:72, 4:7
Cid, the, 1:150, **1:190–91**, 4:87, 93, 150
Cilicia, 1:41
Circassians, 3:113
Cistercians, 1:98, 117, **1:191–92**, 3:90
    communities for women, 4:192
    eremitic tradition and, 2:213
    monastic reform and, 3:148
    Otto of Freising, 3:185–86
    St. Bernard of Clairvaux as abbot of, 1:85–86
    St. Birgitta and, 1:89
Cities and towns, **1:192–99** (*illus.*)
    basic characteristics of medieval towns,
        1:197–99
    bastides, 1:73–74, 216
    boroughs and, 1:104–5
    Byzantine, 1:128, 192–94, 4:126–27
    citizens of, 4:85
    food and food trades in, 1:107–10, 2:84, 103,
        104, 105–6
    government, 1:225, 2:43
    growth and development of, 1:196–99, 2:72,
        182, 183–85, 3:74
    Islamic, 1:194, 198, 3:12, 4:80–81, 175–76
    markets in, 3:121–22 (*illus.*)
    population in, 3:227
    postal service between, 3:232
    relationship with countryside, 1:198–99
    road and bridges, development of, 4:11–13
        (*illus.*)
    social classes in, 4:85
    Swiss Confederation and, 4:98–99
    trade and, 4:124
    types of, 1:197
    walls of, 1:157, 198
    western European, 1:194–96
    See also Castles and fortifications; Commune;
        specific cities and countries
Citizenship, 4:85
City of God (Augustine), 1:54
City-states, 1:72, 3:35
Civil engineering, Islamic, 4:110–11
Civil law, 1:72, 3:9, 78, 85
Clan, 2:77
Clare, Richard Fitzgilbert de (Strongbow), 3:14
Classes, social. *See* Social classes
Classical tradition in the Middle Ages, **1:199–200**
    ancient fables, 2:71–72
    courtly love adapted from, 2:7
    Greek language and, 2:178–79
    Petrarch and, 3:210, 211
    Plato and, 3:222–23
    rhetoric and, 4:7–9
    Troy, story of, 4:140
    See also Plato in the Middle Ages
Clement II, pope, 2:203
Clement III, pope, 4:26, 149
Clement V, pope, 1:57, 2:24, 119, 3:69, 213

Clement VI, pope, 1:172, **1:200–201,** 2:218
Clement VII, pope, 1:57, 143, 172, 2:121, 3:129, 4:45
Clerecia (Spanish poetry form), 4:93
Clergy, **1:201–2**
  cathedral schools to train, 4:46–48
  chaplains, 1:169
  chapters of, 1:163, 170
  literacy among, 3:93
  medicine and, 3:130, 131, 133
  position in royal households, 4:27
  religious instruction from, 4:7
  sermons by, 4:64
  social classes among, 4:85, 86
  taxes paid by, 4:107
  travel by, 4:131
  Wyclif's condemnation of wealth of, 4:198
Clermont, Council of (1095), 1:184 (illus.), 4:149
Climate, influence on history, **1:202–3,** 2:83, 85–87
Clito, William (Norman), 2:99
Clocks and reckoning of time, 1:51, **1:203–6** (illus.), 2:37, 3:146, 4:53, 111–12. See also Calendars
Cloister, monastery, 2:144
Clontarf, Battle of (1014), 3:14
Clothing, **1:206–11** (illus.)
  costumes for dramas, 2:40
  fur trade and, 2:135
  silk, 4:76–77
  sumptuary laws and, 1:210
  textiles for, 4:113–15 (illus.)
  wool, 4:193–94
  See also Armor; Cosmetics and beauty aids; Gems and jewelry; Leather and leather-working
Clotilda, Burgundian princess, 1:183
Clovis, 1:14, 183, **1:211,** 2:114, 125, 3:134–35 (illus.), 139
Cluny, monastery at, 1:83, 117, 184, 2:26, 85, 3:209
  Romanesque style of, 3:146, 4:21, 22
Cnut VI of Denmark, 4:40
Cnut the Great, **1:212–13** (illus.), 2:44, 54, 4:39, 157, 197
Coat of arms, 1:42, 210, 2:206, 207–8 (illus.)
Code of Civil Laws (Justinian Code), 1:49, 122, 3:61, 79, 81, 84, 89
Codex Regius, 4:43
Coins, 3:148–49
Colle Val d'Elsa, Battle of (1265), 2:22
Colleges, 3:200, 4:146, 147, 148
  Muslim, 3:27, 28, 29, 85, 93, 4:7, 49–50, 148–49
  See also Schools; Universities
Cologne, **1:213–14,** 1:216
Coloman of Hungary, king, 2:225
Columba, St., 1:166, 3:144
Columbanus, St., 1:14, **1:214,** 3:144
Columbus, Christopher, 2:71
Combat, trial by, 4:136
Commentary (type of writing), 4:46
Commercial hospitality, rise of, 3:5–6
Commercial production of manuscripts, 1:103–4
Common law, English, 2:200, 3:14, 81–82
Commune, **1:215–17** (illus.)
  consuls and development of, 1:225
  échevins and, 2:43
  in Italy, 2:102–3, 182, 3:35, 140, 4:26, 74

as threat to Papal States, 3:196
  Ypres as, 4:200
Compass, 3:118, 171, 4:52–53, 112
Competition, guilds and regulation of, 2:183
Compline, 2:33
Compurgations, 3:180–81
Comyn, John, lord of Badenoch, 4:14
Conciliarism, 3:195, 4:45
Concordats, **1:217**
Confession, 4:31
Confessor, royal, **1:218**
Congregation of Windesheim, 1:107
Conrad II, Holy Roman Emperor, 2:158, 203, 216
Conrad III, Holy Roman Emperor, 1:75, 2:10, 13 (illus.), 3:180
Conrad IV (Hohenstaufen king), 2:159
Conrad, king of East Francia, 1:147
Conrad of Franconia, duke, 2:157
Conrad of Marburg (priest), 3:7
Consolation of Philosophy (Boethius), 1:22, 176, 2:113
Constable, local, **1:218,** 2:57
Constable of the realm, **1:219**
Constance, Council of (1414–1418), 1:58, 217, 2:162, 211, 229 (illus.), 230, 4:45, 76
Constance of Aragon, 4:72
Constance of Sicily, 2:204, 4:71, 72
Constance (wife of John of Gaunt), 3:56
Constans II, emperor, 1:183
Constantine I the Great, 1:121, 181, 182, **1:219** (illus.), 2:218, 3:193
Constantine V, emperor, 2:237
Constantine VI, emperor, 4:117
Constantine VII, emperor, 1:120, 123, 2:51, 3:108, 4:117
Constantine IX, emperor, 1:185
Constantine XI, emperor, 1:126
Constantine (Basil II's brother), 1:73
Constantine Doukas, 3:70
Constantine the African, 3:131
Constantinople, **1:220–22** (illus.)
  Arab attacks on (626, 674, 717), 1:122
  as art center of medieval world, 1:119–20
  Byzantine Empire and
    Arab attacks, 1:122
    bureaucracy, 1:127
    crusades and fall of city (1204), 1:114, 125, 221
    founding of, 1:121, 219
    Ottoman capture (1453), 1:126, 128, 139, 2:14, 3:187 (map), 188, 190, 4:181
    trade and, 1:221, 4:124, 125, 126
  Byzantine higher education in, 4:148
  decline of, 1:194
  design of, 1:192, 193 (illus.)
  as early Christian center, 1:182
  Hagia Sophia, 2:189–90 (illus.)
  as heir to classical tradition, 1:199
  Latin Empire of, 1:115, 3:172
  library in, 3:89
  Pantokrator hospital in, 2:221
  patriarch of, 1:183
  as pilgrimage destination, 3:216
  prefect of, 1:220
  recovery of, 1:125–26
Constantinople, council in (381), 1:182
Constitution of Melfi (1231), 4:72
Construction, building, **1:222–25** (illus.)
  of bridges, 4:13

building design and techniques, 1:154–57, 223–25
building materials, 1:154–57, 222, 223–24, 3:98, 4:13
castles and fortifications, 1:152–57, 224, 2:14
cathedrals and churches, 1:161–63, 174–75, 224–25, 2:170, 3:176–77
decline of forests and, 2:112
houses in medieval towns, 1:198
Islamic architecture, 1:155, 225, 3:23–29
in Jerusalem, 3:41, 42
Romanesque architecture, 4:18–21 (illus.)
Consuls, consulates, 1:217, **1:225,** 2:43
Convents. See Women's religious orders
Conventuals, 2:125
Conversos, 1:152, **1:225–26,** 3:52
Copernicus, 1:52
Coptic Christianity, 1:131, 2:48 (illus.), 3:179
Corbeil, Treaty of (1258), 3:39
Córdoba, 1:151, **1:226–28** (illus.), 3:86, 90, 4:146
  Great Mosque of, 1:226 (illus.), 227, 3:25, 4:87, 89, 144
Coronation, **2:1** (illus.), 2:125, 3:185
  of Charlemagne by Leo III, 1:170–71, 184, 189–90, 2:1 (illus.), 216, 3:87, 193, 4:25
Corpus juris civilis. See Code of Civil Laws (Justinian Code)
Cortes, 1:150, **2:2,** 2:135, 3:230, 231, 4:150
Cosimo de' Medici, 2:103, 3:129, 4:75, 142
Cosmas (Egyptian monk), 2:64–65
Cosmetics and beauty aids, **2:2–4** (illus.), 2:208–10, 3:1
Council of Basel (1433), 1:96
Council of Clermont (1095), 1:184 (illus.), 4:149
Council of commune, 1:216–17
Council of Constance (1414–1418), 1:58, 217, 2:162, 211, 229 (illus.), 230, 4:45, 76
Count, county, **2:4**
  barons compared to counts, 1:71
  castellans used by, 1:148
  Charlemagne's control of empire through, 1:145–46
  Domesday Book as survey of, 2:34–35 (illus.)
  feudalism and, 2:94–95
  shires replaced by county, 4:69
Counterweights, 4:109
"Counts cycle" (epic poems), 4:93
Couriers, 3:231–32
Courtesy books, **2:4–6**
Courtly love, **2:6–7**
  Arthurian romances and, 1:46–47
  chivalry and, 1:179
  classical influence on, 1:200, 3:211
  Dante and, 2:22–23
  Dinis, king of Portugal and, 2:28
  French literature and, 2:6–7, 131–32, 134, 4:17–18
  German lyric about, 2:152, 153
  Hadewijch of Antwerp and, 2:188
  in Tristan legend, 4:138
  in troubadour songs, 2:6–7, 132, 4:139, 140
  women's position and, 2:82
Courts. See Law; Trials
Covilhão, Pero da, 2:70
Crécy, Battle of (1346), 2:46, 47, 121 (illus.)
Credit sales, 1:66–67
Credit transfer, 1:67, 68
Cresques, Abraham, 3:117 (illus.)
Crime, 2:87, 4:122. See also Law; Trials
Crimea, 3:134

Criminal law, 3:9, 82
Croatia, **2:7–8,** 4:121
Croatian literature, 4:82
Crop rotation systems, 1:7, 8 *(illus.),* 12–13
Crops, 1:7, 9, 11. *See also* Agriculture; Food and drink
Cross-rigged ships, 4:67, 68 *(illus.)*
Crossbow, 1:47–48, 432, 4:112, 180, 181
Cross-in-square church, 1:119, 161–62
Cross-staff, 4:53
Crown of Aragon, 1:37–38, 160
Crown technique for making window glass, 2:166
Crusade(s), 1:184 *(illus.),* **2:8–15** *(map) (illus.)*
    Albigensian, 1:161, 2:211, 3:76–77, 237, 4:123
    anti-Semitism and, 1:27
    armor used during, 1:42–43
    Battle of Hittin (1187), 2:10, 216, 4:33–34
    against Bayazid I, 1:76
    Bohemond I and, 1:97
    Byzantine art taken during, 1:120
    Byzantine Empire and, 1:114–15, 124–25, 154, 4:127
    Byzantine roads used by, 4:12
    Children's Crusade, 1:177–78 *(illus.)*
    chivalric orders and, 1:179–80
    clothing influenced by, 1:210
    counts of Champagne on, 1:167, 168
    against Egypt, 1:76
    Ethiopia and, 2:65
    exploration and, 2:69
    Fifth (1217–1221), 1:56, 2:11–12, 3:4
    First (1095–1099), 1:27, 97, 124, 167, 2:8–10, 69, 3:42, 208–9 *(illus.),* 218, 4:101 *(illus.),* 104, 149
    Fourth (1202–1204), 1:125, 185, 189, 2:11, 69, 3:4, 4:127, 153
    France and, 2:116, 118
    of Frederick II, Thibaut of Champagne, and Richard of Cornwall (1228–1240), 2:12, 128
    Genoa's ships and supplies for, 2:149
    German, into Baltic countries, 1:64
    indulgences based on joining, 3:1
    Innocent III and, 2:11, 3:4, 76–77, 4:123
    interest in Aristotle in era of, 1:40
    Jerusalem in period of (1099–1187), 3:42
    Jewish communities, impact on, 3:50, 58
    of later Middle Ages, 2:13–14
    of Louis IX (1248–1254, 1270–1272), 1:77, 189, 2:12–13, 3:101–2
    missionaries during, 3:145
    Nicene Empire and, 3:172
    noble families in, effect on, 3:173
    political millenialism and, 3:141
    Qala'un al-Mansur and end of, 4:2
    scarcity of wood due to, 1:154–55
    Second (1147–1149), 1:86, 167, 2:10, 13, 116, 3:40, 4:95
    second Bulgarian Empire and, 1:114–15
    Seventh (1248–54), 1:93, 3:101–2
    shepherds', 1:178
    shipping on Mediterranean and, 4:67
    in Spain, 1:150–51, 2:14
    taxes to finance, 4:106, 107
    Third (1189–1192), 1:56, 125, 2:10–11, 127, 3:212, 4:9 *(illus.),* 33, 34
    travel on, 4:134
    Venice during, 2:11, 4:153
    William IX of Aquitaine and, 4:184
Crusade songs, 2:153

Crusader states, 1:97, 124, 2:9–10, 12
Cumberland, literature of, 1:165
Curragh (ship), 4:68
Cyprus, kingdom of, 1:125, **2:15–16**
Cyril and Methodios, Sts., 1:89, 184, **2:16–17,** 3:145, 4:81–82
Cyrillic alphabet, 2:16, 4:81–82
Cyrus the Great, Persian king, 4:34
Czech literature, 4:82
Czechs of Bohemia-Moravia, 1:95–96 *(illus.).* *See also* Hus, Jan

Dafydd ap Gwylym (poet), 1:165
Dagobert I (Merovingian king), 3:135
Dairy products, 2:109
Dalmatia, 2:7
Dalmatian Croatia, 4:121
Damascus, 1:136, **2:17–19** *(illus.),* 4:144
Damascus I, pope, 3:192
Damask fabric, 1:210
Damietta, Egypt, capture in Fifth Crusade, 2:11–12
Dance, **2:19–20** *(illus.),* 2:90, 91
    of death (danse macabre), 2:26, 3:220 *(illus.)*
Danegeld, **2:21,** 2:54, 4:157
Danelaw, 2:53
Danes, 4:39, 155–57
Danish Empire, 1:212–13
Dante Alighieri, 2:6 *(illus.),* **2:21–24** *(illus.),* 3:30–31, 32, 129
    Divine Comedy, 1:22, 2:6 *(illus.),* 21–22, 23, 3:30, 31, 4:150
Dar al-Ilm (House of Science), Cairo, 4:51
David II of Scotland, 4:14, 55 *(illus.)*
Deacon, 1:202
Death and burial in Europe, **2:25–26,** 4:31
    plagues and, 3:219–21
    purgatory and, 4:1–2 *(illus.)*
    Sutton Hoo in England, 4:96–97 *(illus.)*
Debate poems, 2:60, 62
Decameron (Boccaccio), 1:93, 94, 3:7, 31 *(illus.),* 32
Decorated style, 1:110
Decorative arts in Egypt, 3:27
Demography. *See* Population of the medieval world
Dendrites, 3:147
Denmark, 1:212–13 *(illus.),* 3:102–3, 4:39–40, 155–57. *See also* Scandinavia
Desiderius, abbot, 4:71
Devils and demons, **2:27–28** *(illus.),* 3:105–6, 4:187–88
Dhikr (Sufi ritual exercise), 3:166
Dhu'l-Nunid dynasty, 4:120
Dias, Bartholomew, 2:70
Diaspora, office of, 3:47
Dictionaries. *See* Encyclopedias and dictionaries
Diet of Piotrkow (1496), 3:225
Diet of Worms (1495), 2:161
Diet. *See* Food and drink
Differentiation *(ghiyar),* Muslim law of, 1:209
Dinawari, al- (writer), 2:208
Dinis, king of Portugal, **2:28,** 3:230
Diplomacy, **2:28–33** *(illus.),* 2:130, 3:231–32
Diplomatic immunity, 2:31–32
Disease. *See* Black Death; Medicine; Plagues
Divination, 3:106–7
Divine Comedy (Dante), 1:22, 2:6 *(illus.),* 21–22, 23, 3:30, 31, 4:150
Divine Office, 1:107, 2:26, **2:33,** 2:179
Divorce, 2:76, 78, 4:190, 191

Dmitrii Ivanovich Donskoi, **2:33–34,** 3:156
Dobrava of Bohemia, 3:223
Dolgorukii, Yurii, prince of Moscow, 3:155, 156
Dome of the Rock (Jerusalem), 1:136, 3:23, 28 *(illus.),* 41, 4:100
Domesday Book, **2:34–35** *(illus.),* 2:57, 3:226, 4:185
Dominic, St., 1:161, **2:35,** 2:36, 3:8 *(illus.),* 4:192–93
Dominicans, **2:36–37** *(illus.)*
    Aquinas, 1:27–28 *(illus.)*
    in Cologne, 1:214
    emergence of, 1:186
    friars, 2:133
    Innocent IV and, 3:5
    Meister Eckhart, 2:43
    monasteries of, 3:146
    monastic reform and, 3:148
    parishes and, 3:201
    St. Catherine of Siena and, 1:163–64
    St. Dominic and founding of, 2:35, 36
    St. Vincent Ferrer, 4:160–61
    sermons of, 3:32–33, 4:64
    urban grammar schools of, 4:49
    Vincent of Beauvais, 4:161
    women's religious orders, 2:35, 36, 37, 4:192–93
Donation of Constantine, 3:193 *(illus.)*
Donation of Pepin, 3:193, 207–8 *(illus.)*
Dondi, Giovanni de', 1:205, **2:37–38**
Douglas, Sir James, 4:14
Dowry system, 2:76, 3:2
Dracula. *See* Vlad Tepes
Drama, **2:38–40,** 2:130, 132–33, 222, 3:32, 4:7
Drawbridge, 1:156
Drawloom, 4:77
Drogheda, Parliament at, 3:15
Dromedary, 1:30 *(illus.)*
Dualism, 1:160
Dublin, **2:41,** 3:14–15
Duke, duchy, 1:75, **2:42**
Duma, **2:42,** 3:158
Dunbar, William, 2:63, 4:55
Duncan I of Scotland, 3:105
Dungeon, castle, 1:156
Duns Scotus, John, 1:24, 40
Dunstan, archbishop, 1:141
Dürer, Albrecht, 2:85 *(illus.),* 173
Durham Cathedral, 1:109 *(illus.)*
Dusan of Serbia, 4:60
Dynastic archives, 1:39

East Anglia, 1:213, 2:53
East Francia, 1:146–47
East Saxons, 2:53
Easter, 1:134, 2:91
Eastern Orthodox Church. *See* Byzantine Church
Ecclesiastical History of the English Nation (Bede), 1:79, 2:214
Echelon apse plan, 4:20
Échevin, 1:111, 112, 217, **2:43**
Eckhart, Meister, **2:43**
Ecloga (law code issued 741), 2:76
Economy
    Black Death's impact on, 1:91–92
    of Byzantine Empire, 1:127–28
    in England, 2:54, 58
    famine in Islamic world and, 2:86–87
    feasts and festivals, impact on, 2:90

food and drink and, 2:103–10
  guilds and expansion of, 2:185
  See also Agriculture; Cities and towns; Guilds;
    Trade
Eddas (Icelandic poems), 4:42–43
Edgar the Peaceable, 1:141, 2:54
Edictum Theodorici (Edict of Theodoric), 3:80
Education
  Alfred the Great and English tradition of,
    1:18, 19
  Benedictines' role in, 1:83
  Byzantine higher, 4:148
  Dominicans and, 2:37
  legal, 1:72, 3:79, 81, 84–85, 4:48 *(illus.)*
  literacy and, 3:92–94
  medical, 3:130, 131, 132–33, 148
  religious instruction, 4:6–7
  on rhetoric, 4:7–9
  subjects of secular, 4:8
  of women, 4:189
  See also Schools; Universities
Edward the Confessor, St., 1:213, **2:44–45**
  (illus.), 3:176
  Anglo-Saxon dynasty of Wessex under, 2:54
  death of, 2:193
  London under, 3:98
  royal touch of, 4:28
  Westminster Abbey begun by, 4:183
  William I and, 2:45, 4:184
Edward I of England, **2:45**
  defeat of barons in civil war, 2:201
  expulsion of Jews by, 3:53
  Parliament under, 3:202 *(illus.)*
  Scotland and, 4:14, 54
  self-government of Londoners and, 3:99
  Simon de Montfort the Younger and, 4:77, 78
  Wales and, 3:96, 4:170
Edward II of England, **2:45–46,** 3:100, 202,
  4:14, 170
Edward III of England, 2:29 *(illus.)*, **2:46,** 3:213
  Aquitaine and, 1:29
  Chaucer and, 1:175
  claim to French throne, 2:58
  embargo on trade of English wool to Flan-
    ders, 2:100–101, 163
  Hundred Years War and, 2:46, 58
  Parliament under, 3:202
  Scotland and, 4:14, 54
  William of Wykeham, chief minister to, 4:186
Edward IV of England, 1:130, 2:59, 202, 4:11,
  177–78
Edward V of England, 4:11, 178
Edward the Black Prince, 1:25, 151,
  2:46–47 *(illus.)*, 2:223, 224
Egbert, king of Wessex, 2:53
Egypt, **2:47–49** *(illus.)*
  Black Death in, 3:221
  Cairo, 1:131–32 *(illus.)*, 194, 197, 2:89, 4:51
  culture of, 2:49
  early history, 2:47, 48, 3:16
  Islamic art and architecture in, 3:25, 27
  Islamic dynasties, 2:48–49. *See also* Ayyubids;
    Fatimid Empire; Mamluk dynasty
  monasticism's origins in, 3:147
  Nubia and, 3:179
  Qala'un al-Mansur, sultan of, 4:2–3
  Saladin in, 4:33–34
  trade in, 4:125, 128
Einhard, **2:49**
Eldad ha-Dani (traveler), 3:108

Eleanor of Aquitaine, 1:29, **2:50** *(illus.)*, 4:185
  husbands of, 2:116, 199–200
  patronage of troubadours, 2:58, 4:139
Eleanor of Castile, 2:45, 50
Eleanor of Provence, 2:45
Electoral College (German), 2:159
Elias, Brother, 2:124
Emanuel I of Portugal, 3:53
Embossing, 1:45
Emirs, 4:87, 145
Emissaries, diplomatic, 2:29, 30–32
Emma of Normandy, 1:213, 2:44, 3:175
Encyclopedias and dictionaries, 1:94, **2:50–52,**
  2:221, 4:161
  geographic, 3:117–18
  Latin dictionaries, 3:78
  literacy and, 3:94
  on medicine, 3:130, 132
England, **2:52–59** *(map)*
  administrative organization of, 2:54, 57–58
  Anglo-Saxon period, 1:25, 2:52–55
    Alfred the Great and, 1:18–19, 2:53–54
  art and architecture, 1:108–10
  bailiffs in, 1:62, 2:112
  Cade's Rebellion in, 1:130, 2:59
  Canterbury, 1:140–42
  church-state relations in, 1:190, 4:171
  communes in, 1:216, 217
  constitutional crisis of 1258–1265, 4:77–78
  Domesday Book describing, 2:34–35 *(illus.)*,
    57, 3:226, 4:185
  Dublin, conquest of (1170), 2:41
  feudalism in, 2:57, 96–97, 3:110
  Germanic migrations and, 1:183, 3:139
  Gothic architecture in, 1:109–10, 2:170, 4:183
  Gothic painting in, 2:173
  Gothic sculpture in, 2:176
  government
    boroughs, 1:104–5, 2:54
    Exchequer, 1:167, 2:57, 65–66, 4:16
    lord great chamberlain, office of, 1:167
    Parliament, 3:201–3 *(illus.)*
    Roger of Salisbury, 4:16
  Hanseatic League trading rights in, 2:191
  heraldry in, 2:206, 207, 208
  hospitals in, 2:220–21
  inheritance laws and practices in, 3:2–3
  inns in, 3:5, 6
  Ireland and, 3:14–15
  Jewish loan activities, 1:67
  Jews in, expulsion of, 3:52–53
  John of Gaunt and, 3:56–57
  kings of
    Cnut the Great, 1:212–13 *(illus.)*
    Edward the Confessor, St., 2:44–45 *(illus.)*
    Edward I, 2:45
    Edward II, 2:45–46
    Edward III, 2:46
    Edward IV, 1:130, 2:59, 202, 4:11, 177–78
    Edward V, 4:11, 178
    Henry I, 2:198–99
    Henry II, 2:199–200
    Henry III, 2:200–201
    Henry IV, 1:177, 2:59, 3:57, 4:11, 170
    Henry V, 2:201–2 *(illus.)*
    Henry VI, 2:202–3 *(illus.)*
    Henry VII, 2:59, 3:15, 4:11, 178
    John, 3:55–56 *(illus.)*
    Richard I the Lionhearted, 4:9–10 *(illus.)*
    Richard II, 4:10–11

    Richard III, 4:11
    William I the Conqueror, 4:184–85
    William II, 1:26
  law in, 2:54, 57–58
    common law, 2:200, 3:14, 81–82
    local constables, 1:218
    outlaws and outlawry, 3:189
    sheriff and, 2:54, 57, 66, 3:82, 4:66–67
    Wulfstan of York and, 4:197
  London, 2:75, 3:97–100 *(map) (illus.)*, 4:183
  Magna Carta and, 3:110
  mechanical clocks in, 1:205
  money in, 3:149
  mystics in, 3:166
  nobility in, 3:175, 202
  Norman conquest of, 2:45, 193–94 *(illus.)*,
    3:75, 175–76, 4:173
  Normandy, rule over, 2:55–57, 58, 198–99,
    3:212, 4:184–85
  population of, 3:227
  Robin Hood, legend of, 4:15–16
  royal household in, 4:27
  Scotland and, 4:14, 54, 56
  seneschal in, 4:58
  serfs and serfdom in, 4:62
  shires of, 2:54, 4:69
  taxation in, 2:65–66, 4:106–7
  Viking invasions of, 1:18–19, 2:53, 54, 69,
    193, 3:97, 4:39, 156–57
  Wales and, 2:45, 3:95–96, 4:169–70
  Wars of the Roses, 2:59, 202–3 *(illus.)*, 207,
    4:11, 170, 176–78 *(illus.)*
  wool industry in, 4:193–94
English language and literature, **2:59–63**
  Alfred the Great and, 1:14, 15
  Caxton, first English publisher of, 1:164
  golden age of, 2:62–63
  language, 3:203, 4:199
  literature, 2:60–63
    by Chaucer, 1:175–77
    drama, 2:40
    by Gower, 2:62–63, 176
    Lydgate, 3:104–5, 215 *(illus.)*
    by Malory, 1:59, 2:13, 3:111–12
    Robin Hood in, 4:15–16
    by Wyclif, 4:197–99 *(illus.)*
  Middle English, 2:59, 61–63
  Old English (Anglo-Saxon), 2:59, 60–61
English Nation of Merchant Adventurers, 1:164
Ephesus, 1:192, 198
Ephesus, Council of (431), 2:211
Epiphany, feast of, 2:94
Epiros, 1:126
Equatorium, 4:52
Eric of Pomerania, 4:40
Eric the Red, 4:15
Erik Eriksson, 4:43
Estates General, 2:122
Estonia, 1:63, 64, 65
Ethelbert of Kent, king, 1:140, 2:53, 3:144
Ethelred II the Unready, 2:21, 44, 54, 3:175,
  4:157
Ethelred (brother of Alfred the Great), 1:18
Ethelred (grandson of Alfred the Great), 1:212
Ethelred of Rievaulx, 1:192
Ethelwulf, king of Wessex, 1:18
Ethiopia (Abyssinia), **2:63–65** *(illus.)*, 3:234
Étienne du Castel, 1:187
Eucharist (Holy Communion), 3:123, 124, 4:31
Euclid, 3:125–26, 126, 4:51

Eugenius III, pope, 1:86, 192, 2:10
Euphemia, empress, 4:116
Eusebius, 2:214, 215
Evagrius Ponticus, 3:165
Exchequer, 1:167, 2:57, **2:65–66**, 4:16
Excommunication, 1:202, **2:66–67**, 2:210
Exegesis, biblical, 1:89
Exilarch, 3:47
Exorcists, 1:201, 202
Exploration, **2:67–71** *(illus.)*
   Ibn Battuta and, 2:69, 231
   Mandeville's *Travels* and, 3:114
   maps and mapmaking and, 3:116–19 *(illus.)*
   Polo and, 2:69, 3:225–26 *(illus.)*
   Portugal and, 2:70–71, 3:231
   Viking, 4:154–55
Extreme unction, 4:31
Eyck, Jan van, 2:172 *(illus.)*
Eyeglasses, 3:87, 4:111
Ezana of Ethiopia, 2:64

Fables, 1:21, **2:71–72** *(illus.)*, 2:132, 3:120–21
Fabliaux, tradition of, 2:72
Fabrics. *See* Textiles
Fachschrifttum. See Handbooks (*Fachschrifttum*)
Fairs, **2:72–75**
   business correspondence and, 3:232
   international, 1:68, 4:128, 129
   roads to, 4:12
   standard weights and measures for, 4:182
   trade at Byzantine, 2:73, 4:125
   travel between, 4:132–33
Falconry, 2:227, 228
Falkirk, Battle of (1298), 4:54
Family, **2:75–83** *(illus.)*
   in Byzantine world, 2:75–76
   extended and nuclear, 2:75
   in Islamic world, 2:76–78
   Jewish, 2:82–83
   laws about, 2:76, 77–78, 81–82, 83
      inheritance laws and practices, 3:2–3
   marriage patterns, 3:228
   property and, 2:76, 78, 82, 83
   in western Europe, 2:78–82
   women's roles and, 4:189–91 *(illus.)*
Family occupations, 1:127
Famine, 1:13, **2:83–87**, 2:105, 120, 3:74, 77, 222. *See also* Food and drink
Farabi, al-, 1:39, 2:51, **2:87–88**
Farces, 2:38, 39
Farms. *See* Agriculture
Fasting, 2:92, 93, 3:21
Fatimid Empire, **2:88–90** *(map)*
   Abbasids and, 1:3
   Ayyubid defeat of, 1:58
   birthday festivals celebrated in, 2:94
   crusades and, 2:8
   founding of, 1:31
   Islamic art and architecture in, 3:27
   Jewish nagids in, 3:167
   libraries under, 3:90
   Saladin's campaigns against, 4:33
Feast of Corpus Christi, 3:124
Feasts and festivals, **2:90–94** *(illus.)*
   calendars and, 1:133, 134
   carnival tradition, 3:107
   dramas and, 2:39, 40
   in Europe, 2:90–92, 152–53
   in Islam, 2:92–94, 3:21
Fencing, 2:141

Ferdinand I of Aragon, Castile, and León, 1:37, 150, 152, 3:229, 4:90, 161
Ferdinand II of Aragon-Castile, 1:152, 3:170
Ferdinand III of Castile and León, 1:18, 150, 151, 228, 4:87, 93
Ferdinand and Isabella of Spain, 3:53
Fernán González, 1:53, 149
Fernando of Castile, 1:53
Ferrand of Portugal, 2:100
Ferrara, Cathedral of, 4:23
Feudal aids, 4:106
Feudalism, **2:94–97** *(illus.)*
   benefices and, 1:84
   Black Death and, 1:92
   in Catalonia, 1:158–59
   church's association with, 1:184
   communes and, 1:215–16
   in England, 2:57, 96–97, 3:110
   family life in western Europe and, 2:79, 80
   fiefs, 2:95, 3:3
   French representative assemblies and rise of, 2:122
   in Germany, 2:127, 153, 3:80
   growth of villages and, 4:158
   in Hungary, 2:224
   hunting and fowling restrictions under, 2:227
   on kingdom level, 2:95–97, 4:131
   on local level, 2:94–95
   military, 4:172–73
   mining rights under, 3:143
   in Naples, 3:168
   origins of, 2:94–95
   serfs and serfdom, 4:60–63 *(illus.)*
   women's roles in, 2:82, 4:189–90
Fibonacci, Leonardo, 3:126, 4:73
Ficino, Marsilio, 3:223
Fief, 2:95, 3:3
Field systems, 4:159, 160
Fields (social form of land), 3:73
Finger reckoning, 3:125
Firdawsi, Abu'l-Qasim, 4:66
Fireplaces, 2:195–96 *(illus.)*
Fires, stone or masonry building to prevent, 1:222
Fishing, fish trade, **2:97–98**, 2:106, 108–9, 191, 4:41, 129
Flaccus, 2:50
Flagellants, 1:201
Flanders and the Low Countries, **2:98–101** *(illus.)*
   Bruges, 1:11–12
   communes in, 1:216
   France and, 2:99–100, 116–17
   German dialect of, 2:151
   Ghent, 2:163–64
   international fairs in, 4:128, 129
   trade and, 2:191, 4:129–30
   waterworks projects in, 4:178–79
   women mystics in, 3:166
   wool industry in, 4:54, 193–94
   Ypres, 4:200–201
Flodden Hill, Battle of (1513), 4:56
Flooding, efforts to control, 4:178
Florence, **2:101–3** *(illus.)*
   cathedral of, 1:113, 2:164
   Dante and, 2:21, 22–23
   food policies and supply in, 2:84, 105
   Guelphs and Ghibellines conflict in, 2:102, 103, 4:141–42
   guilds in, 2:102–3, 184
   inns in, 3:6

   life expectancy in, 3:228
   Medici family in, 2:101–2, 103, 3:129
   Siena's rivalry with, 4:74–75
Florence, Council of (1441), 2:65
Florin (money), 2:102
Flowers. *See* Gardens
Flue, 2:195
Flying buttresses, 1:174 *(illus.)*, 175, 224, 2:169, 3:177
Folk songs, 1:166
Folklore. *See* Magic and folklore
Fontevrault, religious order at, 4:15, 192
Food and drink, **2:103–10**
   at feasts and festivals, 2:90–94
   fish, 2:97–98, 106, 108–9, 191, 4:41, 129
   food trades, 2:103–6
   herbs and herbals, 2:208–10 *(illus.)*
   hunting and fowling for, 2:227
   kinds of, 2:107–10
   markets and, 3:121–22
   in towns and cities, 1:107–10, 2:84, 103, 104, 105–6
   See also Famine
Food shortages. *See* Famine
Foot combat event at tournament, 2:142
Forestalling, laws against, 2:106
Forests, 1:75, 222, **2:111–12**, 2:196, 227, 3:73–74, 142
Forgaill, Dallan, 1:166
Fortifications. *See* Castles and fortifications
Fortune, **2:113–14** *(illus.)*
Fourth Lateran Council (1215), 1:211, 3:4, 194, 4:136
Fraga, battle of (1134), 1:36
France, **2:114–22** *(illus.)*
   Alsace-Lorraine, 1:147
   Angevins in, 1:25, 4:72
   Aquitaine, region in, 1:28–29 *(illus.)*
   Blanche of Castile, regent of, 1:92–93 *(illus.)*, 2:50, 117, 3:101, 102
   Capetian dynasty, 1:142, 147, 2:97, 114, 115–20, 3:198
   Champagne, county of, 1:167–68
   church-state relations in, 1:190, 3:212–13
   cities of, 2:115, 3:198–200 *(illus.)*, 4:123–24
   communes in, 1:216, 217
   duchies in, 2:42
      Brittany, 1:110–11
   expulsions of Jews from, 3:52, 53
   feudalism in, 2:97
   Flanders and, 2:99–100, 116–17
   forests in, 2:111, 112
   Frankish kingdoms, 2:114
   Gothic style originating in, 2:168, 171–72, 174–75
   inns in, 3:6
   Jacquerie in (1358), 3:205, 4:108
   Joan of Arc and, 3:54–55
   John of England's wars with, 3:55–56
   kings of
      Charles IV, 2:120
      Charles V, 1:171–72
      Charles VI, 1:172, 173, 2:101, 121, 4:170
      Charles VII, 1:172–73 *(illus.)*
      John II, 1:171, 172, 2:120–21
      Louis V, 1:142, 147
      Louis VI, 3:100–101
      Louis VII, 1:29, 92, 2:10, 13 *(illus.)*, 50, 3:101
      Louis IX, 3:101–2 *(illus.)*
      Louis X, 1:168, 3:53

Louis XI, 2:122
Philip II Augustus, 3:211–12
Philip IV the Fair, 3:212–13
Philip V, 4:134
Philip VI, 3:132
Philip of Valois, 3:213
Valois dynasty, 2:120–22
Languedoc, 3:75–77 *(illus.)*, 4:22
legal traditions in, 2:118, 119, 3:80–81
Merovingian dynasty, 3:134–35 *(illus.)*
mining in, 3:142
Navarre, kingdom of, 3:170
nobility in, 3:173, 175
Normans and, 3:175–76
Provence, 1:116, 3:236–38 *(illus.)*, 4:22
representative assemblies, **2:122–23**
Romanesque style in, 4:20–21, 22, 23–24
Scotland and, 4:55–56
seneschal in, 4:58–59
serfs and serfdom in, 4:62
Switzerland and, 4:98
taxation in, 2:123, 4:107
Franche-Comté, 1:116
Francien (dialect), 2:129
Francis of Assisi, St., **2:123–24** *(illus.)*, 2:165,
    4:192 *(illus.)*, 193
Franciscan Second Order, 4:193
Franciscans, 1:186, **2:124–25**, 2:133
in Bosnia, 1:105
Conventuals, 2:125
English songs composed by, 2:62
Grosseteste's influence on, 2:181
Innocent IV and, 3:5
Jacopone da Todi, 3:37
monasteries of, 3:146
parishes and, 3:201
St. Bonaventure and, 1:97, 2:124–25
St. Francis of Assisi and, 2:124
sermons of, 4:64
Spirituals, 1:97, 98, 2:124–25
urban grammar schools of, 4:49
women's religious orders, 4:192–93
Frankfurt, Germany, 2:74
Franks, **2:125–26**
Aachen under, 1:1
Alamanni under, 1:14
Bavaria, invasion of, 1:74–75
Carolingian dynasty. *See* Carolingians
Charlemagne, king of, 1:170–71
Charles Martel, leader of, 1:173–74
Clovis and uniting of, 1:211
control of hunting reserves, 2:227
Italy, invasion of, 3:33, 140, 4:25
kingdoms in France, 1:28–29, 110, 2:114
Languedoc under, 3:76
legal traditions under, 3:80
Merovingians descended from, 3:134–35
migration of, 2:125–26, 3:137, 138 *(map)*, 139
military service among, 4:172
Papal States and, 3:195
Pepin III the Short, king of, 3:207–8 *(illus.)*
St. Gregory of Tours's writings on, 2:180
succession customs of, 1:144
Viking raids on lands of, 4:155–56
See also Charlemagne
Frau Ava, **2:126**
Frederick I Barbarossa, **2:126–27** *(illus.)*
Adrian IV and, 1:5
Austria and, 1:56
Bavaria and, 1:75

canonization of Charlemagne, 1:1
Germany and, 2:158
Guelph-Ghibelline conflict and, 2:182
Hadrian IV, dispute with, 1:84
Holy Roman Empire and, 2:126–27, 217
Hungary and, 2:225
Kingdom of Sicily and, 4:71
Lübeck under, 3:102
Milan subdued by, 3:140
Otto of Freising's book about, 3:185, 186
Frederick II of the Holy Roman Empire, 1:56,
    2:14, **2:127–28,** 2:159, 3:31, 4:72, 73, 108
crusade of, 2:12, 128
diplomacy under, 2:32
Ghibelline forces supporting, 2:182
guilds banned by, 2:184
Innocent IV and, 2:128, 3:5
law school established by, 3:85
Lübeck under, 3:103
Naples under, 3:168
Nuremberg charter granted by, 3:180
resistance of papal authority, 3:194
work on falconry, 2:228
Frederick III, Holy Roman Emperor, 2:160, 188
Frediano, St., 4:178
Free will vs. predestination, 3:21
French language and literature, **2:128–33**
language, 2:129–30
English vernacular and, 2:59–60, 61
Walloon dialect, 2:99
literacy and, 3:94
literature, 2:130–33
Chaucer's translations of, 1:175
by Chrétien de Troyes, 1:180–81
by Christine de Pizan, 1:87–88 *(illus.)*
courtly love in, 2:6–7, 131–32, 134, 4:17–18
drama, 2:39–40, 130, 132–33
by Froissart, 1:189, 2:134, 223 *(illus.)*,
    3:174 *(illus.)*
German romances based on, 2:154
by Machaut, 2:133, 3:106
Marie de Champagne as patroness of,
    1:181, 3:119–20
by Marie de France, 2:72, 131, 3:120–21
    (illus.)
in Provence, 3:238
Roman de la Rose, 1:4 *(illus.)*, 175, 2:131,
    132 *(illus.)*, 146, 4:17–18
Song of Roland, 1:169, 2:130, 3:170,
    4:16–17 *(illus.)*
Tristan, legend of, 4:137–38
of troubadours and trouvères, 4:138–40
    (illus.)
Troy, story of, 4:140
Fresco painting, 2:164–65, 171, 4:23–24, 28–29
Friaries, 2:134
Friars, 1:83, 186, **2:133–34**
breviary for missionary work, 1:107
Dominicans, 2:36–37 *(illus.)*
Franciscans, 2:124–25
lauda sung by, 3:32
Friday prayer, 2:92
Friedrich von Hausen, baron, 2:152
Frisia and Frisians, 1:25, 98, 2:53
Froissart, Jehan, 1:189, **2:134**, 2:223 *(illus.)*,
    3:174 *(illus.)*
Froment, Nicolas, 3:238
Frontiers, tariffs levied at, 4:108
Frotmund, perpetual pilgrimage of, 3:216
Fuel, sources of, 2:196

Fuero, **2:134–35**
Fugitives, right of sanctuary of, 4:36
Fur trade, 1:209, **2:135–36** *(illus.)*
Furniture, **2:136–40** *(illus.)*, 3:6, 4:115. *See also*
    Lighting devices
Fust, Johann, 2:186
Fustat, al-, 1:131
Futhark (runic alphabet), 4:30

Gaddi, Agnolo, 2:27 *(illus.)*
Gaelic literature, 1:165–66
Galen, 3:130, 132
Galicia, 1:52
Gall, St., 1:214
Gallipoli, 3:188
Gama, Vasco da, 2:71
Games and pastimes, 2:90–94, **2:140–43** *(illus.)*
Gan Eden (paradise), 3:197
Gandersheim, Benedictine monastery of, 2:222
Gaon (head of the yeshiva), 3:47, 57, 167
Gaonic period, 3:83
Gardens, **2:143–46** *(illus.)*, 3:197
Garrison cities, Islamic, 4:175–76
Gascony, 2:119. *See also* Aquitaine
Gaul, 2:114, 129
Christian missions in, 3:144
Germanic migrations into, 3:137, 139, 4:162
Huns in, 2:226, 227
Jewish communities in, 3:48
monasticism in, 3:147
See also France
Gediminas (Lithuanian ruler), 3:95
Geert de Groote, 1:106
Gehinnom (hell), 3:197
Gelds, 4:106
Gemma Donati, 2:22
Gems and jewelry, **2:146–47** *(illus.)*, 3:136, 4:43
Genghis Khan, **2:147–48** *(illus.)*, 3:11, 149,
    150–51 *(illus.)*
Genoa, 1:68, **2:148–50** *(illus.)*, 3:218
trade and, 2:70, 149, 4:79, 129
Venice and, 2:148, 3:226, 4:153–54
Genseric, king of Vandals, 4:151
Geoffrey V Plantagenet, 1:24, 2:199
Geoffrey de Villehardouin, 1:189
Geoffrey of Auxerre, 1:86
Geoffrey of Monmouth, 1:46, 2:58, 153
Geoffrey of Winchester, 1:143
Geoffroy de La Tour-Landry, 2:5
Geography and geographers, 2:232–33,
    3:116–19 *(illus.)*, 154–55
Geometry, 3:125
Georgia, **2:150–51**, 4:69–70, 102–3
Georgius Florentius. *See* Gregory of Tours, St.
Gerbert of Aurillac, 3:125
Gerbert of Rheims, archbishop, 3:185
German language and literature, **2:151–55**
    (illus.)
during Hohenstaufens' rule, 2:159
language, 2:151
literature, 2:151–55
allegory, 2:151–52
drama, 2:40, 222
by Einhard, 2:49
by Frau Ava, 2:126
lyric, 2:152–53
by Mechthild von Magdeburg, 3:128–29
by Oswald von Wolkenstein, 3:184
romance, 2:153–55
Tristan, legend of, 4:137–38

by Walther von der Vogelweide, 2:152–53, 4:171
by Wolfram von Eschenbach, 1:47, 2:153, 154–55, 4:188–89
Germanic laws, 3:79–80
Germanic migrations. *See* Migrations, Germanic
Germany, **2:155–61** *(map)*
    Aachen, 1:1
    Bavaria under rulers of, 1:75–76
    Carolingians, 2:155–57
    Christian missions to, 1:98, 3:144
    cities of, 1:213–14, 2:160, 3:102–3, 179–80
    communes in, 1:216
    duchies in, 2:42
    feudalism in, 2:127, 153, 3:80
    forests in, 2:112
    Gothic painting in, 2:173
    Gothic sculpture in, 2:175–76
    Habsburgs and Luxembourgs, 2:159–60, 188
    Hohenstaufens, 1:56, 2:126, 158–59, 204, 4:71–72
    Holy Roman Empire and, 2:216–17
    inheritance law in, 3:2
    kings of
        Frederick I Barbarossa, 2:126–27 *(illus.)*
        Frederick II and, 2:127–28
        Henry II, 2:158
        Henry III, 2:203–4
        Henry IV, 1:95, 140, 190, 2:158, 181, 3:66, 4:25–26, 149
        Henry V, 1:217, 2:158, 3:127
        Henry VI, 2:204–5 *(illus.)*
        Henry VII, 1:96, 2:24, 160
        Maximilian, 2:160, 3:127, 4:99
        Otto I the Great, 3:184–85
        Otto II, 2:157, 216
        Otto III, 3:185
        Otto IV, 2:159, 4:72
    mining in, 3:142
    mystics in, 3:165–66
    nobility in, 2:155–56, 157, 160, 3:175
    representative assemblies, **2:161–62**
    Salians, 2:125, 158, 203, 3:134
    Saxons, 1:25, 2:157–58
    seneschal in, 4:58
    system of electing monarchs, 1:75–76
Gero, Saxon count, 3:223
Gerson, John, **2:162**
Géza II of Hungary, 2:225, 4:94
Ghana, 4:119
Ghazal (lyric poem), 2:189
Ghazali, al-, **2:162**
Ghazis (Muslim volunteers), 3:186
Ghent, **2:163–64**
Ghibellines. *See* Guelphs and Ghibellines
Ghiyar, Muslim law of, 1:209
Ghuta, the (oasis), 2:17
Gilbert of Sempringham, 4:193
Gildas (historian), 1:45
Giordano of Pisa, 3:33
Giorgi III, king, 4:102
Giorgi VI, king, 2:150
Giotto di Bondone, **2:164–65** *(illus.)*, 2:172
Giovanni di Bicci de' Medici, 3:129
Giovanni Pian de Carpine, 2:69
Glass, **2:165–66**, 3:151–52, 4:111
    lenses and eyeglasses, 3:86–87, 4:111
    stained, 2:113, 146, **2:166–67**, 2:169–70, 171, 3:198

Glendower, Owen, 4:170
Godfred (Danish king), 4:39
Godfrey of Bouillon, 2:10, 3:208 *(illus.)*
Godwin of Wessex, 2:44
Gogynfeirdd (bard), 1:165
Goidelic language and literature, 1:165–66
Golden Bull (1222), 2:225
Golden Bull (1356), 2:160, 3:180, 4:57 *(illus.)*
Golden Horde, 2:33–34, **2:167**, 3:151, 156, 4:104
Golden Legend. *See* Saints, lives of
Golden Spurs, Battle of (1302), 2:100
Goldsmiths, 3:136–37 *(illus.)*
Goliards, **2:167–68**
Gospels, 1:88, 181, 3:61
Gothic architecture, 1:163, **2:168–71** *(illus.)*
    building construction and, 1:224, 2:170
    of cathedral of Milan, 3:140 *(illus.)*
    characteristics of, 2:168–69
    of Chartres Cathedral, 1:174–75
    English, 1:109–10, 2:170, 4:183
    late Gothic style, 2:171
    of monasteries, 3:146
    in Paris, 3:176–77, 198–99
    in Provence, 3:238
    spread of, 2:169–70, 4:95
    stained glass and, 2:166, 167, 169–70
Gothic painting, 2:164–65, **2:171–73** *(illus.)*, 3:43
Gothic script, 3:94
Gothic sculpture, **2:174–76** *(illus.)*
Goths, 3:183–84, 4:30, 162–63. *See also* Ostrogoths; Visigoths
Gotland, 2:191, 4:40 *(illus.)*
Gottfried von Strassburg, 1:47, 2:153, 154, 155, 4:137, 138
Gottschalk of Orbais, 2:222
Gower, John, 2:62–63, **2:176**
Grafs (German counts), 2:4
Grail. *See* Arthurian literature
Grammatikos (teacher), 3:93
Granada, 1:19–20, **2:177–78** *(illus.)*, 3:28, 52, 4:88
Grand juries, 2:58
Gratian, emperor, 3:192
Gratian (monk), 3:79
Great Arbitration Act (1258), 1:214
Great Chronicles of France, 1:104, 189, 2:132, 214
Great Mosque of Córdoba, 1:226 *(illus.)*, 227, 3:25, 4:87, 89, 144
Greece, scientific works of ancient, 4:50, 51, 52. *See also* Byzantine Empire
Greek fire, 1:127, 154, 4:109
Greek language, 1:128–29, **2:178–79**, 3:92–93, 124, 125
Greek literature, ancient, 1:128–29, 199
Green Mosque (Bursa), 3:29
Green Tomb of Sultan Mehmed I, 3:29
Greenland, Vikings in, 2:68, 4:15
Gregorian chant, **2:179**, 3:161
Gregory I the Great, pope, 1:22, 82, **2:180**
    Gregorian chant named for, 2:179
    missions under, 3:144
    papacy under, 1:183, 3:192
    Rome under, 4:24
    simony and, 4:78
Gregory II, pope, 1:98
Gregory VI, Pope, 2:181
Gregory VII, pope, 1:185–86, **2:181**, 3:194, 4:149
    Henry IV and Investiture Controversy with, 1:140, 190, 2:158, 3:66, 194, 4:25–26

Gregory IX, pope, 1:80, 2:12, 128, 3:4, 85, 4:193
    Inquisition and, 1:161, 3:7, 4:137
Gregory XI, pope, 1:57, 186, 2:121, 3:187–88, 4:44–45, 197
Gregory XII, pope, 4:45
Gregory of Tours, St., 2:84, **2:180**, 2:214
Grosseteste, Robert, **2:181–82**, 3:86
Gruffydd ap Llywelyn, 4:169
Gruffydd ap yr Ynad Coch, 3:96
Grunwald, Battle of (1410), 3:95, 224
Guadalajara, Treaty of (1207), 3:170
Guelphs and Ghibellines, **2:182**, 3:35
    church-state relations and, 1:190
    Dante and, 2:22
    Florence and, 2:102, 103, 4:141–42
    Naples and, 3:168–69
    Siena and, 4:74–75
    Whites and Blacks (factions), 2:23, 102
Guibert of Nogent, abbot, 4:28
Guido Novello da Polenta, 2:24
Guido of Arezzo, 3:160
Guifred "the Hairy," 1:158
Guildhalls, Gothic, 2:170
Guilds, **2:182–85** *(illus.)*
    borough rights purchased by, 1:104
    communes and, 1:215–16
    craft, 2:182, 184
        specific types of, 1:170, 2:173, 3:85, 137, 4:53, 115
    decline of, 2:184–85
    domination of town life, 1:196
    markets and, 3:121, 122
    merchant, 2:106, 182, 183, 185, 3:6–7
    musicians hired by, 3:162
    rise of, 2:182–83
    tapestry weaving regulated by, 4:105
    trademark or emblem identifying, 2:184 *(illus.)*
    of trouvères, 4:140
Guillaume de Lorris, 1:22, 2:131, 132 *(illus.)*, 4:17
Guillaume de Nangis, 2:85
Guillaume de Poitiers. *See* William IX of Aquitaine, duke
Guillelmine Fanjeux, 4:193
Guittone d'Arezzo, 3:31
Gunpowder, 1:48, 4:174
Gutenberg, Johannes, **2:185–86** *(illus.)*, 3:234
Guthrum, king of Denmark, 1:19, 4:157
Guy de Chauliac, 3:131 *(illus.)*
Guy of Burgundy, 4:184
Guy of Châtillon, count of Blois, 2:134
Guy of crusader states, king, 2:10
Guy of Flanders, 2:100
Guy of Lusignan, 2:15, 216
Guyenne. *See* Aquitaine
Gwynedd, 4:168
Gypsies, **2:187** *(illus.)*

Haakon VI of Norway, 4:41
Habsburg dynasty, 1:56, 2:159–60, **2:187–88**, 4:98–99
Hadamar von Laber, 2:152
Hadewijch of Antwerp, **2:188**
Hadith, 1:33, 2:231–32, 3:20
Hadrian IV, pope, 1:84
Hadrian, Roman emperor, 3:216
Hafiz, **2:189**
Hagia Sophia, 1:118, 122 *(illus.)*, 139, 163, 192, 224–25, **2:189–90** *(illus.)*
Hair-care devices, 2:3–4

Hajj (pilgrimage), 2:93, 3:21, 23, 127–28 (illus.), 216–17
Hajjaj, al-, 3:125
Hakam II, al-, 4:87
Hakim, al- (Fatimid ruler), 2:89
Hamlet, 4:159
Handbooks (Fachschrifttum), 2:143, **2:190–91,** 4:138
Hanifs, 3:19
Hanseatic League, **2:191–92** (illus.)
    cities in, 2:160, 3:102, 103, 177, 178, 4:201
    fish trade and, 2:98
    food trades and, 2:84, 104
    merchant guilds in, 2:183
    ships and shipbuilding and, 4:68
    trade and formation of, 4:129
Hansen's disease. See Leprosy
Harald I Fairhair, 4:41
Harald II Bluetooth, 4:39
Haram al-Sharif, 3:41
Hardecnut, 2:44
Harlech castle (Wales), 4:169 (illus.)
Harold of England, king, 1:77
Harold of Wessex, 2:55, 193–94 (illus.), 4:184
Hartmannvon Aue, 2:154
Harun al-Rashid, 1:2, 61, 2:31, **2:192–93,** 3:113, 4:51
Hasan, mosque of Sultan (Cairo), 1:131 (illus.)
Hasidei Ashkenaz, 3:58, 166
Hasidim, 3:166
Hastings, Battle of (1066), 1:77, 141, 2:55, **2:193–94** (illus.), 3:176, 4:173, 184
Hätzlerin, Klara, **2:194**
Hawking, 2:227, 228
Heating, **2:194–96** (illus.)
Heaven, idea of, 3:197–98
Hebrew Bible, 1:88
Hebrew literacy, 3:93
Hebrew literature, **2:196–98**
    historical writing, 2:215
    illuminated Jewish manuscripts, 3:43
    Jewish libraries and, 3:89–90
    Judaism interpreted in, 3:57–58, 59
    paradise and hell in, 3:197
    by Rashi, 4:4
    religious instruction in Hebrew, 4:7
    rhetoric, 4:8–9
    sermons, 4:65
    Spanish, 4:92, 94
Hegira (emigration), 3:153
Heinrich von Halle, 3:128
Hellenistic tradition. See Classical tradition in the Middle Ages
Heloise. See Abelard and Heloise
Henry II of Castile (Henry of Trastámara), 1:151
Henry IV of Castile, 1:152
Henry I of England, 1:24, 2:55, **2:198–99,** 3:60, 98, 101, 4:16
Henry II of England, 1:25, **2:199–200,** 3:60
    administration of forests under, 2:11–12
    Aquitaine and, 1:29
    Becket and, 1:78–79, 2:200
    Bertran de Born and, 1:86–87
    Castile and, alliance with, 1:150
    church-state relations under, 1:190
    Eleanor of Aquitaine, wife of, 2:50
    as first Angevin, 2:55
    Ireland, overlordship of, 3:14
    legal reforms, 3:82, 4:136

travel by, 4:134
Wales and, 4:170
Henry III of England, 1:29, **2:200–201,** 3:60
    Blanche of Castile and, 1:93
    diplomacy under, 2:31
    Edward I, successor of, 2:45
    Louis IX and, 3:101
    Parliament's emergence under, 2:58
    Simon de Montfort the Younger and, 4:77–78
    Wales and, 4:170
    Westminster Abbey and, 4:183
    William Marshal as guardian to, 4:185
Henry IV of England, 1:177, 2:59, 3:57, 4:11, 170
Henry V of England, 1:117, 172, 2:121, **2:201–2** (illus.), 2:223, 3:176
Henry VI of England, 1:130, **2:202–3** (illus.), 3:54, 4:11, 177 (illus.), 178
Henry VII of England, 2:59, 3:15, 4:11, 178
Henry VIII of England, 3:15
Henry II of Germany, 2:158
Henry III of Germany, 1:84, 2:158, **2:203–4,** 3:179
Henry IV of Germany (Holy Roman Emperor), 1:95, 2:158, 181, 4:149
    Investiture Controversy and, 1:140, 190, 2:158, 3:66, 194, 4:25–26
Henry V of Germany (Holy Roman Emperor), 1:217, 2:158, 3:127
Henry VI of Germany (Holy Roman Emperor), 2:102, 127, 152, 158–59, **2:204–5** (illus.), 4:9 (illus.), 10, 71–72
Henry VII of Germany (Holy Roman Emperor), 1:96, 2:24, 102, 160
Henry I of Champagne, 1:167, 3:119
Henry the Lion of Saxony, 1:75, 2:158, 204, 3:102
Henry I of Saxony, duke, 2:157, 3:184
Henry de Mondeville, **2:205–6**
Henry of Reynes (architect), 4:183
Henry the Navigator, 2:65, 3:230 (illus.), 231
Henry the Proud of Bavaria, 1:75
Henryson, Robert, 4:55
Heraklios, emperor, 1:122
Heraldry, 1:43, 210, **2:206–8** (illus.), 3:107
Heralds' College of Arms, 2:208
Herbs and herbals, **2:208–10** (illus.)
Hercegovina, 1:105, 106
Hereford, Nicholas, 4:198
Heresy and heresies, **2:210–12**
    in Byzantine Empire, 2:211
    in Christian tradition, 2:210–11
    crusades against heretics, 2:14
    excommunication and, 2:66
    Inquisition against, 1:161, 4:137
    in Islam, 2:211–12
    St. Dominic's order to preach against, 2:35, 36–37
    torture of heretics, 4:122
    trials for, 3:7–8 (illus.), 4:137
    western European, 2:210–11
        Arians, 1:182, 183, 227, 3:183
        Beguines and Beghards, 1:80–81, 2:43, 188
        Cathars, 1:160–61
        Hus and Hussites, 1:96, 2:14, 211, 229, 230, 232
        Lollards, 3:96, 4:197
        Meister Eckhart and, 2:43
        Ockham and, 3:181
        Spirituals, 1:98, 2:125
        Waldensians, 3:76, 4:167–68

witchcraft as, 4:187–88
Wyclif and, 2:211, 4:197–99 (illus.)
Hermandades, **2:212**
Hermann of Carinthia, 3:125
Hermits, **2:212–13,** 3:59, 147, 4:14–15
Hesychios, 2:51
Hiberno-Saxon art. See Irish-Saxon art
Hilda of Whitby, 4:191
Hildebrand (monk). See Gregory VII, pope
Hildegard of Bingen, St., **2:213**
Hippocrates, 3:130
Hisdai ibn Shaprut, 3:51
Hispano-Mauresque art, 4:89–90
Historical writing, **2:213–16**
    by Anna Komnena, 3:70–71
    Armenian, 2:215
    Byzantine, 2:214–15, 4:1
    chronicles, 1:188–89
    Islamic, 2:215–16, 232, 4:66 (illus.), 102
    Jewish, 2:215
    about Scandinavia, 4:38, 39, 40
    Slavic, 4:82, 83
    western European, 2:180, 213–14, 3:185–86, 4:91–92
History, climate's influence on, 1:202–3
Hittin, Battle of (1187), 2:10, **2:216,** 4:33–34
Hohenstaufens, 1:56, 2:126, 158–59, 204, 4:71–72
Holidays. See Feasts and festivals
Holy Communion. See Eucharist
Holy Grail, quest for, 1:46
Holy Land. See Palestine
Holy orders, 4:31
Holy Roman Empire, **2:216–17** (map)
    Alfonso X el Sabio and, 1:18
    Austria and, 1:54–56 (illus.)
    Bohemia-Moravia as kingdom in, 1:95–96 (illus.)
    Burgundy as kingdom of, 1:115, 116
    church-state relations in, 1:189–90
    consuls' power in, 1:225
    emperors
        Charlemagne, 1:170–71 (illus.)
        Charles III, 2:155
        Charles IV, 1:95 (illus.), 96, 116, 2:160, 3:180, 4:57 (illus.)
        Conrad II, 2:158, 203, 216
        Conrad III, 1:75, 2:10, 13 (illus.), 3:180
        Frederick I Barbarossa and, 2:126–27, 217
        Frederick II, 2:127–28
        Frederick III, 2:160, 188
        Henry IV, 1:95, 140, 190, 2:158, 181, 3:66, 194, 4:25–26, 149
        Henry V, 1:217, 2:158, 3:127
        Henry VI, 2:204–5 (illus.)
        Henry VII, 1:96, 2:24, 102, 160
        Otto I, 3:184–85
        Otto II, 2:157, 216
        Otto III, 3:185
    formal beginning of, 4:25
    Habsburg dynasty and, 2:187–88
    Hungary and, 2:225
    Italy and, conflicts with, 3:33, 35
    Lübeck and, 3:102–3
    Naples as part of, 3:168
    pope-emperor relationship, 2:181, 3:4, 5, 193. See also Investiture Controversy
    Switzerland under, 4:98
    Tuscany and, 4:141
    See also Germany

Holy Sepulcher, Church of the, 2:89, 3:41
Holy Year, **2:217–18**
Homer, 4:140
Homilies, 2:61, 63
Honoré, Master, 1:104
Honorius III, pope, 2:35, 36
Horsemen. *See* Cavalry warfare
Horses, use of, 1:13, 4:135. *See also* Cavalry
   warfare
Hospitality, rise of commercial, 3:5–6
Hospitals and poor relief, **2:218–21** *(illus.)*,
   3:8–9, 69, 88–89, 130, 4:120
Hostels, 3:5–6
Hours of Divine Office, 2:33
Hours of the Virgin, 1:99
Hrabanus Maurus, **2:221–22**
Hrotswitha von Gandersheim, 2:39, **2:222**
Hsi-hsia in China, 3:150
Hugh of Orleans, 1:143, 2:168
Hugh of Troyes, 1:167
Hulagu, Mongol king, 1:58, 3:11
Humiliati (Christian group), 2:211
Humphrey, duke of Gloucester, 3:90
Hunayn ibn Ishaq, 2:209
Hundred constables, 1:218
Hundred court, 3:81–82
Hundred Years War, **2:222–24** *(illus.)*
   causes of, 1:29
   Clement VI and, 1:200
   diplomacy during, 2:30
   England and
      Cade's Rebellion and, 1:130
      Edward III and, 2:46, 58
      Henry V of England and, 2:202, 223
      Henry VI of England and, 2:202
      Parliament and, 2:58–59
   Flanders and, 2:100–101
   France and, 2:120–22
      Charles V and, 1:171–72
      Charles VII and, 1:172–73, 2:121–22,
         202, 223, 3:54–55
      Froissart's writing on, 2:134
      Jacquerie and, 3:205
      Jacques Coeur and end of war, 3:37
      Joan of Arc and, 1:156, 173, 2:122, 162,
         223, 3:54–55
      Valois dynasty and, 2:120–22, 3:213
   Ghent and, 2:163
   Normandy and, 3:176
   phases of, 2:222–23
   population decrease and, 3:227
   towns and cities, impact on, 1:196
   warfare in, 2:224, 4:173–74, 175
Hundreds, 2:54
Hungary, **2:224–26** *(illus.)*
   Bosnia and, 1:105–6
   Golden Bull of 1222 and, 2:225
   Henry III of Germany's control of, 2:203
   Moldavia and, 4:165–66
   Otto III and Christianization of, 3:185
   St. Stephen of, 4:94–95
   Sigismund, king of, 4:76
   Tomislav's defeat of, 4:121
   Vlad Tepes and, 4:164
   Walachia and, 4:165
Hunger. *See* Famine
Huns, **2:226–27**
   Germanic migrations caused by, 2:226,
      3:137–39 *(map)*
   in Hungary, 2:224

invasion of Italy, 3:33, 139–40
   Odoacer and, 3:182
   Ostrogoths and, 2:226, 3:183
   Paris and, 3:198
Hunting and fowling, 2:111–12, **2:227–28** *(illus.)*
Hus, Jan, 1:187, **2:229–30** *(illus.)*, 4:76, 82
   heresy of, 1:89, 96, 2:211, 229, 230, 3:232
Husayn ibn Ali, al-, 2:93, **2:230**, 4:199–200
Hussites, 1:96, 2:14, 230
Hywel the Good, 4:169

Ibn al-Jawzi, 1:33–34, 4:65
Ibn al-Khatib (writer), 2:177
Ibn al-Nadim, 3:109
Ibn al-Sarraj (grammarian), 2:87
Ibn Battuta, 2:69, 177, **2:231**, 3:118, 4:119
Ibn Hanbal, **2:231–32**
Ibn Ishaq, 2:215
Ibn Khaldun, 1:34, 2:49, 177, **2:232**, 3:109
Ibn Khurdadhbih, **2:232–33**
Ibn Qutayba, 1:33, 2:51
Ibn Rushd, 1:39, **2:233–34** *(illus.)*
Ibn Sad, 2:215
Ibn Sina, 1:16, 39, 2:3, **2:234–35** *(illus.)*, 3:132
Ibn Taymiya, **2:235**
Iceland, 4:15, 41–42
Iconoclasm, 1:119–21, 123, 183–84, 2:211, 237
Iconostasis, 2:235–36
Icons, 1:119, 120, 123, **2:235–37** *(illus.)*, 3:152,
   4:28–29
Idrisi, al- (geographer), 3:118, 4:73
Ifriqiya, 4:70
Ilarion, 4:82
Île de la Cité, 3:176–77, 199 *(illus.)*
Île-de-France, 2:115, 129, 3:100, 101
Ilkhanids, 3:151
Illuminated manuscripts. *See* Books, manuscript
Imam, 1:136, **2:237–38**
   Fatimid, 2:88, 89, 90
   Shi'ite, 1:120, 2:88, 230, 3:22
Immanuel ben Solomon of Rome, 3:197
Imperial Assembly (Reichstag), 2:161
Imru'al-Qays, 1:32–33
Ince Minare madrasa, 3:29
Incense, **3:1**
Incunabula, 3:235
India, 2:70–71, 143, 3:17
Indian Ocean, navigation in, 3:170
Indulgences, 2:217–18, 230, **3:1**, 3:214, 215,
   4:13, 168
Inheritance laws and practices, 2:94, 95, **3:2–3**,
   3:173–74, 4:85–86
Innkeepers, 3:6–7
Innocent II, pope, 1:86
Innocent III, pope, **3:4** *(illus.)*, 4:188
   civil war under, 4:26
   crusades and, 1:161, 2:11, 3:76–77, 4:123
   Francis of Assisi and, 2:123
   John of England's dispute over Langton
      with, 3:56, 75
   Kingdom of Sicily and, 4:72
   papal authority under, 3:194
Innocent IV, pope, 2:128, 182, **3:4–5**, 4:72, 193
Innocent VIII, pope, 3:129
Inns and taverns, **3:5–7**
Inns of Court, 3:82
Inquests, 2:57, 3:82, 4:136–37
Inquisition, 1:161, 2:211, **3:7–8** *(illus.)*
   of Joan of Arc, 3:54–55
   Spanish, 3:7, 8, 53, 4:151

torture used by, 4:122
   trials of, 4:137
   Waldensianism and, 4:168
   witchcraft targeted by, 4:187–88
Insanity, treatment of, **3:8–9**
Insular languages. *See* Celtic languages and
   literature
Interdict, 2:66–67
Invention. *See* Technology
Investiture Controversy, 1:140, 3:66, 194,
   4:25–26
   Concordat of Worms settling, 1:190, 217,
      2:158
   Henry I and, 2:199
   Matilda of Tuscany and, 1:140, 3:126
   simony as issue in, 4:78
Iran, **3:9–11** *(illus.)*
   Armenia as center of trade for, 4:124
   culture of, 1:3
   Georgia and, 2:150
   Islamic art and architecture in, 3:25–26
   Islamic conquest of, 3:9–11, 17
   Jewish communities in, 3:50–51
   literature of, 4:29, 66
   Mongol rule of, 3:11
   Persian Empire, 1:122, 137
   Samarkand, 4:34–35, 51, 104
   Sasanian dynasty in, 3:9, 10 *(illus.)*, 4:37–38
   under Seljuks, 3:11, 4:57, 58
Iraq, **3:11–13**
   cities of, 3:72–73, 4:35–36
   Islamic art and architecture in, 3:24, 26–27
   Jewish communities in, 3:50–51
   Sasanian dynasty in, 3:11–12, 16, 4:37–38
   Zanj slaves' revolt (868–883), 4:201
Ireland, **3:13–15** *(illus.)*
   Dublin, 2:41
   England and, 3:14–15
   John Scottus Eriugena of, 3:57
   literature of, 1:166
   missions and missionaries of, 3:13, 144, 204,
      4:131
   St. Brigit of, 1:107–8
   Vikings in, 2:41, 68, 3:14, 4:154
Irene, Byzantine empress, 1:123, 170, 184, 2:237
Irish art, 1:108, 3:13
Irrigation techniques, 1:10, 11
Isaac I Komnenos, 3:71
Isaac ben Samud of Dampierre, 3:36
Isabella of Angoulême, 3:56
Isabella of Brienne, 2:128
Isabella of France, 2:46
Isabella of Gloucester, 3:56
Isabella of Spain, 1:37, 152, 2:71, 3:53
Isabelle of France, 4:10
Isfahan, 3:26
Isidore of Seville, St., 1:87, 188, 2:52, 214,
   3:118, 4:91
Isidoros of Miletos (architect), 2:189
Islam, conquests of, 1:31, **3:15–17** *(map)*
   Abu Bakr and, 1:5
   in Armenia, 1:40–41, 3:17
   Battle of Siffin and, 1:21, 4:75
   Berbers and, 1:85
   Byzantine Empire and, 1:122–23, 192–93
   Charles Martel's resistance of, 1:174
   Córdoba and, 1:226, 227–28
   Damascus and, 2:17–18, 19
   Egypt and, 2:48, 49
   Ethiopia and, 2:64, 65

fairs allowed in subject lands, 2:73
Genoa and, 2:149
Georgia and, 2:150
Granada and, 2:177–78 *(illus.)*
Iran and, 3:9–11, 17
Iraq and, 3:12
Jews in Islamic world and, 3:49–52
Kufa, founding of, 3:72–73
music and influence of, 3:159
in Nubia, 3:179
Ottomans and Ottoman Empire, 3:183, 186–89 *(map) (illus.)*
Palestine and, 3:191
in Portugal, 3:229, 230
Saladin and, 4:33–34 *(illus.)*
Samarkand as outpost for, 4:34–35, 51, 104
Sasanians and, 4:38
of Sicily, 4:70, 72
slaves acquired through, 4:81
in Spain, 1:149, 150–51, 3:17, 4:86–89 *(illus.)*
the Cid and, 1:190, 191
Toledo and, 4:120, 121
Syria and, 4:100–101
Timbuktu and, 4:119
Toulouse as center of defense against, 4:123
trade and, 4:127–28
travel and transportation necessitated by, 4:130, 134–35
Umar I ibn al-Khattab and, 4:143
Umayyad dynasty and, 1:136–37, 3:17, 4:144–46
warfare during, 4:175–76
Islam, political organization of, **3:18–19,** 3:113
birth of Islamic state, 3:153–54
caliphate and, 1:2–3, 135–38, 3:10
al-Farabi and, 2:88
Fatimid Empire, 2:88–90 *(map)*
imam and, 2:237–38
Mamluk dynasty, 3:19, 112–13 *(illus.)*
principle of priority in, 1:136
Sunna and, 2:88, 3:20, 21, 4:96
ulama and, 4:142
Umar I ibn al-Khattab, founder of state, 3:18, 4:142–43
Umayyads and, 1:136–37, 4:144–46
vizier and, 4:163–64
Islam, religion of, **3:19–22** *(illus.)*
Arabia and rise of, 1:30–31
Arabic rhetoric and, 4:8
Christian missionary activity and rise of, 3:145
devil in, 2:27
European view of, 4:17
family in, 2:76–78
fasting in, 2:92, 93, 3:21
feasts and festivals in, 2:92–94, 3:21
five pillars of, 2:220, 3:21
Golden Horde and, 2:167
heresies in, 2:211–12
historical writing on, 2:215–16
hospitals and poor relief in, 2:219–20
hunting and fowling in, 2:228
inheritance laws in, 3:3
in Iran, 3:9, 10, 11
in Iraq, 3:12, 13
Jerusalem and, 3:41–42
jihad and, 3:53–54
law schools and, 3:85
libraries to preserve, 1:61, 3:89–90, 91 *(illus.),* 4:51

magic and folklore in, 3:109
millenialism in, 3:142
Muhammad, founder of, 1:30, 3:19, 152–54 *(illus.),* 4:3 *(illus.)*
music in, 3:158–59
mysticism and, 2:49, 162, 3:22, 166–67, 4:29
paradise in, 3:197–98
Peter the Venerable's understanding of, 3:209
pilgrimages to Mecca (hajj), 2:93, 3:21, 23, 127–28 *(illus.),* 216–17
purgatory *(barzakh)* in, 4:2
Qur'an and, 3:19–20, 21, 4:3 *(illus.)*
religious instruction in, 4:7
religious law (shari'a) and worship, 2:220, 3:20–21, 82–83
five "pillars," 2:220, 3:21
scholars of, 2:162, 231–32, 234, 4:5–6, 102
sermons in, 4:65
Shi'ism. *See* Shi'ism, Shi'ites
slavery in, 4:80
Sufism, 3:22, 166–67
sundials and time for prayer in, 1:204
Sunna, 2:88, 3:20, 21, 4:96
Sunnites. *See* Sunnite branch of Islam
theology, 3:21–22
Turmeda, convert to, 4:140–41
ulama and, 4:142
Umar I ibn al-Khattab and, 4:142
Islamic art and architecture, **3:23–29** *(illus.)*
Alhambra, 1:19–20
building construction and, 1:155, 225, 3:23–29
calligraphy as decorative form of, 1:101, 138–39, 4:3 *(illus.)*
gardens and, 2:145–46
of Granada, 2:177–78
jewelry, 2:146
Jewish art and, 3:43
lighting devices, 3:92
regional styles, development of, 3:24, 25–29, 4:87, 89–90
Islamic astrology and astronomy, 1:49–51, 4:51
Islamic calendar, 1:133–34
Islamic manuscript books, 1:100, 101–2, 104, 3:24 *(illus.)*
Islamic musical instruments, 3:162–63
Islamic world
agriculture in, 1:8–10, 11
banking in, 1:66–67, 4:128
cities and towns of, 1:194, 198, 3:12, 4:80–81, 175–76
colleges in, 3:93, 4:49–50, 148–49
diplomacy in, 2:30, 32
Jewish communities in, 2:220, 3:47, 48, 49–52, 222
maps and mapmaking in, 3:116–18, 154–55
mathematics in, 3:62, 4:52
nomadic origins of, 2:139
plagues in, 3:221–22
postal service *(barid)* in, 3:231
roads in, 4:12
schools in, 4:49–50
scientific instruments from, 4:52–53 *(illus.)*
sealing in, 4:57
slaves in, 4:78, 80–81, 176
taxation in, 4:108–9, 143
technology in, 4:51, 110–11
textiles in, 4:115
trade and, 1:158, 3:34–35, 217, 4:127–28

travel and transportation in, 4:12, 130, 134–35
women in, 4:190
Ismailis, 1:138, 2:88, 3:22
Isopets (fable collections), 2:72
Istanbul. *See* Constantinople
Italian language and literature, **3:29–33** *(illus.)*
Hebrew literature and, 2:198
language, 3:30–31
literature, 3:31–33, 35
by Boccaccio, 1:93–95
by Dante Alighieri, 2:21–24
influence on Chaucer, 1:175–76
by Jacopone da Todi, 3:37
by Petrarch, 3:209–11 *(illus.)*
Italian Renaissance, 1:112–13, 119, 121, 176, 2:103
Italy, 1:146, **3:33–35** *(map)*
banking in, 1:67–69
church-state relations in, 1:190
cities and towns of, 3:33–35
consuls of, 1:225
Florence, 2:101–3 *(illus.)*
Genoa, 2:148–50 *(illus.)*
Milan, 3:139–41 *(illus.)*
Naples, 3:168–69
Pisa, 3:217–18 *(illus.)*
Ravenna, 4:4–5 *(illus.)*
Rome, 4:24–26 *(illus.)*
Siena, 4:73–75 *(illus.)*
Venice, 4:151–54 *(illus.)*
as commercial leader of western Europe, 4:129
communes in, 1:216
Germanic migrations into, 3:33–35, 137, 138
Lombards, 3:33–34, 139, 140, 4:24–25, 141
Ostrogoths, 3:33, 139–40, 182, 183–84, 4:116–17
Saxons, 2:157
Visigoths, 3:33
glassmaking in, 2:165
Guelph-Ghibelline conflict and, 2:182
Jewish communities in, 3:48
Kingdom of Sicily and, 4:71–73
Lombards, kingdom of, 3:96–97
Papal States, 3:195–96 *(map)*
Romanesque art in, 4:22–23
serfs and serfdom in, 4:62
silk industry in, 4:77
trade and. *See under* Trade
Tuscany, 4:141–42
women mystics in, 3:166
Ivan I Kalita, 2:167
Ivan III of Muscovy, **3:36,** 3:157, 158, 179
Ivan IV of Muscovy, 3:158, 4:63
Ivan Kalita, grand prince of Vladimir, 3:156

Jabir ibn Hayyan, 1:16
Jacob ben Abba Mari Anatoli, 4:65
Jacob ben Meir, **3:36**
Jacopone da Todi, **3:37**
Jacquerie (1358), 3:205, 4:108
Jacques Coeur, **3:37–38,** 3:77
Jadwiga of Poland, queen, 3:224
Jagiello of Lithuania, 3:95, 224
Jahiz, al-, 1:33, **3:38**
Jalal al-Din. *See* Rumi
Jamali, Badr al- (vizier), 2:89
James, St. (apostle), 1:52, 4:36
James I the Conqueror, 1:18, 37, **3:38–39** *(illus.),* 4:87, 150

James II of Aragon, 1:37
James I of Cyprus, 2:16
James of Majorca, 3:39
James III of Scotland, 4:55
James IV of Scotland, 4:55, 56
Jamuqa, 2:147
Janissaries, 3:134, 155, 186–87, 189, 4:79
Jawhar (military strategist), 2:89
Jazari, al-, 4:110
Jean de Joinville, 2:132, 214, **3:40**
Jean de Meun, 1:22, 2:131, 132 *(illus.)*, 4:18
Jean, duke of Berry, 1:99
Jerome, St., 2:214, 3:141
Jerusalem, **3:40–42** *(illus.)*
   Ayyubid, Mamluk, and early Ottoman period
     (1187–1566), 3:42
   Battle of Hittin (1187) and Muslim libera-
     tion of, 2:10, 216, 4:33–34
   Byzantine Christian period (324–638),
     3:40–41
   Christian fair in, 2:73
   crusades, period of (1099–1187), 3:42
   Dome of the Rock, 1:136, 3:23, 28 *(illus.)*, 41,
     4:100
   as early Christian center, 1:182
   early Islamic period (638–1099), 3:41–42
   Frederick II as king of, 2:128
   Jewish community in, 3:41, 42, 50, 168
   Latin kingdom of, 2:10
   pilgrimages to, 3:40–41, 213, 214, 216
   Saladin's recapture of (1187), 1:58, 3:42,
     4:33–34
Jewelry. *See* Gems and jewelry
Jewish art, **3:43–44** *(illus.)*, 4:90
Jewish communities, **3:44–52** *(illus.)*
   during Black Death, 1:91, 200–201, 3:49
   clothing in, 1:207, 209, 211
   conversos and, 1:225–26
   in Europe, 3:47–49
   family and, 2:82–83
   Innocent IV's tolerance of, 3:5
   in Islamic world, 2:220, 3:47, 48, 49–52, 222
   Jacob ben Meir and, 3:36
   in Jerusalem, 3:41, 42, 50, 168
   Jewish banking in western Europe, 1:67,
     3:45, 49
   Jewish law in, 3:45–46, 47, 57–58, 59, 83–84,
     110, 4:4
   Jewish sermons in, 4:64–65
   life in, general characteristics of, 3:44–45
   literacy in, 3:58 *(illus.)*, 93
   magic and folklore in, 3:108–9
   music in, 3:161
   nagid, leader of, 3:167
   schools in, 4:50
   self-government by, 3:45–47
   in Spain, 1:71, 150, 152, 225–26, 3:48, 51–52,
     4:88–89
   traders from, 2:69
   women in, 4:191
   See also Anti-Semitism; Judaism
Jewish manuscript books, 1:101, 3:43–44
Jewish pilgrimages, 3:216
Jewish science, 4:51–52
Jews, expulsion of, **3:52–53**
   anti-Semitism and, 1:27, 3:48–49
   banking and, 1:67
   conversos and, 1:225–26
   from Europe, 2:119, 3:48–49, 180
     Spain, 1:228, 3:52, 53, 4:121

Hebrew literature and, 2:198
   science and, 4:52
Jihad, 2:30, 228, **3:53–54**
Jinn (spirits), 3:109
Joan of Arc, St., 1:156, 173, 2:122, 162, 223,
   3:54–55 *(illus.)*
Joan of Flanders, countess, 2:99–100
Joanna II of Navarre, 3:170
Joanna of Sicily, 2:50
João I of Aviz, 3:231
John VIII, pope, 2:17
John XII, pope, 2:157, 216
John XXII, pope, 1:76, 2:125, 160, 3:181
John XXIII, pope, 4:45
John II Komnenos, emperor, 3:71, 130
John V Palaiologos, emperor, 1:126, 3:188
John II of Castile, 1:152
John of England, king, **3:55–56** *(illus.)*
   borough liberties purchased under, 1:104
   collapse of Angevin Empire under, 2:56–57
   Eleanor of Aquitaine, mother of, 2:50
   forests and, 2:112
   Jewish banking under, 1:67
   Langton and, 3:56, 75
   loss of Normandy to Philip II Augustus,
     3:176, 212
   Magna Carta granted by, 2:57, 3:55, 56, 110
   William Marshal and, 4:185
John II of France, 1:171, 172, 2:120–21, 135
John II of Portugal, 2:65, 70
John Asen II, tsar of Bulgaria, 1:115
John Chrysostom, archbishop of Constantino-
   ple, 2:218
John of Brienne, 2:11
John of Damascus, 1:184
John of Gaunt, 2:47, **3:56–57,** 3:206
John of Luxembourg, 3:106
John of Salisbury, 2:214, 3:66
John Scottus Eriugena, **3:57**
John the Grammarian, 1:221
Jonas (monk), 1:214
Jongleur, 2:130, 3:143, 161
Jordan River, pilgrimage to, 3:214
Jordanes (historian), 4:40
Jordanus de Nemore (Nemorarius), 3:126
Joseph ibn Zabara (writer), 2:198
Journeyman, 2:184, 3:100
Joust, 2:141–42
Jubilee indulgences, 3:1
Judah al-Harizi (writer), 2:198
Judah ben Jehiel, 4:8–9
Judah Halevi (poet), 2:197, 3:58
Judah he-Hasid, rabbi, 4:65
Judaism, **3:57–59** *(illus.)*
   cabala, 1:130, 2:197–98, 3:58–59, 166, 167
   conversos from, 1:152, 225–26, 3:52
   Hebrew Bible of, 1:88
   Hebrew literature and, 2:196–98, 3:57–58,
     59
   Jacob ben Meir and, 3:36
   Jewish calendar, 1:133
   Jewish mysticism, 3:166
   law in, 3:45–46, 47, 57–58, 59, 83–84, 110,
     4:4
   libraries to preserve, 3:89–90
   liturgy, 2:196
   magic and folklore in, 3:108–9
   mysticism in, 3:58–59, 166
   paradise in, 3:197
   philosophy of, 3:58

pilgrimages in, 3:216
   rabbinic, 3:57–58
   Rashi's influence on, 3:84, 4:4
   religious instruction in, 4:7
   schools teaching, 4:50
   sermons in, 4:64–65
   spread of, 3:57–58
   Talmud, 1:89, 3:36, 50, 57, 108, 167, 4:4, 7, 50
Judgment Day, rites preparing for, 2:25–26
Judicial pilgrimage, 3:214
Judicial torture, 4:122, 123
Julian calendar, 1:134
Julian of Norwich, 2:62, **3:59**
Jury system, 2:58, 3:80–81, 82, 181, 4:136–37,
   197
Justiciar, **3:60,** 4:16, 171
Justin I, emperor, 3:60
Justin II, emperor, 3:61
Justinian I, **3:60–61** *(illus.)*
   Anatolia and, 1:22
   archives under, 1:38
   Byzantine Empire under, 1:122
   Constantinople in reign of, 1:220
   Corpus juris civilis (Body of Civil Law), 3:79
     Code of Civil Law in, 1:49, 122, 3:61, 79,
      81, 89
   inheritance laws under, 3:3
   law schools under, 3:84
   libraries under, 3:89
   plague during reign of, 3:220, 221
   Vandals, defeat of, 4:151
   waterworks in Constantinople and, 4:178
Justinian Code, 1:49, 122, 3:61, 79, 81, 89
Justiniana Prima, 1:197
Justinian's Plague, 3:220, 221
Jutes, 1:25, 2:53, 3:139

Kaaba, 3:128 *(illus.)*, 152, 217
Kalbites, 4:70
Kalka River, Battle of (1223), 3:65
Kallir (poet), 2:197
Kalojan of Bulgaria, king, 1:115
Karaites, 3:50–51, 58, 59
Karbala, Battle of (680), 2:230
Karlmann (Carolingian ruler), 1:147
Kells, Book of, 1:108, 3:13, **3:61**
Kempe, Margery, 2:62, 79, **3:62**
Kent, kingdom of, 1:140, 2:53
Khadija (wife of Muhammad), 3:153
Khans, 2:33
Kharijites, 1:21, 85, 136, 137, 138, 4:75
Khayzuran, al-, 2:192
Khazars, 3:17
Khosrow II, Sasanian king, 3:10 *(illus.)*
Khwarezm people of Afghanistan, 2:147
Khwarizmi, al-, 1:34, 3:62, 3:125–26
Khwarizmshah (Muslim ruler), 3:150
Kievan Rus, **3:62–65** *(map)*
   conversion to Byzantine Christianity, 1:73, 3:64
   invasion of Baltic countries from, 1:64
   literature in, 4:82–83
   Novgorod ruled by princes of, 3:177
   roots of serfdom in Russia in, 4:63
   Russian pilgrimages, 3:216
   Vikings in, 2:68, 3:64, 4:157
   Vladimir, principality of, 3:155–56
   Yaroslav the Wise, grand prince of, 3:64, 4:199
Kildare, Anglo-Irish earls of county, 3:15
King's Bench, 3:82 *(illus.)*
King's evil. *See* Royal touch

King's Wardrobe, 3:98
Kingship, theories of, **3:65–67**
  anointing of kings, 1:25–26, 3:65–66
  conflicts between pope and king, 3:66–67
  coronation ceremonies, 2:1 (illus.)
  feudalism and relationship with great lords,
    2:95–97
  German representative assemblies and, 2:161
  Germanic migrations and, 3:137
  hereditary kingship, 3:137
  John of Salisbury on, 3:66
  "mirrors of princes," 3:65–66
  Parliament's emergence and, 2:58–59
  Philip IV the Fair and, 3:212–13
  royal households and, 4:26–28 (illus.)
  royal touch and, 3:65–66, 4:28
Kirman, Seljuk state in, 4:58
Kirtles (dresses), 1:209
Knighthood, **3:67–68** (illus.)
  armor and, 1:41–45 (illus.), 3:68
  chivalry and, 1:178–80 (illus.), 3:67
  coats of arms of, 2:206, 207–8 (illus.)
  courtesy books for knights, 2:5
  Edward III of England and, 2:46
  during Hundred Years War, 2:224
  Knights of the Round Table, 1:45,
    46 (illus.)
  social class and, 3:67–68, 4:84
  tournaments and, 1:179, 2:141–42
  warfare and, 4:172–73
Knights Hospitalers, 1:179, 2:10, 3:69
Knights of Christ, 1:179
Knights of Malta, 1:179, 3:69
Knights of Rhodes, 1:179
Knights of St. John of Jerusalem. See Knights
  Hospitalers
Knights of the Holy Sepulcher, 1:180
Knights of the Sword of Cyprus, 1:180
Knights, orders of, **3:69–70**
  chivalric orders, 1:179–80, 186, 2:10, 3:70
  Grail knights, 2:155
  hospitals operated by, 2:221
  Knights Hospitalers, 1:179, 2:10, 3:69
  Knights Templars, 1:86, 179, 2:10, 119, 3:69
  pilgrimages by knights, 3:214
  in Portugal, 3:230–31
  prestige of knighthood and, 3:67, 68
  Teutonic Knights, 1:64 (illus.), 65, 179, 2:191,
    3:69, 94–95, 224
  Truce of God and, 3:204
Knights Templars, 1:86, 179, 2:10, 119, 3:69
Koloman of Hungary, king, 2:8
Komnena, Anna, 1:129, 2:214, **3:70–71**
Komnenos family, **3:71–72**
  Alexios I, 1:96–97, 124, 2:8–10, 75, 3:70, 71,
    4:149
  Alexios II, 3:71
  Andronikos I, 3:71, 72
  Hungary and, 2:225
  Isaac I, 3:71
  John II, 3:71, 130
  Manuel I, 2:225, 3:71, 72, 4:127
  Tamar, queen of Georgia, and, 4:103
Kontore (countinghouses), 2:192
Koran. See Qur'an
Koriwn (writer), 2:215
Kosovo, Battle of (1389), 1:76, 126, 3:155, 188,
  4:60
Kotromanic, Stjepan, 1:105–6
Krak de Montreal, 2:14

Krak des Chevaliers, 2:14, 3:69
Kremlin, 3:157, 4:28
Krum, 1:113, 114, **3:72**
Kublai Khan, 2:69, 3:225–26
Kufa, 1:60–61, 3:12, **3:72–73**
Kufi (style of lettering), 1:138
Kulikovo, Battle of (1380), 2:34, 3:156

La Fontaine, fables as influence on, 2:72
Ladislas I of Hungary, 2:225
Lais, 3:120 (illus.)
Lammas Day, 2:92
Land tax, 4:108
Land use, 2:95, 96–97, **3:73–74** (illus.), 3:227–28,
  4:83. See also Agriculture; Forests
Lanfranc of Bec, 1:26, 141, 3:60, **3:75**
Lanfrance of Canterbury. See Lanfranc of Bec
Langland, William, 1:22, 2:63
Langton, Stephen, 1:141, 3:56, **3:75**, 3:110
Languages. See individual languages
Langue d'oc, 2:129, 130
Langue d'oïl, 2:129, 130
Languedoc, **3:75–77** (illus.), 4:22
Las Navas de Tolosa, Battle of (1212), 1:37, 151,
  3:230
Last rites, 2:25
Lateen (fore-and-aft) rigging ships, 4:67, 68
  (illus.)
Lateran Councils, 1:186
Latin cross design church, 1:162
Latin Empire of Constantinople, 1:115, 3:172
Latin Kingdom of Jerusalem, 2:10
Latin language, **3:77–78**
  classical tradition preserved in, 1:200
  evolution of Italian from, 3:29–30
  French language and, 2:129
  instruction at cathedral schools in, 4:47
  literature in
    Boccaccio's encyclopedias, 1:94
    Christian books, 1:102, 103
    herbals, 2:208
    liberal arts handbooks, 2:190
    by St. Columbanus, 1:214
    Scandinavian religious literature, 4:44
  printing books in, 3:235
  sermons in, 4:64
  Vulgar Latin, 2:129, 3:30, 77, 78
  western European literacy in, 3:93–94
Latin liturgy, drama as part of, 2:39
Latvia, 1:63, 64, 65
Laude, 3:32, 37
Law, **3:78–84** (illus.)
  banking and, 1:66
  Bartolo da Sassoferrato and, 1:72
  borough courts in England, 1:105
  Byzantine, 1:72, 2:76, 3:3, 79
  canon, 3:2, 78, 79, 81, 85
  civil, 1:72, 3:9, 78, 85
  in communes, 1:216–17
  criminal, 3:9, 82
  European, 3:78–82, 84
  about family, 2:76, 77–78, 81–82, 83
  of food trades, 2:105–8, 110
  on forests, 2:111
  Franks and, 2:125
  fuero in Spain, 2:134–35
  inheritance, 3:2–3
  on insane persons, 3:9
  Islamic, 3:54, 154, 4:128, 142, 190
    shari'a, 1:138, 3:20–21, 82–83

  on jewelry wearing according to rank, 2:147
  Jewish, 3:45–46, 47, 57–58, 59, 83–84, 110,
    4:4
  Justinian Code, 1:49, 122, 3:61, 79, 81, 89
  lepers, sanctions on, 3:88–89
  local constable and, 1:218
  maritime, 1:71
  marketplace regulations, 3:121
  mining, 3:143
  oaths and compurgations, 3:180–81, 4:136
  outlaws and outlawry, 3:189, 4:15–16
  papal courts, 1:143
  prisons and, 3:235–36
  public health and sanitation, 3:221
  Roman, 3:79, 80, 81, 84
  sanctuary, right of, 1:218, 4:36
  Slavic, 4:83
  status of serfs under, 4:62
  sumptuary, 1:210
  Timbuktu, legal scholars of, 4:119
  on torture, 4:122–23
  trials, 4:136–37
  universities teaching, 3:79, 81, 84–85,
    4:147
  on usury, 4:149–50
  village justice, 4:159
  women's rights under, 4:189–90
Law schools, 1:72, 3:79, 81, **3:84–85,**
  4:48 (illus.), 147
Layamon (chronicler), 1:46, 2:61
Leagues of Peace, 2:212
Leagues, town, 1:196
Leaning tower of Pisa, 3:218 (illus.)
Learned heresy, 2:210
Leather and leatherworking, **3:85–86**
Lechfeld, Battle of (955), 2:157, 3:185
Lecterns, 2:138
Legate, 2:31
Leif Eiriksson, 2:68, 4:15
Leipzig, fairs in, 2:74
Lenses and eyeglasses, **3:86–87,** 4:111
Lent. See Christianity
Leo I, pope, 2:226, 3:192
Leo III, pope, 2:216, **3:87**
  coronation of Charlemagne, 1:170–71, 184,
    189–90, 2:1 (illus.), 3:87, 193, 4:25
Leo VI, pope, 2:76
Leo IX, pope, 1:184–85, 2:181
Leo X, pope, 2:125, 3:129
Leo I, emperor, 4:6
Leo III, emperor, 1:123, 183, 2:237
Leo V, emperor, 2:237
Leo VI the Wise, 1:123
Leo the Deacon, 2:214
Leo the Mathematician, 1:221
León, Empire of, 1:52
Leonor López de Córdoba, 4:94
Leopold V of Austria, duke, 1:56
Leopold VI of Austria, duke, 1:56, 2:11, 153
Leopold of Babenberg, 1:55
Leopold of Habsburg, duke, 4:98
Leprosariums, 3:88–89
Leprosy, 2:123, 220, **3:88–89** (illus.)
Les Halles, 3:121
Letter writing, art of, 1:129, 4:8
Levi ben Gershom, 4:52
Liberal arts, 2:190, 4:47
Libraries, 1:38, 61, **3:89–91** (illus.), 3:94, 131,
  133, 4:51
Life expectancy, 3:228

Lighting devices, **3:91–92** (*illus.*), 3:142. *See also* Furniture
Limbourg brothers, 1:99, 2:172
Literacy, 3:58 (*illus.*), 89–91 (*illus.*), **3:92–94,** 3:234
   musical, 3:160
   schools promoting, 4:46–50 (*illus.*)
   See also Books, manuscript
Literary Latin, 3:78
Literature. *See individual nationalities*
Lithuania, 1:63, 64, 65, **3:94–95,** 3:157, 224
Little Domesday, 2:35
Liturgical drama, 3:32
Liutpoldings, 1:75
Liutprand of Lombard kingdom, king, 3:97, 4:141
Livestock, 1:9, 10 (*illus.*), 11, 2:104
Llull, Ramón. *See* Lull, Ramon
Llywelyn ap Gruffydd, 2:45, **3:95–96,** 3:202 (*illus.*), 4:170
Llywelyn the Great, 4:170
Logothete, 2:29, 32
Lögrétta (legislative body), 4:42
Lokietek, 3:224
Lollards, **3:96,** 4:197
Lombard League, 1:225, 2:158, 3:35, 141
Lombards, kingdom of, **3:96–97**
   Byzantine Empire and, 1:122, 3:96
   Florence, rule of, 2:102
   Germany and, 2:158, 159
   Gregory I the Great and, 2:180
   jewelry of, 2:146–47
   Liutprand, king, 3:97, 4:141
   migrations of Lombards, 2:84, 3:139
      England, 1:183, 3:139
      Italy, 3:33–34, 139, 140, 4:24–25, 141
   military service among, 4:172
   Naples and, 3:168
   Pepin III's defeat of, 3:207
Lombardy, 3:96, 139–41 (*illus.*), 4:22–23
London, 2:75, **3:97–100** (*map*) (*illus.*), 4:183
London Bridge, 3:98, 4:13
Longbow, 4:181
Looms, 4:114–15
Lords, feudalism and, 2:94–97. *See also* Nobility and nobles
Lorenzetti, Ambrogio, 1:215 (*illus.*), 2:172
Lorenzo de' Medici, the Magnificent, 2:103 (*illus.*), 3:129, 4:142
Loros (clothing), 1:206
Lorraine, 1:147, 2:157, 203
Lothar I of Burgundy, 1:115, 116, 146, 147
Louis I the Pious of Aquitaine, 1:29, 70, 110, 145 (*illus.*), 146, 2:49, 4:49
Louis II the Stammerer (Carolingian ruler), 1:147
Louis III (Carolingian ruler), 1:147
Louis V of France, 1:142, 147
Louis VI of France, 1:154, 2:99, 115–16, **3:100–101,** 3:198, 4:28
Louis VII of France, 1:29, 92, 2:10, 13 (*illus.*), 50, 3:101, 211
Louis VIII of France, 2:117, 3:77
Louis IX of France, 1:25, 2:117–18, **3:101–2** (*illus.*)
   Aigue-Mortes built by, 3:76 (*illus.*), 77
   crusades of (1248–1254, 1270–1272), 1:77, 189, 2:12–13, 3:101–2
   Gothic manuscript painting and, 2:172
   James I the Conqueror's treaty with, 3:39

Jean de Joinville, biographer of, 3:40
   Paris under, 3:200
Louis X of France, 1:168, 3:53
Louis XI of France, 2:122
Louis IV the Bavarian, 1:76, 2:160, 188
Louis of Anjou, 3:174 (*illus.*)
Louis of Male, 2:101
Louis of Nevers, 2:100–101, 163
Louis of Orleans, 2:121
Louis the Child, 1:147, 2:157
Louis the German, 1:116, 146–47, 2:16, 129, 155
Low German, 2:151
Lübeck, 2:192, **3:102–3**
Lucerne, Switzerland, 4:99
Lull, Ramon, 2:5, **3:104**
Lumphanan, Battle of (1057), 3:106
Luther, Martin, 1:187, 2:43
Luxembourgs, 2:160
Lydgate, John, **3:104–5,** 3:215 (*illus.*)

Ma'arri, al-, **3:105**
Macarius of Egypt, 3:165
Macbeth, **3:105–6**
Macedonian dynasty, 1:23, 72, 123–24
Machaut, Guillaume de, 2:133, **3:106**
Machines. *See* Technology
Madeiras, 2:70
Madinat al-Salam (City of Peace), 1:61
Madinat al-Zahra (palace city), 3:25, 4:89–90
Madrasa (college), 3:27, 28, 29, 85, 93, 4:7, 50
Magic and folklore, 2:27, 3:1, **3:106–9,** 4:30 (*illus.*), 186–88 (*illus.*)
Magna Carta (1215), 1:141, 2:58, 96, 112, **3:110**
   John of England and, 2:57, 3:55, 56, 110
   Langton and, 3:75
   Londoners and, 3:98
Magnetic compass, 4:112
Magnifying lenses, 3:86
Magnus II Eriksson, 4:43
Magyars, 1:55, 2:7, 157, 224–25, 3:185
Mahdi, al- (caliph), 1:61, 2:192
Mahdi, idea of the coming of, 3:142
Mahmud of Ghazna, 2:234
Maimonides, Moses, 1:39, 2:49, 197, 3:58, 59, 84, **3:110**
Mainz, 1:216
Majorca, 3:39 (*illus.*), 4:79–80
Malcolm, king of Scotland, 3:106
Mali, **3:111** (*illus.*), 4:119
Malik al-Salih, al-, 1:77
Malik al-Zahir, al-. *See* Baybars al-Bunduqdari
Malikshah (Seljuk sultan), 4:58
Malory, Sir Thomas, 1:47, 2:63, **3:111–12**
Mamluk dynasty, 1:59, 2:13, **3:112–13** (*illus.*)
   in Arabia, 1:31
   Baybars al-Bunduqdari, founder of, 1:77
   Circassian period (1382–1517), 3:113
   Damascus under, 2:19
   in Egypt, 1:132, 2:48–49, 3:112–13 (*illus.*)
   Golden Horde and, 2:167
   Ibn Taymiya and, 2:235
   Islamic administration under, 3:19, 112–13 (*illus.*)
   Islamic books of, 1:102
   Jerusalem under, 3:42
   al-Ma'mun's introduction of Mamluks in army and, 3:113
   Mecca under, 3:128
   Palestine under, 3:191

Qala'un al-Mansur, ruler of, 4:2–3
   Syria under, 3:112–13 (*illus.*), 4:101
   Turkish period (1240–1382), 3:112–13
Ma'mun, al-, 1:2, 2:232, 3:38, **3:113–14,** 4:120
Mandeville, John, 2:62, 69, 3:114
Mandeville's *Travels*, 2:69, **3:114**
Manfred, king of Sicily, 2:14, 3:169
Mangonels (torsion device), 1:47
Maniera greca (Greek manner), 1:121
Manners, courtesy books on, 2:4–6
Mannyng, Robert, 2:62
Manors, 2:79, 96 (*illus.*), 4:158
Manrique, Jorge, 4:94
Mansa Musa, 3:111 (*illus.*)
Mansa Sulayman, 3:111
Mansa Uli, king of Mali, 3:111
Mansur, al-, 1:2, 2:31, **3:114–15**
   in Spain, 1:53, 149, 158, 4:146
Mansura, al-, 2:12
   Battle of (1250), 1:77
Manuel I Komnenos, 2:225, 3:71, 72, 4:127
Manuel, Don Juan, **3:115–16,** 4:93, 94
Manumission, 4:62, 81
Manuscript books. *See* Books, manuscript
Manzikert, Battle of (1071), 1:23, 124, 2:8, 4:57
Maps and mapmaking, **3:116–19** (*illus.*), 3:154–55, 171
Maqamat (secular Islamic book), 1:102
Marcion at Arles, 3:237
Margaret of Anjou, 4:177–78
Margaret of Denmark, 4:40, 41
Margaret of Flanders, 2:99, 100
Margaret of Provence, 3:101
Mari Jata, king of Mali, 3:111
Mari Jata II, king of Mali, 3:111
María de Molina, 1:151
Marica, Battle of (1371), 4:60
Marie de Champagne, 1:181, **3:119–20**
Marie de France, 2:72, 131, **3:120–21** (*illus.*)
Marie of Savoy, 2:135
Marienburg Castle (Poland), 1:64 (*illus.*), 3:69
Marinid sultans of Morocco, 2:177
Maritime chart makers, 3:119
Maritime law, 1:71
Markets, 1:198–99, 2:74–75, **3:121–22** (*illus.*), 3:154, 232, 4:133
Marriage
   church law on, 2:76
   in Islam religion, 2:77–78
   patterns of, 3:228
   property and, 2:82
   of serfs, 4:62
   woman's role in, 2:5, 4:190, 191
Marsilius of Padua, 3:67
Martianus Capella, 3:124
Martin of Tours, St., 2:180, 3:144
Martin I, pope, 1:183
Martin V, pope, 3:196, 4:26, 45
"Martyr's shrines," 1:118
Marwan ibn Muhammad, 4:146
Marwanids, 4:145
Mary, cult of, **3:122–23**
Mary of Burgundy, 2:160, 3:127
Masonry, 1:222
Mass, liturgy of, 2:179, 3:1, **3:123–24**
   transubstantiation, 2:210, 3:181, 4:198
   votive, 2:26
Mass sermons, 4:64
Massys, Quentin, 1:66 (*illus.*)

Mastoc, 2:215
Mathematics, **3:124–26**
  Bacon and, 1:60
  Greek and Arabic heritage, 1:34 *(illus.)*,
    3:125–26
  instruction at school in, 4:47
  Islamic, 3:62, 4:52
  Jewish, 4:52
  music and, 3:159–60
  Oresme and, 3:182
  Roman heritage, 3:124–25, 4:18
Matilda (daughter of Henry I), 1:24, 2:55, 199
Matilda of Flanders, 4:184
Matilda of Tuscany, 1:140, 2:102, **3:126–27,**
  3:195, 4:141
Matins, 2:33
Matthew of Paris (monk), 1:189
Mawlawiya (mystical brotherhood), 4:29
Maximian, archbishop, 4:5 *(illus.)*
Maximilian I, emperor, 2:160, **3:127,** 4:99
May Day, 2:91
Measures. *See* Weights and measures
Mecca, 1:30, **3:127–28** *(illus.)*
  Muhammad and, 3:127–28 *(illus.)*, 152, 153
  pilgrimage to, 2:73, 93, 3:21, 23, 127–28
    (illus.), 216–17
  Umayyads and, 4:144
Mechanical clocks, 1:203, 204–6, 2:37, 3:146,
  4:111–12
Mechthild von Magdeburg, **3:128–29**
Medici family, 2:101–2, 103 *(illus.)*, **3:129,** 4:75,
  142
Medicine, **3:129–33** *(illus.)*
  barber-surgeons and, 1:69–70 *(illus.)*, 3:132,
    133
  Henry de Mondeville and, 2:205–6
  herbs and herbals, 2:208–10 *(illus.)*
  history of, 3:130–32
  hospitals and poor relief, 2:218–21 *(illus.)*
  Ibn Sina on, 2:234
  insanity, treatment of, 3:9
  Islamic, 4:5
  Jewish authorities on, 4:52
  lepers, care of, 3:88–89
  medical education, 3:130, 131, 132–33, 148
  medical practice, 3:133
  royal touch as, 4:28
  Trota and *Trotula*, 4:138
Medina, 3:23, 217
Mediterranean shipbuilding, 4:67–68
Mediterranean trade, 4:128
Mehmed I, Green Tomb of, 3:29
Mehmed II the Conqueror, 1:126, 128, 221–22,
  3:134, 3:188 *(illus.)*
Melancholy, 3:9
Mena, Juan de, 4:94
Mendoza, Íñigo López de, 4:94
Mental illness, treatment of, 3:8–9
Mercenary troops in warfare, 4:173
Merchant class, 1:213, 2:79
Mercia, 1:213, 2:53
Merovich (Merovingian chieftain), 3:134
Merovingians, 1:144, **3:134–35** *(illus.)*
  Alamanni under, 1:14
  Bavaria under, 1:75
  Charles Martel, last of, 1:173–74
  Gaul and, 2:114
  Jewish communities under, 3:48
  legal traditions under, 3:80
  restrictions on use of forests, 2:111

Meseta, Spanish, 3:142
Messalians, 2:211
Metals and metalworking, **3:135–37** *(illus.)*
  for building tools, 1:224
  Irish-Saxon, 1:108
  Islamic, 3:26
  lighting devices and advances in German,
    3:92
  mining and, 3:142–43
  money and, 3:148–49
  in Nuremberg, 3:180
  for weapons, 4:179–80
Methodios, St. *See* Cyril and Methodios, Sts.
Metz, France, siege of (1324), 1:48
Mevlevi (Muslim order), 3:159
Michael II, emperor, 4:117
Michael III, emperor, 1:72, 3:145
Michael IV, emperor, 4:1
Michael VII Doukas, emperor, 4:1
Michael VIII Palaiologos, 1:126, 3:190
Middle Eastern musical instruments, 3:162–63
Middle English, 2:59, 61–63
Middle High German period, 2:151
Midrash (Hebrew writing discipline), 2:197, 3:108
Midsummer Eve, 2:92
Mieszko (Misaca), king of Poland, 3:223
Migrations, Germanic, 1:74–75, **3:137–39** *(map)*
  of Alamanni, 1:14–15, 3:137, 138 *(map)*
  of Franks, 2:125–26, 3:137, 138 *(map)*, 139
  Huns and, 2:226, 3:137–39 *(map)*
  of Lombards, 1:183, 2:84, 3:33–34, 139, 140,
    141, 4:24–25
  Odoacer and, 3:182
  of Ostrogoths, 3:33, 137, 138 *(map)*, 139–40,
    182, 183–84
  Paris and, 3:198
  into Portugal, 3:228–29
  travel following, 4:130
  of Vandals, 1:227, 3:33, 138–39, 4:151
  of Visigoths, 3:137–38 *(map)*, 139, 4:162–63
Migrations, Viking, 4:154–57 *(map)*
Mihrab, 3:23
Milan, 1:216, 3:35, **3:139–41** *(illus.)*
Military architecture. *See* Castles and
  fortifications
Military feudalism, 4:172–73
Military service. *See* Warfare
Military strategy, Byzantine, 4:174–75
Military technology, 4:111
Millennialism, **3:141–42**
Mining, 1:105, 106, 3:111, **3:142–43**
Ministerials, 1:148
Minnesingers, 2:152
Minstrels, **3:143–44** *(illus.)*
  ballads and, 1:63
  chansons de geste and, 1:169
  German, 2:153
  music of, 3:161–62
  Robin Hood legend and, 4:15
  schools for, 3:159
  tales of Prester John and, 2:65
  travel by, 4:132
Mi-parti, 1:210
Miracle plays, 2:39
Miracles, French, 2:132
Mircea the Old, 4:165
Mirrors, 2:3 *(illus.)*
"Mirrors of princes," 3:65–66
Misericord, 2:138
Mishrad. *See* Judaism

Miskawayh, 2:215
Missions and missionaries, Christian, 1:183,
  3:144–45
  of Cyril and Methodios, 1:184, 2:16–17
  explorations of Asia and, 2:69
  Franciscan, 2:124
  Irish, 3:13, 144, 204, 4:131
  Lull and, 3:104
  religious instruction from, 4:6
  St. Boniface, 1:98, 3:144
  St. Columbanus, 1:214, 3:144
  of St. Dominic's Dominican order, 2:35
  in Scandinavia, 4:44
  travel and transportation, 4:131, 134
Mitigations, 2:67
Moats, 1:155
Modena, Cathedral of, 4:22–23
Moldavia, 4:164–67
Monarchs. *See* Kingship, theories of
Monasteries, **3:145–46**
  in Anglo-Saxon England, 2:54
  book production in, 1:102–3, 188–89, 2:151
  Byzantine, 1:119, 128, 3:146
  in Catalonia, 1:159 *(illus.)*
  chapters of, 1:163, 170
  Cistercian, 1:191
  cloister of, 2:144
  double, 4:191
  gardens of, 2:144–45
  hospitals built outside of, 2:218, 219, 221
  libraries in, 3:90, 91, 131
  literacy and, 3:94
  parishes formed around, 3:201
  in Provence, 3:237
  reform movement, 1:184
  Robert d'Arbrissel and, 4:14–15
  St. Birgitta and, 1:89–90
  St. Columbanus and, 1:214
  sermons in, 4:64
  Sufi, 3:22
  Windesheim, 1:107
Monastery colleges, Islamic, 4:50
Monastic architecture, 3:146, 4:21
Monastic church in Bosnia, 1:105
Monastic schools, 4:48–49
Monasticism, 1:186, **3:147–48**
  Augustine and, 1:53
  Benedictines, 1:82–84
  Cistercian order, 1:191–92
  Dominican order, 2:36–37 *(illus.)*
  food trades and, 2:104
  Franciscan order, 2:124–25
  hermits and spread of, 2:212–13
  in Ireland, 3:13
  monasteries and, 3:145–46
  reform movements, 1:117, 3:148
  St. Brigit and, 1:108
  in Sicily, 4:71
  women's religious orders, 4:191–93 *(illus.)*
Mondino dei Luzzi, **3:148**
Money, 2:65–66, 102, **3:148–49,** 4:128, 153. *See
  also* Banking
Möngke Temür (Tatar ruler), 2:167
Mongol Empire, **3:149–51** *(illus.)*
  Abbasid caliphate defeated by, 1:3
  Armenia and, 1:41, 4:125
  Ayyubids, defeat of, 1:58
  Baybars's defeat of, 1:77
  exploration and European contact with, 2:69
  Genghis Khan and, 2:147–48

Georgia and, 2:150–51
Golden Horde and, 2:33–34, 167
Hungary, invasion of, 2:226
Ibn Taymiya and resistance against, 2:235
Iran as part of, 3:11
Iraq as part of, 3:13
Islamic administration and invasions from, 3:19
Islamic art and architecture and, 3:26
Kievan Rus and, decline of, 3:65
Muscovy and, overlordship of, 3:156
Novgorod under, Nevsky and, 3:171
plague carried by invaders from, 3:220–21
Polo as emissary of Kublai Khan, 3:225–26 (illus.)
pressure on Poland from, 3:224
Samarkand under, 4:35
Syria under, 4:101
Tamerlane and, 4:103–4 (illus.)
Monks, 2:133–34, 4:131. See also Monasticism
Monophysites, 2:211
Montaperti, Battle of (1260), 4:74
Monte Cassino, abbey of, 3:131, 4:71
Montgomery, Treaty of (1267), 3:95
Moors, 3:39, 4:162–63
Morality plays, 2:38, 39, 40
Moravia. See Bohemia-Moravia
Morocco, Marinid sultans of, 2:177
Morte Darthur, Le (The Death of Arthur) (Malory), 1:47, 3:111
Mosaics, 1:119, 3:26, **3:151–52**, 4:23–24
Moscow, 2:33–34, 42, 3:155–58 (illus.)
Moses ibn Ezra, 4:8
Moshe ben Asher codex, 3:43
Moshe ben Nachman. See Nahmanides, Moses
Mosques, 1:194, 3:23, 25, 26, 27–28, 4:49, 148
Motte-and-bailey design for forts, 1:153–54
Mount Badon, Battle of (516), 1:45
Mozarabs, 4:88, 120, 121
Mu'awiya, 2:17, 3:21, **3:152**
    Ali ibn Abi Talib, defeat of, 1:21, 3:152, 4:75
    caliphate under, 1:136, 4:144, 145
Mu'awiya II, 4:145
Mudejars, 4:88
Muhammad, **3:152–54** (illus.)
    Abbasids as descendants of, 1:1
    Abu Bakr and, 1:5
    A'isha, wife of, 1:13–14
    Ali ibn Abi Talib and, 1:20
    at Badr, Battle of, 1:60, 3:153
    Islam and, 1:30, 3:19, 152–54 (illus.), 4:3 (illus.)
    Islamic law and, 3:83
    Jews and, 3:50
    magic and folklore and, 3:109
    Mecca and, 3:127–28 (illus.), 152, 153
    mosque in Medina founded by, 3:23
    Mu'awiya and, 3:152
    on music, 3:158
    night of ascension festival and, 2:93
    Sunna of, 4:96
    Umar I ibn al-Khattab and, 4:142
    Umayyads and, 4:144
Muhammad V, 2:177
Muhammad al-Amin (caliph), 3:113–14
Muhammad ibn al-Ahmar (prince of Jaén), 2:177
Muhammad of Cabra, 4:92
Muhtasib, **3:154**
Mu'izz, al- (imam), 2:89
Muqaddam, 3:47

Muqaddasi, al-, **3:154–55**
Muqtadi, al-, 4:95
Murad I, 1:76, 126, **3:155**, 3:186–87, 188
Murad II, 3:134
Murcia, 3:39
Musa al-Hadi, 2:192
Musa ibn Nusayr, 4:86
Muscovy, rise of, 2:167, 3:36, **3:155–58** (illus.), 3:178–79
Music, **3:158–62** (illus.)
    courtly love lyrics, 2:131–32
    dance and, 2:19–20 (illus.)
    European, 3:159–60
        German, 4:171
        Gregorian chant, 2:179
        Middle English period, 2:61–62
        minstrels, 3:143–44 (illus.)
        troubadours and trouvères, 4:139 (illus.)
    folk songs, 1:166
    Islamic, 2:88, 3:158–59
    sacred vs. secular, 3:159, 161–62
Musical instruments, 2:19, 20, 139, 3:143, **3:162–64** (illus.)
Musical notation, 3:160, 161 (illus.)
Mustansir, al- (caliph), 2:89
Musta'sim, al- (caliph), 1:138, 3:11, 13
Mu'tadid, al-, 1:62, 4:35, 36
Mu'tasim, al-, 1:2, 61, 3:12, **3:164**, 4:35
Mutawakkil, al-, 2:232
Mu'tazila (theological group), 2:231–32, 3:21
Muwaqqit (timekeeper), 1:51
Muwashshah (type of poem), 4:92
Myriokephalon, Battle of (1176), 3:71
Mysticism, **3:165–67**
    Byzantine, 3:165
    devils and demons and, 2:27
    Islamic, 2:49, 162, 3:22, 166–67, 4:29
    Jewish, 1:130, 2:97–98, 3:58–59, 166
    western European, 3:165–66
        Beguines and Beghards and, 1:80
        Hadewijch of Antwerp, 2:188
        Julian of Norwich and, 2:62, 3:59
        Kempe and, 2:62, 3:62
        Lull and, 3:104
        Mechthild von Magdeburg, 3:128–29
        Meister Eckhart and, 2:43
        St. Birgitta and, 1:89–90
        St. Bonaventure's writings on, 1:97
        St. Catherine of Siena and, 1:163–64
        St. Francis of Assisi and, 2:124, 165
        St. Hildegard of Bingen and, 2:213

Nagid, **3:167**
Nahmanides, Moses, **3:167–68**
Nancy, Battle of (1477), 4:174
Naples, **3:168–69**
Nasir Muhammad, al-, sultan, 3:112
Nasrids of Granada, 2:177, 3:28
Naumburg Cathedral, 2:176
Navarre, kingdom of, 1:35, **3:169–70**
Navigation, 2:191, 3:116–19 (illus.), **3:170–71** (illus.), 4:52–53, 154–55
Nehor, Rabbi Isaac Saggi ("Isaac the Blind"), 1:130
Nemanja family in Serbia, 4:59–60
Nennius (writer), 1:45
Neoplatonism, 2:87
Nestorius, archbishop of Constantinople, 2:211
Netherlandish dialect, 2:99

Neustria, 3:135
Neville's Cross, Battle of (1346), 4:55 (illus.)
Nevsky, Alexander, 3:155, **3:171**
New High German period, 2:151
New Testament, 1:88
New Year's Day, 2:94
Newfoundland, 4:155
Nicaea, councils of
    first (325), 1:182, 219
    second (787), 1:123, 2:237
Nicaea, Empire of, 1:125, 2:9, **3:172**
Niccolò da Verona, 4:23
Nicene Creed, 2:210, 3:87
Nicholas I, pope, **3:172–73**
Nicholas II, pope, 3:194, 4:71
Nicholas, Master (handbook author), 2:143
Nicholas (of German Children's Crusade), 1:177
Nicopolis, battle of (1396), 1:76
Niger River, 4:119
Nika Revolt (532), 3:60, 4:116
Nikephoros I, emperor, 3:72
Nikephoros II Phokas, 1:123, 4:117
Nikephoros Bryennios, 3:70
Nikephoros Gregoras, 2:214
Niklot of Mecklenburg, 3:102
Nine, the (political regime in Siena), 4:75
Ninian, St. (Welsh bishop), 3:144
Ninoslav, Ban, 1:105
Nizam al-Mulk (vizier), 2:162
Nobility and nobles, **3:173–75** (illus.)
    castellans and, 1:148
    German, 2:155–56, 157, 160, 3:175
    growth of noble class, 4:84–85
    hunting and fowling by, 2:227–28
    laws of primogeniture and, 3:3
    palace schools for, 3:90, 4:49
    peasant rebellions against, 3:205–6 (illus.)
    troubadours and trouvères, patronage of, 4:139
    types of, 1:71, 2:4, 42
    villages and, growth of, 4:158
    western European family life among, 2:79, 81
    wine consumption by, 2:109
    women of, 4:189, 191–93 (illus.)
Noble Sanctuary (Haram al-Sharif), 3:41
Noghay (Mongol ruler), 2:167
Nomadic origins of Islamic world, 2:139
Nomads, 2:187 (illus.), 3:149–50
Nominalism, 3:181
Normandy, 1:110, 3:175
    English rule over, 2:55–57, 58, 198–99, 3:212, 4:184–85
    French rule over, 2:116, 117–18
    Hundred Years War and, 3:176
    Viking raids of, 1:110, 2:69
Normans, 1:110, **3:175–76**
    achievements of, 2:57–58
    Byzantine Empire and, 1:124
    in England, 2:55, 57–58
        art and architecture and, 1:109–10
        conquest (1066), 1:141, 2:45, 193–94 (illus.), 3:75, 175–76, 4:173
        Domesday Book and, 2:34–35 (illus.)
        English common law and, 3:81, 82
        justiciars serving as kings' representatives in, 3:60
        Scotland and, 4:54
        taxation under, 4:106
    forest laws of, 2:227
    Ghent, raid on, 2:163

Komnenos dynasty defeated by, 3:71–72
Naples and, conquest of, 3:168
Papal States and, 3:195
Sicily under, 4:70–71
Viking settlers known as, 4:156
in Wales, 4:169–70
warfare and military skills of, 4:173
Norse sagas. *See* Scandinavia
North Africa, 1:85, 3:17, 25, 27–28, 51, 4:151
Northampton, Battle of (1460), 4:177 *(illus.)*
Northumbria, 1:213, 2:53
Norway, 4:41, 42, 154
Notarial archive, 1:39
Notary, institution of, 3:81
Notre Dame de Paris, cathedral, 2:170, 3:160,
      3:176–77, 3:199
Notre-Dame du Port in France, 4:19 *(illus.)*
Novgorod, **3:177–79** *(illus.)*
fur trade and, 2:135–36
Nevsky, prince of, 3:171
Rurik and, 3:177, 4:30–31
as trading center, 2:74
Vikings in, 3:63 *(map)*, 64, 4:157
Nubia, **3:179**
Numerals, Arabic and Roman, 1:34 *(illus.)*,
      3:125, 4:18
Nuncius, 2:31
Nuns. *See* Women's religious orders
Nur al-Din, 1:58, 4:33
Nur al-Din Mahmud, 2:19
Nuremberg, 2:166, **3:179–80**

Oaths and compurgations, **3:180–81,** 4:136
Oberammergau passion play, 2:130
Observants, 2:125
Ockham, William of, 1:40, **3:181**
Ockham's razor, 3:181
O'Connor, Rory (Irish chieftain), 3:14
Odo (Carolingian king), 1:147, 2:114
Odo. *See* Urban II, pope
Odoacer, **3:182,** 3:183
Offa of Wales, king, 2:53, 4:169
Offa's Dyke, 2:53, 4:169
Ögödai (Mongol ruler), 3:151
Olaf IV of Norway, 4:40, 41
Olaf Tryggvason, king, 4:15
Old Church Slavic, 4:81
Old English (Anglo-Saxon), 2:59, 60–61
Old French, 2:129–30
Old High German, 2:151
Old Slavic, 4:81
Old Spanish, 4:90–91
Oldcastle, Sir John, 3:96
Oleg (grand prince of Kievan Rus), 3:64
Oliphant, 3:163
Oman, 1:138
Omurtag (Bulgar), 1:113, 114
Oporto, Portugal, 3:229
Ordeal, trial by, 3:81, 82, 4:136
Order of Friars Preachers. *See* Dominicans
Order of St. Clare, 2:124, 4:192 *(illus.)*, 193
Order of the Garter, 1:180, 2:46, 3:68
Order of the Golden Fleece, 1:180
Order of the Most Holy Savior, 1:90
Order of the White Elephant, 1:180
Ordinances of 1311, 3:202
Ordinances of Justice, 2:102
Ordination, 1:201–2
Ordoño I of Asturias-León, 1:53
Ordoño II of Asturias-León, 1:53

Oreibasios of Pergamum, 3:130
Oresme, Nicole, 3:126, **3:182**
Orkhan (Ottoman leader), 3:183
Orleans, Hundred Years War and, 2:122, 223,
      3:54
Orthodox Church, Russian, 1:185, 3:156
Osbern of Gloucester, 2:51
Osman I, **3:183,** 3:186
Ostmen, 2:41
Ostrogoths, **3:183–84**
Huns and, 2:226, 3:183
Jewish communities under, 3:48
migration of, 3:33, 137, 138 *(map)*, 139–40,
      182, 183–84
Theodoric, king of, 4:116–17
Oswald von Wolkenstein, **3:184**
Otto I the Great, emperor, 1:1, 55, 2:99, 157,
      216, **3:184–85,** 4:25
Otto II, Holy Roman Emperor, 2:157, 216
Otto III, Holy Roman Emperor, 1:1, 2:157–58,
      3:185, 4:25
Otto IV (Otto of Brunswick), 2:159, 4:72
Otto of Freising, **3:185–86,** 3:233
Otto of Wittelsbach, 1:75
Ottokar II of Bohemia, king, 1:56, 95–96
Ottomans and Ottoman Empire, **3:186–89**
      (map) *(illus.)*
Abbasid caliphate defeated by, 1:3
Armenia, conquest of, 1:41
in Bosnia, 1:106
crusades in later Middle Ages against, 2:14
Damascus conquered by (1516), 2:19
in Egypt, 2:49
expansion into Europe, 3:155, 187–88
fall of Constantinople to (1453), 1:126, 128,
      221–22, 2:14
Byzantine art and, 1:119–20
Golden Horde and, 2:167
Hungary, invasion of, 2:225 *(illus.)*, 226
Iraq as part of, 3:13
Janissaries in, 3:134, 155, 186–87, 189, 4:79
Jerusalem under, 3:42
Mamluk dynasty defeated by, 3:113
Moldavia under, 4:166
Serbia under, 4:60
Sigismund, defeat of, 4:76
social hierarchy, 3:188–89
sultans of, 1:76, 3:134, 155, 183
Syria under, 4:102
Walachia under, 4:165
Ottonian architecture, 4:20
Outlaws and outlawry, **3:189,** 4:15–16
Owain Gwynedd (Welsh prince), 4:170
Oxford University, 2:181, 3:96, 4:147, 186, 197
Özbeg (Mongol ruler), 2:167

Pact of Umar, 3:47
Pages, proper behavior for, 2:5
"Palace" churches, 1:118
Palace schools, 3:90, 4:49
Palaiologos family, 1:126, 194, 3:188, **3:190**
Palatinate, 1:76
Pale, the (fortified area around Dublin), 2:41,
      3:14–15
Palestine, 3:50, **3:190–91** *(illus.)*, 3:216
Palladius (bishop), 3:204
Pandemics of plague, 3:219–22
Panegyrics, 1:129
Pannonia, 2:7
Pannonian Croatia, 4:121

Pantokrator hospital in Constantinople, 2:221
Papacy, origins and development, **3:192–95**
      (illus.)
ascendancy of papal power (11th–14th cen-
      tury), 1:185–86, 2:203–4, 3:194–95,
      4:25–26
Avignon and, 1:57–58
Charles V and, 1:172
church-state relations and, 1:189–90.
      See also Investiture Controversy
concordats and, 1:217
crusades and, 2:8–9, 10, 11, 12, 14–15
declining power (800s–900s), 3:193–94
early church and, 1:182–83
election of pope, 1:142–43
Great Schism and, 1:186–87, 3:195, 4:44–45,
      161
Gregory I the Great and, 2:180
Gregory VII and, 2:181
Holy Roman Empire and, 2:216–17
Holy Year and, 2:217–18
indulgences and, 3:1
Innocent III and, 3:4
Innocent IV and, 3:4–5
kingship theories and, 3:66–67
Leo III and, 3:87
Medici family and, 3:129
Nicholas I and, 3:172–73
papal coronation of kings, 2:1 *(illus.)*, 3:185
Papal States and, 3:195–96 *(map)*
political support for (700s–800s), 1:184, 3:193
Portugal's conflicts with, 3:230
taxes collected by, 4:107
Papal courts, 1:143
Papal States, 2:14, 15, 3:4, 34 *(illus.)*, 35, 193,
      3:195–96 *(map)*, 3:207 *(illus.)*, 208, 4:25
Papermaking, 4:110, 150, 195, 196
Papyrus, 4:195, 196
Paradise, idea of, 2:22, **3:197–98**
Parchment, 4:195 *(illus.)*, 196
Paris, 2:116, 3:121, 176–77, **3:198–200** *(illus.)*,
      4:160
Paris Psalter, 1:120
Paris, Treaty of (1229), 2:118, 4:123
Paris, University of, 2:120, 162, 3:199–200, 4:64,
      147, 148 *(illus.)*
Parish, **3:200–201**
Parisii tribe of ancient Gaul, 3:198
Parlement of Paris, 2:118, 119
Parliament at Drogheda, 3:15
Parliament, English, 2:45–46, 58–59, 66, 123,
      3:201–3 *(illus.)*, 4:77–78. *See also* Repre-
      sentative assemblies
Parzival (Wolfram von Eschenbach), 1:47,
      2:154–55, 4:188–89
Paschal I, pope, 4:25
Paschal II, pope, 3:69
Passover Haggadah, 3:43, 49 *(illus.)*
Paston family and letters, **3:203**
Patriarchs, 1:182, 183, 207, 220
Patrick, St., 3:13, 144, **3:204**
Paul I, pope, 4:25
Paulicians, 2:211
Paulus Alvarus, 4:91
Peace of Athis (1305), 2:100
Peace of God, Truce of God, **3:204**
Peasantry, 2:80, 81, 4:85, 86, 189
Peasants' Crusade, 2:9
Peasants' rebellions and uprisings, 1:92,
      3:205–6 *(illus.)*

English Peasants' Revolt (1381), 2:184–85, 3:56, 205–6, 4:10, 108
Jacquerie (1358), 3:205, 4:108
Pedro I of Aragon, 1:35–36
Pedro II of Aragon, 1:37
Pedro III of Aragon, 1:37, 2:14, 15, 3:39, 4:72
Pedro IV the Ceremonious of Aragon, 1:37, **3:207**
Pedro I of Castile, 1:151
Pelagius II, pope, 2:180
Pelayo (Visigothic noble), 1:52
Penance, 4:31
Pendentives, 1:118
Pentateuch, Rashi's commentary on, 4:4
Pepin I, 1:144
Pepin II, 1:144, 173
Pepin III the Short, 1:144–45, 174, 184, 3:97, **3:207–8** (illus.)
    diplomatic missions of, 2:31
    Donation of Pepin to papacy, 3:193, 207–8 (illus.)
    end of Merovingian dynasty and, 3:135
    invasion of Italy, 3:33
Perfumes, 2:2, 3, 3:1
"Permanent prayer," doctrine of, 3:165
Perpendicular style, 1:110
Persia. See Iran
Peter III of Aragon. See Pedro III of Aragon
Peter I de Lusignan of Cyprus, 2:13–14, 15–16
Peter II of Cyprus, 2:16
Peter of Bulgaria, king, 1:114
Peter (Slavic bishop), 3:156
Peter, St., 1:182, 3:215
Peter the Hermit, 2:9, **3:208–9** (illus.)
Peter the Venerable, **3:209**
Peter's Pence, 4:107
Petrarch, 3:30–32, **3:209–11** (illus.), 3:221
Petru I Musat, 4:166
Pfaffenbrief (priest's charter) of 1370, 4:99
Phaedrus, 2:71
Philip (archbishop of Cologne), 1:213
Philip I of France, 2:115
Philip II Augustus, 2:116–17, **3:211–12**
    coronation of, 2:117
    duchy of Brittany and, 1:110–11
    England and, 2:56–57, 200, 3:56, 176, 212, 4:9–10
    expulsion of Jews by, 3:52
    Flanders and, 2:99–100
    Germany and, 2:159
    Paris under, 3:199
    perfumers' guild chartered by, 2:3
Philip IV the Fair, 1:179, 186, 2:100, 119–20, **3:212–13**
    church-state relations under, 1:190, 3:194–95
        Boniface VIII, conflict with, 1:98, 2:119, 3:66, 212–13
    expulsion of Jews by, 3:53
    Flanders and, 2:100
Philip V of France, 4:134
Philip of Valois, 2:29 (illus.), 95 (illus.), 120, 3:132, **3:213**
Philip I the Handsome (Habsburg ruler), 2:188
Philip of Flanders, 2:99
Philip of Swabia, 2:127, 159
Philip the Bold of Burgundy, 1:116, 117, 2:101, 3:106
Philip the Good, 2:101
Philippa of Hainault, 1:189, 2:46

Philippe of Comines, 1:189
Philosopher's stone, 1:17
Philosophy, 3:58, 222–23
Phoenix, 1:87
Photios of Constantinople, 2:51
Physiologus (Physiologist), 1:87, 3:108
Piast dynasty in Poland, 3:223–24
Pica, Lady, 2:123
Piers Plowman (Langland), 1:22, 2:63
Pietro di Bernardone, 2:123
Pilgrimage, **3:213–17** (illus.)
    Christian, 3:213–16
    destinations, 3:214–17
        Canterbury, 1:141, 3:215–16 (illus.)
        Jerusalem, 3:40–41, 213, 214, 216
        Mecca (hajj), 2:73, 93, 3:21, 23, 127–28 (illus.), 216–17
        Palestine, 3:191
        Rome, 2:218, 3:214–15
        Santiago de Compostela, 3:169, 215, 4:36–37
    Holy Year and, 2:217–18
    by the insane, 3:9
    Jewish, 3:216
    messages carried by travelers, 3:232
    as penance imposed by Inquisition, 3:8
    roads to, 4:12
    to see relics, 4:6
    as symbolic journey toward heaven, 3:198
    travel for, 3:114, 4:131, 133, 135
Pilgrimage churches, 1:162
"Pillars" of Islam, 2:220, 3:21
Pinar, Florencia, 4:94
Pipes (musical instruments), 3:164
Pisa, 1:216, 2:70, **3:217–18** (illus.)
Pisa, Council of (1409), 4:45
Pisanello, Antonio, 3:184
Pius II, pope, 2:14
Plagues, 2:87, 3:77, 89, **3:219–22** (illus.), 4:159.
    See also Black Death
Plainsong, 3:161
Planetarium of de' Dondi, 2:37, 38
Planned towns, 1:197
Plantagenets, 1:25, 4:9–10 (illus.)
Plato in the Middle Ages, 2:88, **3:222–23,** 4:161
Plays. See Drama
Plenary indulgence, 2:217–18, 3:1
Pliny (Roman writer), 2:52, 4:38
Pneumonic plague, 1:90, 3:221
Poetry. See literature of specific countries
Pogroms, 1:91
Poitiers, Battle of (1356), 1:171, 2:46, 47
Poland, 2:158, 3:95, 185, **3:223–25,** 4:166
Polish literature, 4:82
Polo, Marco, 2:69, **3:225–26** (illus.)
Polycandelon (light fixture), 3:92
Polygamy, 2:77
Poor Clares. See Order of St. Clare
Poor relief. See Hospitals and poor relief
Pope. See Papacy, origins and development
Population of the medieval world, 1:13, 2:85, 3:74, **3:226–28** (illus.), 4:41
Portcullis, 1:156
Porter, 1:201
Portolano sailing charts, 3:119
Portolanos, 3:171
Portugal, 1:150, **3:228–31** (illus.)
    Alfonso III of, 1:53, 2:28
    Dinis, king of, 2:28, 3:230
    explorations and, 2:70–71, 3:231

expulsion of Jews from, 3:53
    Mamluk dynasty and, 3:113
Portuguese language, 2:28
Posse, 1:218
Postal services, 2:232–33, **3:231–32**
Poulaines, 1:210
Pourpoint, 1:210
Poynings' Law, 3:15
Prague, 1:95 (illus.), 96, 2:229–30, **3:232–33** (illus.)
Prague, University of, 1:96, 2:160, 229–30, 4:82
Prayer of the two festivals, 2:92
Preaching. See Sermons
Predestination vs. free will, 3:21
Prefabrication techniques, use of, 1:156
Prefect of Constantinople, 1:220
Premonstratensians, order of, 4:192
Premyslid dynasty in Bohemia, 1:95–96, 3:232
Prester John, 2:65, 70, **3:233–34** (illus.)
Prévôts, 2:115
Prijezda, Ban, 1:105
Primogeniture, laws of, 2:115, 3:3
Printing, origins of, **3:234–35,** 4:151
    Caxton, first English publisher, 1:164, 2:63
    libraries and, growth of, 3:90
    literacy and, 3:94
    mapmaking and, 3:119
    in Nuremberg, 3:180
    printing press, 1:52, 104
        Gutenberg, inventor of, 2:185–86 (illus.), 3:234
    Wynkyn de Worde and, 4:199
Priory, 2:36, 37, 3:145–46
Priscian (Latin grammarian), 3:78
Prisons, **3:235–36**
Private archives, 1:39
Private churches, 3:201
Procopius (historian), 4:40
Procurators, 2:31
Property, ownership of, 2:76, 78, 82, 83, 3:2–3
Provence, 1:116, **3:236–38** (illus.), 4:22
Prudentius (Spanish poet), 1:22
Prussia, 1:64, 65, 3:224
Psellos, Michael, 2:214, 3:130, 222, **4:1**
Pseudo-Dionysius the Areopagite, 1:23
Pskov, city-state of, 3:36
Ptocheia, 2:219
Ptolemy, 1:49, 52, 3:116, 4:51
Public health and sanitation, 3:221
Pucelle, Jean, 1:133 (illus.)
Purgatory, idea of, 2:22, 92, **4:1–2** (illus.), 4:168
Puy d'Arras (guild), 4:140

Qaba (coat), 1:209
Qabus ibn Washmgir, tomb of, 3:25
Qahira, al-. See Cairo
Qalansuwa (hat), 1:207, 209
Qala'un al-Mansur, **4:2–3**
Qanats (underground canals), 1:10
Qansuh al-Ghawri, sultan, 3:113
Qara Qitai in Transoxania, 3:150
Qarmations (Shi'ite group), 1:31
Qayrawan, al-, 3:51, 58
Quarries, 1:222
Quires, 1:100
Qur'an, 1:138, 3:209, **4:3** (illus.)
    Ali ibn Abi Talib and, 1:21
    angels in, 1:23, 24
    Arabic dictionaries to explain words from, 2:51

Arabic rhetoric and, 4:8
chanting of, 3:159
on charity, 2:220
on famine, 2:86
geographical concepts in, 3:116
as holy book of Islam, 3:19–20, 21, 4:3 *(illus.)*
Ibn Hanbal, theologian of, 2:231–32
interpretation of, 2:88, 3:85, 4:142
Islamic book production and, 1:101
Islamic law and, 3:3, 83
Islamic mystical tradition from, 3:166
language of, 1:32, 33
on magic, 3:109
on marriage, 2:77, 78
Muhammad's revelations in, 3:153
night of divine decree commemorating, 2:93
paradise in, 3:197
slavery in, 4:80
al-Tabari's writings on, 4:102
Quraysh (Arab tribe), 1:5, 30, 60, 2:237, 3:152
Qusayr Amra (palace), 3:23–24
Qutuz (Mamluk sultan), 1:77, 3:112

Rabbenu Tam. *See* Jacob ben Meir
Rabbinic Judaism, 3:57–58
Rabbinic period, 3:84
Rabbis, 3:46–47
Radewijns, Florens, 1:106
Raedwald, East Anglian king, 4:97
Rahewin (secretary of Otto of Freising), 3:186
Rahman, al-, 1:30
Raimbaut d'Aurenga, 3:238
Raimondo de' Liuzzi. *See* Mondino dei Luzzi
Rainulf (Norman leader), 4:71
Ramadan, 3:21
Ramban. *See* Nahmanides, Moses
Ramiro of Aragon, 1:35, 36–37
Ramon Berenguer I of Catalonia, 1:159
Ramon Berenguer III of Catalonia, 1:159
Ramon Berenguer IV of Catalonia, 1:160
Randolph, Thomas (earl of Moray), 4:14
Rashi, 2:197, 3:36, 84, **4:4**
Rasuls (emissary), 2:30
Rationalism, 3:58
Ravenna, 2:24, 106, **4:4–5** *(illus.)*
Raymond IV of St. Gilles, count, 3:75, 76
Raymond VI, count of Toulouse, 3:76, 4:123
Raymond VII, count of Toulouse, 4:123
Razi, al-, 1:16, **4:5–6**
Recanati, Rabbi Menahem, 1:130
Red Sea, navigation in, 3:171
Reeves, 2:54, 57, 4:106, 158
Regno. See Sicily
Regrating, laws against, 2:106
Regula sancti Benedicti (Benedictine Rule), 1:82, 3:147–48, 4:191
Reichstag, 2:161
Relics, 3:214, 215, **4:6** *(illus.)*, 4:131, 133
Religious archives, 1:38
Religious instruction, **4:6–7**, 4:46–50 *(illus.)*, 64–65
Reliquaries, 4:6 *(illus.)*
Renaissance, Italian, 1:112–13, 119, 121, 2:103
Representative assemblies, 2:2, 122–23, 161–62, 4:38–39, 42, 85. *See also* Parliament, English
Rheims Cathedral, 1:162 *(illus.)*, 2:175
Rhetor (teacher), 3:93
Rhetoric, 1:129, **4:7–9**
Rhys ap Gruffydd (Welsh prince), 4:170

Richard I the Lionhearted, 2:50, 55–56, **4:9–10** *(illus.)*
Bertran de Born and, 1:86–87
borough liberties purchased under, 1:104
Cyprus, conquest of, 1:125, 2:15
Henry VI of Germany and, 2:204
Saladin and, 1:58, 4:9 *(illus.)*, 10
Third Crusade and, 1:56, 2:10–11, 3:212, 4:9 *(illus.)*
Walter's service to, 4:171
William Marshal and, 4:185
Richard II, 1:25, 176, 2:47, 3:56, 57, 206, **4:10–11**
Richard III, 2:59, 208, **4:11**, 4:178
Richard I of Normandy, duke, 3:175
Richard of Burgundy, duke, 1:116
Richard of Capua, prince, 4:71
Richard of Cornwall, 2:12, 159
Richard of York, 1:130, 2:202, 4:177
Rigord of St. Denis, 2:117
Riksdag (Swedish parliament), 4:85
Ripuarians, 2:125
Rites of death and burial, 2:25–26
Rites of Mass, 3:123
Roads and bridges, 1:22, 198, 3:232, **4:11–13** *(illus.)*, 4:179. *See also* Travel and transportation
Robert I of Scotland, **4:14**
Robert II of Flanders, prince, 2:99
Robert II the Pious of France, king, 4:28
Robert I of Normandy, duke, 4:184
Robert Curthose of Normandy, 2:55, 198–99
Robert d'Arbrissel, **4:14–15**, 4:192
Robert Guiscard (duke of Sicily), 1:96, 159, 3:71, 4:71
Robert le Bougre, 3:7
Robert of Anjou, 2:164
Robert of Béthune, 2:100
Robert the Frisian, 2:99
Robert the Strong, 2:114
Robertinian family, 1:147
Robin Hood, **4:15–16**
Roderick, king of Visigoths, 3:17
Rodrigo Díaz de Vivar. *See* Cid, the
Roger I Guiscard of Sicily, 4:71
Roger II of Sicily, 2:127, 3:71, 4:71 *(illus.)*, 73
Roger of Salisbury, 3:60, **4:16**
Roger, Pierre. *See* Clement VI, pope
Roland, Song of, 1:169, 2:130, 3:170, **4:16–17** *(illus.)*
Rollo (Viking leader), 1:147, 3:175, 4:156
Roman architecture, 4:20
Roman Church, 1:182–83, 185–87, 189
Roman civil law, 1:72
Roman de la Rose, 1:4 *(illus.)*, 22, 175, 2:131, 132 *(illus.)*, 146, **4:17–18**
Roman Empire
Byzantine Empire as direct descendant of, 1:121, 122
Constantine I, emperor of, 1:219
Germanic migrations into, 3:137, 173, 4:162
Huns' raids in, 2:227
inheritance law in, 3:2
London and, 3:97
Portugal under, 3:228
roads, 4:12, 130
Syria and, 4:100
Roman fortifications, 1:154
Roman law, influence of, 3:79, 80, 81, 84
Roman liturgy, Gregorian chant of, 2:179
Roman numerals, 1:34, 3:124, **4:18**

Roman system of measures, 4:181
Roman tradition of bookmaking, 1:102
Romance languages, 2:129, 3:30, 77, 78. *See also* French language and literature; Italian language and literature; Spanish language and literature
Romances in literature, 1:129, 2:7, 131, 153–55, 228, 3:32
Romanesque architecture, 1:117, 3:146, **4:18–21** *(illus.)*
churches, 1:109, 162–63
Gothic architecture as successor to, 2:168–69
Provençal, 3:237 *(illus.)*
in Spain, 4:37, 90
Romanesque art, 2:171, 174, 3:43, **4:21–24** *(illus.)*
Romania, 4:164
Romanies, 2:187
Romanos I Lekapenos, emperor, 1:123, 128
Romanos II, emperor, 4:117
Rome, **4:24–26** *(illus.)*
ancient relics of, 4:25
bishop of. *See* Papacy, origins and development
Byzantine architecture and heritage of, 1:117–18
calendar of ancient, 1:134
as early Christian center, 1:182–83
Great Schism and, 4:44–45
Lombards and, 3:97
as pilgrim destination, 2:218, 3:214–15
Romanesque painting in, 4:23
Romulus Augustulus, 3:182
Roosebeke, Battle of (1382), 2:101
Round City (Baghdad), 1:61, 3:24, 115
Royal coronations, 2:1 *(illus.)*
Royal forests, 2:111, 112, 227
Royal households, **4:26–28** *(illus.)*, 4:131, 133–34
Royal touch, 3:65–66, **4:28**
Rublev, Andrei, **4:28–29**
Rudolf II, Czech emperor, 3:232
Rudolf I of Habsburg, 1:18, 56, 96, 2:159, 188
Rudolf IV of Austria, duke, 1:56
Rudolf II of Fenis, 2:152
Rudolf I of Welf, duke, 1:115
Ruiz, Juan, **4:29**, 4:93–94
Rule of St. Augustine, 1:53
Rumi, **4:29**
Runes, 2:60–61, **4:30** *(illus.)*
Rurik, 2:68, 3:63 *(map)*, 64, 177, **4:30–31**, 4:157
Russia, 2:33–34, 42, 4:30–31, 63. *See also* Kievan Rus; Muscovy, rise of; Novgorod
Russian fur trade, 2:135–36
Russian Orthodox Church, 1:185, 3:156
Russian pilgrimages, 3:216
Ryazan, territory of, 3:36

Saadiah Gaon (Hebrew writer), 2:197, 3:58
Sabbath candles, origins of, 3:59
Sabinius, pope, 1:81
Sabuhr I, 4:37
Sabuhr II, 4:37
Sabunde, Raymond, 4:92
Sacraments, **4:31**
Sacrificing, festival of, 2:93
Sacrobosco, 3:118
Safavids, 3:11
Safirs (emissary), 2:30
St. Albans, Battle of (1455), 4:177

St. Denis, abbey of, 1:189, 2:169–70, 4:22, 95
St. Denis, October fair at, 2:74
St. Gilles, 3:76
St. Pierre, monastery of (Moissac), 4:22
St. Savin-sur-Gartempe, church of, 4:23–24
St. Sernin, church of (Toulouse), 4:22 (illus.)
St. Swithin's Day, 2:92
St. Valentine's Day, 2:91
St. Victor, abbey of, 3:237
Sainte Chapelle (church), 3:102
Saints' days, 1:134
Saints, lives of, 4:13, **4:32–33** (illus.)
    canonization of saints, 1:139
    literature on, 2:130–31, 132, 180, 222, 4:44
    relics of, 4:6
    See also specific saints
Sakkos (garment), 1:206
Sakura, king of Mali, 3:111
Saladin, **4:33–34** (illus.)
    Ayyubid dynasty in Egypt and, 1:58, 2:48,
        4:33, 34
    Battle of Hittin (1187), 2:10, 216, 4:33–34
    Cairo under, 1:132
    Damascus under, 2:19
    recapture of Jerusalem (1187), 1:58, 3:42,
        4:33–34
    Richard I the Lionhearted and, 1:58,
        4:9 (illus.), 10
Salat (ritual prayer), 3:21
Salces, fortress of, 1:153 (illus.), 157
Salerno, Italy, 3:131–32
Salians, 2:125, 158, 203, 3:134
Salih Ayyub, al- (Ayyubid ruler), 3:112
Sallust (historian), 2:213
Sama (Sufi ritual exercise), 3:166
Samarkand, **4:34–35**, 4:51, 104
Samarra, 1:2 (illus.), 3, 3:24–25, 164, **4:35–36**
Samuel ben Meir, rabbi, 3:36
Samuel ha-Nagid, 3:51–52
Samuil (Bulgarian ruler), 1:73
San Marco, cathedral of (Venice), 4:152
San Vitale (Ravenna), 1:120 (illus.), 3:61 (illus.),
    4:4
Sancho I of Portugal, 3:229–30
Sancho II of Portugal, 3:230
Sancho III of Aragon and Navarre, 1:35, 53,
    150, 3:169
Sancho V of Aragon and Navarre, 3:169
Sancho Garcia, 1:149
Sancho Ramirez, 1:35
Sanctuary, right of, 1:218, **4:36**
Sant'Apollinare in Classe, basilica of, 4:5
    (illus.)
Santiago de Compostela, 1:52, 150, 3:169, 215,
    4:36–37, 4:90
Santo Spirito, church of (Florence), 1:112 (illus.)
São Mamede, Battle of (1128), 3:229
Sapping, 1:155
Sarajevo Haggadah, 2:197
Sarat Canal, 1:61
Sasanians, 3:9, 10 (illus.), 11–12, 16, **4:37–38**
Satan, 2:27. See also Devils and demons
Sava, archbishop of Serbia, 4:60
Savonarola, Girolamo, 3:33
Sawm (fasting), 3:21
Saxo Grammaticus, 4:39
Saxons, 1:25, 2:157–58
Scandinavia, 2:191–92, 3:144–45, **4:38–42** (illus.)
    culture of, 4:30 (illus.), **4:42–44**
    Vikings of, 4:154–57 (map)

Schism between Eastern and Western
        Churches, 1:184–85, 186, 220–21
Schism, Great, **4:44–45**
    Avignon and, 1:57–58, 186–87, 4:44–45
    Charles V and, 1:172
    France and, 2:121
    papacy and, 1:186–87, 3:195, 4:44–45, 161
    Papal States and, 3:196
    resolution of, 2:162, 4:76, 161
    St. Birgitta and, 1:89
Scholasticism, **4:45–46** (illus.)
    Albertus Magnus and, 1:15
    Aquinas and, 1:28
    biblical exegesis and start of, 1:89
    development of, 1:39, 40
    French literature and rise of, 2:132
    Gothic sculpture and, 2:174
    Grosseteste and, 2:181
    Meister Eckhart and, 2:43
    Ockham's break with, 3:181
    on witchcraft, 4:187
Schools, 3:90, 131, **4:46–50** (illus.), 4:186
    law, 1:72, 3:79, 81, 84–85, 4:48 (illus.), 147
    literacy and, 3:92–94
    medical, 3:130, 131, 132–33, 148
    for minstrels, 3:159
    religious instruction in, 4:6, 7
    See also Universities
Science, **4:50–52**
    Bacon and, 1:59, 60
    Greek, influence on Judaism, 3:58
    Grosseteste and, 2:181–82
    maps and mapmaking and, 3:116–19 (illus.)
    St. Hildegard of Bingen and, 2:213
    See also Technology
Scientific instruments, 3:118, 171, **4:52–53** (illus.)
Scotland, **4:54–56** (illus.)
    Christian missions in, 3:144
    England and, 4:14, 54, 56
    literature of, 1:166
    Macbeth, ruler of, 3:105–6
    Robert I, king of, 4:14
    Vikings in, 2:68, 4:154
Script (handwriting), 3:93–94
Scriptoria, 1:102, 103
Scrofula, royal touch to cure, 4:28
Sculpture. See British Isles, art and architecture;
        Byzantine architecture; Gothic sculp-
        ture; Islamic art and architecture;
        Romanesque art; Spanish art and
        architecture
Scutage, 4:106
Seals and charters, **4:56–57** (illus.)
Second Council of Nicaea (787), 2:237
Second Temple (Jerusalem), 3:40–41
Secular books, 1:102, 103
Secular music, 3:159, 161–62
Secular painting, 2:173
Self-government by Jewish communities,
    3:45–47
Seljuk ibn Doqaq (tribal warlord), 4:57
Seljuks, **4:57–58**
    Abbasids and, 1:3
    in Arabia, 1:31
    Armenia and, 1:41, 4:125
    caliphate and, 1:138
    crusades and, 2:8, 3:208–9 (illus.)
    Damascus under, 2:18–19
    Georgia and, 2:150
    in Iran, 3:11, 4:57, 58

in Iraq, 3:13
    Islamic art and architecture under, 3:28–29
    Syria under, 4:57, 58, 101
    warfare of, 4:176
Sempach, Battle of (1386), 4:99
Seneschal, 2:115–16, 4:27, **4:58–59**
Septuagesima, 2:91
Septuagint, 1:88
Serbia, 3:155, 188, **4:59–60** (illus.)
Serbian literature, 4:82
Serfs and serfdom, 1:127–28, 3:225,
    4:60–63 (illus.), 4:79, 85, 86
Sericulture, 4:76–77
Sermons, 1:129, 2:61, 3:32–33, 4:6, 7, 8,
    4:64–65, 4:82
Seven Deadly Sins, 4:162
Severinus, St., 1:75
Shafi'i, Muhammad ibn Idris, al- (jurist), 4:96
Shahada (statement of faith), 3:21
Shahnama, **4:66** (illus.)
Shakespeare, William, 3:105, 4:176
Shams al-Dawla (Buyid prince), 2:234
Shams al-Din Muhammad. See Hafiz
Shams-i-Tabrizi (mystic), 4:29
Sharbush (cap), 1:209
Shari'a (Islamic law), 1:138, 3:20–21, 82–83
Shawm (musical instrument), 3:163
Shem Tov ben Yitzhak Ardutiel, 4:94
Shepherds' crusade, 1:178
Sheriff, 2:54, 57, 66, 3:82, **4:66–67**
Shi'ism, Shi'ites, 1:61, 137, 4:101, 144
    Ali ibn Abi Talib and, 1:20, 21
    Berber conversion to, 1:85
    emergence of, 1:136
    Fatimid Empire and, 2:88–90 (map)
    al-Husayn ibn Ali as imam of, 2:230
    imam, meaning in, 2:238
    in Iran, 3:10, 11
    in Iraq, 3:12, 13
    in Kufa, 3:72, 73
    political decline of caliphate and, 1:138
    split between Sunnites and, 1:31, 135–36,
        2:48, 88, 3:10, 11, 12, 13, 22, 142
Ships and shipbuilding, 2:149, 4:40,
    4:67–69 (illus.), 4:112, 154
Shire, 2:54, 4:66, **4:69**
Shirkuh (Kurdish warrior), 1:58, 4:33
Shota Rustaveli, **4:69–70**
Sicilian Vespers, 1:126
Sicily, **4:70–73** (illus.)
    under Angevins, 1:25
    Byzantine Empire and, 1:126
    Frederick II of Holy Roman Empire and,
        2:127–28, 3:31
    Germany and, 2:158, 204
    Naples as part of, 3:168
    Norman invasions of, 4:173
    scientific instruments from, 4:52
Siena, 1:163–64, **4:73–75** (illus.)
Siffin, Battle of (657), 1:21, **4:75**
Sigismund, emperor, **4:76**
Signori (despots), 3:35
Silk, 1:210, 221, **4:76–77**, 4:115, 124, 125
Silver coins, 3:148–49
Simeon, St., 4:6
Simon de Montfort III, 3:76–77, 4:77, 123
Simon de Montfort the Younger, 3:95, **4:77–78**
Simony, **4:78**
Sinibaldo Fieschi. See Innocent IV, pope
Sir Gawain and the Green Knight, 1:47, 2:63

Sisters of the Common Life, 1:106, 107
Sitting games, 2:142–43
Siward, earl of Northumbria, 3:105, 106
Sixtus IV, pope, 4:166
Skanör, Sweden, fish fair at, 2:75
Slavery, 4:60, 61–62, **4:78–81** *(illus.)*, 4:130, 176, 201
Slavic language, 2:16
Slavic literature, **4:81–83**
Slavs, 1:54, **4:83**
  Bulgars and, 1:113
  Byzantine Empire threatened by, 1:122
  conversion by Cyril and Methodios, 1:184
  East, Kievan Rus emerging among, 3:62–65 *(map)*
  German defeat of, 2:157
  invasions of, 1:13, 2:7
  Lithuanians and, 3:95
  as slaves, 4:79
Sluis, naval battle of (1340), 2:223
Sluter, Claus, 2:175 *(illus.)*
Smallpox, 3:219
Snorra Edda. *See* Eddas (Icelandic poems)
Snorri Sturluson, 4:43
Social classes, **4:83–86** *(illus.)*
  in Byzantine Empire, 1:127–28, 4:85–86
  diplomatic personnel and, 2:30
  family life and, 2:75, 79–80, 81
  French representative assemblies and, 2:122
  under Germanic laws, 3:80
  merchant class, 1:213, 2:79
  middle class, 2:79, 81, 82, 4:189
  in Muslim Spain, 4:88
  in Novgorod, 3:178
  in Ottoman Empire, 3:188–89
  peasantry, 2:80, 81, 4:85, 86, 189
  pilgrims from all, 3:214
  in Scandinavia, 4:38, 39
  seating in Muslim society by, 2:140
  serfs and serfdom, 4:60–63 *(illus.)*, 85, 86
  sumptuary laws and, 1:210
  in Walachia and Moldavia, 4:165
  in western Europe, 4:84–85
  women's roles and, 4:189
  See also Nobility and nobles
Soissons, Council of, 1:3
Solomon ben Isaac. *See* Rashi
Song of Roland, 1:169, 2:130, 3:170, 4:16–17 *(illus.)*
Songhai, 4:119
Sophia, wife of Ivan III of Muscovy, 3:36
Sorbon, Robert de, 3:90, 200
Sorcery, tradition of, 4:186–87. *See also* Magic and folklore; Witchcraft, European
Spain
  Christian states in northern, 4:87
    Aragon, 1:35–38 *(map)*
    Asturias-León, 1:52–53
    Castile, 1:149–52
    Catalonia, 1:158–60 *(illus.)*
    Navarre, 3:169–70
  the Cid, hero of, 1:190–91
  cities and towns in
    Barcelona, 1:70–71
    fuero and, 2:134–35
    hermandades, 2:212
    Santiago de Compostela, 4:36–37
    Toledo, 4:120–21
  cortes of, 2:2
  crusades in, 1:150–51, 2:14

  expulsion of Jews from, 1:228, 3:52, 53, 4:121
  Inquisition in, 3:7, 8, 53, 4:151
  Jewish communities in, 1:71, 150, 152, 225–26, 3:48, 51–52, 4:88–89
  scientific instruments from, 4:52
  serfs and serfdom in, 4:62
  synagogues in, 3:43
  Vandals in, 4:151
  Visigoths in, 4:162–63
Spain, Muslim kingdoms of, **4:86–89** *(illus.)*
  art and architecture in, 3:25, 27–28, 4:87, 89–90
    Alhambra, 1:19–20 *(illus.)*
  Berbers and, 1:85
  conquest and reconquest, 1:149, 150–51, 190, 191, 3:17, 4:86–88, 120, 121
  Córdoba and, 1:226, 227–28
  diverse populations of, 3:51–52, 4:88–89
  Granada, 2:177–78 *(illus.)*
  libraries in, 3:90
  literature of, 4:91–92
  Navarre's independence of, 3:169
  Toledo and, 4:120, 121
  Umayyad dynasty in, 4:146
  Valencia, 4:150–51
Spanish art and architecture, 2:170, 173, 4:23, **4:89–90** *(illus.)*
Spanish language and literature, **4:90–94** *(illus.)*
  Hebrew literature and, 2:197
  language, 4:90–91
    Castilian, 1:151, 2:28, 3:115
  literature, 4:91–94
    in Latin, 4:91–92
    by Lull, 3:104
    by Manuel, 3:115–16
    by Ruiz, 4:29
    in Spanish, 4:92–94
Speculum maius (Vincent of Beauvais), 2:52, 4:161
Sphrantzes, George, 2:214
Spinning wheel, 4:114
Spirituals, 1:97, 98, 2:124–25
Squinches, 1:118
Squires, courtesy books on behavior of, 2:5
Stained glass. *See under* Glass
Starvation. *See* Famine
State archives, 1:38
Stationer, 1:103
Statute of Gloucester (1278), 2:45
Statute of York (1322), 3:202
Statutes of Kilkenny (1366), 3:14
Stave churches, wooden, 1:162
Stefan Tomasevic, 1:106
Stela, Scandinavian, 4:40 *(illus.)*
Stem duchies, 1:75, 2:42
Stephen II, pope, 3:207
Stephen III, pope, 4:25
Stephen (king of England), 2:55, 4:16
Stephen I of Hungary, St., 2:225, **4:94–95**
Stephen II of Hungary, 2:225
Stephen III the Great of Moldavia, 4:166, 167
Stephen of Blois, 1:24, 2:199
Stephen (of French Children's Crusade), 1:177–78
Stephen of Garlande, 2:116
Stoicism, 1:49
Stokton, Elizabeth, 2:79
Stone and masonry construction, 1:155, 222, 224, 3:98, 4:13
Strabo (Greek geographer), 4:38

  Strasbourg Oaths, 2:129, 130
Streets. *See* Roads and bridges
Stylites, 3:147
Stylus, 4:196
Styria, 1:567
Sufism, 3:22, 166–67
Sufyanid branch of Umayyads, 4:144
Suger of St. Denis, 2:116, 169–70, 214, 3:101, 4:23, **4:95**
Süleyman I the Magnificent, 2:225 *(illus.)*, 3:42, 4:166
Sulpicius Severus, 4:32
Sultan, **4:95**
  Mamluk, 2:48
  Ottoman, power of, 3:188, 189
  Seljuk, 1:3, 4:57–58
Summa (type of writing), 4:46
Sumptuary laws, 1:210
Sundials, 1:203, 204
Sunna, 2:88, 3:20, 21, **4:96**
Sunnite branch of Islam, 1:58, 59, 3:22, 4:96, 101, 144
  Cairo as center for, 1:132
  emergence of, 1:136
  in Fatimid Empire, 2:88, 89, 90
  split between Shi'ites and, 1:31, 135–36, 2:48, 88, 3:10, 11, 12, 13, 22, 142
Surcoats, 1:42, 43
Surgeons. *See* Barber-surgeons
Sussex, 2:53
Sutton Hoo, **4:96–97** *(illus.)*
Svyatoslav I of Kievan Rus, 3:64
Swabian League, 2:160
Sweden, 4:40–41, 85, 157
Sweyn I Forkbeard, 1:212, 2:54, 4:39
Sweyn II Estridsen, 4:39
Swiss Confederation, 4:98–99
Switzerland, 2:188, **4:98–100** *(illus.)*, 4:174
Swynford, Katherine, 3:56
Syagrius (Celtic ruler), 1:211
Sylvester I, pope, 3:193 *(illus.)*
Sylvester II, pope, 3:185
Symeon of Bulgaria, king, 1:114
Symeon (abbot in Constantinople), 3:165
Symeon Seth, 3:130
Sympathetic magic, 3:107
Synagogues, 3:43, 47, 57, 233 *(illus.)*, 4:50
Synod of Whitby (664), 1:140, 2:54
Synods, 1:182
Syria, **4:100–102** *(illus.)*
  Ayyubids in, 1:58–59
  Damascus, 2:17–19 *(illus.)*
  Islamic art and architecture in, 3:27
  Islamic conquest into, 3:15–16
  Jewish communities in, 3:50
  Mamluk dynasty in, 3:112–13 *(illus.)*, 4:101
  Mu'awiya as governor of, 3:152
  Qala'un al-Mansur, sultan of, 4:2–3
  under Seljuks, 4:57, 58, 101
  Tamerlane's conquests in, 4:101, 104
  Tancred's control of, 4:104
Syriac language, 4:101

Tabari, al-, **4:102**
Tabors (musical instruments), 3:164
Taifas (principalities), 1:227
Taliesin (writer), 1:165
Tallage, 4:106
Talmud, 1:89, 3:50, 57, 108, 4:7
  scholars of, 3:36, 167, 4:4, 50

Tamar, queen of Georgia, 2:150, 4:69–70, **4:102–3**
Tamerlane, **4:103–4** *(illus.)*
  campaigns of
    defeat of Bayazid I, 1:76
    in Egypt, 2:49
    in Georgia, 2:151
    in Iran, 3:11
    in Iraq, 3:13
    against Mamluks, 3:113
    in Syria, 4:101, 104
  Golden Horde and, 2:167
  Islamic art and architecture and, 3:26
  Samarkand under, 4:35
Tancred, **4:104**
Tapestries, 2:146, **4:105** *(illus.)*
Targe (shield), 1:44
Tariq ibn Ziyad, 4:86
Tatars, 2:147, 167, 3:156
Taula de Canvi (Exchange Table), 1:68
Tawing of leather, 3:86
Taxation, 2:123, **4:106–9** *(illus.)*, 4:143
  bread-tax law, 2:107
  danegeld as, 2:21
  English Exchequer and, 2:65–66
  tithes, 4:120
Technology, **4:109–12** *(illus.)*
  agricultural, 1:7–12
  Byzantine, 1:7–8, 4:109–10
  decline of guilds with improvements in, 2:184
  glassmaking, 2:165–66
  Gothic style and, 2:168
  handbooks to explain, 2:190–91
  heating, 2:194–96 *(illus.)*
  Islamic, 4:51, 110–11
  metalworking, 3:136
  mining, 3:142–43
  printing, 2:185–86 *(illus.)*, 3:234–35
  shipbuilding, 4:67–69 *(illus.)*
  silk-throwing machine, 4:77
  transportation, inventions for, 4:132 *(illus.)*
  western European, 4:111–12
Temüjin. *See* Genghis Khan
Teutonic Knights, 1:64 *(illus.)*, 65, 179, 2:191, 3:69, 94–95, 224
Textbooks, **4:113**
Textiles, **4:113–15** *(illus.)*
  for clothing, 1:206, 207, 210, 211
  Flanders and, 2:99, 100–101
  furniture fabrics, 2:136, 137, 138, 139
  Islamic industrial technology in, 4:110
  silk, 4:76–77
  tapestries, 4:105 *(illus.)*
  wool, 2:163–64, 4:193–94
  of Ypres, 4:201
Theodebert II, king of Franks, 4:97
Theodora I, empress, 1:122, 4:1, **4:116** *(illus.)*
Theodora II, empress, 4:126
Theodore I Laskaris, 3:172
Theodoric I of Visigoths, 4:162
Theodoric II of Visigoths, 3:80
Theodoric the Ostrogoth, 1:148, 3:33, 182, 183, **4:116–17**
Theodoros Meliteniotes (astronomer), 3:107–8
Theodosian Code, 3:46
Theodosius I, emperor, 1:181, 3:192
Theological millennialism, 3:141
Theophano, empress, **4:117**
Theophano (Otto III's mother), 2:157

Theophilus (Benedictine monk), 2:165–66, 3:137
Theophrastus of Eresus, 2:209
Thibaut, count of Champagne, 1:167, 2:12
Thierry of Alsace, 2:99
Third Order of Penance of St. Dominic, 2:37
Third Order of the Franciscan Friars, 1:80
Thomas of Brittany, 4:138
Thomas of Gloucester, duke, 4:10
Thomas the Slav, **4:117–18**
Thousand and One Nights, 2:49, 192, 3:109, 117, **4:118–19** *(illus.)*
Timbuktu, **4:119–20**
Timekeeping. *See* Clocks and reckoning of time
Timur Leng (Timur the Lame). *See* Tamerlane
Tintinnabula, 1:81–82
Tiraz (embroidered fabric), 1:207, 209
Tirel, Walter, 2:198
Tithes, 4:107, **4:120**
Todros ben Judah Halevi (writer), 2:198
Toghril (sultan), 4:57
Toghril-Beg, 4:95
Tolbiac, Battle of (506), 1:211
Toledo, 4:87, 88 *(illus.)*, **4:120–21**
Tomás ze Štítného, 4:82
Tomislav, 2:7, **4:121**
Tonsure, 1:201, 202
To'oril, ruler of Kereyid tribe, 2:147
Topiary, 2:144
Torah, 3:57
Torquetum, 4:52
Torture, **4:122–23** *(illus.)*, 4:136, 137
Tosafot, 3:36
Toslunda helmet plate, 1:86
Toulouse, 1:73, 2:118, 3:76, 77, **4:123–24**
Toulouse, University of, 3:85
Tournaments, 1:179, 2:141–42
Tower of London, 3:98, 100 *(illus.)*
Towns. *See* Cities and towns
Towton, Battle of (1461), 4:177
Trade, **4:124–30** *(map) (illus.)*
  Armenian, 4:124–25
  with Asia, 2:71
  banking and, 1:65–69 *(illus.)*
  Barcelona and, 1:70, 71
  bastides and, 1:73–74
  boroughs as centers of, 1:104
  Bruges and, 1:111–12
  in Burgundy, 1:116
  Byzantine, 1:221, 4:124, 125–27
  clothing styles influenced by, 1:206, 210
  in Croatia, 2:7
  Dublin as center of, 2:41
  exploration and, 2:67–71 *(illus.)*
  fairs and, 2:72–75
  fish, 2:97–98
  in food and drink, 2:103–10
  fur, 2:135–36 *(illus.)*
  in gems and jewelry, 2:147
  Ghent and, 2:163–64
  guilds and expansion of, 2:182, 183–84
  Hanseatic League and control of, 2:191–92 *(illus.)*, 3:178
  Islamic, 1:158, 3:34–35, 217, 4:127–28
  in Italy, 2:69, 70
    Genoa, 2:70, 149, 4:79, 129
    Pisa as center of, 3:217–18 *(illus.)*
    Polo family and, 3:225–26
    rise of cities and, 3:34–35
    Venice, 2:70, 3:34, 4:129, 151–54 *(illus.)*, 179

  Jews and international, 3:45, 49
  London as center of, 3:97, 98, 99–100
  Lübeck and, 3:102, 103
  markets and, 3:121–22
  money and, 3:149
  navigation and, 3:170–71
  plagues and, 3:219
    Black Death, 1:190, 191 *(illus.)*, 4:129–30
  in Poland, 3:224
  regulating, 4:128
  roads and bridges and, 4:11–13 *(illus.)*
  Samarkand on route of, 4:34
  in Scotland, 4:55
  silk, 4:76–77
  slave, 4:79
  standard weights and measures for, 4:182
  in Sweden, 4:40
  textile, 4:113
  Timbuktu and, 4:119–20
  trans-Saharan, Mali and, 3:111
  travel and, 4:132–33, 134, 135
  urban growth and, 1:195–96
  Walachia and Moldavia and, 4:167
  western European, 4:128–30
  Ypres and, 4:200–201
Trancoso, Battle of (1385), 3:231
Transubstantiation, 2:210, 3:181, 4:198
Trastámara dynasty in Castile, 1:151–52
Travel and transportation, **4:130–35** *(illus.)*
  canals and, 4:178, 179
  inns and taverns and, 3:5–7
  pilgrimages, 3:213–17 *(illus.)*
  plagues spread through, 3:219
  Polo and, 3:225–26 *(illus.)*
  postal service and, 3:232
  western European, 4:130–34
Travel books, 2:191
Travels of Sir John Mandeville, The. *See* Mandeville's *Travels*
Trebizond, 2:73, 4:103
Très Riches Heures, 1:99, 2:172
Trials, **4:136–37**
  European witch, 4:186
  for heresy, 3:7–8 *(illus.)*, 4:137
  Jewish courts, 3:45–46
  jury, 2:58, 3:80–81, 82, 181, 4:136–37, 197
  oaths and compurgations at, 3:180–81
  by ordeal, 3:81, 82, 4:136
  outlawry and, 3:189
  Parliament as highest English court, 3:203
  torture used in, 4:122–23
Tribal warfare, 4:172
Trinity Sunday, 2:91
Tripoli, 2:10
Tristan, legend of, 1:46, 2:131, 155, **4:137–38** *(illus.)*
Troilus and Criseyde (Chaucer), 1:176, 2:63
Trota and *Trotula*, **4:138**
Troubadour, trouvère, **4:138–40** *(illus.)*
  Alfonso X el Sabio and, 1:18
  ballads from songs of, 1:63
  chansons de geste and, 1:169
  courtly love lyrics and, 2:6–7, 132, 4:139, 140
  Dinis's support of, 2:28
  Eleanor of Aquitaine and, 2:58, 4:139
  German lyrics and, 2:153
  music of, 3:162
  in Provence, 3:236, 238
  William IX of Aquitaine, 4:183–84
Troy, story of, 2:153, **4:140**

Troyes, Treaty of (1420), 2:121, 202
Truce of God, 3:204
Tsiganes (Tsihanes). See Gypsies
Tunisia, Louis IX's crusade to, 2:13
Turan-Shah, 1:77
Turkey, 1:23, 3:28–29. *See also* Ottomans and
     Ottoman Empire; Seljuks
Turmeda, Anselm, **4:140–41**
Tuscany, 3:96, **4:141–42**
     cities of, 2:101–3 *(illus.)*, 3:217–18 *(illus.)*,
         4:73–75 *(illus.)*
     Matilda of Tuscany, 3:126–27
     Romanesque sculpture in, 4:23
Tutush (Turkish prince), 2:18
Tvrtko (Bosnian ruler), 1:106
Twelfth Night, 2:91, 92
Tyler, Wat, 3:205, 206
Tzimiskes, John, 1:123, 4:117

Ubayd Allah, 2:88
Uguccione da Lodi, 3:31
Ulama, 1:135, 136, 137–38, **4:142**
Umar I ibn al-Khattab, 1:5, 135, 3:16, 18, 41, 47,
     50, **4:142–43**
Umar Khayyam, **4:143**
Umayyads, **4:144–46**
     Abbasids' defeat of, 1:1–2
     art and architecture under, 3:23–24
     beginning of dynasty, 1:21, 31
     caliphate under, 1:136–37, 4:144–46
     in Córdoba, 1:227
     Damascus under, 2:17
     Granada under, 2:177
     hospitals and poor relief under, 2:220
     hunting under, 2:228
     al-Husayn's rebellion and death, impact on,
         2:230
     Iraq under, 3:12
     Islamic conquests under, 1:136–37, 3:17,
         4:144–46
     Islamic sermons under, 4:65
     libraries under, 3:90
     Mu'awiya, caliph of, 3:152
     Palestine under, 3:191
     Syria under, 4:100
     taxation under, 4:109
     Yazid I, caliph of, 4:199–200
Umma (community of faithful), 2:77
Unicorn, 1:87
Universities, **4:146–49** *(illus.)*
     biblical exegesis and start of, 1:89
     Black Death's effect on, 1:90–91
     book production by, 1:103
     Byzantine higher education, 4:148
     development of, 4:48, 49
     European, 1:196, 4:147–48
         Bologna, 3:79, 81, 84–85, 4:147
         Charles, 3:232
         Naples, 2:128, 4:73
         Paris, 2:120, 162, 3:199–200, 4:64, 147,
           148 *(illus.)*
         Prague, 1:96, 2:160, 229–30, 4:82
         Toulouse, 3:85
     Islamic colleges, 3:27, 28, 29, 85, 93, 4:7,
         49–50, 148–49
     law schools at, 3:79, 81, 84–85, 4:147
     libraries at, 3:90
     literacy and, 3:94
     medical education at, 3:132, 133
     Oxford, 2:181, 3:96, 4:147, 186, 197

postal service used by, 3:232
Scholasticism at, 4:45, 46 *(illus.)*
     in Scotland, 4:55
     sermons in, 4:64
     students at inns and taverns, 3:7
     textbooks used by, 4:113
     travel to study at, 4:134
Urban II, pope, 1:81, 184 *(illus.)*, 3:1, 214, **4:149**
     First Crusade and, 1:97, 124, 2:8–9, 3:213
Urban IV, pope, 1:15
Urban VI, pope, 1:57, 143, 172, 2:121, 4:45
Usury, 1:66, 3:349, **4:149–50**
Uthman ibn Affan (caliph), 1:20, 135–36,
     2:211–12, 3:21, 4:3, 144

Valencia, 1:190, 191, 3:39, **4:150–51**
Valentinian III, emperor, 4:151
Valois dynasty, 2:120–22, 3:213
Vandals, 1:227, 3:33, 138–39, **4:151**
Varangians, explorations of, 2:68
Vasilii of Muscovy, 3:156
Vasilii II the Blind of Muscovy, 3:156, 179
Vassals, lords and, 2:94–95
Vatican City, 3:196
Vaults, architectural, 1:224, 4:20
Veche (tribal assembly of freemen), 3:178
Venerable Bede. *See* Bede
Venice, **4:151–54** *(illus.)*
     Byzantine Empire and, 4:126, 127, 152, 153
     crusades and, 2:11, 4:153
     de' Dondi as Paduan ambassador to, 2:37
     as first commune, 1:216
     food policies and supply in, 2:84, 106
     Genoa and, 2:148, 3:226, 4:153–54
     glassmaking in, 2:165
     Ottomans as threat to, 3:188
     as printing center, 3:235
     trade and, 2:70, 3:34, 4:79, 129
Verdun, Treaty of (843), 1:145 *(illus.)*, 146
Vernacular
     in Christian liturgy, 2:16
     Dante on use of, 2:22, 23–24
     dramas in, 2:39
     histories in, 2:214
     Jewish writings in, 2:197
     literacy and written, 3:94
     manuscript books in, 1:104
     mechanical arts handbooks in, 2:190–91
     printing and standard forms of, 3:235
     sermons in, 4:64
     See also English language and literature;
         French language and literature; Italian
         language and literature
Veronica, St., 4:32 *(illus.)*
Vespers, 2:33
Vices. *See* Virtues and vices
Vikings, **4:154–57** *(map)*
     Carolingians and, 1:147
     climate and, influence on voyages of, 1:203
     danegeld to buy off, 2:21
     Danes, 4:39, 155–57
     early traders and explorers, 2:67, 68–69
     Flanders as defense against, 2:98
     fur trade and, 2:135
     invasions of
         agricultural development and, 1:13
         cities and towns and, effect on, 1:195
         in England, 1:18–19, 2:53, 54, 69, 193,
           3:97, 4:39, 156–57
         in Kievan Rus, 2:68, 3:64, 4:157

     in Normandy, 1:110, 2:69
     in North Atlantic, 4:155–56
     in Paris, 3:198
     in Scotland and Ireland, 2:41, 68, 3:14,
         4:154
     outlawry introduced by, 3:189
     Rurik, founder of Russian state, 4:30–31
     sagas of, 4:43
     trade and, 4:129
     See also Normans; Scandinavia
Villages, 1:8, **4:157–60**
Villard de Honnecourt, 4:111 *(illus.)*
Villes neuves, 1:216
Villon, François, 2:133, **4:160**
Vincent Ferrer, St., **4:160–61**
Vincent of Beauvais, 2:52, **4:161**
Virtues and vices, **4:161–62**
Visigoths, **4:162–63**
     in Aquitaine, 1:28
     Carcassonne dynasty in Catalonia, 1:158
     Clovis's defeat of, 1:211
     invasion of Italy, 3:33
     jewelry of, 2:146–47
     Jewish communities under, 3:48
     Languedoc under, 3:75–76
     law codes of, 3:80
     migration of, 3:137–38 *(map)*, 139, 4:162–63
     military service among, 4:172
     Muslim invasion of empire of, 1:52
     in Portugal, 3:228
     Spanish art and, 4:90 *(illus.)*
     Toledo under, 4:102
Visions, **4:163**
Viticulture, 2:104
Vizier, 1:3, 137, 3:18, 134, **4:163–64**
Vlachs, 4:165, 167
Vlad II Dracul, 4:164
Vlad Tepes, **4:164** *(illus.)*, 4:165
Vladimir I of Kievan Rus, 3:64, 4:157
Vladimir II Monomakh of Kievan Rus, prince,
     1:73, 185, 3:65, 155
Vladimir, principality of, 3:155–56
Vladimir-Suzdal, 3:178 *(illus.)*
Vladislav I, prince of Walachia, 4:165
Vlastimir (Serb leader), 4:59
Votive Masses, 2:26
Vsevolod III, 3:155
Vukan (Serbian noble), 4:59
Vulgar Latin, 2:129, 3:30
Vulgate, 1:88 *(illus.)*, 89
Vytautas (Lithuanian ruler), 3:95

Wace (poet), 1:46
Waiving, 3:189
Wake ceremony, 2:26
Wakefield, Battle of (1460), 4:177
Walachia and Moldavia, **4:164–67** *(illus.)*
Waldemar I of Denmark, 4:39–40
Waldemar II of Denmark, 3:103, 4:40
Waldemar IV of Denmark, 4:40
Waldensians, 3:76, **4:167–68**
Waldstätte (forest districts), 4:98
Wales, 1:165, 2:45, 3:95–96, **4:168–70** *(illus.)*
Walid I, al-, 2:18 *(illus.)*, 220
Wallace, William, 4:54
Walloon dialect, 2:99
Walter, Hubert, 3:60, 4:10, **4:171**
Walter of England (writer), 2:72
Walther von der Vogelweide, 2:152–53, **4:171**

Warfare, **4:172–76** (illus.)
  armor as protection in, 1:41–44
  games as practice for, 2:141–42, 143
  handbooks on, 2:191
  heraldry and, 2:206–8 (illus.)
  during Hundred Years War, 2:222–24 (illus.)
  Peace of God, Truce of God movements
     against, 3:204
  siege, 2:223–24, 4:174 (illus.)
  slavery and, 4:79, 81
  taxes to finance, 4:106, 107
  technological advances and, 4:111, 112
  See also Castles and fortifications; Weapons
Wars of the Roses, 2:59, 202–3 (illus.), 207,
    4:11, 170, **4:176–78** (illus.)
Water clocks, 1:203, 204, 4:111
Waterworks, 4:110, **4:178–79**
Weapons, **4:179–81** (illus.)
  armor as protection against, 1:41–45 (illus.)
  artillery, 1:47–48
    Byzantine, 1:127, 154, 4:109
    cannons, 1:47, 48, 81, 157, 222, 4:174, 181
    crossbow, 1:47–48, 432, 4:112, 180, 181
  for hunting and fowling, 2:227
  metals and metalworking for, 3:136
  siege, 1:47–48, 157
  technological advances in, 4:111, 112
  See also Warfare
Weather. See Climate, influence on history
Weights and measures, 4:109, **4:181–83** (illus.)
Welfs, 1:75, 2:126
Wenceslas IV of Bohemia, 2:230
Wenceslas of Luxembourg and Brabant, duke,
  2:134
Wessex, 1:18, 213, 2:53–54
West Francia, 1:147
West Saxons, 2:53
Western Church. See Roman Church
Western Europe
  agriculture in, 1:10–13
  astrology and astronomy in, 1:51–52
  cities and towns of, 1:194–96
  climate in Middle Ages, 1:203
  diplomacy in, 2:30–31
  family in, 2:78–82
  famine in, 2:83–86
  heresies in. See under Heresy and heresies
  hospitals and poor relief in, 2:220–21
  inheritance laws in, 3:2–3
  lighting devices in, 3:92
  magic and folklore in, 3:106–7
  maps and mapmaking in, 3:118–19
  medicine in, 3:131–32
  monasticism in, 3:147–48
  mysticism in. See under Mysticism
  taxation in, 4:106–8
  technology in, 4:111–12
  travel and transportation in, 4:130–34
Westminster Abbey, 2:44, 176, 3:98, 203, **4:183**
Whirling Dervishes, 3:159, 166, 4:29

Whitby, Synod of (663), 1:140, 2:54
White magic, 3:107
White monks. See Cistercians
Whittington, Richard, mayor of London, 3:98
Wildwood, 3:73–74 (illus.)
Wiligelmo, Master, 4:22
William I of England, the Conqueror, **4:184–85**
  Bayeux Tapestry and, 1:177
  coronation of, 3:98
  Domesday Book of, 2:34–35 (illus.), 3:226
  as first Norman king of England, 2:55, 57
  invasion of England, 1:141, 2:44 (illus.), 45,
    193–94 (illus.), 3:176
  justiciar of, 3:60
  quotas of knights under, 3:67–68
  restrictions on use of forests under, 2:111
  Wales and, 4:169
William II Rufus of England, king, 1:26, 2:55,
  198, 199
William I of Sicily, 1:6
William II of Sicily, 1:124, 4:71
William IX of Aquitaine, duke, **4:183–84**
William X of Aquitaine, duke, 1:29, 3:143
William Marshal, 2:200, **4:185**
William of Dampierre, 2:100
William of Malmesbury, 1:45
William of Paris, 1:218
William of Rubruck, 2:69
William of Toulouse (William of Orange),
  1:158, 169
William of Wykeham, **4:186**
William Tell, 4:99 (illus.)
William the Breton, 2:117
William "the Liberator" of Provence, 3:236
Wilton Diptych, 2:173
Winchester College School, 4:186
Winchester, Treaty of (1153), 2:55, 199
Windsor Castle, 4:186
Witchcraft, European, 2:28, **4:186–88** (illus.)
Wittelsbach family, 1:75, 76
Wladyslaw I "the Short" (Lokietek), 3:224
Wolfram von Eschenbach, 1:47, 2:153, 154–55,
  4:188–89
Women, roles of, **4:189–91** (illus.)
  Blanche of Castile and, 1:92–93 (illus.)
  chivalry and, 2:82
  Christine de Pizan on, 1:187–88 (illus.)
  as clergy, 1:201
  early Middle English works on, 2:62
  in Europe, 4:189–90
  in family, 2:75, 78, 79, 80, 81, 82, 83
  inheritance laws and practices and, 3:2, 3,
    4:189–90
  in Islamic world, 2:78, 4:190
  in Jewish society, 2:83, 4:191
  Julian of Norwich and, 3:59
  Kempe and, 3:62
  life expectancy, 3:228
  marriage patterns, 3:228
  in middle class, 2:82

  right to property, 2:82
  Theodora I and, 4:116
Women's religious orders, **4:191–93** (illus.)
  Beguines, 1:80–81
  Cistercian, 1:191
  Dominican, 2:35, 36, 37, 4:192–93
  Franciscan, 4:192–93
  mysticism and, 3:165–66
  Robert d'Arbrissel and, 4:14, 15
  St. Francis of Assisi and, 2:124
Wood, scarcity of, 1:154–55, 222, 2:111, 112.
  See also Forests
Wooden construction, 1:154, 222, 223–24
Wool, **4:193–94** (illus.)
  Hanseatic League and, 2:191
  industrial centers for, 2:163–64, 4:201
  Scottish, 4:54
  stages of weaving, 4:114 (illus.)
  for tapestries, 4:105
  textiles of, 2:99, 100–101, 4:113–14
Writing materials and techniques, 1:100–101,
  139, 3:93–94, 4:110, **4:194–96** (illus.)
Wulfstan of York, 2:61, **4:197**
Wyclif Bible, 4:198
Wyclif, John, 1:89, 187, 2:211, **4:197–99** (illus.)
  supporters of, 2:229, 230, 3:56, 96
Wynkyn de Worde, **4:199**

Xusro I, 4:38
Xusro II, 4:38

Yagut (scholar), 3:117
Yannai (poet), 2:197
Ya'qub ibn Killis, 2:89
Yaroslav the Wise, 3:64, **4:199**
Yazid I ibn Mu'awiya, 2:230, 4:144, 145,
  4:199–200
Yeomen (free farmers), 4:38, 39
Yersinia pestis, plague caused by, 1:90, 3:219
Yeshivas, 3:57, 58
Yesügei Baghatur, 2:147
Yose ben Yose (poet), 2:196–97
Yosef al-Katib, 4:92
Ypres, **4:200–201**
Yuhanna ibn Haylan (logician), 2:87

Zacharias I, pope, 1:184, 3:97, 207, 4:24
Zahir Barquq, al-, sultan, 3:113
Zähringens, 4:98
Zakat (giving of alms), 3:21
Zanj, **4:201–2**
Zara, capture by crusaders (1202), 2:11
Zawiyyas (hermitages), 3:28
Zeno, Eastern Roman emperor, 3:182, 183
Ziyadat Allah I, 4:70
Zoroastrianism, 3:9, 4:37
Zosimus of Panopolis, 1:16
Zuhri, Ibn Shihab al- (historian), 2:17
Zunnar (belt), 1:209
Zupas in Bosnia, 1:105